Mayne Reid

Odd People

Being a Popular Description of Singular Races of Man

Mayne Reid

Odd People
Being a Popular Description of Singular Races of Man

ISBN/EAN: 9783744692199

Printed in Europe, USA, Canada, Australia, Japan

Cover: Foto ©ninafisch / pixelio.de

More available books at **www.hansebooks.com**

THE CENTAURS OF THE "GRAN CHACO."

ODD PEOPLE.

BEING

A Popular Description

OF

SINGULAR RACES OF MAN.

BY

CAPTAIN MAYNE REID,

AUTHOR OF "THE DESERT HOME," "THE BUSH BOYS," ETC.

With Illustrations.

NEW YORK:

HARPER & BROTHERS, PUBLISHERS,

FRANKLIN SQUARE.

1860.

CONTENTS.

THE BOSJESMEN, OR BUSHMEN.

ODD PEOPLE.

BOSJESMEN, OR BUSHMEN.

PERHAPS no race of people has more piqued the
curiosity of the civilized world than those little yellow savages of South Africa, known as the *Bushmen*. From the first hour in which European nations became acquainted with their existence, a keen
interest was excited by the stories told of their peculiar character and habits: and although they have
been visited by many travellers, and many descriptions have been given of them, it is but truth to say,
that the interest in them has not yet abated, and the
Bushmen of Africa are almost as great a curiosity
at this hour as they were when Di Gama first doubled the Cape. Indeed there is no reason why this
should not be, for the habits and personal appearance of these savages is just now as it was then,
and our familiarity with them is not much greater.
Whatever has been added to our knowledge of their
character, has tended rather to increase than diminish our curiosity.

At first the tales related of them were supposed
to be filled with wilful exaggerations, and the early
travellers were accused of dealing too much in the
marvellous. This is a very common accusation
brought against the early travellers; and in some
instances it is a just one. But in regard to the accounts given of the Bushmen and their habits there

has been far less exaggeration than might be supposed; and the more insight we obtain into their peculiar customs and modes of subsistence, the more do we become satisfied that almost everything alleged of them is true. In fact, it would be difficult for the most inventive genius to contrive a fanciful account, that would be much more curious or interesting, than the real and *bonâ fide* truth that can be told about this most peculiar people.

Where do the Bushmen dwell? what is their country? These are questions not so easily answered, as in reality they are not supposed to possess any country at all, any more than the wild animals amidst which they roam, and upon whom they prey. There is no Bushman's country upon the map, though several spots in Southern Africa have at times received this designation. It is not possible, therefore, to delineate the boundaries of their country, since it has no boundaries, any more than that of the wandering Gipsies of Europe.

If the Bushmen, however, have no country in the proper sense of the word, they have a " range," and one of the most extensive character—since it covers the whole southern portion of the African continent, from the Cape of Good Hope to the twentieth degree of south latitude, extending east and west from the country of the Caffres to the Atlantic Ocean. Until lately it was believed that the Bushman-range did not extend far to the north of the Orange river; but this has proved an erroneous idea. They have recently " turned up " in the land of the Dammaras, and also in the great Kalahari desert, hundreds of miles north from the Orange river; and it is not certain that they do not range still nearer to the equatorial line—though it may be remarked that the country in that direction does not favour the supposition, not being of the peculiar nature of a

Bushman's country. The Bushman requires a desert for his dwelling-place. It is an absolute necessity of his nature, as it is to the ostrich and many species of animals; and north of the twentieth degree of latitude, South Africa does not appear to be of this character. The heroic Livingstone has dispelled the long-cherished illusion of the geography about the " *Great-sanded level*" of these interior regions; and, instead, disclosed to the world a fertile land, well watered, and covered with a profuse and luxuriant vegetation. In such a land there will be no Bushmen.

The limits we have allowed them, however, are sufficiently large—fifteen degrees of latitude, and an equally extensive range from east to west. It must not be supposed, however, that they *populate* this vast territory. On the contrary, they are only distributed over it *in spots*, in little communities, that have no relationship or connection with one another, but are separated by wide intervals, sometimes of hundreds of miles in extent. It is only in the desert tracts of South Africa that the Bushmen exist—in the karoos, and treeless, waterless plains —among the barren ridges and rocky defiles—in the ravines formed by the beds of dried-up rivers —in situations so sterile, so remote, so wild and inhospitable as to offer a home to no other human being save the Bushman himself.

If we state more particularly the localities where the haunts of the Bushman are to be found, we may specify the barren lands on both sides of the Orange river—including most of its head-waters, and down to its mouth—and also the Great Kalahari desert. Through all this extensive region the *kraals* of the Bushmen may be encountered. At one time they were common enough within the limits of the Cape colony itself, and some half-caste remnants still ex-

ist in the more remote districts; but the cruel persecution of the *boers* has had the effect of extirpa-
ting these unfortunate savages; and, like the elephant, the ostrich, and the eland, the true wild
Bushman is now only to be met with beyond the
frontiers of the colony.

About the origin of the Bushmen we can offer no
opinion. They are generally considered as a branch
of the great Hottentot family; but this theory is
far from being an established fact. When South
Africa was first discovered and colonized, both Hottentots and Bushmen were found there, differing
from each other just as they differ at this day; and
though there are some striking points of resemblance between them, there are also points of dissimilarity that are equally as striking, if we regard
the two people as one. In personal appearance
there is a certain general likeness: that is, both are
woolly-haired, and both have a Chinese caste of
features, especially in the form and expression of
the eye. Their colour, too, is nearly the same; but,
on the other hand, the Hottentots are larger than
the Bushmen. It is not in their persons, however,
that the most essential points of dissimilarity are to
be looked for, but rather in their mental characters;
and here we observe distinctions so marked and
antithetical, that it is difficult to reconcile them
with the fact that these two people are of one race.
Whether a different habit of life has produced this
distinctive character, or whether *it* has influenced
the habits of life, are questions not easly answered.
We only know that a strange anomaly exists—the
anomaly of two people being personally alike—that
is, possessing physical characteristics that seem to
prove them of the same race, while intellectually,
as we shall presently see, they have scarce one character in common. The slight resemblance that ex-

ists between the languages of the two is not to be
regarded as a proof of their common origin. It
only shows that they have long lived in juxtaposition, or contiguous to each other; a fact which
cannot be denied.

In giving a more particular description of the
Bushman, it will be seen in what respect he resembles the true Hottentot, and in what he differs from
him, both physically and mentally, and this description may now be given.

The Bushman is the smallest man with whom
we are acquainted; and if the terms "dwarf" and
"pigmy" may be applied to any race of human beings, the South-African Bushman presents the fairest claim to these titles. He stands only 4 feet 6
inches upon his naked soles—never more than 4
feet 9, and not unfrequently is he encountered of
still less height—even so diminutive as 4 feet 2. His
wife is of still shorter stature, and this Lilliputian
lady is often the mother of children when the crown
of her head is just 3 feet 9 inches above the soles of
her feet. It has been a very common thing to contradict the assertion that these people are such pig-
mies in stature, and even Dr. Livingstone has done
so in his late magnificent work. The doctor states,
very jocosely, that they are "not dwarfish—that the
specimens brought to Europe have been selected,
like costermongers' dogs, for their extreme ugliness."

But the doctor forgets that it is not from "the
specimens brought to Europe" that the above standard of the Bushman's height has been derived, but
from the testimony of numerous travellers—many
of them as trustworthy as the doctor himself—from
actual measurements made by them upon the spot.
It is hardly to be believed that such men as Spar-
mann and Burchell, Barrow and Lichtenstein, Har-

ris, Campbell, Patterson, and a dozen others that might be mentioned, should all give an erroneous testimony on this subject. These travellers have differed notoriously on other points, but in this they all agree, that a Bushman of 5 feet in height is a *tall* man in his tribe. Dr. Livingstone speaks of Bushmen "6 feet high," and these are the tribes lately discovered living so far north as the Lake Nagami. It is doubtful whether these are Bushmen at all. Indeed, the description given by the doctor, not only of their height and the colour of their skin, but also some hints about their intellectual character, would lead to the belief that he has mistaken some other people for Bushmen. It must be remembered that the experience of this great traveller has been chiefly among the *Bechuana* tribes, and his knowledge of the Bushman proper does not appear to be either accurate or extensive. No man is expected to know everybody; and amid the profusion of new facts, which the doctor has so liberally laid before the world, it would be strange if a few inaccuracies should not occur. Perhaps we should have more confidence if this was the only one we are enabled to detect; but the doctor also denies that there is anything either terrific or majestic in the "roaring of the lion." Thus speaks he: "The same feeling which has induced the modern painter to caricature the lion has led the sentimentalist to consider the lion's roar as the most terrific of all earthly sounds. We hear of the 'majestic roar of the king of beasts.' To talk of the majestic roar of the lion is mere majestic twaddle."

The doctor is certainly in error here. Does he suppose that any one is ignorant of the character of the lion's roar? Does he fancy that no one has ever heard it but himself? If it be necessary to go to South Africa to take the true measure of a Bushman, it is not necessary to make that long journey in order to obtain a correct idea of the compass of the lion's voice. We can hear it at home in all its modulations; and any one who has ever visited the Zoological Gardens in Regent's Park—nay, any one who chances to live within half a mile of that magnificent menagerie,—will be very much disposed to doubt the correctness of the doctor's assertion. If there be a sound upon the earth above all others "majestic," a noise above all others "terrific," it is certainly the *roar* of the lion. Ask Albert Terrace and St. John's Wood. .

But let us not be too severe upon the doctor. The world is indebted to him much more than to any other modern traveller, and all great men indulge occasionally in the luxury of an eccentric opinion. We have brought the point forward here for a special purpose—to illustrate a too much neglected truth. Error is not always on the side of exaggeration; but is sometimes also found in the opposite extreme of a too-squeamish moderation. We find the learned Professor Lichtenstein ridiculing poor old Hernandez, the natural historian of Mexico, for having given a description of certain fabulous animals—*fabulous*, he terms them, because to him they were odd and unknown. But it turns out that the old author was right, and the *animals exist!* How many similar misconceptions might be recorded of the Buffons, and other closet philosophers—urged, too, with the most bitter zeal! Incredulity carried too far is but another form of credulity.

But to return to our proper theme, and complete the portrait of the Bushman. We have given his height. It is in tolerable proportion to his other dimensions. When young, he appears stout enough; but this is only when a mere boy. At the age of sixteen he has **reached all the** manhood he **is ever** destined to attain; **and then** his **flesh disappears;** his **body** assumes a meagre outline; **his arms and** limbs grow thin; **the** calf disappears **from his legs;** the plumpness from **his** cheeks; **and altogether he** becomes as wretched-looking an object **as it is** possible **to conceive in human** shape. **Older, his** skin grows **dry,** corrugated, **and** scaly; **his bones protrude; and his** knee, elbow, and ankle-joints **appear** like **horny knobs placed** at the end of what **more** resemble **long straight** sticks than the arms and **limbs of a human being.**

The colour of this **creature may be** designated a yellow-brown, though it **is not easy to** determine it to a shade. The Bushman **appears** darker **than he** really is; since his **skin serves him for a towel, and** every species of **dirt that discommodes his fingers** he gets rid **of by wiping it off on his arms, sides, or** breast. The **result is, that his whole body is** usually coated over with **a stratum of grease and** filth, which has led to the **belief that he regularly** anoints himself—a custom common **among** many savage tribes. This, however, the Bushman does not do: **the** smearing toilet is merely occasional or accident**al, and** consists simply in the fat of whatever flesh **he has been** eating being transferred from **his** fingers **to the cuticle** of his body. This **is never** washed off **again—for water** never **touches** the Bushman's **hide. Such a** use of water **is entirely** unknown **to him,** not even **for** washing his face. Should **he** have occasion to cleanse **his** hands—which the handling of gum or some like substance sometimes compels him **to** do—he performs the operation, not with soap **and** water, but with the dry dung of cattle or some wild animal. A little rubbing **of this** upon **his** skin is all the purification the Bushman believes to be needed.

Of course, the dirt darkens his complexion; but
he has the vanity at times to brighten it up—not
by making it whiter—but rather a brick-red. A
little ochreous earth produces the colour he requires; and with this he smears his body all over
—not excepting even the crown of his head, and
the scant stock of wool that covers it.

Bushmen have been washed. It requires some
scrubbing, and a plentiful application either of soda
or soap, to reach the true skin and bring out the
natural colour; but the experiment has been made,
and the result proves that the Bushman is not so
black as, under ordinary circumstances, he appears.
A yellow hue shines through the epidermis, somewhat like the colour of the Chinese, or a European
in the worst stage of jaundice—the eye only not
having that complexion. Indeed, the features of
the Bushman, as well as the Hottentot, bear a strong
similarity to those of the Chinese, and the Bushman's eye is essentially of the Mongolian type. His
hair, however, is entirely of another character. Instead of being long, straight, and lank, it is short,
crisp, and curly,—in reality, wool. Its scantiness
is a characteristic; and in this respect the Bushman
differs from the woolly-haired tribes both of Africa
and Australasia. These generally have " fleeces" in
profusion, whereas both Hottentot and Bushman
have not enough to half cover their scalps; and between the little knot-like " kinks" there are wide
spaces without a single hair upon them. The Bushman's " wool" is naturally black, but red ochre and
the sun soon convert the colour into a burnt reddish
hue.

The Bushman has no beard or other hairy en-
cumbrances. Were they to grow he would root
them out as useless inconveniences. He has a low-
bridged nose, with wide flattened nostrils; an eye

B

that appears a mere slit between the eyelids; a pair of high cheek-bones, and a receding forehead. His lips are not thick, as in the negro, and he is furnished with a set of fine white teeth, which, as he grows older, do not decay, but present the singular phenomenon of being regularly worn down to the stumps—as occurs to the teeth of sheep and other ruminant animals.

Notwithstanding the small stature of the Bushman, his frame is wiry and capable of great endurance. He is also as agile as an antelope.

From the description above given, it will be inferred that the Bushman is no beauty. Neither is the Bushwoman; but, on the contrary, both having passed the period of youth, become absolutely ugly —the woman, if possible, more so than the man.

And yet, strange to say, many of the Bush-girls, when young, have a cast of prettiness, almost amounting to beauty. It is difficult to tell in what this beauty consists. Something, perhaps, in the expression of the oblique almond-shaped eye, and the small well-formed mouth and lips, with the shining white teeth. Their limbs too, at this early age, are often well rounded; and many of them exhibit forms that might serve as models for a sculptor. Their feet are especially well-shaped, and in point of size, they are by far the smallest in the world. Had the Chinese ladies been gifted by Nature with such little feet, they might have been spared the torture of compressing them.

The foot of a Bushwoman rarely measures so much as 6 inches in length; and full-grown girls have been seen whose feet, submitted to the test of an actual measurement, proved but a very little over 4 inches!

Intellectually, the Bushman does not rank so low as is generally believed. He has a quick, cheerful mind, that appears ever on the alert—as may be judged by the constant play of his little piercing black eye—and though he does not always display much skill in the manufacture of his weapons, he can do so if he pleases. Some tribes construct their bows, arrows, fish-baskets, and other implements and utensils, with admirable ingenuity; but in general, the Bushman takes no pride in fancy weapons. He prefers having them effective, and to this end he gives proof of his skill in the manufacture of most deadly poisons with which to anoint his arrows. Furthermore, he is ever active and ready for action; and in this his mind is in complete contrast with that of the Hottentot, with whom indolence is a predominant and well-marked characteristic. The Bushman, on the contrary, is always on the *qui vive;* always ready to be doing where there is anything to do; and there is not much opportunity for him to be idle, as he rarely ever knows where the next meal is to come from. The ingenuity which he displays in the capture of various kinds of game—far exceeding that of other hunting tribes of Africa—as also the cunning exhibited by him while engaged in cattle-stealing and other plundering forays, prove an intellectual capacity more than proportioned to his diminutive body; and, in short, in nearly every mental characteristic does he differ from the supposed cognate race—the Hottentot.

It would be hardly just to give the Bushman a character for high courage; but on the other hand, it would be as unjust to charge him with cowardice. Small as he is, he shows plenty of "pluck," and when brought to bay, his motto is "No surrender." He will fight to the death, discharging his poisoned arrows as long as he is able to bend a bow. Indeed, he has generally been treated to

shooting, or clubbing to death, wherever and whenever caught, and he knows nothing of *quarter.*
Just as a badger he ends his life—his last struggle
being an attempt to do injury to his assailant. This
trait in his character has no doubt been strengthened by the inhuman treatment that for a century he
has been receiving from the brutal boers of the colonial frontier.

The costume of the Bushman is of the most primitive character—differing only from that worn by
our first parents, in that the fig-leaf used by the
men is a patch of jackal-skin, and that of the wom-
en, a sort of fringe or bunch of leather thongs suspended around the waist by a strap, and hanging
down to the knees. It is in reality a little apron of
dressed skin—or, to speak more accurately, two of
them, one above the other, both cut into narrow
strips or thongs, from below the waist downward.
Other clothing than this they have none, if we except a little skin *kaross* or cloak which is worn over
their shoulders—that of the women being provided
with a bag or hood at the top, that answers the naked "piccaninny" for a nest or cradle. Sandals
protect their feet from the sharp stones, and these
are of the rudest description—merely a piece of the
thick hide cut a little longer and broader than the
soles of the feet, and fastened at the toes and round
the ankles by thongs of sinews. An attempt at ornament is displayed in a leathern skullcap, or more
commonly a circlet around the head, upon which
are sewed a number of "cowries," or small shells
of the *Cyprea moneta.*

It is difficult to say where these shells are procured—as they are not the product of the Bushman's country, but are only found on the far shores
of the Indian Ocean. Most probably he obtains
them by barter, and after they have passed through

many hands; but they must cost the **Bushman dear,**
as he sets the highest value upon **them.** Other ornaments consist of old brass or copper **buttons, at-**
tached to the little curls of his woolly **hair:** and,
among the women, strings of little **pieces of** ostrich
egg-shells, fashioned to resemble beads; besides a
perfect load of leathern bracelets **on** the arms, and
a like profusion of similar circlets on the limbs, **oft-**
en reaching from the knee to the ankle-joint.

Red ochre over the face and hair is the fashionable toilette, and a perfumery is obtained by rubbing
the skin with the powdered leaves of the "buku"
plant, a species of *diosma.* According to a quaint
old writer, this causes them to "stink like a pop-
py," and would be highly objectionable **were** it not
preferable to the odour which they have without it.

They do not *tattoo,* nor yet perforate **the ears,**
lips, or nose—practices so common **among savage**
tribes. Some instances of nose-piercing have **been**
observed, with the usual appendage of a piece **of**
wood or porcupine's quill inserted in the septum,
but this is a custom rather of the Caffres than Bushmen. Among **the** latter it is rare. A grand ornament is obtained by smearing the face and head
with a **shining** micaceous paste, which is procured
from a cave in one particular part of the Bushman's
range; but this, being a "far-fetched" article, is pro-
portionably scarce and dear. **It** is only a fine belle
who can afford to give herself a coat of *blink-slip*—
as this sparkling pigment is called by the colonists.
Many of the women, and men as well, carry in their
hands the bushy tail of a jackal. The purpose is to
fan off the flies, and serve also as a "wipe," to disembarrass their bodies of perspiration when the
weather chances to be over hot.

The domicile of the Bushman next merits description. It is quite as simple and primitive as his dress,

and gives him about equal trouble in its construction. If a cave or cleft **can be** found in the rocks—of sufficient capacity **to** admit his own body and those of his family—**never** a very large one—he builds **no** house. The cave contents him, be it ever **so** tight a squeeze. If there be no cave handy, an overhanging rock will answer equally as well. He regards not the open sides, nor the draughts. It **is** only **the rain** which he does not relish; and any sort **of** a **shed that** will shelter him from that will serve him **for a d**welling. If neither cave, crevice, nor **impending cliff** can be found in the neighbourhood, **he then** resorts **to** the alternative of house-building, **and his** style of architecture does not differ greatly from that of the orang-outang. A bush is chosen that grows near to two or three others—the branches of all meeting **in** a common centre. Of these branches the builder takes advantage, fastening them together at the ends, and wattling some into the others. Over this framework a quantity **of** grass is scattered in such a fashion **as to cast off** a **good shower** of rain, and **then the** "carcass" **of** the **building is** considered complete. The inside work remains yet to be done, and that is next set about. **A** large roundish or oblong hole is scraped out in the middle of the floor. It is made wide enough and deep enough to hold the bodies of three or four Bush-people—though a single large Caffre or Dutchman would scarcely find room in it. Into this hole is flung a quantity of dry grass, and arranged so as to present the appearance of a gigantic nest. This nest, or lair, becomes the **bed** of the Bushman, his wife or wives—for he frequently keeps two—and **the other** members of his family. Coiled together like monkeys, and covered with their skin karosses, they all sleep in it, whether "sweetly" or "soundly" I shall not take upon me to determine.

It is supposed to be this fashion of literally "sleeping in the bush," as also the mode by which he skulks and hides among bushes—invariably taking to them when pursued—that has given origin to the name Bushman, or *Bosjesman*, as it is in the language of the colonial Dutch. This derivation is probable enough, and no better has been offered.

The Bushman sometimes constructs himself a more elaborate dwelling; that is, some Bushmen— for it should be remarked that there are a great many tribes or communities of these people, and they are not all so very low in the scale of civilization. None, however, ever arrive at the building of a house—not even a hut. A tent is their highest effort in the building line, and that is of the rudest description, scarce deserving the name. Its covering is a mat, which they weave out of a species of rush that grows along some of the desert streams; and in the fabrication of the covering they display far more ingenuity than in the planning or construction of the tent itself. The mat, in fact, is simply laid over two poles, that are bent into the form of an arch by having both ends stuck into the ground. A second piece of matting closes up one end; and the other, left open, serves for the entrance. As a door is not deemed necessary, no further construction is required, and the tent is "pitched" complete. It only remains to scoop out the sand, and make the *nest* as already described.

It is said that the Goths drew their ideas of architecture from the aisles of the oak forest; the Chinese from their Mongolian tents; and the Egyptians from their caves in the rocks. Beyond a doubt, the Bushman has borrowed his from the nest of the ostrich!

It now becomes necessary to inquire how the Bushman spends his time? how he obtains subsist-once? and what is the nature of his food? All these questions can be answered, though at first it may appear difficult to answer them. Dwelling, as he always does, in the very heart of the desert, remote from forests that might furnish him with some sort of food—trees that might yield fruit—far away from a fertile soil, with no knowledge of agriculture, even if it were near—with no flocks or herds, neither sheep, cattle, horses, nor swine—no domestic animals but his lean, diminutive dogs—how does **this** Bushman procure enough to eat? What are his sources of supply?

We shall see. Being neither a grazier nor a farmer, he has other means of subsistence, though **it** must be confessed that they are of a precarious character, and often during his life does the Bushman find himself on the very threshold **of** starvation. This, however, results less from the parsimony of Nature than the Bushman's own improvident habits—a trait in his character which is, perhaps, more strongly **developed in** him than any other. We shall have **occasion to refer to it** presently.

His first and chief mode of procuring his food is by the chase; for, although he is surrounded by the sterile wilderness, he is not the only animated being who has chosen the desert for his home. Several species of birds—one the largest of all—and quadrupeds share with the Bushman the solitude and safety of this desolate region. The rhinoceros can dwell there; and in numerous streams are found **the** huge hippopotami; whilst quaggas, zebras, and several species of antelope frequent the desert plains as their favorite "stamping" ground. Some of these animals **can** live almost without water; but when they do require it, what to them is a gallop of fifty miles to some well-known "vley" or pool? It will

be seen, therefore, **that the** desert has its numerous denizens. **All these** are objects of the Bushman's pursuit, who follows them with incessant pertinacity—as if he were a beast of prey, furnished by nature with the most carnivorous propensities.

In the capture of these animals he displays an almost incredible dexterity and cunning. His mode of approaching the sly ostrich, by disguising himself in the skin of one of these birds, is so **well** known that I need not describe it here; but **the** *ruses* he adopts for capturing or killing other sorts of game are many of them equally ingenious. The pit-trap is one of his favorite contrivances; and this, too, has been often described, but often very erroneously. The pit is not a large hollow, as is usually asserted, but rather of dimensions proportioned to the size of the animal that is expected to **fall into** it. For game like the rhinoceros or *eland* antelope it is dug of six feet in length and three **in** width at the top, gradually narrowing to the **bottom**, where it ends in a trench of only twelve inch**es** broad. Six or seven feet is considered deep enough; and the animal, once into it, gets so wedged at the narrow bottom part as to be unable to make use of its legs for the purpose of springing **out** again. Sometimes a sharp stake or two are used with the view of *impaling* the victim; but this plan is not always adopted. There is not much danger of a quadruped that drops in ever getting out again till he is dragged out by the Bushman in the shape of a carcass.

The Bushman's ingenuity does not end here. Besides the construction of the trap, it is necessary the game should be guided into it. Were this not done, the pit might remain a long time empty, and, as a necessary consequence, so too might the belly of the Bushman. In the wide plain few of the gregarious animals have a path which they follow habitually; only where there is a pool may such beaten trails be found, and of these the Bushman also avails himself; but they are not enough. Some artificial means must be **used** to make the traps pay, **for** they are not constructed without much labor and patience. The plan adopted by the Bushman to accomplish this exhibits some points of originality. He first chooses a part of the plain which lies between **two** mountains. No matter **if** these be **distant** from each other; a mile, or even two, will not deter **the** Bushman from his design. By the help of his **whole** tribe—men, women, and children —**he** constructs a fence from one mountain to the other. The material used is whatever may be most ready to the hand: stones, sods, brush, or dead timber, if this be convenient. No matter how rude the fence; it **need not either be** very high. He leaves several gaps in it; **and** the wild animals, however easily they might **leap over** such a puny barrier, will, in their ordinary way, prefer to walk leisurely through the gaps. In each **of** these, however, there is a dangerous hole—dangerous from its **depth as** well **as** from the cunning way in which it is concealed from the view—in short, in each gap there is a *pitfall*. No one—at least, no animal except the elephant—would ever suspect its presence; the **grass** seems to grow over it, and the sand lies unturned, just as elsewhere upon **the plain**. What quadruped could **detect** the cheat? **Not** any one except the sagacious **elephant**. The stupid eland tumbles through; the gemsbok goes under; and the rhinoceros rushes into it as if destined to destruction. The Bushman sees this from his elevated perch, glides forward over the ground, and spears the struggling victim with his *poisoned assagai*.

Besides the above method of capturing game the

Bushman also uses the bow and arrows. This is a weapon in which he is greatly skilled ; and although both bow and arrows are as tiny as if intended for children's toys, they are among the deadliest of weapons. Their fatal effect lies not in the *size* of the wound they are capable of inflicting, but in the peculiar mode in which the barbs of the arrows are prepared. I need hardly add that they are dipped in poison—for who has not heard of the poisoned arrows of the African Bushmen ?

Both bow and arrows are usually rude enough in their construction, and would appear but a trumpery affair, were it not for a knowledge of their effects. The bow is a mere round stick, about three feet long, and slightly bent by means of its string of twisted sinews. The arrows are mere reeds tipped with pieces of bone, with a split ostrich-quill lapped behind the head, and answering for a barb. This arrow the Bushman can shoot with tolerable certainty to a distance of a hundred yards, and he can even project it farther by giving a slight elevation to his aim. It signifies not whether the force with which it strikes the object be ever so slight, if it only makes an entrance. Even a scratch from its point will sometimes prove fatal.

Of course the danger dwells altogether in the poison. Were it not for that, the Bushman, from his dwarfish stature and pigmy strength, would be a harmless creature indeed.

The poison he well knows how to prepare, and he can make it of the most " potent spell," when the "materials" are within his reach. For this purpose he makes use of both vegetable and animal substances, and a mineral is also employed—but the last is not a poison, and is only used to give consistency to the liquid, so that it may the better adhere to the arrow. The vegetable substances are of various kinds. Some are botanically known: the bulb of *Amaryllis disticha*—the gum of a *Euphorbia*—the sap of a species of sumac (*Rhus*)—and the nuts of a shrubby plant, by the colonists called *Woolf-gift* (Wolf-poison).

The animal substance is **the** fluid found in the fangs of venomous serpents, several species of which serve the purpose of the Bushmañ: **as** the little "Horned Snake"—so called from the scales rising prominently **over** its eyes; the "Yellow Snake," or South African Cobra (*Naga haje*); the "Puff Adder," and others. From all these he obtains the ingredients of his deadly ointment, and mixes them, not all together—for he cannot always procure them all in any one region of the country in which he dwells. He makes his poison, also, of different degrees of potency—according to the purpose for which he intends it: whether for hunting or war. With sixty or seventy little arrows, well imbued with this fatal mixture, and carefully placed in his quiver of tree bark or skin—or, what is not uncommon, stuck like a coronet around his head—he sallies forth, ready to deal destruction either to game, animals, or to human enemies.

Of these last he has no lack. Every man, not a Bushman, he deems his enemy; and he has some reason for thinking so. Truly may it be said of him, as of Ishmael, that his "hand is against every man, and every man's hand against him;" and such has been his unhappy history for ages. Not alone have the boers been his pursuers and oppressors, but all others upon his borders who are strong enough to attack him—colonists, Caffres, and Bechuanas, all alike—not even excepting his supposed kindred, the Hottentots. Not only does no fellow-feeling exist between Bushman and Hottentot, but, strange to say, they hate each other with the most rancorous hatred. The Bushman will plunder a Namaqua Hottentot, a Griqua, or a Gonaqua—plunder and murder him with as much ruthlessness, or even more, than he would the hated Caffre or boer. All are alike his enemies—all to be plundered and massacred, whenever met, and the thing appears possible.

We are speaking of plunder. This is another source of supply to the Bushman, though one that is not always to be depended upon. It is his most dangerous method of obtaining a livelihood, and often costs him his life. He only resorts to it when all other resources fail him, and food is no longer to be obtained by the chase.

He makes an expedition into the settlements—either of the frontier boers, Caffres, or Hottentots—whichever chance to live most convenient to his haunts. The expedition, of course, is by night, and conducted, not as an open *foray*, but in secret, and by stealth. The cattle are stolen, not *reeved*, and driven off while the owner and his people are asleep.

In the morning, or as soon as the loss is discovered, a pursuit is at once set on foot. A dozen men, mounted and armed with long muskets (*röers*), take the *spoor* of the spoilers, and follow it as fast as their horses will carry them. A dozen boers, or even half that number, is considered a match for a whole tribe of Bushmen, in any fight which may occur in the open plain—as the boers make use of their long-range guns at such a distance that the Bushmen are shot down without being able to use their poisoned arrows; and if the thieves have the fortune to be overtaken before they have got far into the desert, they stand a good chance of being terribly chastised.

There is no quarter shown them. Such a thing as mercy is never dreamt of—no sparing of lives any more than **if they were** a pack of hyenas. The Bushmen may escape to the rocks, such of them as are not hit by the bullets; and there the boers know it **would** be idle to follow **them.** Like the klipspringer antelope, the little savages can bound from rock to rock, and cliff to cliff, or hide like partridges **among crevices, where** neither man **nor** horse can pursue them. **Even** upon the level plain — if it chance **to** be stony or intersected with breaks and ravines—a horseman would endeavour **to** overtake them in **vain,** for these yellow imps are as swift as ostriches.

When the spoilers scatter thus, the boer may re-cover his cattle, but in **what** condition? That he **has** surmised already, without going among the herd. He does not expect to drive home one-half of them—perhaps not one head. On reaching **the** flock, he finds there is not one without a wound **of** some kind or other: a gash in the flank, the cut of a knife, the stab of an assagai, or **a** poisoned arrow —intended for the boer himself—sticking between the ribs. This is the sad spectacle that meets his **eyes;** but he never reflects that **it is the** result of **his** own cruelty—he never regards it in the light of retribution. Had he not first hunted the Bushman to make him a slave—to make bondsmen and bondsmaids of his sons and daughters—to submit them to the caprice and tyranny of his great strapping *frau,* perhaps his cattle would have been browsing quietly in his fields. The poor Bushman, in attempting to **take** them, followed but his instincts of hunger: **in** yielding them **up,** he obeyed but the promptings of revenge.

It is not always that the Bushman is thus over-taken. He frequently succeeds in carrying the whole herd to his desert fastness; and the skill which he exhibits in getting them there is perfectly surprising. The cattle themselves are more afraid of him than of a wild beast, and run at his approach; but the Bushman, swifter than they, can glide all around them, and keep them moving at a rapid rate.

He uses stratagem also to obstruct or baffle the pursuit. The route he takes is through the driest part of the desert—if possible, where water does not exist at all. The cattle suffer from thirst, and bellow from the pain; but the Bushman cares not for that, so long as he is himself served. But how is he served? There is no water, and a Bushman can no more go without drinking than a boer: how then does he provide for himself on these long expeditions?

All has been pre-arranged. While off to the settlements, the Bushman's wife has been busy. The whole *kraal* of women—young and old—have made an excursion half-way across the desert, each carrying ostrich egg-shells, as much as her kaross will hold, each shell full of water. These have been deposited at intervals along the route in secret spots known by marks to the Bushmen, and this accomplished the women return home again. In this way the plunderer obtains his supply of water, and thus is he enabled to continue his journey over the arid *Karroo*.

The pursuers become appalled. They are suffering from thirst—their horses sinking under them. Perhaps they have lost their way? It would be madness to proceed further. "Let the cattle go this time!" and with this disheartening reflection they give up the pursuit, turn the heads of their horses, and ride homeward.

There is a feast at the Bushman's kraal — and such a feast! not *one* ox is slaughtered, but a score of them all at once. They kill them, as if from very wantonness; and they no longer eat, but raven on the flesh.

For days **the** feasting is kept up almost continuously—even at night they must wake up to have a midnight meal! and thus runs the tale, till every ox has been eaten. They have not the slightest idea of a provision for the future; even the lower animals seem wiser in this respect. They do not think of keeping a few of the plundered cattle at pasture to serve them for a subsequent occasion. They give the poor brutes neither food nor drink; but, having penned them up in some defile of the rocks, leave them **to** moan and bellow, to droop down and die.

On goes the feasting, till all are finished; and **even** if the flesh has turned putrid, this forms not the slightest objection: it is eaten all the same.

The kraal now exhibits an altered spectacle. The starved, meagre wretches, who were seen flitting among its tents but a week ago, have all disappeared. Plump bodies and distended abdomens are the order of the day; and the profile of the Bushwoman, taken from the neck to the knees, now exhibits **the** outline of the letter S. The little imps leap about, tearing raw flesh—their yellow cheeks besmeared with blood—and the lean curs seem to have been exchanged for a pack of fat petted poodles.

But this scene must some time come to an end, and at length it does end. All the flesh is exhausted, and the bones picked clean. A complete reaction comes over the spirit of the Bushman. He falls into a state of languor—the only time when he knows such a feeling,—and he keeps his kraal, and remains idle for days. Often he sleeps for twenty-four hours **at a** time; and wakes, only to go to sleep again. He need not rouse himself with the idea of getting something to eat: there is **not a** morsel in the whole kraal, and **he** knows it. He lies still, therefore—

weakened with hunger, and overcome with the drowsiness of a terrible lassitude.

Fortunate for him, while in this state, if those bold vultures—attracted by the *débris* of his feast, and now high wheeling in the air—be not perceived from afar ; fortunate if they do not discover the whereabouts of his kraal to the vengeful pursuer. If they should do so, he has made his last foray and his last feast.

When the absolute danger of starvation at length compels our Bushman to bestir himself, he seems to recover a little of his energy, and once more takes to hunting, or, if near a stream, endeavours to catch a few fish. Should both these resources fail, he has another — without which he would most certainly starve — and perhaps this may be considered his most important source of supply, since it is the most constant, and can be depended on at nearly all seasons of the year. Weakened with hunger, then, and scarce equal to any severer labour, he goes *out hunting—this time insects, not quadrupeds.* With a stout stick inserted into a stone at one end and pointed at the other, he proceeds to the nests of the white ants (*termites*), and using the point of the stick—the stone serving by its weight to aid the force of the blow—he breaks open the hard gummy clay of which the hillock is formed. Unless the *aard-vark* and the *pangolin* — two very different kinds of ant-eaters—have been there before him, he finds the chambers filled with the eggs of the ants, the insects themselves, and perhaps large quantities of their *larvæ.* All are equally secured by the Bushman, and either devoured on the spot, or collected into a skin bag, and carried back to his kraal.

He hunts also another species of ants that do not build nests or " hillocks," but bring forth their young in hollows under the ground. These make

C

long galleries or **covered ways just** under the surface, and at certain **periods—which** the Bushman **knows by unmistakable signs —they** become very **active, and traverse these underground** galleries in thousands.   **If the passages** were **to** be opened **above,** the **ants would soon** make **off to** their caves, **and but a very** few could **be** captured.   The Bushman knowing this, adopts a stratagem.   **With the** stick already **mentioned** he pierces holes **of a** good depth **down ; and works** the stick about, until **the** sides **of the holes are** smooth and even.   These **he** intend's shall **serve him as pitfalls ; and they** are **therefore made in** the **covered ways** along which **the** insects are passing.   The **result** is, that the little creatures, not suspecting the existence of these deep wells, tumble head foremost into them, **and are** unable to mount up the steep smooth sides again— so that in **a** few minutes **the** hole **will** be filled with ants, which **the** Bushman scoops out at his leisure.

Another source **of** supply which he has, and **also** a **pretty** constant **one,** consists of **various** roots of **the** tuberous kind, but more especially bulbous roots **which** grow in the desert.   **They are** several species **of *Ixias*** and *Mesembryanthemums*—some of them **producing** bulbs of a large size, and deeply buried **underground.** Half the Bushman's and Bushwoman's **time is** occupied **in** digging for these **roots ; and the spade** employed is the **stone-headed staff** already **described.**

Ostrich eggs **also furnish** the Bushman with **many** a meal ; and **the huge shells** of these eggs serve him **for** water-vessels, cups, and dishes.   He is exceedingly expert in tracking up the ostrich, and discovering **its** nest.   Sometimes he finds a nest in the **absence of** the birds ; and **in a** case of this kind he **pursues** a course of conduct that is *peculiarly Bushman.*   Having removed all **the** eggs to a distance,

and concealed them under some bush, he returns to
the nest and ensconces himself in it. His diminutive body, when close squatted, cannot be perceived
from a distance—especially when there are a few
bushes around the nest, as there usually are. Thus
concealed he awaits the return of the birds—holding his bow and poisoned arrows ready to salute
them as soon as they come within range. By this
ruse he is almost certain of killing either the cock
or hen, and not unfrequently both—when they do
not return together.

Lizards and land-tortoises often furnish the Bushman with a meal; and the shell of the latter serves
him also for a dish; but his period of greatest plenty
is when the *locusts appear.* Then, indeed, the Bushman is no longer in want of a meal; and while these
creatures remain with him, he knows no hunger.
He grows fat in a trice, and his curs keep pace with
him—for they too greedily devour the locusts.
Were the locusts a constant, or even an annual visitor, the Bushman would be a rich man—at all
events his wants would be amply supplied. Unfortunately for him, but fortunately for everybody else,
these terrible destroyers of vegetation only come
now and then—several years often intervening between their visits.

The Bushmen have no religion whatever; no form
of marriage—any more than mating together like
wild beasts—but they appear to have some respect
for the memory of their dead, since they bury them
—usually erecting a large pile of stones, or " cairn,"
over the body.

They are far from being of a melancholy mood.
Though crouching in their dens and caves during
the day, in dread of the boers and other enemies,
they come forth at night to chatter and make merry. During fine moonlights they dance all night,

keeping up the *ball* till morning; and in their kraals may be seen a circular spot — beaten hard and smooth with their feet—where these dances are performed.

They have no form of government—not so much as a head man or chief. Even the father of the family possesses no authority, except such as superior strength may give him; and when his sons are grown up and become as strong as he is, this, of course, also ceases.

They have no tribal organization; the small communities in which they live being merely so many individuals accidentally brought together, often quarrelling and separating from one another. These communities rarely number over a hundred individuals, since, from the nature of their country, a large number could not find subsistence in any one place. It follows, therefore, that the Bushman race must ever remain widely scattered—so long as they pursue their present mode of life—and no influence has ever been able to win them from it. Missionary efforts made among them have all proved fruitless. The desert seems to have been created for them, as they for the desert; and when transferred elsewhere, to dwell amidst scenes of civilized life, they always yearn to return to their wilderness home.

Truly are these pigmy savages an odd people!

THE AMAZONIAN INDIANS.

In glancing at the map of the American continent, we are struck by a remarkable analogy between the geographical features of its two great divisions—the North and the South—an analogy amounting almost to a symmetrical parallelism.

Each has its "mighty" mountains—the *Cordilleras of the Andes* in the south, and the *Cordilleras of the Sierra Madre* (Rocky Mountains) in the north—with all the varieties of volcano and eternal snow. Each has its secondary chain: in the north, the *Nevadas* of California and Oregon; in the south, the *Sierras* of Caraccas and the group of Guiana; and, if you wish to render the parallelism complete, descend to a lower elevation, and set the Alleghanies of the United States against the mountains of Brazil—both alike detached from all the others.

In the comparison we have exhausted the mountain-chains of both divisions of the continent. If we proceed farther, and carry it into minute detail, we shall find the same correspondence—ridge for ridge, chain for chain, peak for peak;—in short, a most singular equilibrium, as if there had been a design that one half of this great continent should balance the other!

From the mountains let us proceed to the rivers, and see how *they* will correspond. Here again, we discover a like parallelism, amounting almost to a rivalry. Each continent (for it is proper to style them so) contains the largest river in the world. If we make *length* the standard, the north claims

precedence for the Mississippi; if *volume of water*
is to be the criterion, the south is entitled to it upon
the merits of the Amazon. Each, too, has its numerous branches, spreading into a mighty "tree;"
and these, either singly or combined, form a curious
equipoise, both in length and magnitude. We have
only time to set list against list, tributaries of the
great northern river against tributaries of its great
southern compeer,—the Ohio and Illinois, the Yel-
lowstone and Platte, the Kansas and Osage, the
Arkansas and Red, against the Madeira and Purus,
the Ucayali and Huallaga, the Japura and Negro,
the Xingu and Tapajos.

Of other river systems, the St. Lawrence may be
placed against the La Plata, the Oregon against the
Orinoco, the Mackenzie against the Magdalena, and
the Rio Bravo del Norte against the Tocantins;
while the two Colorados—the Brazos and Alabama
—find their respective rivals in the Essequibo, the
Paranahybo, the Pedro, and the Patagonian Negro;
and the San Francisco of California, flowing over
sands of gold, is balanced by its homonyme of
Brazil, that has its origin in the land of diamonds.
To an endless list might the comparison be carried.

We pass to the plains. *Prairies* in the north,
llanos and *pampas* in the south, almost identical in
character. Of the *plateaux* or table-lands, those of
Mexico, La Puebla, Perote, and silver Potosi in the
north; those of Quito, Bogota, Cusco, and gold
Potosi in the south; of the desert plains, Utah and
the Llano Estacado against Atacama and the deserts of Patagonia. Even the Great Salt Lake has
its parallel in Titicaca; while the "Salinas" of New
Mexico, and the upland prairies, are represented
by similar deposits in the Gran Chaco and the
Pampas.

We arrive finally at the forests. Though unlike

in other respects, we have here also a rivalry in
magnitude—between the vast timbered expanse
stretching from Arkansas to the Atlantic shores,
and that which covers the válley of the Amazon.
These *were* the two greatest forests on the face of
the earth. I say *were*, for one of them no longer
exists—at least, it is no longer a continuous tract,
but a collection of forests, opened by the axe, and
intersected by the clearings of the colonist. The
other still stands in all its virgin beauty and primeval vigour, untouched by the axe, undefiled by
fire, its path scarce trodden by human feet, its silent
depths to this hour unexplored.

It is with this forest and its denizens we have to
do. Here then let us terminate the catalogue of
similitudes, and concentrate our attention upon the
particular subject of our sketch.

The whole *valley* of the Amazon—in other words,
the tract watered by this great river and its tributaries—may be described as one unbroken forest.
We now know the borders of this forest with considerable exactness, but to trace them here would
require a too lengthened detail. Suffice it to say,
that lengthwise it extends from the mouth of the
Amazon to the foot-hills of the Peruvian Andes, a
distance of 2,500 miles. In breadth it varies, beginning on the Atlantic coast with a breadth of 400
miles, which widens towards the central part of the
continent till it attains to 1,500, and again narrowing to about 1,000, where it touches the eastern
slope of the Andes.

That form of leaf known to botanists as "obovate"
will give a good idea of the figure of the great Amazon forest, supposing the small end or shank to rest
on the Atlantic, and the broad end to extend along
the semicircular concavity of the Andes, from Bolivia on the south to New Granada on the north.

In all this **vast expanse of territory** there **is scarce
an acre of open ground,** if we except the water-sur-
face of the rivers **and** their bordering "lagoons,"
which, were they to bear their due proportions on
a map, could **scarce be represented** by the narrowest lines, or **the most** inconspicuous dots. The grass
plains which **embay the** forest on its southern edge
along **the** banks **of some** of its Brazilian tributaries,
or those which proceed like spurs from the Llanos
of Venezuela, do not in any place approach the Amazon itself, and there are many points on the great
river which may **be** taken **as** centres, and around
which circles may **be** drawn, having diameters 1,000
miles in length, the circumference of which will in-
close nothing but timbered land. The main stream
of the Amazon, though it intersects this grand forest, does not *bisect* it, speaking with mathematical
precision. There is rather more timbered surface
to the southward than that which extends northward, though the inequality of the two divisions is
not great. It would not be much of an error to say
that the Amazon river cuts the forest in halves. At
its mouth, however, this would not apply; since for
the first 300 miles above the embouchure of the river, the country on the northern side is destitute of
timber. This is occasioned by the projecting spurs
of the Guiana mountains, which on that side approach the Amazon in the shape of naked ridges
and grass-covered hills and plains.

It is not necessary to say that the great forest of
the Amazon is a tropical one—since the river itself,
throughout its whole course, almost traces the line
of the equator. Its vegetation, therefore, is emphatically of a tropical character; and in this respect it
differs essentially from that of North America, or
rather, we should say, of Canada and the United
States. It is necessary to make this limitation, be-

cause the forests of the tropical parts of **North**
America, including the West-Indian islands, present
a great similitude to that of the Amazon. It is not
only in the genera and species of trees that the *sylva*
of the temperate zone differs from that of the torrid;
but there is a very remarkable difference in the dis-
tribution of these genera and species. **In** a great
forest of the north, it is not uncommon **to** find a
large tract covered with **a** single species **of trees,**—
as with pines, oaks, poplars, or the red cedar (*Juniperus virginiana*). This arrangement is rather
the rule than the exception; whereas, in the trop-
ical forest, the rule is reversed, except in the case
of two or three species of palms (*Mauritia* and
Euterpe), which sometimes exclusively cover large
tracts of surface. Of other trees, it is rare to find
even a clump or grove standing together—often
only two or three trees, **and** still more frequently,
a single individual is observed, separated **from** those
of its own kind by hundreds of others, **all** differing
in order, genus, and species. I note this peculiarity of the tropic forest, because it exercises, as may
easily be imagined, a direct influence upon the econ-
omy of its human occupants—whether these be savage **or** civilized. Even the habits of the lower animals—beasts and birds—are subject to a **similar**
influence.

It would be out of place here to enumerate the
different kinds of trees that compose this mighty
wood,—a bare catalogue of their names would alone
fill many pages—and it would be safe to say, **that**
if the list were given as now known to botanists, it
would comprise scarce half the species that actually exist in the valley of the Amazon. In real truth,
this vast Garden of God is yet unexplored by man.
Its border walks and edges have alone been examined; and the enthusiastic botanist need not fear

that he is too late in the field. A hundred years will elapse before this grand *parterre* can be exhausted.

At present, a thorough examination of the botany of the Amazon valley would be difficult, if not altogether impossible, even though conducted on a grand and expensive scale. There are several reasons for this. Its woods are in many places absolutely impenetrable—on account either of the thick tangled undergrowth, or from the damp, spongy nature of the soil. There are no roads that could be traversed by horse or man; and the few paths are known only to the wild savage—not always passable even by him. Travelling can only be done by water, either upon the great rivers, or by the narrow creeks (igaripes) or lagoons; and a journey performed in this fashion must needs be both tedious and indirect, allowing but a limited opportunity for observation. Horses can scarce be said to exist in the country, and cattle are equally rare—a few only are found in one or two of the large Portuguese settlements on the main river—and the jaguars and blood-sucking bats offer a direct impediment to their increase. Contrary to the general belief, the tropical forest is not the home of the larger mammalia; it is not their proper *habitat*, nor are they found in it. In the Amazon forest but few species exist, and these not numerous in individuals. There are no vast herds—as of buffaloes on the prairies of North America, or of antelopes in Africa. The tapir alone attains to any considerable size,—exceeding that of the ass,—but its numbers are few. Three or four species of small deer represent the ruminants, and the hog of the Amazon is the peccary. Of these there are at least three species. Where the forest impinges on the mountain regions of Peru, bears are found of at least two kinds, but not on the lower plains of the great "Montaña"—for by this general designation is the vast expanse of the Amazon country known among the Peruvian people. "Montes" and "montañas," literally signifying "mountains," are not so understood among Spanish Americans. With them the "montes" and "montañas" are tracts of forest-covered country, and that of the Amazon valley is the "Montaña" *par excellence*.

Sloths of several species, and opossums of still greater variety, are found all over the Montaña, but both thinly distributed as regards the number of individuals. A similar remark applies to the ant-eaters or "ant-bears," of which there are four kinds,—to the armadillos, the "agoutis," and the "cavies," one of which last, the *capibara*, is the largest rodent upon earth. This, with its kindred genus, the "paca," is not so rare in individual numbers, but, on the contrary, appears in large herds upon the borders of the rivers and lagoons. A porcupine, several species of spinous rats, an otter, two or three kinds of badger-like animals (the *potto* and *coatis*), a "honey-bear" (*Galera barbara*), and a fox, or wild dog, are widely distributed throughout the Montaña.

Everywhere exists the jaguar, both the black and spotted varieties, and the puma has there his lurking-place. Smaller cats, both spotted and striped, are numerous in species, and squirrels of several kinds, with bats, complete the list of the terrestrial mammalia.

Of all the lower animals, monkeys are the most common, for to them the Montaña is a congenial home. They abound not only in species, but in the number of individuals, and their ubiquitous presence contributes to enliven the woods. At least thirty different kinds of them exist in the

Amazon valley, from the "coatas," and other howlers as large as baboons, to the tiny little "ouistitis" and "säimiris," not bigger than squirrels or rats.

While we must admit a paucity in the species of the quadrupeds of the Amazon, the same remark does not apply to the birds. In the ornithological department of natural history, a fulness and richness here exist, perhaps not equalled elsewhere. The most singular and graceful forms, combined with the most brilliant plumage, are everywhere presented to the eye, in the parrots and great macaws, the toucans, trogons, and tanagers, the shrikes, humming-birds, and orioles; and even in the vultures and eagles: for here are found the most beautiful of predatory birds,—the king vulture and the harpy eagle. Of the feathered creatures existing in the valley of the Amazon there are not less than one thousand different species, of which only one half have yet been caught or described.

Reptiles are equally abundant—the serpent family being represented by numerous species, from the great water boa (*anaconda*), of ten yards in length, to the tiny and beautiful but venomous *lachesis*, or coral snake, not thicker than the shank of a tobacco-pipe. The lizards range through a like gradation, beginning with the huge "jacare," or crocodile, of several species, and ending with the turquoise-blue *anolius*, not bigger than a newt.

The waters too are rich in species of their peculiar inhabitants—of which the most remarkable and valuable **are** the *manatees* (two or three species), the great and smaller turtles, the porpoises of various kinds, and an endless catalogue of the finny tribes that frequent the rivers of the tropics. It is mainly from this source, and not from four-footed creatures of the forest, that the human denizen of the great Montaña draws his supply of food,—at

least that portion of **it** which may be termed the
" meaty." Were it not for the *manatee*, the great
porpoise, and other large fish, he would often have
to " eat his bread dry."

And now it is *his* turn to be " talked about." I
need not inform you that the aborigines who inhabit the valley of the Amazon, are all of the so-called
Indian race—though there are so many distinct
tribes of them that almost every river of any considerable magnitude has a tribe of its own. In
some cases a number of these tribes belong to one
nationality; that is, several of them may be found
speaking nearly the same language, though living
apart from each other ; and of these larger divisions or nationalities there are several occupying the
different districts of the Montaña. The tribes even
of the same nationality do not always present a
uniform appearance. There are darker and fairer
tribes ; some in which the average standard of
height is less than among Europeans ; and others
where it equals or exceeds this. There are tribes
again where both men and women are ill-shaped
and ill-favoured—though these are few—and other
tribes where both sexes exhibit a considerable degree of personal beauty. Some tribes are even distinguished for their good looks, the men presenting
models of manly form, while the women are equally
attractive by the regularity of their features, and
the graceful modesty of expression that adorns
them.

A minute detail of the many peculiarities in
which the numerous tribes of the Amazon differ
from one another would fill a large volume ; and in
a sketch like the present, which is meant to include
them all, it would not be possible to give such a detail. Nor indeed would it serve any good purpose ;
for although there are many points of difference be-

tween the different tribes, yet these are generally
of slight importance, and are far more than counterbalanced by the multitude of resemblances. So
numerous are these last, as to create a strong *idiosyncrasy* in the tribes of the Amazon, which not
only entitles them to be classed together in an ethnological point of view, but which separates them
from all the other Indians of America. Of course,
the non-possession of the horse—they do not even
know the animal—at once broadly distinguishes
them from the Horse Indians, both of the Northern
and Southern divisions of the continent.

It would be idle here to discuss the question as
to whether the Amazonian Indians have all a common origin. It is evident they have not. We
know that many of them are from Peru and Bogota—runaways from Spanish oppression. We know
that others migrated from the south—equally fugi-
tives from the still more brutal and barbarous dom-
ination of the Portuguese. And still others were
true aboriginals of the soil, or if emigrants, when
and whence came they? An idle question, never
to be satisfactorily answered. There they now are,
and *as they are* only shall we here consider them.

Notwithstanding the different sources whence
they sprang, we find them, as I have already said,
stamped with a certain idiosyncrasy, the result, no
doubt, of the like circumstances which surround
them. One or two tribes alone, whose habits are
somewhat "odder" than the rest, have been treated
to a separate chapter; but for the others, whatever
is said of one, will, with very slight alteration, stand
good for the whole of the Amazonian tribes. Let it
be understood that we are discoursing only of those
known as the "Indios bravos," the fierce, brave,
savage, or wild Indians—as you may choose to
translate the phrase,—a phrase used throughout all

Spanish America to distinguish those tribes, or sections of tribes, who refused obedience to Spanish tyranny, and who preserve to this hour their native independence and freedom. In contradistinction to the "Indios bravos" are the "Indios mansos," or "tame Indians," who submitted tamely both to the cross and sword, and now enjoy a rude demi-semi-civilization under the joint protectorate of priests and soldiers. Between these two kinds of American aborigines, there is as much difference as between a lord and his serf—the true savage representing the former, and the demi-semicivilized savage approximating more nearly to the latter. The meddling monk has made a complete failure of it. His ends were purely political, and the result has proved ruinous to all concerned;—instead of civilizing the savage, he has positively demoralized him.

It is not of his neophytes, the "Indios mansos," we are now writing, but of the "infidels," who would not hearken to his voice or listen to his teachings—those who could never be brought within "sound of the bell."

Both "kinds" dwell within the valley of the Amazon, but in different places. The "Indios mansos" may be found along the banks of the main stream, from its source to its mouth—but more especially on its upper waters, where it runs through Spanish (Peruvian) territory. There they dwell in little villages or collections of huts, ruled by the missionary monk with iron rod, and performing for him all the offices of the menial slave. Their resources are few, not even equalling those of their wild but independent brethren; and their customs and religion exhibit a ludicrous *mélange* of savagery and civilization. Farther down the river, the "Indio manso" is a "tapuio," a hireling of the Portuguese, or, to speak more correctly, a *slave;* for the latter treats

him as such, considers him as such, and, though
there is a law against it, often drags him from his
forest-home and keeps him in life-long bondage.
Any human law would be a dead letter among such
white-skins as are to be encountered upon the banks
of the Amazon. Fortunately they are but few; a
town or two on the lower Amazon and Rio Negro
—some wretched villages between—scattered *estancias* along the banks—with here and there a paltry
post of "militarios," dignified by the name of a
"fort:" these alone speak the progress of the Portuguese civilization throughout a period of three
centuries!

From all these settlements the wild Indian keeps
away. He is never found near them—he is never
seen by travellers, not even by the settlers. You
may descend the mighty Amazon from its source to
its mouth, and not once set your eyes upon the true
son of the forest—the "Indio bravo." Coming in
contact only with the neophyte of the Spanish missionary, and the skulking *tapuio* of the Portuguese
trader, you might bring away a very erroneous impression of the character of an Amazonian Indian.

Where is he to be seen? where dwells he? what-
like is his home? what sort of a house does he
build? His costume? his arms? his occupation?
his habits? These are the questions you would put.
They shall all be answered, but briefly as possible
—since our limited space requires brevity.

The wild Indian, then, is not to be found upon
the Amazon itself, though there are long reaches of
the river where he is free to roam—hundreds of
miles without either town or *estancia*. He hunts,
and occasionally fishes by the great water, but does
not there make his dwelling—though in days gone
by, its shores were his favourite place of residence.
These happy days were before the time when Orel-

lana floated down past the door of his "malocca"—
before that dark hour when the Brazilian slave-hunter found his way into the waters of the mighty *Soli-
moes*. This last event **was** the cause of his disappearance. It drove him **from** the shores of **his** beloved
river-sea; forced him to withdraw his dwelling from
observation, and rebuild it far up, on those tributaries where he might live a more peaceful life, secure from the trafficker in human flesh. Hence it
is that the home of the Amazonian Indian is now
to be sought for—not on the Amazon itself, but on
its tributary streams—on the "caños" and "igaripes," the canals and lagoons that, with a labyrinthine ramification, intersect the mighty forest of
the Montaña. Here dwells he, and here is he to be
seen by any one bold enough to visit him in his fastness home.

How is he domiciled? Is there anything peculiar about the style of his house or his village?

Eminently peculiar; for in this respect he differs
from all the other savage people of whom we have
yet written, or of whom we may have occasion to
write.

Let us proceed at once to describe his dwelling.
It is not a tent, nor is it a hut, nor a cabin, nor a
cottage, nor yet a cave! His dwelling can hardly
be termed a house, nor his village a collection of
houses—since both house and village are one and
the same, and both are so peculiar that we have no
name for such a structure in civilized lands, unless
we should call it a "barrack." But even this appellation would give but an erroneous idea of the
Amazonian dwelling; and therefore we shall use
that by which it is known in the "Lingoa geral,"
and call it a *malocca*.

By such name is his house (or village rather)
known among the *tapuios* and traders of the Ama-

zon. Since it is both house and village at the same
time, it must needs be a large structure; and so is
it, large enough to contain the whole tribe—or at
least the section of it that has chosen one particular
spot for their residence. It is the property of the
whole community, built by the labour of all, and
used as their common dwelling—though each family has its own section specially set apart for itself.
It will thus be seen that the Amazonian savage is,
to some extent, a disciple of the Socialist school.

I have not space to enter into a minute account
of the architecture of the *malocca*. Suffice it to
say, that it is an immense temple-like building, raised
upon timber uprights, so smooth and straight as to
resemble columns. The beams and rafters are also
straight and smooth, and are held in their places by
"sipos" (tough creeping plants), which are whipped
around the joints with a neatness and compactness
equal to that used in the rigging of a ship. The
roof is a thatch of palm-leaves, laid on with great
regularity, and brought very low down at the eaves,
so as to give to the whole structure the appearance
of a gigantic beehive. The walls are of split palms
or bamboos, placed so closely together as to be im-
pervious to either bullet or arrows.

The plan is a parallelogram, with a semicircle at
one end; and the building is large enough to accommodate the whole community, often numbering
more than a hundred individuals. On grand festive occasions several neighboring communities can
find room enough in it—even for dancing—and
three or four hundred individuals not unfrequently
assemble under the roof of a single *malocca*.

Inside the arrangements are curious. There is a
wide hall or avenue in the middle—that extends
from end to end throughout the whole length of the
parallelogram—and on both sides of the hall is a

row of partitions, separated from each other by split palms, or canes, closely placed. Each of these sections is the abode of a family, and the place of deposit for the hammocks, clay pots, calabash-cups, dishes, baskets, weapons, and ornaments, which are the private property of each. The hall is used for the larger cooking utensils—such as the great clay ovens and pans for baking the cassava, and boiling the *caxire* or *chicha*. This is also a neutral ground, where the children play, and where the dancing is done on the occasion of grand "balls" and other ceremonial festivals.

The common doorway is in the gable end, and is six feet wide by ten in height. It remains open during the day, but is closed at night by a mat of palm fibre suspended from the top. There is another and smaller doorway at the semicircular end; but this is for the private use of the chief, who appropriates the whole section of the semicircle to himself and his family.

Of course the above is only the general outline of a *malocca*. A more particular description would not answer for that of all the tribes of the Amazon. Among different communities, and in different parts of the Montaña, the *malocca* varies in size, shape, and the materials of which it is built; and there are some tribes who live in separate huts. These exceptions, however, are few, and, as a general thing, that above described is the style of habitation throughout the whole Montaña, from the confines of Peru to the shores of the Atlantic. North and south we encounter this singular house-village, from the head-waters of the Rio Negro to the highlands of Brazil.

Most of the Amazonian tribes follow agriculture, and understood the art of tillage before the coming of the Spaniards. They practise it, however, to a very limited extent. They cultivate a little manioc, and know how to manufacture it into *farinha* or *cassava* bread. They plant the *musaceæ* and yam, and understand the distillation of various drinks, both from the plantain and several kinds of palms. They can make pottery from clay—shaping it into various forms, neither rude nor inelegant—and from the trees and parasitical twiners that surround their dwellings, they manufacture an endless variety of neat implements and utensils.

Their canoes are hollow trunks of trees, sufficiently well shaped, and admirably adapted to their mode of travelling—which is almost exclusively by water, by the numerous *caños* and *igaripes*, which are the roads and paths of their country—often as narrow and intricate as paths by land.

The Indians of the tropic forest dress in the very lightest costume. Of course each tribe has its own fashion; but a mere belt of cotton cloth, or the inner bark of a tree, passed round the waist and between the limbs, is all the covering they care for. It is the *guayuco*. Some wear a skirt of tree-bark, and, on grand occasions, feather tunics are seen, and also plume head-dresses, made of the brilliant wing and tail feathers of parrots and macaws. Circlets of these also adorn the arms and limbs. All the tribes paint, using the *anotto*, *caruto*, and several other dyes which they obtain from various kinds of trees, elsewhere more particularly described.

There are one or two tribes who *tattoo* their skins; but this strange practice is far less common among the American Indians than with the natives of the Pacific isles.

In the manufacture of their various household utensils and implements, as well as their weapons for war and the chase, many tribes of Amazonian Indians display an ingenuity that would do credit to the most accomplished artisans. The hammocks made by them have been admired everywhere; and it is from the valley of the Amazon that most of these are obtained, so much prized in the cities of Spanish and Portuguese America. They are the special manufacture of the women, the men only employing their mechanical skill on their weapons.

The hammock, "rede," or " maqueira," is manufactured out of strings obtained from the young leaves of several species of palms. The *astrocaryum*, or " tucum" palm furnishes this cordage, but a still better quality is obtained from the " miriti," (*Mauritia flexuosa*). The unopened leaf, which forms a thick pointed column growing up out of the crown of the tree, is cut off at the base, and this being pulled apart, is shaken dexterously until the tender leaflets fall out. These being stripped of their outer covering, leave behind a thin tissue of a pale-yellowish colour, which is the fibre for making the cordage. After being tied in bundles this fibre is left awhile to dry, and is then twisted by being rolled between the hand and the hip or thigh. The women perform this process with great dexterity. Taking two strands of fibre between the fore finger and thumb of the left hand, they lay them separated a little along the thigh; a roll downwards gives them a twist, and then being adroitly brought together, a roll upwards completes the making of the cord. Fifty fathoms in a day is considered a good day's spinning. The cords are afterwards dyed of various colours, to render them more ornamental when woven into the maqueira.

The making of this is a simple process. Two horizontal rods are placed at about seven feet apart, over which the cord is passed some fifty or sixty times, thus forming the " woof." The warp is then worked in by knotting the cross strings at equal

distances apart, until there are enough. Two strong
cords are then inserted where the rods pass through,
and these being firmly looped—so as to draw all
the parallel strings together—the rod is pulled out,
and the hammock is ready to be used.

Of course, with very fine "redes," and those intended to be disposed of to the traders, much pains
are taken in the selection of the materials, the dyeing the cord, and the weaving it into the hammock. Sometimes very expensive articles are made
ornamented with the brilliant feathers of birds cun-
ningly woven among the meshes and along the borders.

Besides making the hammock—which is the universal couch of the Amazonian Indian—the women
also manufacture a variety of beautiful baskets.
Many species of palms and *calamus* supply them
with materials for this purpose, one of the best being the "Iu" palm (*Astrocaryum acaule*). They
also make many implements and utensils, some for
cultivating the plantains, melons, and *manioc* root,
and others for manufacturing the last-named vegetable into their favourite "farinha" (*cassava*). The
Indians understood how to separate the poisonous
juice of this valuable root from its wholesome fari-
na, before the arrival of white men among them;
and the process by which they accomplish this purpose has remained without change up to the present hour—in fact, it is almost the same as that practised by the Spaniards and Portuguese, who simply
adopted the Indian method. The work is performed by the women, and thus: the roots are brought
home from the manioc "patch" in baskets, and then
washed and peeled. The peeling is usually performed by the teeth; after that the roots are grated
—the grater being a large wooden slab about three
feet long, a foot wide, a little hollowed out, and the

hollow part covered all over with sharp pieces of quartz set in regular diamond-shaped patterns. Sometimes a cheaper grater is obtained by using the aërial root of the pashiuba palm (*Iriartea exhorhiza*), which, being thickly covered over with hard spinous protuberances, serves admirably for the purpose.

The grated pulp is next placed to dry upon a sieve made of the rind of a water-plant, and is afterwards put into a long elastic cylinder-shaped basket or net, of the bark of the "jacitara" palm (*Desmoncus macroacanthus*). This is the *tipiti;* and at its lower end there is a strong loop, through which a stout pole is passed; while the *tipiti* itself, when filled with pulp, is hung up to the branch of a tree, or to a firm peg in the wall. One end of the pole is then rested against some projecting point, that serves as a fulcrum, while the Indian woman, having seated herself upon the other end, with her infant in her arms, or perhaps some work in her hands, acts as the lever power. Her weight draws the sides of the *tipiti* together, until it assumes the form of an inverted cone; and thus the juice is gradually pressed out of the pulp, and drops into a vessel placed underneath to receive it. The mother must be careful that the little imp does not escape from under her eye, and perchance quench its thirst out of the vessel below. If such an accident were to take place, in a very few minutes she would have to grieve for a lost child; since the sap of the manioc root—the variety most cultivated by the Indians—is a deadly poison. This is the "yucca amarga," or bitter manioc; the "yucca dulce," or sweet kind, being quite innoxious, even if eaten in its raw state.

The remainder of the process consists in placing the grated pulp—now sufficiently dry—on a large pan or oven, and submitting it to the action of the fire. It is then thought sufficiently good for Indian use; but much of it is afterwards prepared for. commerce, under different names, and sold as *semonilla* (erroneously called *semolina*), sago, and even as arrow-root.

At the bottom of that poisonous tub, a sediment has all the while been forming. That is the *starch* of the manioc root—the *tapioca* of commerce: of course that is not thrown away.

The men of the tropic forest spend their lives in doing very little. They are idle and not much disposed to work—only when war or the chase calls them forth do they throw aside for awhile their indolent habit, and exhibit a little activity.

They hunt with the bow and arrow, and fish with a harpoon spear, nets, and sometimes by poisoning the water with the juice of a vine called barbasco. The "peixe boy," "vaca marina," or "manatee,"— all three names being synonyms—is one of the chief animals of their pursuit. All the waters of the Amazon valley abound with manatees, probably of several species, and these large creatures are captured by the harpoon, just as seals or walrus are taken. Porpoises also frequent the South-American rivers; and large fresh-water fish of numerous species. The game hunted by the Amazonian Indians can scarcely be termed noble. We have seen that the large *mammalia* are few, and thinly distributed in the tropical forest. With the exception of the jaguar and peccary, the chase is limited to small quadrupeds—as the capibara, the paca, agouti— to many kinds of monkeys, and an immense variety of birds. The monkey is the most common game, and is not only eaten by all the Amazonian Indians, but by most of them considered as the choicest of food.

In procuring their game the hunters sometimes use the common bow and arrow, but most of the tribes are in possession of a weapon which they prefer to all others for this particular purpose. It is an implement of death so original in its character and so singular in its construction as to deserve a special and minute description.

The weapon I allude to is the "blow-gun," called "pucuna" by the Indians themselves, "gravitana" by the Spaniards, and "cerbatana" by the Portuguese of Brazil.

When the Amazonian Indian wishes to manufacture for himself a *pucuna* he goes out into the forest and searches for two tall straight stems of the "pashiuba miri" palm (*Iriartea setigera*). These he requires of such thickness that one can be contained within the other. Having found what he wants, he cuts both down and carries them home to his malocca. Neither of them is of such dimensions as to render this either impossible or difficult.

He now takes a long slender rod—already prepared for the purpose—and with this pushes out the pith from both stems, just as boys do when preparing their pop-guns from the stems of the elder-tree. The rod thus used is obtained from another species of *Iriartea* palm, of which the wood is very hard and tough. A little tuft of fern-root, fixed upon the end of the rod, is then drawn backward and forward through the tubes, until both are cleared of any pith which may have adhered to the interior; and both are polished by this process to the smoothness of ivory. The palm of smaller diameter, being scraped to a proper size, is now inserted into the tube of the larger, the object being to correct any crookedness in either, should there be such; and if this does not succeed, both are whipped to some straight beam or post, and thus left till they become

straight. One end of the bore, from the nature of
the tree, is always smaller than the other; and to
this end is fitted a mouth-piece of two peccary tusks
to concentrate the breath of the hunter when blowing into the tube. The other end is the muzzle;
and near this, on the top, a sight is placed, usually
a tooth of the " paca" or some other rodent animal.
This sight is glued on with a gum which another
tropic tree furnishes. Over the outside, when desirous of giving the weapon an ornamental finish,
the maker winds spirally a shining creeper, and then
the *pucuna* is ready for action.

Sometimes only a single shank of palm is used,
and instead of the pith being pushed out, the stem
is split into two equal parts throughout its whole
extent. The heart substance being then removed,
the two pieces are brought together, like the two
divisions of a cedar-wood pencil, and tightly bound
with a sipo.

The *pucuna* is usually about an inch and a half
in diameter at the thickest end, and the bore about
equal to that of a pistol of ordinary calibre. In
length, however, the weapon varies from eight to
twelve feet.

This singular instrument is designed, not for pro-
pelling a bullet, but an arrow; but as this arrow
differs altogether from the common kind it also
needs to be described.

The blow-gun arrow is about fifteen or eighteen
inches long, and is made of a piece of split bamboo;
but when the " patawa" palm can be found, this tree
furnishes a still better material, in the long spines
that grow out from the sheathing bases of its leaves.
These are 18 inches in length, of a black color, flat-
tish though perfectly straight. Being cut to the
proper length—which most of them are without
cutting—they are whittled at one end to a sharp

point. This point is dipped about three inches deep in the celebrated "curare" poison; and just where the poison mark terminates, a notch is made, so that the head will be easily broken off when the arrow is in the wound. Near the other end a little soft down of silky cotton (the floss of the *bombax ceiba*) is twisted around into a smooth mass of the shape of a spinning-top, with its larger end towards the nearer extremity of the arrow. The cotton is held in its place by being lightly whipped on by the delicate thread or fibre of a *bromelia*, and the mass is just big enough to fill the tube by gently pressing it inward.

The arrow thus made, is inserted, and whenever the game is within reach the Indian places his mouth to the lower end or mouthpiece, and with a strong "puff," which practice enables him to give, he sends the little messenger upon its deadly errand. He can hit with unerring aim at the distance of forty or fifty paces; but he prefers to shoot in a direction nearly vertical, as in that way he can take the surest aim. As his common game—birds and monkeys—are usually perched upon the higher branches of tall trees, their situation just suits him. Of course it is not the mere wound of the arrow that kills these creatures, but the poison, which in two or three minutes after they have been hit, will bring either bird or monkey to the ground. When the latter is struck he would be certain to draw out the arrow; but the notch, already mentioned, provides against this, as the slightest wrench serves to break off the envenomed head.

These arrows are dangerous things—even for the manufacturer of them to play with; they are therefore carried in a quiver, and with great care—the quiver consisting either of a bamboo joint or a neat wicker case.

The weapons of war used by the forest tribes are the common bow and arrows, also tipped with *curare*, and the "macana," or war-club, a species peculiar to South America, made out of the hard heavy wood of the *piassaba* palm.   Only one or two tribes use the spear; and both the "bolas" and lazo are quite unknown, as such weapons would not be available among the trees of the forest.   These are the proper arms of the Horse Indian, the dweller on the open plains; but without them, for all war purposes, the forest tribes have weapons enough, and, unfortunately, make a too frequent use of them.

THE WATER-DWELLERS OF MARACAIBO.

THE Andes mountains, rising in the extreme southern point of South America, not only extend throughout the whole length of that continent, but continue on through Central America and Mexico, under the name of "Cordilleras de Sierra Madre;" and still farther north to the shores of the Arctic Sea, under the very inappropriate appellation of the "Rocky Mountains." You must not suppose that these stupendous mountains form one continuous elevation. At many places they furcate into various branches, throwing off spurs, and sometimes parallel "sierras," between which lie wide "valles," or level plains of great extent. It is upon these high plateaux—many of them elevated 7,000 feet above the sea—that the greater part of the Spanish-American population dwells; and on them too are found most of the large cities of Spanish South America and Mexico.

These parallel chains meet at different points, forming what the Peruvians term "nodas" (knots); and, after continuing for a distance in one great cordillera, again bifurcate.

One of the most remarkable of these bifurcations of the Andes occurs about latitude 2° N. There the gigantic sierra separates into two great branches, forming a shape like the letter Y, the left limb being that which is usually regarded as the main continuation of these mountains through the Isthmus of Panama, while the right forms the eastern boundary of the great valley of the Magdalena river; and then,

trending in an eastwardly direction along the whole
northern coast of South America to the extreme
point of the promontory of Paria.

Each of these limbs again forks into several
branches or spurs—the whole system forming a
figure that may be said to bear some resemblance
to a genealogical tree containing the pedigree of
four or five generations.

It is only with one of the bifurcations of the right
or eastern sierra that this sketch has to do. On
reaching the latitude of 7° north, this chain separates itself into two wings, which, after diverging
widely to the east and west, sweep round again towards each other, as if desirous to be once more
united. The western wing advances boldly to this
reunion; but the eastern, after vacillating for a
time, as if uncertain what course to take, turns its
back abruptly on its old comrade, and trends off in
a due east direction, till it sinks into insignificance
upon the promontory of Paria.

The whole mass of the sierra, however, has not
been of one mind; for, at the time of its indecision,
a large spur detaches itself from the main body, and
sweeps round, as if to carry out the union with the
left wing advancing from the west. Although they
get within sight of each other, they are not permitted to meet—both ending abruptly before the circle is completed, and forming a figure bearing a
very exact resemblance to the shoe of a racehorse.
Within this curving boundary is enclosed a vast
valley—as large as the whole of Ireland—the central portion of which, and occupying about one-third
of its whole extent, is a sheet of water known, from
the days of the discovery of America, as the *Lake
of Maracaibo.*

It obtained this appellation from the name of an
Indian cacique, who was met upon its shores by the

first discoverers; but although this lake was known to the earliest explorers of the New World,—although it lies contiguous to many colonial settlements both on the mainland and the islands of the Caribbean Sea,—the lake itself, and the vast territory that surrounds it, remain almost as unknown and obscure as if they were situated among the central deserts of Africa.

And yet the valley of Maracaibo is one of the most interesting portions of the globe,—interesting not only as a *terra incognita*, but on account of the diversified nature of its scenery and productions. It possesses a *fauna* of·a peculiar kind, and its *flora* is one of the richest in the world, not surpassed—perhaps not equalled—by that of any other portion of the torrid zone. To give a list of its vegetable productions would be to enumerate almost every species belonging to tropical America. Here are found the well-known medicinal plants—the sassafras and sarsaparilla, guaiacum, copaiva, cinchona, and cuspa, or *Cortex Angosturæ;* here are the deadly poisons of *barbasco* and *mavacure*, and alongside them the remedies of the "palo sano," and *mikania guaco*. Here likewise grow plants and trees producing those well-known dyes of commerce, the blue indigo, the red arnotto, the lake-coloured chica, the brazilletto, and dragon's blood; and above all, those woods of red, gold, and ebon tints, so precious in the eyes of the cabinet and musical-instrument makers of Europe.

Yet, strange to say, these rich resources lie, like treasures buried in the bowels of the earth, or gems at the bottom of the sea, still undeveloped. A few small lumbering establishments near the entrance of the lake—here and there a miserable village, supported by a little coast commerce in dye-woods, or cuttings of ebony—now and then a hamlet of fish-

ermen—a "hato" of goats and sheep; and at wider
intervals, a "ganaderia" of cattle, or a plantation
of cocoa-trees (*cocale*), furnish the only evidence
that man has asserted his dominion over this interesting region.   These settlements, however, are
sparsely distributed, and widely distant from one
another.   Between them stretch broad savannas
and forests—vast tracts, untilled and even unexplored—a very wilderness, but a wilderness rich in
natural resources.

The Lake of Maracaibo is often, though erroneously, described as an arm of the sea.   This description only applies to the *Gulf of Maracaibo*, which
is in reality a portion of the Caribbean Sea.   The
lake itself is altogether different, and is a true fresh-
water lake, separated from the gulf by a narrow
neck or strait.   Within this strait—called "boca,"
or mouth—the salt-water does not extend, except
during very high tides or after long-continued *nortes*
(north winds), which have the effect of driving the
sea-water up into the lake, and imparting to some
portions of it a saline or brackish taste.   This, however, is only occasional and of temporary continuance; and the waters of the lake, supplied by a
hundred streams from the horse-shoe sierra that
surrounds it, soon return to their normal character
of freshness.

The shape of Lake Maracaibo is worthy of remark.   The main body of its surface is of oval outline—the longer diameter running north and south
—but, taken in connection with the straits which
communicate with the outer gulf, it assumes a shape
somewhat like that of a Jew's harp, or, rather, of a
kind of guitar, most in use among Spanish Americans, and known under the name of "mandolin" (or
"bandolon").   To this instrument do the natives
sometimes compare it.

Another peculiarity of Lake Maracaibo is the extreme shallowness of the water along its shores. It
is deep enough toward the middle part; but at
many points around the shore a man may wade for
miles into the water without getting beyond his
depth. This peculiarity arises from the formation
of the valley in which it is situated. Only a few
spurs of the sierras that surround it approach near
the edge of the lake. Generally from the bases of
the mountains the land slopes with a very gentle
declination—so slight as to have the appearance of
a perfectly horizontal plain—and this is continued
for a great way under the surface of the water.
Strange enough, however, after getting to a certain
distance from the shore, the shoal water ends as
abruptly as the escarpment of a cliff, and a depth
almost unfathomable succeeds, as if the central part
of the lake was a vast subaqueous ravine, bounded
on both sides by precipitous cliffs. Such, in reality, is it believed to be.

A singular phenomenon is observed in the Lake
Maracaibo, which, since the days of Columbus, has
not only puzzled the curious, but also the learned
and scientific, who have unsuccessfully attempted to
explain it. This phenomenon consists in the appearance of a remarkable light, which shows itself
in the middle of the night, and at a particular part
of the lake, near its southern extremity. This light
bears some resemblance to the *ignis fatuus* of our
own marshes; and most probably is a phosphores-
cence of a similar nature, though on a much grander scale, since it is visible at a vast distance across
the open water. As it is seen universally in the
same direction, and appears fixed in one place, it
serves as a beacon for the fishermen and dye-wood
traders who navigate the waters of the lake—its
longitude being precisely that of the straits leading

E.

outward to the gulf. Vessels that have strayed
from their course often regulate their reckoning by
the mysterious "Farol de Maracaibo" (Lantern of
Maracaibo), for by this name is the natural beacon
known to the mariners of the lake.

Various explanations have been offered to account
for this singular phenomenon, but none seem to explain it in a satisfactory manner. It appears to be
produced by the exhalations that arise from an extensive marshy tract lying around the mouth of the
river Zulia, and above which it universally shows
itself. The atmosphere in this quarter is usually
hotter than elsewhere, and supposed to be highly
charged with electricity; but whatever may be the
chemical process which produces the illumination,
it acts in a perfectly silent manner. No one has
ever observed any explosion to proceed from it, or
the slightest sound connected with its occurrence.

Of all the ideas suggested by the mention of Lake
Maracaibo, perhaps none are so interesting as those
that relate to its native inhabitants, whose peculiar
habits and modes of life not only astonished the
early navigators, but eventually gave its name to
the lake itself, and to the extensive province in
which it is situated. When the Spanish discoverers, sailing around the shores of the gulf, arrived
near the entrance of Lake Maracaibo, they saw, to
their amazement, not only single houses, but whole
villages, apparently floating upon the water! On
approaching nearer, they perceived that these houses
were raised some feet above the surface, and supported by posts or piles driven into the mud at the
bottom. The idea of Venice—that city built upon
the sea, to which they had been long accustomed—
was suggested by these *superaqueous* habitations;
and the name of *Venezuela* (Little Venice) was at
once bestowed upon the coast, and afterwards ap-

plied to the whole province now known as the Republic of Venezuela.

Though the " water villages" then observed have long since disappeared, many others of a similar kind were afterwards discovered in Lake Maracaibo itself, some of which are in existence to the present day. Besides here and there an isolated habitation situated in some bay or "laguna," there are four principal villages upon this plan still in existence, each containing from fifty to a hundred habitations. The inhabitants of some of these villages have been " Christianized"—that is, have submitted to the teaching of the Spanish missionaries; and one in particular is distinguished by having its little church —a regular *water* church—in the centre, built upon piles, just as the rest of the houses are, and only differing from the common dwellings in being larger and of a somewhat more pretentious style. From the belfry of this curious ecclesiastical edifice a brazen bell may be heard at morn and eve tolling the "oracion" and "vespers," and declaring over the wide waters of the lake that the authority of the Spanish monk has replaced the power of the cacique among the Indians of the Lake Maracaibo. Not to all sides of the lake, however, has the cross extended its conquest. Along its western shore roams the fierce unconquered Goajiro, who, a true warrior, still maintains his independence; and even encroaches upon the usurped possessions both of monk and "militario."

The *water-dweller*, however, although of kindred race with the Goajiro, is very different, both in his disposition and habits of life. He is altogether a man of peace, and might almost be termed a civilized being—that is, he follows a regular industrial calling, by which he subsists. This is the calling of a fisherman, and in no part of the world could he

follow it with more certainty of success, since the
waters which surround his dwelling literally swarm
with fish.

Lake Maracaibo has been long noted as the resort
of numerous and valuable species of the finny tribe,
in the capture of which the Indian fisherman finds
ample occupation.   He is betimes a fowler—as we
shall presently see—and he also sometimes indulges,
though more rarely, in the chase, finding game in
the thick forests or on the green savannas that surround the lake, or border the banks of the numerous "riachos" (streams) running into it.   On the
savanna roams the graceful roebuck and the " ve-
nado," or South American deer, while along the
river banks stray the capibara and the stout tapir,
undisturbed save by their fierce feline enemies, the
puma and spotted jaguar.

But hunting excursions are not a habit of the
water Indian, whose calling, as already observed, is
essentially that of a fisherman and "fowler," and
whose subsistence is mainly derived from two kinds
of *water-dwellers*, like himself—one with fins, living
below the surface, and denominated *fish ;* another
with wings, usually resting *on* the surface, and
known as *fowl.*   These two creatures, of very different kinds and of many different species, form the
staple and daily food of the Indian of Maracaibo.

In an account of his habits we shall begin by
giving a description of the mode in which he constructs his singular dwelling.

Like other builders he begins by selecting the
site.   This must be a place where the water is of
no great depth ; and the farther from the shore he
can find a shallow spot the better for his purpose,
for he has a good reason for desiring to get to a
distance from the shore, as we shall presently see.
Sometimes a sort of subaqueous island, or elevated

sandbank, is found, which gives him the very site
he is in search of. Having pitched upon the spot,
his next care is to procure a certain number of tree-
trunks of the proper length and thickness to make
"piles." Not every kind of timber will serve for
this purpose, for there are not many sorts that would
long resist decay and the wear and tear of the water insects, with which the lake abounds. Moreover, the building of one of these aquatic houses,
although it be only a rude hut, is a work of time
and labour, and it is desirable therefore to make it
as permanent as possible. For this reason great
care is taken in the selection of the timber for the
"piles."

But it so chances that the forests around the lake
furnish the very thing itself, in the wood of a tree
known to the Spanish inhabitants as the "vera," or
"palo sano," and to the natives as "gnaiac." It
is one of the zygophyls of the genus *Guiacum*, of
which there are many species, called by the names
of "ironwood" or "lignum-vitæ;" but the species
in question is the *tree* lignum-vitæ (*Guiacum arbo-
reum*), which attains to a height of 100 feet, with a
fine umbrella-shaped head, and bright orange flowers. Its wood is so hard that it will turn the edge
of an axe, and the natives believe that if it be buried for a sufficient length of time under the earth it
will turn to iron! Though this belief is not literally true, as regards the *iron*, it is not so much of an
exaggeration as might be supposed. The "palo de
fierro," when buried in the soil of Maracaibo or im-
mersed in the waters of the lake, in reality does undergo a somewhat similar metamorphose; in other
words, it turns into stone; and the petrified trunks
of this wood are frequently met with along the
shores of the lake. What is still more singular—
the piles of the water-houses often become petrified,

so that the dwelling **no longer** rests upon wooden posts, but upon real columns of stone!

Knowing all this by experience, the Indian selects the guaiac for his uprights, cuts them of the proper length; and then, launching them in the water, **transports** them to the site of his dwelling, **and fixes them** in their places.

Upon this a platform is erected, out of split boards **of some less** ponderous timber, usually the "ceiba," or "silk-cotton tree" (*Bombax ceiba*), or the "cedro negro" (*Cedre-la odorata*) of the order *Meliaceæ*. Both kinds grow in abundance upon the shores of the lake—and the huge trunks of the former are also used by the water Indian for the constructing of his canoe.

The platform, or floor, being thus established, about two or three **feet** above the surface **of** the water, it then only **remains to** erect the walls and cover them over with a roof. The former are **made** of the slightest materials—light saplings or bamboo poles—usually left **open at** the interstices. There **is no** winter or cold **weather here—why** should the **walls** be thick? There are heavy rains, however, at certain seasons of the year, and these require to be guarded against; but this is not a difficult matter, since the broad leaves of the "enea" and "vihai" (a species of *Heliconia*) serve the purpose of a roof just as **well as** tiles, slates, or shingles. **Nature** in these **parts is bountiful, and** provides her human creatures **with a** spontaneous supply **of** every want. Even ropes **and cords** she furnishes, for binding the beams, joists, and **rafters together, and** holding on the thatch against **the most** furious assaults of the **wind.** The numerous species of creeping and twining plants ("llianas" or "sipos") serve admirably for this purpose. They are applied in their green state, and when contracted by exsiccation draw the timbers as closely together as if held by spikes of iron. In this manner and of such materials does the water Indian build his house.

Why he inhabits such a singular dwelling is a question that requires to be answered. With the *terra firma* close at hand, and equally convenient for all purposes of his calling, why does he not build his hut there? So much easier too of access would it be, for he could then approach it either by land or by water; whereas, in its present situation, he can neither go away from his house or get back to it without the aid of his "periagua" (canoe). Moreover, by building on the beach, or by the edge of the woods, he would spare himself the labor of transporting those heavy piles and setting them in their places—a work, as already stated, of no ordinary magnitude. Is it for personal security against human enemies—for this sometimes drives a people to seek singular situations for their homes? No; the Indian of Maracaibo has his human foes, like all other people; but it is none of these that have forced him to adopt this strange custom. Other enemies? wild beasts? the dreaded jaguar, perhaps? No, nothing of this kind. And yet it is in reality a living creature that drives him to this resource— that has forced him to flee from the main land and take to the water for security against its attack— a creature of such small dimensions, and apparently so contemptible in its strength, that you will no doubt smile at the idea of its putting a strong man to flight—a little insect exactly the size of an English gnat, and no bigger, but so formidable by means of its poisonous bite, and its myriads of numbers, as to render many parts of the shores of Lake Maracaibo quite uninhabitable. You guess, no doubt, the insect to which I allude? You cannot fail to recognize it as the *mosquito?* Just so; it is

the mosquito I mean, and in no part of South America do these insects abound in greater numbers, and
nowhere are they more blood-thirsty than upon the
borders of this great fresh-water sea.   Not only one
species of mosquito, but all the varieties known as
"jejens," "zancudos," and "tempraneros," here
abound in countless multitudes—each kind making
its appearance at a particular hour of the day or
night—"mounting guard" (as the persecuted natives say of them) in turn, and allowing only short
intervals of respite from their bitter attacks.

Now, it so happens, that although the various
kinds of mosquitoes are peculiarly the productions
of a marshy or watery region—and rarely found
where the soil is high and dry—yet as rarely do
they extend their excursions to a distance from the
land.   They delight to dwell under the shadow of
leaves, or near the herbage of grass, plants, or trees,
among which they were hatched.   They do not
stray far from the shore, and only when the breeze
carries them do they fly out over the open water.
Need I say more?   You have now the explanation
why the Indians of Maracaibo build their dwellings
upon the water.   It is simply to escape from the
"plaga de moscas" (the pest of the flies).

Like most other Indians of tropical America, and
some even of colder latitudes, those of Maracaibo
go naked, wearing only the *guayuco*, or "waist-
belt."   Those of them, however, who have submitted to the authority of the monks, have adopted a
somewhat more modest garb—consisting of a small
apron of cotton or palm-fibre, suspended from the
waist, and reaching down to their knees.

We have already stated, that the water-dwelling
Indian is a fisherman, and that the waters of the
lake supply him with numerous kinds of fish of excellent quality.   An account of these, with the

method employed in capturing them, may not prove uninteresting.

First, there is the fish known as "liza," a species of skate. It is of a brilliant silvery hue, with bluish corruscations. It is a small fish, being only about a foot in length, but is excellent to eat, and when preserved by drying, forms an article of commerce with the West-Indian islands. Along the coasts of Cumana and Magarita, there are many people employed in the *pesca de liza* (skate-fishery) ; but although the liza is in reality a sea fish, it abounds in the fresh waters of Maracaibo, and is there also an object of industrial pursuit. It is usually captured by seines, made out of the fibres of the *cocui aloe* (*agave cocuiza*), or of cords obtained from the unexpanded leaflets of the moriche palm (*Mauritia flexuosa*), both of which useful vegetable products are indigenous to this region. The roe of the liza, when dried in the sun, is an article in high estimation, and finds its way into the channels of commerce.

A still more delicate fish is the "pargo." It is of a white colour tinged with rose ; and of these great numbers are also captured. So, too, with the "doncella," one of the most beautiful species, as its pretty name of "doncella" (young maiden) would indicate. These last are so abundant in some parts of the lake, that one of its bays is distinguished by the name of *Laguna de Doncella*.

A large ugly fish, called the "vagre," with an enormous head and wide mouth, from each side of which stretches a beard-like appendage, is also an object of the Indian's pursuit. It is usually struck with a spear, or killed by arrows, when it shows itself near the surface of the water. Another monstrous creature, of nearly circular shape, and full three feet in diameter, is the "carite," which is harpooned in a similar fashion.

Besides these there is the " viegita," or " old-woman fish," which itself **feeds** upon lesser creatures of the finny tribe, and especially upon the smaller species of shell-fish. It has obtained its odd appellation from a singular noise which it gives forth, and which resembles the voice of an old woman debilitated with extreme age.

" The " dorado," or gilded fish—so called on account **of its** beautiful colour—is taken by a hook, with **no** other bait attached than a piece of white **rag.** This, however, must be kept constantly in motion, **and the** bait is played by simply paddling the canoe over the surface of the lake, until the dorado, attracted by the white meteor, follows in its track, and eventually hooks itself.

Many other species of fish are taken by the water-Indians, as the " lebranche" **which goes in large** " **schools,**" and **makes its** breeding-place **in the** lagunas **and up** the rivers, **and the** " guabina," **with** several **kinds of sardines that** find their way into the tin **boxes of** Europe; **for the** Maracaibo fisherman **is** not contented with an exclusive fish diet. He likes **a** little " casava," or maize-bread, along **with it;** besides, he **has a** few other wants to satisfy, and the means he readily obtains in exchange for the surplus produce of his nets, harpoons, and arrows.

We have already stated that he is a fowler. At certain seasons of the year this is essentially his occupation. The fowling season with him is the period of northern winter, when the migratory aquatic birds come down from the boreal regions of Prince Rupert's **Land to** disport their bodies in the more agreeable **waters** of Lake Maracaibo. There **they** assemble in large flocks, darkening the air **with their** myriads of numbers, now fluttering over the lake, or, at other times, seated on its surface silent and motionless. Notwithstanding their great numbers, however, they are too shy to be approached near enough for the "carry" of an Indian arrow, or a gun either; and were it not for a very cunning stratagem which the Indian has adopted for their capture, they might return again to their northern haunts without being *minus* an individual of their "count."

But they are not permitted to depart thus unscathed. During their sojourn within the limits of Lake Maracaibo their legions get considerably thinned, and thousands of them that settle down upon its inviting waters are destined never more to take wing.

To effect their capture, the Indian fowler, as already stated, makes use of a very ingenious stratagem. Something similar is described as being practised in other parts of the world; but in no place is it carried to such perfection as upon the Lake Maracaibo.

The fowler first provides himself with a number of large gourd-shells of roundish form, and each of them at least as big as his own skull. These he can easily obtain, either from the herbaceous squash (*Cucurbita lagenaris*) or from the calabash-tree (*Crescentia cujete*), both of which grow luxuriantly on the shores of the lake. Filling his periagua with these, he proceeds out into the open water to a certain distance from the land, or from his own dwelling. The distance is regulated by several considerations. He must reach a place which, at all hours of the day, the ducks and other waterfowl are not afraid to frequent; and, on the other hand, he must not go beyond such a depth as will bring the water higher than his own chin when wading through it. This last consideration is not of so much importance, for the water Indian can swim almost as well as a duck, and dive like one, if need be; but it is connected with another matter of greater importance —the convenience of having the birds as near as possible, to save him a too long and wearisome "wade." It is necessary to have them so near, that at all hours they may be under his eye.

Having found the proper situation—which the vast extent of shoal water (already mentioned) enables him to do—he proceeds to carry out his design by dropping a gourd here and another there, until a large space of surface is covered by these floating shells. Each gourd has a stone attached to it by means of a string, which, resting upon the bottom, brings the buoy to an anchor, and prevents it from being drifted into the deeper water or carried entirely away.

When his decoys are all placed, the Indian paddles back to his platform dwelling, and there, with watchful eye, awaits the issue. The birds are at first shy of these round yellow objects intruded upon their domain; but, as the hours pass, and they perceive no harm in them, they at length take courage and venture to approach. Urged by that curiosity which is instinctive in every creature, they gradually draw nigher and nigher, until at length they boldly venture into the midst of the odd objects and examine them minutely. Though puzzled to make out what it is all meant for, they can perceive no harm in the yellow globe-shaped things that only bob about, but make no attempt to do them any injury. Thus satisfied, their curiosity soon wears off, and the birds, no longer regarding the floating shells as objects of suspicion, swim freely about through their midst, or sit quietly on the water side by side with them.

But the crisis has now arrived when it is necessary the Indian should act, and for this he speedily

equips himself. He first ties a stout rope around
his waist, to which are attached many short strings
or cords. He then draws over his head a large
gourd-shell, which, fitting pretty tightly, covers his
whole skull, reaching down to his neck. This shell
is exactly similar to the others already floating on
the water, with the exception of having three holes
on one side of it—two on the same level with the
Indian's eyes, and the third opposite his mouth, intended to serve him for a breathing hole.

He is now ready for work; and, thus oddly accoutred, he slips quietly down from his platform,
and laying himself along the water, swims gently
in the direction of the ducks.

He swims only where the water is too shallow to
prevent him from crouching below the surface;
for were he to stand upright, and wade — even
though he were still distant from them—the shy
birds might have suspicions about his after-ap-
proaches.

When he reaches a point where the lake is sufficiently deep, he gets upon his feet and wades, still
keeping his shoulders below the surface. He makes
his advance very slowly and warily, scarce raising
a ripple on the surface of the placid lake, and the
nearer he gets to his intended victims he proceeds
with the greater caution.

The unsuspecting birds see the destroyer approach without having the slightest misgiving of
danger. They fancy that the new comer is only
another of those inanimate objects by their side—
another gourd-shell drifting out upon the water to
join its companions. They have no suspicion that
this wooden counterfeit—like the horse of Troy—
is inhabited by a terrible enemy.

Poor things! how could they? A stratagem so
well contrived would deceive more rational intel-

lects than theirs ; **and, in fact,** having no idea of danger, they perhaps **do not** trouble themselves even to notice the **new** arrival.

Meanwhile the **gourd** has drifted silently into their midst, **and is seen** approaching the odd individuals, first **one and** afterwards another, as **if it** had some special **business** with each. **This** business appears to be of a very mysterious character ; **and in** each case is abruptly brought to a conclusion, **by the duck** making a sudden dive under the water— **not head foremost,** according to **its** usual practice, **but in the reverse** way, as if jerked **down** by the feet, and so rapidly that **the** creature **has** not time to utter a single "quak."

After quite a number of individuals have disappeared in this mysterious manner, the others **sometimes** grow suspicious of the moving **calabash, and** either take to wing, or swim off to a less dangerous neighbourhood ; but if the gourd performs its **office** in a skilful **manner, it** will be **seen** passing **several** times to and fro between **the birds** and the water-**village** before this **event** takes **place.** **On** each re-**turn** trip, when **far from the flock, and** near the habitations, it will be seen to **rise** high above the surface of the water. It will then be perceived that it covers the skull of a copper-coloured savage, around whose hips may be observed a double tier of dead ducks dangling by their necks **from** the rope upon his **waist, and** forming **a sort of** plumed skirt, the **weight of** which **almost drags its** wearer back into **the water.**

Of course **a** capture **is followed** by **a** feast ; and during the fowling **season of** the year the Maracaibo Indian enjoys roast-duck at discretion. He does not trouble his head much about the green peas, nor is he particular to have his ducks stuffed with sage and **onions ;** but a hot seasoning of red pepper

is one of the indispensable ingredients of the **South**
American *cuisine ;* and this he usually obtains from
a small **patch** of capsicum which he cultivates upon
the **adjacent** shore; or, if he be not possessed of
land, **he** procures it by barter, exchanging his fowls
or fish for that and a little maize or manioc flour,
furnished by the coast-traders.

The Maracaibo Indian is not a stranger to commerce. He has been " Christianized"—to use **the**
phraseology of his priestly proselytizer—and this
has introduced him to new wants and necessities.
Expenses that in his former pagan state were entirely unknown to him, have now become necessary, and a commercial effort is required to meet them.
The Church must have its dues. Such luxuries, as
being baptized, married, and buried, are **not to be**
had without expense, and the padre takes good care
that none of these shall be had for nothing. **He has**
taught his proselyte to believe that unless all **these**
rites have been officially performed there is not the
slightest chance for him in the next world; and under the influence of this delusion, the simple savage
willingly yields up his tenth, his fifth, or, perhaps it
would be more correct to say, his all. Between
fees **of** baptism and burial, mulcts for performance
of the marriage **rite,** contributions towards the
shows **and** ceremonies of *dias de fiesta,* extravagant
prices for blessed beads, leaden crucifixes, and **im-**
ages of patron saints, the poor Christianized Indian
is compelled to part with nearly the whole of his
humble gains; and the fear of not being able to pay
for Christian burial after death, is often **one** of the
torments of his life.

To satisfy the numerous demands of the Church,
therefore, he is forced into a little action in the commercial line. With the water-dweller of Maracaibo,
fish forms one of the staples of export trade—of

course in the preserved state, as he is too distant
from any great town or metropolis to be able to
make market of them while fresh. He understands,
however, the mode of curing them—which he accomplishes by sun-drying and smoking—and, thus
prepared, they are taken off his hands by the trader,
who carries them all over the West Indies, where,
with boiled rice, they form the staple food of thousands of the dark-skinned children of Ethiopia.

The Maracaibo Indian, however, has still another
resource, which occasionally supplies him with an
article of commercial export. His country—that
is, the adjacent shores of the lake—produces the finest *caoutchouc*. There the India-rubber tree, of
more than one species, flourishes in abundance; and
the true "seringa," that yields the finest and most
valuable kind of this gummy juice, is nowhere found
in greater perfection than in the forests of Maracaibo. The caoutchouc of commerce is obtained from
many other parts of America, as well as from other
tropical countries; but as many of the bottles and
shoes so well known in the india-rubber shops, are
manufactured by the Indians of Maracaibo, we may
not find a more appropriate place to give an account
of this singular production, and the mode by which
it is prepared for the purposes of commerce and
manufacture.

As already mentioned, many species of trees yield
india-rubber, most of them belonging either to the
order of the "Morads," or *Euphorbiaceæ*. Some are
species of *ficus*, but both the genera and species are
too numerous to be given here. That which supplies the "bottle india-rubber" is a euphorbiaceous
plant—the *seringa* above mentioned—whose proper botanical appellation is *Siphonia elastica*. It is
a tall, straight, smooth-barked tree, having a trunk
of about a foot in diameter, though in favourable

situations reaching to much larger dimensions. The process of extracting its sap—out of which the caoutchouc is manufactured—bears some resemblance to the tapping of sugar-maples in the forests of the north.

With his small hatchet, or tomahawk, the Indian cuts a gash in the bark, and inserts into it a little wedge of wood to keep the sides apart. Just under the gash, he fixes a small cup-shaped vessel of clay, the clay being still in a plastic state, so that it may be attached closely to the bark. Into this vessel the milk-like sap of the *seringa* soon commences to run, and keeps on until it has yielded about the fifth of a pint. This, however, is not the whole yield of a tree, but only of a single wound; and it is usual to open a great many gashes, or "taps," upon the same trunk, each being furnished with its own cup or receiver. In from four to six hours the sap ceases to run.

The cups are then detached from the tree, and the contents of all, poured into a large earthen vessel, are carried to the place where the process of making the caoutchouc is to take place—usually some dry open spot in the middle of the forest, where a temporary camp has been formed for the purpose.

When the dwelling of the Indian is at a distance from where the india-rubber tree grows—as is the case with those of Lake Maracaibo—it will not do to transport the sap thither. There must be no delay after the cups are filled, and the process of manufacture must proceed at once, or as soon as the milky juice begins to coagulate—which it does almost on the instant.

Previous to reaching his camp, the "seringero" has provided a large quantity of palm-nuts, with which he intends to make a fire for smoking the

F

caoutchouc. These **nuts are** the fruit of several **kinds of** palms, but the best are those afforded by two magnificent species—the "Inaja" (*Maximilliana regia*), **and** the "Urucuri" (*Attalea excelsa*).

A fire **is** kindled of **these** nuts, and an earthen pot, with a hole in the bottom, is placed mouth downward over the pile. Through the **aperture now** rises a strong pungent smoke.

If it is a shoe that is intended to be made, a clay-**last is** already prepared, with a stick standing out of the top of it, to serve as a handle, while the operation is going on. Taking the stick in his hand, the seringero dips the last lightly into the milk, or with a cup pours the fluid gently over it, so as to give a regular coating to the whole surface; and then, holding it over the smoke, he keeps turning it, jack-fashion, till the fluid has become dry and adhesive. Another **dip is then** given, and the smoking done as before; **and this** goes on, **till forty or fifty** different coats **have** brought the sides and soles **of the shoe to** a proper thickness. The soles, requiring **greater** weight, are, **of** course, oftener dipped than the "upper leather."

The whole process of making the shoe does not occupy half an hour; but it has afterwards to receive some farther attention in the way of ornament; **the lines** and figures are yet to be executed, and **this is** done about two days after the smoking process. **They are** simply traced out with a piece of smooth wire, or oftener with the spine obtained from some tree—as the thorny point of the *bromelia* leaf.

In about a week the shoes **are** ready to be taken **from** the last; and this is accomplished at the expense and utter ruin of the latter, which is broken into fragments, and then cleaned **out**. Water is used sometimes to soften the last, and the inner surface of the shoe is washed after the clay has been taken out.

Bottles are made in precisely the same manner— a round ball, or other shaped mass of clay, serving as the mould for their construction. It requires a little more trouble to get the mould extracted from the narrow neck of the bottle.

It may be remarked that it is not the smoke of the palm-nuts that gives to the India-rubber its peculiar dark colour; that is the effect of age. When freshly manufactured, it is still of a whitish or cream colour; and only attains the dark hue after it has been kept for a considerable time.

We might add many other particulars about the mode in which the Indian of Maracaibo employs his time, but perhaps enough has been said to show that his existence is altogether an *odd* one.

THE ESQUIMAUX.

THE Esquimaux are emphatically an "odd people," perhaps the oddest upon the earth. The peculiar character of the regions they inhabit has naturally initiated them into a system of habits and modes of life different from those of any other people on the face of the globe; and from the remoteness and inaccessibility of the countries in which they dwell, not only have they remained an unmixed people, but scarce any change has taken place in their customs and manners during the long period since they were first known to civilized nations.

The Esquimaux people have been long known and their habits often described. Our first knowledge of them was obtained from Greenland—for the native inhabitants of Greenland are true Esquimaux—and hundreds of years ago accounts of them were given to the world by the Danish colonists and missionaries—as also by the whalers who visited the coasts of that inhospitable land. In later times they have been made familiar to us through the Arctic explorers and whale-fishers, who have traversed the labyrinth of icy islands that extend northward from the continent of America. The Esquimaux may boast of possessing the *longest* country in the world. In the first place, Greenland is theirs, and they are found along the western shores of Baffin's Bay. In North America proper their territory commences at the straits of Belle Isle, which separate Newfoundland from Labrador,

and thence extends all around the shore of the Arctic Ocean, not only to Behring's Straits, but beyond these, around the Pacific coast of Russian America, as far south as the great mountain St. Elias. Across Behring's Straits they are found occupying a portion of the Asiatic coast, under the name of Tchutski, and some of the islands in the northern angle of the Pacific Ocean are also inhabited by these people, though under a different name. Furthermore, the numerous ice islands which lie between North America and the Pole are either inhabited or visited by Esquimaux to the highest point that discovery has yet reached.

There can be little doubt that the Laplanders of northern Europe, and the Samoyedes, and other litoral peoples dwelling along the Siberian shores, are kindred races of the Esquimaux; and taking this view of the question, it may be said that the latter possess all the line of coast of both continents facing northward; in other words, that their country extends around the globe—though it cannot be said (as is often boastingly declared of the British empire) that "the sun never sets upon it;" for, over the "empire" of the Esquimaux, the sun not only sets, but remains out of sight of it for months at a time.

It is not usual, however, to class the Laplanders and *Asiatic Arctic* people with the Esquimaux. There are some essential points of difference; and what is here said of the Esquimaux relates only to those who inhabit the northern coasts and islands of America, and to the native Greenlanders.

Notwithstanding the immense extent of territory thus designated, notwithstanding the sparseness of the Esquimaux population, and the vast distances by which one little tribe or community is separated from another, the absolute similarity in their habits, in their physical and intellectual conformation, and, above all, in their languages, proves incontestably that they are all originally of **one** and the same race.

Whatever, therefore, may be said of a "Schelling," or native Greenlander, will be equally applicable to an Esquimaux of Labrador, to an Esquimaux of the Mackenzie River or Behring's Straits, or we might **add**, to a Khadiak islander, or a Tuski of the opposite **Asiatic coast**; always taking into account such **differences** of costume, dialect, modes of life, &c., **as may** be brought about by the different circumstances in which **they** are placed. In all these things, however, they are wonderfully alike; their dresses, weapons, boats, houses, and house implements, being almost the same in material and **construction** from East Greenland to the Tchutskoi Noss.

If their country **be** the longest in the world, it is **also** the *narrowest*. Of course, if we take into account **the** large **islands** that thickly stud the Arctic **Ocean**, it may be deemed broad enough; but I am **speaking** rather of the territory which they possess **on the** continents. This may be regarded as a mere strip following the outline of the coast, and never extending beyond the distance of a day's journey inland. Indeed, they only seek the interior in the few short weeks of summer, for the purpose of hunting the reindeer, the musk-ox, and other animals; after each excursion, returning again to the shores of the sea, where they have their winter-houses and more permanent home. They are, truly and emphatically, a *litoral* people, and it is to the sea they look for their principal means of support. But for this source of supply, they could not long continue to exist upon land altogether incapable of supplying the wants even of the most limited population.

The name *Esquimaux*—or, as it is sometimes written, "Eskimo,"—like many other national appellations, is of obscure origin. It is supposed to have been given to them by the Canadian voyageurs in the employ of the Hudson's Bay Company, and derived from the words *Ceux qui miaux* (those who mew), in relation to their screaming like·cats. But the etymology is, to say the least, *suspicious*. They generally call themselves "Inuit" (pronounced enn-oo-eet), a word which signifies "men;"—though different tribes of them have distinct tribal appellations.

In personal appearance they cannot be regarded as at all prepossessing—though some of the younger men and girls, when cleansed of the filth and grease with which their skin is habitually coated, are far from ill-looking. Their natural colour is not much darker than that of some of the southern nations of Europe—the Portuguese, for instance—and the young girls often have blooming cheeks, and a pleasing expression of countenance. Their faces are generally of a broad roundish shape, the forehead and chin both narrow and receding, and the cheeks very prominent, though not angular. On the contrary, they are rather fat and round. This prominence of the cheeks gives to their nose the appearance of being low and flat; and individuals are often seen with such high cheeks, that a ruler laid from one to the other would not touch the bridge of the nose between them!

As they grow older their complexion becomes darker — perhaps from exposure to the climate. Very naturally, too, both men and women grow uglier, but especially the latter—some of whom in old age present such a hideous aspect, that the early Arctic explorers could not help characterizing them as *witches*.

The average stature of the Esquimaux is far below that of European nations, though individuals are sometimes met with nearly six feet in height. These, however, are rare exceptions; and an Esquimaux of such proportions would be a giant among his people. The more common height is from 4 feet 8 inches to 5 feet 8; and the women are still shorter, rarely attaining the standard of 5 feet. The shortness of both men and women appears to be a deficiency in length of limb, for their bodies are long enough; but, as the Esquimaux is almost constantly in his canoe, or "kayak," or upon his dog-sledge, his legs have but little to do, and are consequently stunted in their development.

A similar peculiarity is presented by the Comanche, and other Indians of the prairies, and also in the Guachos and Patagonian Indians, of the South American Pampas, who spend most of their time on the backs of their horses.

The Esquimaux have no religion, unless we dignify by that name a belief in witches, sorcerers, "Shamans," and good or evil spirits, with some confused notion of a good and bad place hereafter. Missionary zeal has been exerted among them almost in vain. They exhibit an apathetic indifference to the teachings of Christianity.

Neither have they any political organization; and in this respect they differ essentially from most savages known—the lowest of whom have usually their chiefs and councils of elders. This absence of all government, however, is no proof of their being lower in the scale of civilization than other savages; but, perhaps, rather the contrary, for the very idea of chiefdom, or government, is a presumption of the existence of vice among a people, and the necessity of coercion and repression. To one another these rude people are believed to act in the most honest manner; and it could be shown that such **was** likewise their behaviour towards strangers **until they** were corrupted by **excessive** temptation. **All Arctic** voyagers record instances of what they term petty theft, on the part of certain tribes of Esquimaux—that is, the pilfering of nails, hatchets, pieces of iron hoops, &c.—but **it** might be worth while reflecting that these articles are, in the eyes of the Esquimaux, what ingots **of** gold **are to** Europeans, and worth while inquiring if a **few** bars of the last-mentioned metal were laid **loosely and** carelessly upon the pavements of London, **how** long they would **be** in changing their owners? Theft should be regarded along with the amount of temptation; and it appears **even in these** recorded cases that only a *few* of the Esquimaux took part in it. I apprehend that something **more** than **a** few Londoners would be **found** picking **up** the golden ingots. How many thieves have **we** among us, with no greater temptation than a cheap cotton kerchief?—more than a few, it is to be feared.

In truth, the Esquimaux are by no means the **savages they** have been represented. The only **important point** in which **they** at all assimilate **to the** purely savage **state is in** the filthiness of their persons, and perhaps also in the **fact** of their **eating** much of their food (fish and flesh-meat) **in a raw** state. For the latter habit, however, they **are partially** indebted to the circumstances in which **they** are placed—fires or cookery being at times altogether impossible. They are not the only people who have been forced to eat raw flesh; and Europeans who have travelled in that inhospitable country soon get used to the practice, at the same time getting quite cured of their *dégoût* for it.

It is certainly not correct to characterize the

Esquimaux as mere *savages*.   On the contrary, they
may be regarded as a civilized people—that is, so
far as civilization is permitted by the rigorous climate in which they live—and it would be safe to
affirm that a colony of the most polished people in
Europe, established as the Esquimaux are, and left
solely to their own resources, would in a single gen-
eration exhibit a civilization not one degree higher
than that now met with among the Esquimaux.
Indeed, the fact is already established: the Danish
and Norwegian colonists of West Greenland, though
backed by constant intercourse with their mother-
land, are but little more civilized than the "Skel-
lings," who are their neighbours.

   In reality, the Esquimaux have made the most of
the circumstances in which they are placed, and
continue to do so.   Among them agriculture is impossible, else they would long since have taken to
it.   So too is commerce; and as to manufactures, it
is doubtful whether Europeans could excel them
under like circumstances.   Whatever raw material
their country produces, is by them both strongly
and neatly fabricated—as indicated by the surprising skill with which they make their dresses, their
boats, their implements for hunting and fishing; and
in these accomplishments—the only ones practicable
under their hyperborean heaven—they are perfect
adepts.   In such arts civilized Europeans are perfect
simpletons to them, and the theories of fire-side speculators, so lately promulgated in our newspapers,
that Sir John Franklin and his crew could not fail
to procure a living where the simple Esquimaux
were able to make a home, betrayed only ignorance
of the condition of these people.   In truth, white
men would starve, where the Esquimaux could live
in luxurious abundance—so far superior to ours is
their knowledge both of fishing and the chase.   It

is a well-recorded fact, that while our Arctic voyagers, at their winter stations, provided with **good**
guns, nets, and every appliance, could but rarely
kill a reindeer or capture a seal, the Esquimaux obtained both in abundance, and apparently without
an effort! and we shall presently note the causes
of their superiority in this respect.

The very dress of the Esquimaux is a proof **of**
their superiority over other savages. At no season
of the year do they go either naked, or even "rag-
ged." They have their changes to suit the seasons
—their summer dress, and one of a warmer kind
for winter. Both are made in a most complicated
manner; and the preparation of the material, as
well as the manner by which it is put together,
prove the Esquimaux women—for they **are alike**
the tailors and dressmakers—to be among the **best**
seamstresses in the world.

Captain Lyon, one of the most observant of Arctic voyagers, has given a description of the costume
of the Esquimaux of Savage Island, and those of
Repulse Bay, where he wintered, and his account is
so graphic and minute in details, that it would be
idle to alter a word of his language. His description, with slight differences in make and material,
will answer pretty accurately for the costume of
the whole race.

"The clothes of both sexes are principally composed of fine and well-prepared reindeer pelts; the
skins of bears, seals, wolves, foxes, and marmottes,
are also used. The seal-skins are seldom employed
for any part of the dress except boots and shoes, as
being more capable of resisting water, and of far
greater durability than other leather.

"The general winter dress of the men is an ample outer coat of deer-skin, having no opening in
front, and a large hood, which is drawn over the

head at pleasure. This hood is invariably bordered
with white fur from the thighs of the deer, and thus
presents a lively contrast to the **dark** face which it
encircles. The front or belly part of **the** coat is cut
off square with **the upper** part of the thighs, but
behind it is **formed into a** broad **skirt, rounded at
the lower end,** which reaches to within a **few inches of the ground. The** lower edges and tails of
these dresses are in some cases bordered with bands
of fur of an opposite colour to the body; and it is a
favourite ornament to hang a fringe of little strips of
skin beneath the border. The embellishments give
a very pleasing appearance to the **dress.** It is customary in blowing weather to tie a piece of skin or
cord tight round the waist of the coat; but in other cases the dress hangs loose.

"Within the covering I have just described is
another, of precisely **the same** form; but though
destitute of ornaments of leather, it has frequently
little **strings** of beads hanging to it from the shoul-
ders or small of the back. This dress is of thinner
skin, and acts as a shirt, the hairy part being placed
near the body: **it is** the in-doors habit. When
walking, the tail is tied up by two strings to the
back, so that it may not incommode the legs. Be-
sides these two coats, they have also a large cloak,
or, in **fact,** an open deer-skin, with sleeves; this,
from its size, is **more** frequently used as a blanket;
and **I but once saw it** worn by a man at the ship,
although **the** women throw **it over** their shoulders
to shelter themselves and **children** while sitting **on
the** sledge.

"The trowsers, which **are** tightly tied round the
loins, have **no** waistbands, but depend entirely by
the drawing-string; they are generally of deer-skin,
and ornamented in the same manner as the coats.
One of the most favourite patterns is an arrangement

of the skins of deers' legs, so as to form very pretty
stripes. As with the jackets, there are two pair of
these indispensables, reaching no lower than the
knee-cap, which is a cause of great distress in cold
weather, as that part is frequently severely frost-
bitten; yet, with all their experience of this bad
contrivance, they will not add an inch to the established length.

"The boots reach to the bottom of the breeches,
which hang loosely over them. In these, as in other parts of the dress, are many varieties of colour,
material, and pattern, yet in shape they never vary.
The general winter boots are of deer-skin; one having the hair next the leg, and the other with the
fur outside. A pair of soft slippers of the same kind
are worn between the two pair of boots, and outside of all a strong seal-skin shoe is pulled to the
height of the ankle, where it is tightly secured by a
drawing-string. For hunting excursions, or in summer when the country is thawed, one pair of boots
only is worn. They are of seal-skin, and so well
sewed and prepared without the hair, that although
completely saturated, they allow no water to pass
through them. The soles are generally of the tough
hide of the walrus, or of the large seal called Oŏ-
ghĭoo, so that the feet are well protected in walking over rough ground. Slippers are sometimes
worn outside. In both cases the boots are tightly
fastened round the instep with a thong of leather.
The mittens in common use are of deer-skin, with
the hair inside; but, in fact, every kind of skin is
used for them. They are extremely comfortable
when dry; but if once wetted and frozen again, in
the winter afford as little protection to the hands as
a case of ice would do. In summer, and in fishing,
excellent seal-skin mittens are used, and have the
same power of resisting water as the boots of which

I have just spoken. The dresses I have just described are chiefly used in winter. During the summer it is customary to wear coats, boots, and even breeches, composed of the prepared skins of ducks, with the feathers next the body. These are comfortable, light, and easily prepared. The few ornaments in their possession are worn by the men. These **are some** bandeaus which encircle the head, and are composed of various-coloured leather, plaited in a mosaic pattern, and in some cases having human hair woven in them, as a contrast to the white skins. **From the** lower edge foxes' teeth hang suspended, arranged as a fringe across the forehead. Some wear a musk ox-tooth, a bit of ivory, or a small piece of bone.

" The clothing of the women is of the same materials as that of the men, but in shape almost every part is different **from** the male dress. An inner jacket is worn next the skin, and the fur of the other is outside. The hind-flap, or tail, is of the same form before described, but there is also a small flap in front, extending **about half-way** down the thigh. The **coats** have each an immense hood, which, as well as covering the head, answers the purpose of a child's cradle for two or three years after the birth of an infant. In order to keep the burden of the child **from** drawing the dress tight across the throat, a contrivance, in a great measure resembling the slings of a soldier's knapsack, is affixed to the collar or neck part, whence it passes beneath the hood, crosses, and, being brought under the arms, is secured on each side the breast by a wooden button. The shoulders of the women's coat have a bag-like **space,** for the purpose of facilitating the removal of **the child** from the hood round to the breast without taking it out of the jacket.

" A girdle is sometimes worn round the waist:

it answers the double purposes of comfort and ornament; being composed of what they consider valuable trinkets, such as foxes' bones (those of the rableeaghioo), or sometimes of the ears of deer, which hang in pairs to the number of twenty or thirty, and are trophies of the skill of the hunter, to whom the wearer is allied. The inexpressibles of the women are of the same form as those of the men, but they are not ornamented by the same curious arrangement of colours; the front part is generally of white, and the back of dark fur. The manner of securing them at the waist is also the same; but the drawing-strings are of much greater length, being suffered to hang down by one side, and their ends are frequently ornamented with some pendant jewel, such as a grinder or two of the musk-ox, a piece of ivory, a small ball of wood, or a perforated stone.

"The boots of the fair sex are, without dispute, the most extraordinary part of their equipment, and are of such an immense size as to resemble leather sacks, and to give a most deformed, and, at the same time, ludicrous appearance to the whole figure, the bulky part being at the knee; the upper end is formed into a pointed flap, which, covering the front of the thigh, is secured by a button or knot within the waistband of the breeches.

"Some of these ample articles of apparel are composed with considerable taste, of various coloured skins; they also have them of parchment — seals' leather. Two pairs are worn; and the feet have also a pair of seal-skin slippers, which fit close, and are tightly tied round the ankle.

"Children have no kind of clothing, but lie naked in their mothers' hoods until two or three years of age, when they are stuffed into a little dress, generally of fawn-skin, which has jacket and breeches in

G

one, the back part being open; into this they are
pushed, when a string or two closes all up again.
A cap forms an indispensable part of the equipment,
and is generally of some fantastical shape; the skin
of a fawn's head is a favourite material in the composition, and is sometimes seen with the ears perfect; the nose and holes for the eyes lying along
the **crown** of the wearer's head, which, in consequence, looks like that of an animal."

The **same** author also gives a most graphic description **of** the curious winter dwellings of the Esquimaux, which on many parts of the coast are built
out of the only materials to be had—*ice and snow!*
Snow for the walls and ice for the windows! you
might fancy the house of the Esquimaux to be a
very cold dwelling; such, however, is by no means
its character.

"The entrance to the dwellings," says **Captain**
Lyon, "was by a hole, about a yard in diameter,
which led through a low-arched passage of sufficient
breadth for two to pass in a stooping posture, and
about sixteen feet in length; another hole then presented itself, and led through a similarly-shaped, but
shorter passage, having at its termination a round
opening, about two feet across. Up this hole we
crept one step, and found ourselves in a dome about
seven feet in height, and as many in diameter, from
whence the three dwelling-places, with arched roofs,
were entered. It must be observed that this is the
description of a large hut, the smaller ones, containing one or two families, have the domes somewhat
differently arranged.

" Each dwelling might be averaged at fourteen
or sixteen feet in diameter by six or seven in height,
but as snow alone was used in their construction,
and was always at hand, it might be supposed that
there was no particular size, that being of course at

the option of the builder. The laying of the arch was performed in such a manner as would have satisfied the most regular artist, the key-piece on the top, being a large square slab. The blocks of snow used in the buildings were from four to six inches in thickness, and about a couple of feet in length, carefully pared with a large knife. Where two families occupied a dome, a seat was raised on either side, two feet in height. These raised places were used as beds, and covered in the first place with whalebone, sprigs of andromeda, or pieces of seals'-skin—over these were spread deer-pelts and deer-skin clothes, which had a very warm appearance. The pelts were used as blankets, and many of them had ornamental fringes of leather sewed round their edges.

"Each dwelling-place was illumined by a broad piece of transparent fresh-water ice, of about two feet in diameter, which formed part of the roof, and was placed over the door. These windows gave a most pleasing light, free from glare, and something like that which is thrown through ground glass. We soon learned that the building of a house was but the work of an hour or two, and that a couple of men—one to cut the slabs and the other to lay them—were labourers sufficient.

"For the support of the lamps and cooking apparatus, a mound of snow is erected for each family; and when the master has two wives or a mother, both have an independent place, one at each end of the bench.

"I find it impossible to attempt describing everything at a second visit, and shall therefore only give an account of those articles of furniture which must be always the same, and with which, in five minutes, any one might be acquainted. A frame, composed of two or three broken fishing-spears, sup-

ported in the first place a large hoop of wood or
bone, across which an open-meshed and ill-made
net was spread or worked for the reception of wet
or damp clothes, skins, &c., which could be dried
by the heat of the lamp. On`this contrivance the
master of each hut placed his gloves on entering,
first carefully clearing them of snow.

"From the frame above mentioned, one or more
coffin-shaped stone pots were suspended over lamps
of the same material, crescent-shaped, and having a
ridge extending along their back; the bowl part
was filled with blubber, and the oil and wicks were
ranged close together along the edge. The wicks
were made of moss and trimmed by a piece of as-
bestos, stone, or wood; near at hand a large bundle of moss was hanging for a future supply. The
lamps were supported by sticks, bones, or pieces of
horn, at a sufficient height to admit an oval pot of
wood or whalebone beneath, in order to catch any
oil that might drop from them. The lamps varied
considerably in size, from two feet to six inches in
length, and the pots were equally irregular, holding from two or three gallons to half a pint. Although I have mentioned a kind of scaffolding, these
people did not all possess so grand an establishment,
many being contented to suspend their pot to a
piece of bone stuck in the wall of the hut. One
young woman was quite a caricature in this way:
she was the inferior wife of a young man, whose
senior lady was of a large size, and had a corresponding lamp, &c., at one corner; while she herself, being short and fat, had a lamp the size of half
a dessert-plate, and a pot which held a pint only.

"Almost every family was possessed of a large
wooden tray, resembling those used by butchers in
England; its offices, however, as we soon perceived,
were more various, some containing raw flesh of seals

and blubber, and others, skins which were steeping
in urine. A quantity of variously-sized bowls of
whalebone, wood, or skin, completed the list of vessels, and it was evident that they were made to
contain *anything.*"

The Esquimaux use two kinds of boats,—the
" oomiak" and "kayak." The oomiak is merely a
large species of punt, used exclusively by the wom-
en; but the kayak is a triumph in the art of naval
architecture, and is as elegant as it is ingenious. It
is about twenty-five feet in length, and less than
two in breadth of beam. In shape it has been compared to a weaver's shuttle, though it tapers much
more elegantly than this piece of machinery. It is
decked from stem to stern, excepting a circular
hole very nearly amidships, and this round hatch-
way is just large enough to admit the body of an
Esquimaux in a sitting posture. Around the rim
of the circle is a little ridge, sometimes higher in
front than at the back, and this ridge is often ornamented with a hoop of ivory. A flat piece of wood
runs along each side of the frame, and is, in fact,
the only piece of any strength in a kayak. Its depth
in the centre is four or five inches, and its thickness
about three-fourths of an inch; it tapers to a point
at the commencement of the stem and stern projec-
tions. Sixty-four ribs are fastened to this gunwale
piece; seven slight rods run the whole length of
the bottom and outside the ribs. The bottom is
rounded, and has no keel; twenty-two little beams
or cross-pieces keep the frame on a stretch above,
and one strong batten runs along the centre, from
stem to stern, being, of course, discontinued at the
seat part. The ribs are made of ground willow,
also of whalebone, or, if it can be procured, of good-
grained wood. The whole contrivance does not
weigh over fifty or sixty pounds; so that a man

easily carries his **kayak on his** head, which, by the form of the rim, he **can do without** the assistance of his hands.

An Esquimaux prides **himself in** the neat appearance of his boat, and **has a warm** skin placed in its bottom to sit on. **His** posture is with **the** legs pointed forward, and he cannot change his position without **the** assistance of another person: **in** all cases where a weight is to be lifted, an alteration of stowage, or any movement to be made, it is customary for two kayaks to lie together; and the paddle of each being placed across the other, they form a steady double boat. An inflated seal's bladder forms, invariably, part of the equipage of a canoe, and the weapons are confined in their places **by** small lines of whalebone, stretched tightly **across** the upper covering, so as to receive the points **or** handles of the spears beneath them. Flesh is **fre**quently stowed within the **stem** or stern, as are **also** birds and eggs; but a seal, although round, **and** easily made to roll, is **so neatly** balanced on the upper part of the boat as **seldom to require a** lashing. When Esquimaux **are** not paddling, their balance must be nicely preserved, and a trembling motion is always observable in the boat. The most difficult position for managing a kayak is when going before the wind, and with a little swell running. Any inattention would instantly, by exposing the broadside, overturn this frail vessel. The dexterity with which **they are** turned, the velocity of their way, and the extreme elegance **of** form of the kayaks, render an Esquimaux an object of the highest **interest** when sitting independently, and urging his course towards his prey.

"The paddle is double-bladed, **nine** feet three inches in length, small at the grasp, and widening to **four** inches **at** the blades, which are thin, and

edged with ivory **for strength as** well as ornament.

"The next object of importance to the boat is
the sledge, which finds occupation during at least
three-fourths of the year. A man who possesses
both this and **a canoe** is considered **a** person of
property. To give a particular description of the
sledge would be impossible, as there are no two
actually alike; and the materials of which they are
composed are as various as their form. The best
are made of the jaw-bones of the whale, sawed **to
about** two inches in thickness, and in depth from six
inches to a foot. These are the runners, and are
shod with a thin plank of the same material; the
side-pieces are connected by means **of** bones, pieces
of wood, or deers' horns, lashed across, with a few
inches space between each, and they yield **to any**
great strain which the sledge may **receive.** The
general breadth of the upper part of the sledge **is**
about twenty inches; but the runners lean inwards,
and therefore at bottom it is rather greater. The
length of bone sledges is from four feet to fourteen.
Their weight is necessarily great; and one of mod-
erate size—that is to say, about ten or twelve feet
—was found to be 217 lbs. The skin of the walrus
is very commonly used during the coldest part of
the winter, as being hard-frozen, and resembling an
inch board, with ten times the strength, for runners.
Another ingenious contrivance is, by casing moss
and earth in seal's skin, so that by pouring a little
water, a round hard bolster is easily formed. **Across**
all these kinds of runners there is the same arrangement of bones, sticks, &c., on the upper part; and
the surface which passes over the snow is coated
with ice, by mixing snow with fresh water, which
assists greatly in lightening the load for the dogs,
as it slides forward with ease. Boys frequently

amuse themselves by **yoking several** dogs to a small piece of seal's skin, **and sitting on** it, holding by the traces. Their **plan is then to set** off at full speed, **and** he who bears **the** greatest number of bumps before he relinquishes his hold is considered a **very** fine fellow.

"The Esquimaux possess various kinds **of spears,** but their difference is chiefly in consequence **of the substances** of which they are composed, and **not in their** general form.

"**One** called kā-tĕ-tēek, is a large and strong-handled spear, with an ivory point made for despatching any wounded animal in **the water.** It is never thrown, but has a place **appropriated for** it on the kayak.

"The oonak is a lighter **kind** than the former; also ivory-headed. It has **a** bladder fastened to **it,** and has **a** loose head with a line attached; this being darted into an animal, is instantly liberated from the handle which gives the impetus. Some few **of** these weapons are constructed **of** the solid ivory of **the** unicorn's horn, **about four feet in** length, and remarkably well **rounded** and polished.

"Ip-pŏo-tōo-yŏo, **is** another kind of hand-spear, varying but little from the one last described. It has, however, no appendages.

"The Noōgh-wĭt is of two kinds; but both are used **for** striking birds, young animals, or fish. The first has **a** double **fork** at the extremity, **and** there are three other **barbed** ones at about half its length, diverging in different directions, so that if the end **pair** should **miss, some of the** centre ones might **strike. The** second kind has only three barbed forks at the head. All the points are of ivory, and the **natural curve** of the walrus tusk favours and facilitates their construction.

"Amongst the minor instruments of the ice-hunt-

ing are a long bone feeler for plumbing any cracks
through which seals are suspected of breathing, and
also for trying the safety of the road. Another contrivance is occasionally used with the same effect
as the float of a fishing-line. Its purpose is to warn
the hunter, who is watching a seal-hole, when the
animal rises to the surface, so that he may strike
without seeing, or being seen, by his prey. This is
a most delicate little rod of bone or ivory, of about
a foot in length, and the thickness of a fine knit-
ting-needle. At the lower end is a small knob like
a pin's head, and the upper extremity has a fine
piece of sinew tied to it, so as to fasten it loosely to
the side of the hole. The animal, on rising, does
not perceive so small an object hanging in the water, and pushes it up with his nose, when the watchful Esquimaux, observing his little beacon in motion, strikes down, and secures his prize.

"Small ivory pegs or pins are used to stop the
holes made by the spears in the animal's body;
thus the blood, a great luxury to the natives, is
saved.

"The same want of wood which renders it necessary to find substitutes in the construction of
spears, also occasions the great variety of bows.
The horn of the musk-ox, thinned horns of deer, or
other bony substances, are as frequently used or met
with as wood, in the manufacture of these weapons,
in which elasticity is a very secondary consideration. Three or four pieces of horn or wood are frequently joined together in one bow—the strength
lying alone in a vast collection of small plaited sinews; these, to the number of perhaps a hundred,
run down the back of the bow, and being quite
tight, and having the spring of catgut, cause the
weapon, when unstrung, to turn the wrong way;
when bent, their united strength and elasticity are

amazing. The bow-string is of fifteen to twenty
plaits, each loose from the other, but twisted round
when in use, so that a few additional turns will at
any time alter its length. The general length of
the bows is about three feet and a half.

"The arrows are short, light, and formed according to no general rule as to length or thickness. A
good one has half the shaft of bone, and a head of
hard slate, or a small piece of iron; others have
sharply - pointed bone heads: none are barbed.
Two feathers are used for the end, and are tied opposite each other, with the flat sides parallel. A
neatly-formed case contains the bow and a few arrows. Seal-skin is preferred for this purpose, as
more effectually resisting the wet than any other.
A little bag, which is attached to the side, contains
a stone for sharpening, and some spare arrow-heads
carefully wrapped up in a piece of skin.

"The bow is held in a horizontal position, and
though capable of great force, is rarely used at a
greater distance than from twelve to twenty yards."

Their houses, clothing, sledges, boats, utensils,
and arms, being now described, it only remains to
be seen in what manner these most singular people
pass their time, how they supply themselves with
food, and how they manage to support life during
the long dark winter, and the scarce less hospitable
summer of their rigorous clime. Their occupations
from year to year are carried on with an almost
unvarying regularity, though, like their dresses,
they change according to the season.

Their short summer is chiefly employed in hunting the reindeer, and other quadrupeds,—for the
simple reason that it is at this season that these appear in greatest numbers among them, migrating
northward as the snow thaws from the valleys and
hill-sides. Not but that they also kill the reindeer

in other seasons, for these animals do not all migrate southward on the approach of winter, a considerable number remaining all the year upon the shores of the Arctic Sea, as well as the islands to the north of them. Of course, the Esquimaux kills a reindeer when and where he can; and it may be here remarked, that in no part of the American continent has the reindeer been trained or domesticated as among the Laplanders and the people of Russian Asia. Neither the northern Indians (*Tinné*) nor the Esquimaux have ever reached this degree in domestic civilization, and this fact is one of the strongest points of difference between the American Esquimaux and their kindred races in the north of Asia. One tribe of true Esquimaux alone hold the reindeer in subjection, viz., the Tuski, already mentioned, on the Asiatic shore; and it might easily be shown that the practice reached them from the contiguous countries of northern Asia. The American Esquimaux, like those of Greenland, possess only the dog as a domesticated animal; and him they have trained to draw their sledges in a style that exhibits the highest order of skill, and even elegance. The Esquimaux dog is too well known to require particular description. He is often brought to this country in the return ships of Arctic whalers and voyagers; and his thick, stout body, covered closely with long stiff hair of a whitish or yellowish colour, his cocked ears and smooth muzzle, and, above all, the circle-like curling of his bushy tail, will easily be remembered by any one who has ever seen this valuable animal.

In summer, then, the Esquimaux desert their winter houses upon the shore, and taking with them their tents make an excursion into the interior. They do not go far from the sea—no farther than is necessary to find the valleys browsed by the

reindeer, and the fresh-water lakes, which, at this
season, are frequented by flocks of swans, geese of
various kinds, ducks, and other aquatic birds. Hunting the reindeer forms their principal occupation at
this time; but, of course, "all is fish that comes
into the net" of an Esquimaux; and they also employ themselves in capturing the wild fowl and the
fresh-water fish, in which these lakes abound. With
the wild fowl it is the breeding and moulting season, and the Esquimaux not only rob them of their
eggs, but take large numbers of the young before
they are sufficiently fledged to enable them to fly,
and also the old ones while similarly incapacitated
from their condition of "moult." In their swift
kayaks which they have carried with them on their
heads, they can pursue the fluttering flocks over
any part of a lake, and overtake them wherever
they may go. This is a season of great plenty in
the larder of the *Inuit*.

The fresh-water fish are struck with spears out of
the kayaks, or, when there is ice on the water strong
enough to bear the weight of a man, the fish are captured in a different manner. A hole is broken in the
ice, the broken fragments are skimmed off and cast
aside, and then the fisherman lets down a shining
bauble—usually the white tooth of some animal—to
act as a bait. This he keeps bobbing about until the
fish, perceiving it afar off through the translucent
water, usually approaches to reconnoitre, partly
from curiosity, but more, perhaps, to see if it be
anything to eat. When near enough the Esquimaux adroitly pins the victim with his fish-spear,
and lands it upon the ice. This species of fishing is
usually delivered over to the boys—the time of the
hunters being too valuable to be wasted in waiting
for the approach of the fish to the decoy, an event
of precarious and uncertain occurrence.

In capturing the reindeer the Esquimaux practises no method very different from that used by
" still hunters" in other parts of America. He has
to depend alone upon his bow and arrows, but with
these poor weapons he contrives to make more hav-
oc among a herd of deer than would a backwoods
hunter with his redoubtable rifle. There is no mystery about his superior management. It consists
simply in the exhibition of the great strategy and
patience with which he makes his approaches, crawling from point to point and using every available
cover which the ground may afford.

But all this would be of little avail were it not
for a *ruse* which he puts in practice, and which
brings the unsuspecting deer within reach of his
deadly arrows. This consists in a close imitation
of the cries of the animal, so close that the sharp-
eared creature itself cannot detect the counterfeit,
but, drawing nearer and nearer to the rock or bush
from which the call appears to proceed, falls a victim
to the deception. The silent arrow makes no audi-
ble sound; the herd, if slightly disturbed at seeing
one of their number fall, soon compose themselves,
and go on browsing upon the grass or licking up
the lichen. Another is attracted by the call, and
another, who fall in their turn victims either to their
curiosity or the instinct of amorous passions.

For this species of hunting, the bow far excels
any other weapon; even the rifle is inferior to it.

Sometimes the Esquimaux take the deer in large
numbers, by hunting them with dogs, driving the
herd into some defile or *cul de sac* among the rocks,
and then killing them at will with their arrows
and javelins. This, however, is an exceptional case,
as such natural "pounds" are not always at hand.
The Indians farther south construct artificial in-
closures; but in the Esquimaux country there is

neither time nor material for such elaborate contrivances.

The **Esquimaux** who dwell **in** those parts frequented by the musk-oxen, hunt these animals very much as they do the reindeer; but killing a musk bull, or cow either, is a feat of far grander magnitude, and requires more address than shooting a tiny deer.

I **have** said that the Esquimaux **do not,** even in these hunting excursions, stray very far into the interior. There is a good reason for their keeping **close to** the seashore. Were they to penetrate far **into** the land they **would be** in danger of meeting with their bitter foemen, the *Tinné* Indians, who in this region also hunt reindeer and musk oxen. War to the knife is the practice between these two races of people, and has ever been since the **first** knowledge of either. They often meet in conflict upon the rivers inland, and these conflicts are of so cruel and sanguinary a nature as to imbue each with a wholesome fear of the other. The Indians, however, dread **the** Esquimaux more than the latter fear them; and up to a late period took good care **never to** approach their coasts; but the musket and rifle have now got into the hands of some of the northern tribes, who avail themselves of these superior weapons, not only to keep the Esquimaux at bay, **but** also to render them more cautious about extending their range towards the interior.

When the dreary winter begins to make its appearance, and the reindeer grow scarce upon the snow-covered plains, the Esquimaux return to their winter villages upon the coast. Quadrupeds and birds **no** longer occupy their whole attention, for the drift **of** their thoughts is now turned towards the inhabitants of the great deep. The seal and the walrus are henceforth the main objects of pursuit.

Perhaps during the summer, when the water was open, they may have visited the shore for the purpose of capturing that great giant of the icy seas— a whale. If so, and they have been successful in only one or two captures, they may look forward to a winter of plenty—since the flesh of a full-grown whale, or, better still, a brace of such ample creatures, would be sufficient to feed a whole tribe for months.

They have no curing process for this immense carcass; they stand in need of none. Neither salt nor smoking is required in their climate. Jack Frost is their provision-curer, and performs the task without putting them either to trouble or expense. It is only necessary for them to hoist the great flitches upon scaffolds, already erected for the purpose, so as to keep the meat from the wolves, wolveranes, foxes, and their own half-starved dogs. From their aërial larder they can cut a piece of blubber whenever they feel hungry, or they have a mind to eat, and this *mind* they are in so long as a morsel is left.

Their mode of capturing a whale is quite different from that practised by the whale-fishers. When the huge creature is discovered near, the whole tribe sally forth, and surround it in their kayaks; they then hurl darts into its body, but instead of these having long lines attached to them, they are provided with seal-skins sewed up air-tight and inflated, like bladders. When a number of these become attached to the body of the whale, the animal, powerful though he be, finds great difficulty in sinking far down, or even progressing rapidly through the water. He soon rises to the surface, and the seal-skin buoys indicate his whereabouts to the occupants of the kayaks, who in their swift little crafts soon dart up to him again, and shoot a fresh

volley into his body.   In this way the whale is soon
"wearied out," and then falls a victim to their
larger spears—just as in the case where a capture
is made by regular whalers.

I need scarcely add that a success of this kind is
hailed as a jubilee of the tribe, since it not only
brings a benefit to the whole community, but is
also a piece of fortune of somewhat rare occurrence.

When no whales have been taken, the long dark
winter may justly be looked forward to with some
solicitude: and it is then that the Esquimaux requires to put forth all his skill and energies for the
capture of the walrus or the seal—the latter of which
may be regarded as the staff of his life, furnishing
him not only with food, but with light, fuel, and
clothing for his body and limbs.

Of the seals that inhabit the Polar Seas there are
several species; but the common seal (*Calocephalus
vitulina*) and the harp-seal (*C. Grœnlandicus*) are
those most numerous, and consequently the principal object of pursuit.

The Esquimaux uses various stratagems for taking these creatures, according to the circumstances
in which they may be encountered; and simpletons
as the seals may appear, they are by no means easy
of capture.   They are usually very shy and suspicious, even in places where man has never been seen
by them.   They have other enemies, especially in
the great polar bear; and the dread of this tyrant
of the icy seas keeps them ever on the alert.   Notwithstanding their watchfulness, however, both the
bear and the biped make great havock among them,
and each year hundreds of thousands of them are
destroyed.

The bear, in capturing seals, exhibits a skill and
cunning scarce excelled by that of the rational be-

ing himself. When this great quadruped perceives
a seal basking on the edge of an ice-field, he makes
his approaches, not by rushing directly towards it,
which he well knows would defeat his purpose. If
once seen by the seal, the latter has only to betake
itself to the water, where it can soon sink or swim
beyond the reach of the bear. To prevent this, the
bear gets well to leeward, and then diving below
the surface, makes his approaches under water, now
and then cautiously raising his head to get the true
bearings of his intended victim. After a number
of these subaqueous " reaches," he gets close in to
the edge of the floe in such a position as to cut off
the seal's retreat to the water. A single spring
brings him on the ice, and then, before the poor
seal has time to make a brace of flounders, it finds
itself locked in the deadly embrace of the bear.
When seals are thus detected asleep, the Esquimaux approaches them in his kayak, taking care to
paddle cautiously and silently. If he succeed in
getting between them and the open water, he kills
them in the ordinary way—by simply knocking
them on the snout with a club, or piercing them
with a spear. Sometimes, however, the seal goes
to sleep on the surface of the open water. Then the
approach is made in a similar manner by means of
the kayak, and the animal is struck with a harpoon.
But a single blow does not always kill a seal—especially if it be a large one, and the blow has been
ill directed. In such cases the animal would undoubtedly make its escape, and carry the harpoon
along with it, which would be a serious loss to the
owner, who does not obtain such weapons without
great difficulty. To prevent this, the Esquimaux
uses a contrivance similar to that employed in the
capture of the whale—that is, he attaches a float or
buoy to his harpoon by means of a cord, and this so

impedes the passage of the seal through the water,
that it can neither dive nor swim to any very great
distance. The float is usually a walrus bladder inflated in the ordinary way, and wherever the seal
may go, the float betrays its track, enabling the
Esquimaux to follow it in his shuttle-shaped kayak,
and pierce it again with a surer aim.

In winter, when the sea is quite covered with ice,
you might fancy that the seal-fishery would be at
an end—for the seal is essentially a marine animal;
and although it can exist upon the ice or on dry
land, it could not *subsist* there. Access to the water it must have, in order to procure its food, which
consists of small fish and molluscs. Of course,
when the ice forms on the surface, the seal is in its
true element—the water underneath—but when
this ice becomes, as it often does, a full yard in
thickness, extending over hundreds of miles of the
sea, how then is the seal to be got at? It could not
be reached at all; and at such a season the Esquimaux people would undoubtedly starve, were it not
for a habit peculiar to this animal, which, happily
for them, brings it within their reach.

Though the seal can live under water like a fish
—and probably could pass a whole winter under
the ice without much inconvenience—it likes now
and then to take a little fresh air, and have a quiet
nap upon the upper surface in the open air. With
this design it breaks a hole through the ice, while
the latter is yet thin, and this hole it keeps carefully open during the whole winter, clearing out each
new crust as it forms. No matter to what thickness the ice may attain, this hole always forms a
breathing-place for the seal, and a passage by which
he may reach the upper surface, and indulge himself in his favourite siesta in the open air. Knowing
this habit, the Esquimaux takes advantage of it to

make the seal his captive. When the animal is discovered on the ice, the hunter approaches with the greatest stealth and caution. This is absolutely necessary; for if the enemy is perceived, or makes the slightest noise, the wary seal flounders rapidly into his hole, and is lost beyond redemption. If badly frightened, he will not appear for a long time, denying himself his open air exercise until the patience of his persecutor is quite worn out, and the coast is again clear.

In making his approaches, the hunter uses all his art, not only taking advantage of every inequality —such as snow-drifts and ice-hillocks—to conceal himself; but he also practises an ingenious deception by dressing himself in the skin of a seal of like species, giving his body the figure of the animal, and counterfeiting its motions, by floundering clumsily over the ice and oscillating his head from side to side, just as seals are seen to do.

This deception often proves successful, when the hunter under any other shape would in vain endeavour to get within striking distance of his prey. When seals are scarce, and the supply greatly needed, the Esquimaux often lies patiently for hours together on the edge of a seal-hole waiting for the animal to come up. In order to give it time to get well out upon the ice, the hunter conceals himself behind a heap of snow, which he has collected and piled up for the purpose. A float-stick, ingeniously placed in the water of the breathing-hole, serves as a signal to tell when the seal is mounting through his trap-like passage, the motion of the stick betraying its ascent. The hunter then gets himself into the right attitude to strike, and summons all his energies for the encounter.

Even during the long, dark night of winter this mode of capturing the seal is practised. The hunter, having discovered a breathing-hole—which its dark color enables him to find—proceeds in the following manner: he scrapes **away** the snow from around it, and lifting up some water pours it **on the** ice, so as to make a circle of **a** darker hue around **the** orifice.   He then makes a sort of cake of pure white snow, and with this covers **the** hole as with **a lid.**   In the centre of this lid he punches **a** small opening **with** the shaft-end of his spear, and then sits **down** and patiently awaits the issue.

The **seal** ascends unsuspiciously as before.   The **dark water,** bubbling up through the small central orifice, betrays its approach, which can be perceived **even** in the darkest night.   The hunter does not wait for its climbing out upon the ice.   Perhaps if he did so, the suspicious creature might detect the device, and dive down again.   But it is not allow**ed** time for reflection.   Before it can turn its unwieldy body, the heavy spear of the hunter—struck through the yielding snow—descends **upon its skull, and** kills it **on** the instant.

The great "walrus" or "morse" (*Trichecus rosmarus*) is another important product of the Polar Seas, and is hunted by the Esquimaux with great assiduity.   This splendid amphibious animal is taken by contrivances very similar to those used for the seal: but the capture of a walrus is an event of importance, second only to the striking of a whale. Its great **carcass not** only supplies food to a whole village, **but an oil** superior to that of the whale, be- **sides various other** useful articles.   Its skin, bones, **and** intestines are employed by the Esquimaux for many domestic purposes—and, in addition, there **are** the huge molar **tusks, that** furnish one of the most valuable ivories of commerce, from which are manufactured those beautiful sets of teeth, of dazzling whiteness, that, gleaming between vermilion lips, you may often see at a ball or an evening party!

MUNDRUCUS, OR BEHEADERS.

In our general sketch of the Amazonian Indians it was stated that **there** were some few tribes who differed in certain customs from all the rest, and who might even be regarded as *odd among the odd*. One of these tribes is the *Mundrucu*, which, from its numbers and warlike strength, **almost** deserves to be styled a nation. It is, at all events, **a** powerful confederacy, of different tribes, linked together in one common nationality, and including in their league other Indians which the Mundrucus **themselves** first conquered, and afterwards **associated** with themselves on terms of equality; **in other** words, "annexed" them. The same sort of annexation or alliance is common among the tribes of North America; as in the case of the powerful Comanche nation, who extend their protecting alliance over the Wacoes, Washites, and Cayguäas or Kioways.

The *Mahüe* is the principal tribe that is patronized in this fashion by the Mundrucus, and the two together number at least 20,000 souls.

Before the days of the Portuguese slave-hunting, the Mundrucus occupied the south bank of the Amazon, from the mouth of the Tapajos to that of the Madeira. This infamous traffic had the effect of clearing the banks of the great river of its native inhabitants—except such of them as chose to submit to slavery, or become *neophytes*, by adopting the monkish faith. Neither of these courses appeared pleasing in the eyes of the Mundrucus, and

they adopted the **only** alternative that was likely
to insure their independence—by withdrawing from
the dangerous **proximity of** the sanguinary **slave-**
trade.

This retreat of the Mundrucus, however, was by
no means an ignominious flight. The withdrawal
was voluntary on their part, and not compulsory, as
was the case with weaker tribes. From the earliest times they had presented a firm front to the
Portuguese encroachments, and the latter were even
forced into a sort of nefarious alliance with them.
The leaving the Amazon on the part of the Mundrucus was rather the result of a negotiation, by
which they conceded their territory—between the
mouths of the Tapajos and Madeira—to the Brazilian government; and to this hour they are not exactly unfriendly to Brazilian *whites*, though **to the**
mulattoes and negroes, who constitute a large proportion of the Brazilian population, the Mundrucu
knows no other feeling than that of a deadly hostility. The origin of their hatred of the Brazilian
blacks is to be found in a revolt which occurred in
the provinces of the Lower Amazon (at Para) in
1835. It was a *caste* revolution against whites, but
more especially against *European* Portuguese. In
this affair the Mundrucus were employed against
the darker-skinned rebels — the *Cabanos*, as they
were called—and did great service in putting down
the rebellion. Hence they retain a lingering spark
of friendship for their *ci-devant* white allies; or perhaps it would be more correct to say they do not
actually hate them, but carry on a little commerce
with their traders. For all that, they occasionally
cut the throats of a few of the latter — especially
those who do not come to deal directly with them,
but who pass through their country in going from
the Amazon to the diamond mines of Brazil. These

last are called *Monçaos*, and their business is to carry supplies from the towns on the Amazon (Santarem and Para) to the miners of gold and washers of diamonds in the district of Matto Grosso, of which Cuiaba is the capital. Their route is by water and "portage" up the Tapajos river, and through the territory of the dreaded Mundrucus—requiring a journey of six months, as perilous and toilsome as it is tedious.

The present residence of the Mundrucus is between the Tapajos and Madeira, as formerly, but far up on both rivers. On the Tapajos, above what are known as the "Caxoeiras," or Cataracts, their villages are found. There they dwell, free from all molestation on the part of the whites; their borders extending widely around them, and limited only by contact with those of other warlike tribes like themselves, who are their deadly enemies. Among these last are the *Muras*, who dwell at the mouths of the Madeira and Rio Negro.

The Mundrucus build the *malocca*, elsewhere described; only in their case it is not used as a dwelling, but rather as a grand arsenal, a council-chamber, a ball-room, and, if need be, a fortress. When fearing an attack, all sleep in it "under arms." It is a structure of large size and great strength, usually rendered more unassailable by being "chinked" and plastered with clay. It is in this building that are deposited those horrid trophies which have given to the Mundrucus their terrible title of *decapitadores*, or "beheaders." The title and its origin shall be presently explained.

Around the great malocca the huts are placed, forming a village, and in these the people ordinarily dwell.

The Mundrucus are not without ample means of subsistence. Like most other Amazonian tribes, they cultivate a little manioc, plantains, and even maize; and they know how to prepare the *farinha* meal, and, unfortunately, also the detestable *chicha*, the universal beverage of the South American aborigines. They have their vessels of calabash—both of the vegetable and arborescent kinds—and a full set of implements and utensils for the field and kitchen. Their war weapons are those common to other Amazonian tribes, and they sometimes also carry the spear. They have canoes of hollow trees; and, of course, fishing and hunting are the employments of the men—the women, as almost everywhere else among the Indians, doing the drudgery—the tilling and reaping, the "hewing of wood and the drawing of water," the making the household utensils and using them—all such offices being beneath the dignity of the "lordly," or rather *lazy* savage.

I have said that they carry on a commercial intercourse with the white traders. It is not of much magnitude, and their exports consist altogether of the native and spontaneous productions of the soil, sarsaparilla being one of the chief articles. They gather this (the women and children do) during six months of the year. The other six months no industry is followed—as this period is spent in hostile excursions against the neighbouring tribes. Their imports consist of iron tools and pieces for weapons; but they more especially barter the product of their labour for ornamental gewgaws—such as savages universally admire and desire. Their sarsaparilla is good, and much sought for in the medical market.

Every one is acquainted with the nature and character of this valuable medicinal root, the appearance of which must also be known to almost everybody—since it is so very common for our druggists

to display the bundles of it in their shop windows.
Perhaps every one is not acquainted with the fact,
that the sarsaparilla root is the product of a great
many different species of plants, most of them of
the genus *Simlax*, but not a few belonging to plants
of other genera, as those of *Carex* and *Herreria* the
roots of which are also sold as sarsaparilla. The
species of simlax are widely distributed throughout
the whole torrid zone, in Asia, Africa, and America,
and some kinds are found growing many degrees
outside the tropics—as is the case in Virginia and
the valley of the Mississippi, and also on the other
side of the Pacific, on the great continent-island of
Australia.

The best sarsaparilla, however, is that which is
produced in tropical countries, and especially in
moist situations, where the atmosphere is at once
hot and humid. It requires these conditions to
concentrate the virtue of its sap, and render it more
active.

It would be idle to give a list of the different
species of simlax that furnish the sarsaparilla root
of the pharmacopeia. There is an almost endless
number of them, and they are equally varied in respect to excellence of quality; some kinds are in reality almost worthless, and for this reason, in using
it as a medicine, great care should be taken in the
selection of the species. Like all other articles, either of food or medicine, the valuable kinds are the
scarcest; the reason in this case being that the best
sarsaparilla is found in situations not only difficult
of access, but where the gathering of its root is attended with considerable danger, from the unhealthy nature of the climate and the hostility of
the savages in whose territory it grows. As to the
quantity that may be obtained, there is no limit, on
the score of any scarcity of the plant itself, since it

is found throughout all the countries of tropical
America plenteously distributed both in species and
individual plants. Such quantities of it grow along
the banks of some South-American rivers, that the
Indians have a belief that those streams, known as
black waters—such as the Rio Negro and others—
derive their peculiar colour from the roots of this
plant. This, however, is an erroneous supposition,
as there are many of the *white water* rivers that
run through regions abundantly supplied with the
sarsaparilla root. The black water, therefore, must
arise from some other cause, as yet unknown.

As observed, the sarsaparilla of the Mundrucu
country is of the very best quality. It is the *Simlax papyracea* of Soiret, and is known in commerce
as the "Lisbon," or "Brazilian." It is a climbing
plant or under-shrub, the stem of which is flattened
and angular, with rows of prickles standing along
the prominent edges. Its leaves are of an oval
acuminated shape, and marked with longitudinal
nerves. It shoots up without any support, to a
height of fifteen or twenty feet, after which it em-
braces the surrounding branches of trees and
spreads to a great distance in every direction. The
main root sends out many long tendrils, all of like
thickness covered with a brownish bark, or sometimes of a dark-grey colour. These tendrils are
fibrous, and about as thick as a quill. They present a constant tendency to become crooked, and
they are also wrinkled longitudinally, with here and
there some smaller lateral fibres branching off from
the sides.

It is in the bark or epidermis of the rhizomes
that the medicinal virtue lies; but the tendrils—
both rhizome and bark—are collected together, and
no attempt is made to separate them, until they
have reached their commercial destination. Indeed,

even these are sold together, the mode of preparing the root being left to the choice of the consumer, or the apothecary who procures it.

The Mundrucus collect it during the six months of the rainy season, partly because during the remaining six they are otherwise employed, and partly for the reason that, in the time of rain, the roots are more easily extracted from the damp soil. The process simply consists in digging them up or dragging them out of the earth—the latter mode especially where the tendrils lie near the surface, and they will pull up without breaking. If the main root be not dug out, it will send forth new tendrils, which in a short time would yield a new crop; but the improvident savages make no prudential calculations of this kind—present convenience forming their sole consideration; and on this account both the root and plant are generally destroyed by them during the operation of collecting.

As already stated, this labour devolves upon the women, who are also assisted in it by their children. They proceed into the depths of the forest—where the simlax grows in greatest abundance—and after collecting as much root as they can carry home with them, they return with their bundles to the malocca. When fresh gathered the sarsaparilla is heavy enough—partly on account of the sap which it then contains, and partly from the quantity of the mud or earth that adheres to the corrugated surface of the roots.

It is extremely probable that in this fresh state the virtue of the sarsaparilla, as a blood-purifier, is much greater than after it has passed through the channels of commerce; and the writer of this sketch has some reason, derived from personal experience, to believe that such is the case. Certain it is, that the reputation of this invaluable drug is far less in

countries where the plant does not grow, than in
those **where** it is common and **can** be obtained in
its fresh state.   In **all** parts of Spanish America its
virtues are unquestioned, and experience has led to
a more extensive use **of** it there than elsewhere.   **It**
is probable, therefore, that the virtue exists in the
juice rather than the cortical integument of the rhizome; **and** this of course would be materially altered and deteriorated, if not altogether destroyed, in
the process of exsiccation, which must necessarily
take place in the time required for transporting it
to distant parts of the world.   **In** the European
pharmacopeia it is the epidermis of the root which
is supposed to contain the sanitary principle; and
this, which is of a mucilaginous nature and slightly
bitter taste, is employed, both in decoctions and in-
fusions, as a tonic and alterative.   In America, however, it is generally taken for what is termed *puri-
fying the blood*—for the same purpose as the rhizomes of the *Laurus sassafras* and other plants are
used; but the sarsaparilla is generally considered
the best, and it certainly *is* **the best** of all known
medicines for this purpose.   Why it has fallen in
the estimation of the Old World practitioners, or
why it never obtained so great a reputation as it
has in America, may arise from two circumstances.
First, that the root offered for sale is generally the
product of the less valuable species; and second,
that the sap, and not the rhizome, may be the part
that contains the virtuous principle.

When the collected roots have **been** kept for
awhile they become **dry and** light, **and** for the convenience **of stowage and** carriage—an important
consideration to the trader in his eight-ton *garratea*
—it is necessary to have the roots done up in packages of a uniform length and thickness.   These
packages are formed by laying the **roots** side by

side, and doubling in the ends of the longer ones.
A bundle of the proper size for stowage contains an
arroba of twenty-five pounds, though the weight varies according to the condition of the root.   Uniformity in size is the chief object aimed at, and the
bundles are made of a round or cylindrical shape,
about five inches in diameter, and something more
than a yard in length.   They are trimmed off small
at the ends—so as to admit of stowage without
leaving any empty space between two tiers of them
—and each bundle is tightly corded round from one
end to the other with a "sipo," or creeping plant.

It has been stated that this "sipo" is a root of
the sarsaparilla itself, with the bark scraped off;
and, indeed, its own root would serve well enough
—were it not that putting it to such a use would
destroy its medicinal value, and thus cause a considerable waste of the costly material.   The sarsaparilla is not to be had for nothing even upon the
banks of the Tapajos.   A bundle of the best quality does not leave the hands of the Mundrucu until
about four dollars' worth of exchange commodities
have been put into them, which would bring the
price of it to something over sixpence a pound.   He
is, therefore, a little particular about wasting a material that has cost him—or rather his wife and
children—so much trouble in collecting.   His cordage is obtained more cheaply, and consists of the
long flexible roots of a species of *pothos,* which
roots—being what are termed *aërial* and not buried
in the ground—require no labour or digging to get
at them.   It is only necessary to stretch up the
hand, and pull them down from the tops of lofty
trees, from which they hang like streamers, often to
the length of a hundred feet.   These are toughened
by the bark being scraped off; and when that is
done they are ready for use, and serve not only to

tie up the bundles of sarsaparilla, but for many other purposes in the domestic economy of the Mundrucus.

In addition to the sarsaparilla, the Mundrucu furnishes the trader with several other items of commercial value—for his climate, although one of the
most unhealthy in all the Amazon region, on account
of its great heat and humidity, is for that very reason one of the most fertile. Nearly all those tropical vegetable products which are characteristics of
Brazilian export commerce can here be produced
of the most luxuriant kind; but it is only those
that grow spontaneously at his very doors that
tempt the Mundrucu to take the trouble of collecting them.

There is one article, however, which he not only
takes some trouble to collect, but also to manufacture
into an item of commercial exchange—a very rare
item indeed. This is the *guarana*, which is manufactured from the fruit of a tree almost peculiar to
the Mundrucu territory—since nowhere is it found
so abundantly as on the Tapajos. It is so prized in
the Brazilian settlements as to command almost its
weight in silver when transported thither. It is
the constituent element of a drink, which has a
stimulating effect on the system, somewhat more
powerful than tea or coffee. It will prevent sleep;
but its most valuable property is, that it is a good
febrifuge, equal to the best quinine. *Guarana* is
prepared from the seeds of an inga—one of the
Mimosaceæ. It is a low wide-spreading tree like
most of the mimosa family. The legumes are gathered, and the seeds roasted in them. The latter
are then taken out, and after being ground to powder, are mixed with water so as to make a tough
paste, which is moulded into little bricks, and when
dried is ready for use. The beverage is then pre-

pared by scraping a table-spoonful of dust from the brick, and mixing it with about a pint of water; and the dry paste, keeping for any length of time, is ready whenever wanted.

The *quarana* bush grows elsewhere in the Amazon valley, and on some headwaters of the Orinoco, where certain tribes also know how to prepare the drink. But it is sparingly distributed, and is nowhere so common as on the upper Tapajos; hence its high price in the markets of Brazil. The Mundrucu manufactures it, not only for "home use," but for "exportation."

He prepares another singular article of luxury, and this he makes exclusively for his own use—not for the gratification of his lips or palate, but for his nose—in other words a snuff. Do not fancy, however, that it is snuff of the ordinary kind—the pulverized produce of innocent tobacco. No such thing; but a composition of such a powerful and stimulating character, that he who inhales it feels as if struck by an electric shock; his body trembles; his eyes start forward as if they would forsake their sockets; his limbs fail to support him; and he drops to the earth like one in a state of intoxication! For a short time he is literally mad; but the fit is soon over—lasting usually only a few minutes—and then a feeling of renewed strength, courage, and joyousness succeeds. Such are the consequences of taking snuff with a Mundrucu.

And now to describe the nature of the substance which produces these powerful effects.

Like the *quarana* this snuff is a preparation, having for its basis the seeds of a leguminous tree. This time, however, it is an *acacia*, not an *inga*. It is the *acacia niopo*; so called because "niopo" is the name given to the snuff itself by certain tribes (the Ottomacs and others), who, like the Mundru-

cus, are snuff-takers. It is also called *curupa*, and
the apparatus for preparing and taking it—for there
is an apparatus of an extensive kind—is termed
parica, in the general language (*lingoa geral*) of the
Amazonian regions.

We shall describe the preparation, the apparatus,
and the ceremonial.

The pods of the *Acacia niopo*—a small tree, with
very delicate pinnate leaves—are plucked when
ripe. They are then cut into small pieces and flung
into a vessel of water. In this they remain until
macerated, and until the seeds have turned black.
These are then picked out, pounded in a mortar,
which is usually the pericarp of the *sapuçaia*, or
"monkey-pot" tree (*Lecythis ollaria*). The pound-
ing reduces them to a paste, which is taken up,
clapped between the hands and formed into little
cakes—but not until it has been mixed with some
manioc flour, some lime from a burnt shell (a *helix*),
and a little juice from the fresh leaves of the "abu-
ta"—a menispermous plant of the genus *Cocculus*.
The cakes are then dried or "barbecued" upon a
primitive gridiron—the bars of which are saplings
of hard wood—and when well-hardened the snuff is
ready for the "box." In a box it is actually carried—usually one made out of some rare and beautiful shell.

The ceremonial of taking the snuff is the most
singular part of the performance. When a Mundrucu feels inclined for a "pinch"—though it is
something more than a *pinch* that he inhales when
he *does* feel inclined—he takes the cake out of the
box, scrapes off about a spoonful of it into a shallow saucer-shaped vessel of the calabash kind, and
then spreads the powder all over the bottom of the
vessel in a regular "stratification." The spreading
is not performed by the fingers, but with a tiny pen-

cil-like brush made out of the bristles of the great
ant-eater (*Myrmecophaga jubata*).

He is in no hurry, but takes his time—for as you
may guess from its effects, the performance is not
one so often repeated as that of ordinary snuff-taking. When the *niopo* dust is laid to his liking, another implement is brought into play, the construction of which it is also necessary to describe. It is
a "machine" of six to eight inches in length, and is
made of two quills from the wing of the *gaviao real*,
or "harpy eagle" (*Harpyia destructor*). These quills
are placed side by side for the greater part of their
length, forming two parallel tubes, and they are
thus neatly whipped together by a thread. At one
end they are pressed apart so as to diverge to a
width corresponding to the breadth between the
Mundrucu's nostrils—where it is intended they shall
be placed during the ceremony of snuff-taking.

And thus are they placed—one end of each quill
being slightly intruded within the line of the septum, while the other end rests upon the snuff, or
wanders over the surface of the saucer, till all the
powder placed there is drawn up and inhaled, producing the convulsive effects already detailed.

The shank-bone of a species of bird—thought to
be a plover—is sometimes used instead of the
quills. It is hollow, and has a forking-tube at the
end. This kind is not common or easily obtained,
for the niopo-taker who has one, esteems it as the
most valuable item of his apparatus.

Snuffing the niopo is not exclusively confined to
the Mundrucu. We have seen elsewhere that it is
also a habit of the dirt-eating Ottomacs; and other
tribes on the upper Amazon practise it. But the
Mahües, already mentioned as the allies of the
Mundrucus, are the most confirmed snuff-takers of
all.

I

Another odd custom of the Mundrucus is their habit of "tatooing." I speak of real tatooing—that is, marking the skin with dots and lines that cannot be effaced, in contradistinction to mere *painting*, or staining, which can easily be washed off. The Mundrucus paint also, with the *anotto*, *huitoc*, *caruta*, and other pigments, but in this they only follow the practice of hundreds of other tribes. The true *tatoo* is a far different affair, and scarcely known among the aborigines of America, though common enough in the islands of the South Sea. A few other Indian tribes practise it to a limited extent—as is elsewhere stated—but among the Mundrucus it is an "institution;" and painful though the process be, it has to be endured by every one in the nation, "every mother's son," and daughter as well, that are cursed with a Mundrucu for their father.

It is upon the young people the infliction is performed—when they are about eight or ten years of age.

The *tatoo* has been so often described, that I should not repeat it here; but there are a few "points" peculiar to Mundrucu tatooing, and a few others, not elsewhere understood.

The performance is usually the work of certain old crones who, from long practice, have acquired great skill in the art.

The chief instrument used is a comb of thorns—not a single thorn, as is generally stated—but a tier or row of them set comb-fashion. These thorns are the spines of the "murumuru," or "pupunha" palm (*Gullielmia speciosa*). Humboldt states that this palm is smooth and spineless, but in this the great good man was in error. Its trunk is so covered with thorns or spines, that when the Indians require to climb it—for the purpose of procuring the valuable fruits, which they eat variously prepared—they have to erect a staging, or rude sort of ladder, to be able to get at them.

The comb, then, is pressed down upon the skin of the "tatooee," till all the points have penetrated the flesh, and a row of holes is laid open, from which the blood flows profusely. As soon as this can be wiped off, ashes of a burnt gum or pitch are rubbed into the wounds, which, when healed, appear like so many dots of a deep bluish or black colour. In this way the young Mundrucus, both boys and girls, get those regular rows of dotted lines, which traverse their forehead and cheeks, their arms and limbs, breasts and bodies in such eccentric fashion. It has often been asked how these lines of dots were carried over the skin in such straight and symmetrical rows, forming regular parallel lines, or other geometrical patterns. The "comb" will explain the mystery.

The tatoo, with a few strings of shell-beads or necklaces, and bracelets of monkey and jaguar teeth, is all the dress which is permitted to the Mundrucu belle. In Mundrucu-land it is the reverse of what is practised among civilized people : the men are the exponents of the fashions, and keep exclusively to themselves the cosmetics and bijouterie. Not content with being tatooed, these also *paint* their bodies by way of " overcoat," and also adorn themselves with the bright feathers of birds. They wear on their heads the beautiful circlet of macaw-plumes, and on grand occasions appear in the magnificent "feather dress," so long celebrated as the peculiar costume of the tropical-forest Indian. These dresses their women weave and border, at a sacrifice of much tedious labour. They also ornament their arms and legs with rows of feathers around them, the tips turned upward and backward.

The tatooing is confined to the Mundrucus proper—their allies the Mahües not following the practice, but contenting themselves with a simple "coat"
of paint.

It is difficult to say what motive first inducted
human beings into this singular and barbarous custom. It is easier to tell why it is still followed, and
the "why" is answered by saying that the Mundrucus "scarify" themselves, because their fathers
did so before them. Many a custom among civilized nations, but little less ridiculous, if we could
only think so, rests upon a similar basis. Perhaps our modern abominable hat—though it has a
different origin—is not less ludicrous than the tatooed patterns of the savage. Certainly it is quite
equal to it in ugliness, and is likely to rival it in per-
manence—to our sorrow be it said. But even *we*
deal slightly in the tatoo. Our jolly Jack would be
nobody in the forecastle without "Polly," in blue,
upon his weather-beaten breast, and the *foul anchor*
upon his arm.

But the Mundrucu baptizes his unfortunate offspring in a still more savage fashion. The tatoo
may be termed the *baptism in blood*, performed at
the tender age of ten. When the youth—fortunately it does not extend to the weaker sex—has attained to the age of eighteen, he has then to undergo the *tocandeira*, which deserves to be called *the
baptism of fire!*

This too merits description. When the Mundrucu youth would become a candidate for manhood,
a pair of "gloves" is prepared for him. These consist of two pieces of a palm-tree bark, with the
pith hollowed out, but left in at one end. The
hollow part is of sufficient diameter to draw over
the hands loosely, and so long as to reach up to
mid-arm, after the fashion of gauntlets.

The "gloves" being got ready, are nearly filled with ants—not only the venomous red ants, but all other species, large or small, that can either bite or sting, of which tropical South America possesses an endless variety. With this "lining" the "mittens" are ready for use, and the "novice" is compelled to draw them on. Should he refuse, or even exhibit a disposition to shrink from the fiery trial, he is a lost man. From that hour he need never hold up his head, much less offer his hand and heart, for there is not a maiden in all Mundrucu-land that would listen to his softest speech. He is for ever debarred from the pleasure of becoming a benedict. Of course he does not refuse, but plunging his hands into the "mittens," into the very midst of the crawling host, he sets about the ceremony.

He must keep on the gloves till he has danced before every door in the village. He must sing as if from very joy; and there is plenty of music to accompany him—drums and fifes, and human voices —for his parents and relatives are by his side encouraging him with their songs and gestures. He is in pain—in positive agony—for these venomous ants both sting and bite, and have been busy at both from the very first moment. Each moment his agony grows more intense—his sufferings more acute, for the poison is thrilling through his veins —he turns pale—his eyes become bloodcast—his breast quivers with emotion and his limbs tremble beneath him; but despite all this, woe to him if he utter a cry of weakness! It would brand him with an eternal stigma—he would never be suffered to carry the Mundrucu lance to battle—to poise upon its point the ghastly trophy of the *Beheaders*. On — on — through the howling throng, amidst friends and relatives with faces anxious as his own

—on to the sound of the shrill-piping reed and the
hoarse booming of the Indian drum—on till he
stands in front of the cabin of the chief! There
again the song is sung—the "jig" is danced—both
proudly prolonged till the strength of the perform-
er becomes completely exhausted. Then, and not
till then, the gloves are thrown aside, and the wearer falls back, into the arms of his friends—" sufficiently punished!"

This is the hour of congratulation. Girls gather
round him, and fling their tatooed arms about his
neck. They cluster and cling upon him, singing his
song of triumph; but just at that crisis he is not in
the mood for soft caresses; and, escaping from their
blandishments, he makes a rush towards the river.
On reaching its bank he plunges bodily in, and
there remains up to his neck in the water—till the
cooling fluid has to some extent eased his aching
arms, and tranquillized the current of his boiling
blood. When he emerges from the water, he is a
man—fit stuff for a Mundrucu warrior, and eligible
to the hand of a Mundrucu maiden!

It may be remarked that this terrible ordeal of
the Mundrucus, though, perhaps, peculiar among
South-American Indians, has its parallel among certain tribes at the north,—the Mandans and others,
as detailed by Catlin—one of the most acute of ethnological observers.

The *scalp trophy*, too, of the Northern Indian has
its analogy in a Mundrucu custom—that which distinguishes him most of all, and which has won for
him the terrible title of " Beheader."

This singular appellation is now to be explained.

When a Mundrucu has succeeded in killing an
enemy, he is not, like his northern compeer, satisfied with only the skin of the head. *He must have
the whole head*—scalp and skull, bones, brains, and

all! And he takes all, severing the head with his knife by a clean cut across the small of the neck, and leaving the trunk to the vulture king. With the ghastly trophy poised upon the point of his lance, he returns triumphant to the malocca to receive the greetings of his tribe and the praises of his chief.

But the warlike exploit requires a memento—some token by which he may perpetuate its fame. The art of printing does not exist among the Mundrucus, and there is no *friendly* pen to record the deed. It has been done—behold the evidence! much clearer than often accompanies the exploits of civilized heroes. There is the evidence of an enemy slain—there is the grim gory voucher, palpable both to sight and touch—proof positive that there is a dead body somewhere.

Of course, such evidence is sufficient for the present; but how about the future? As time passes, the feat may be forgotten, as great deeds are elsewhere. Somebody may even deny it. Some slanderous tongue may whisper, or insinuate, or openly declare that it was no exploit after all—that there was no dead man; for the vultures by this time would have removed the body, and the white ants (*termites*) would have equally extinguished all traces of the bones. How, then, are the proofs to be preserved? *By preserving the head!* And this is the very idea that is in the mind of the Mundrucu warrior. He is resolved not to permit his exploit to be buried in oblivion by *burying the head* of his enemy. That tongue, though mute, will tell the tale to posterity; that pallid cheek, though, perhaps, it may become a little shrivelled in the "drying," will still be smooth enough to show that there is no *tatoo*, and to be identified as the skin of an enemy. Some young Mundrucu, yet unborn, will

read in the countenance of that grinning and gory
witness the testimony of his father's prowess. The
head, therefore, must **be preserved**; and it is preserved with as much **care as the** cherished portrait
of a famous ancestor. The cranial relic is even *em-
balmed*, as if out of affection for him **to** whom it
belonged. The brains and eye-balls **are** removed,
to facilitate the process of desiccation; **but false**
eyes **are** inserted, and the tongue, **teeth**, and ears,
scalp, **skull**, and hair, are all retained,—not only retained, **but** "titivated" out in the most approved
style **of** fashion. The long hair is carefully combed
out, parted, and arranged; brilliant feathers of rock-
cock and macaw are planted behind the ears and
twisted in the hanging tresses. An ornamental
string passes through the **tongue, and** by this the
trophy is suspended from the **beams of the great**
malocca.

It **is not permitted to** remain there. **In some**
dark **niche of this** Golgotha—this Mundruquin
Westminster—it **might** be overlooked and forgotten. **To prevent this it is often** brought forth, and
receives many **an airing. On** all warlike and fes-
tive occasions does **it** appear, poised **upon** the point
of **the** warrior's lance; and even in peaceful times
it may be seen—along with hundreds of its like—
placed in the circular row around the manioc clearing, and lending its demure countenance to the la-
bours **of** the field.

It **is not a** little singular **that** this custom of em-
balming the heads **of their** enemies **is** found among
the Dyaks of Borneo, **and the** process in both places
is ludicrously **similar.** Another rare coincidence
occurs between the Amazonian tribes and the Bor-
nean **savages,** viz. in both being provided with the
blow-gun. The *gravitana* of the American tribes is
almost identical with the sumpitan of Borneo. It

furnishes a further proof of our theory regarding an original connection between the **American** Indians and the savages of the great South **Sea.**

The Mundrucu is rarely ill off in the way of food. When he is so, it is altogether his own fault, **and** chargeable to his indolent disposition. The soil **of** his territory is of the most fertile kind, and produces many kinds of edible fruits spontaneously, as the nuts of the *pupunha* palm and the splendid fruits of the *Bertholetia excelsa*, or juvia-tree, known in Europe as " Brazil nuts." Of these there are **two** kinds, as mentioned elsewhere, the second being a tree of the genus *Lecythys*,—the *Lecythys ollaria*, or " monkey-pot" tree. It obtains this trivial name from **the** circumstance—first, of its great pericarp, almost as large as a **child's head,** having a movable top or lid, which falls off when **the fruit** ripens; and secondly, from the monkeys being **often** seen drawing the seeds or nuts out of that part of the shell which remains attached to the tree, and which, bearing a considerable resemblance to a pot in its shape, is thus very appropriately designated the **pot** of the monkeys. The common Indian name **of the** monkey-pot tree is *sapucaya*, and the nuts **of this** species **are** so called in commerce, though they are also termed **Brazil** nuts. They are of a more agreeable flavour than the true Brazil nuts, **and not so** easily obtained, as the *Lecythys* is less generally distributed over the Amazonian valley. It requires a peculiar soil, and grows only in those tracts that are subject to the annual inundations of the rivers.

The **true Brazil nuts** are the "juvia" trees of the Indians; **and the** season for collecting them is one of the *harvests* **of the** Mundrucu people. The great pericarps—resembling large cocoa-nuts when stripped of the fibres—do not open and shed their seeds,

as is the case with the monkey-pot tree. The whole
fruit falls at once; and as it is **very** heavy, and the
branches on which it grows are often nearly a hundred feet **from the** ground, it may easily be imagined
that it comes **down** like a ten-pound shot; in fact,
one of them falling upon the head of a Mundrucu
would be very likely **to** crush his cranium, **as** a bullet would an egg-shell; and such accidents not unfrequently occur to persons passing imprudently
under **the** branches of the Bertholetia when its nuts
are ripe. Sometimes the monkeys, when on the
ground looking after those that have fallen, become
victims to the like accident; but **these** creatures
are cunning reasoners, and being **by** experience
aware of the danger, will scarce ever go under a
juvia-tree, but when passing one, always make a
wide circuit around it. The monkeys cannot **of**
themselves open the **great** pericarp, as they **do that**
of the "sapucuya," but are crafty enough to get **at**
the precious contents, notwithstanding. In doing
this they avail themselves of **the** help of other crea-
tures, that have also **a motive** in opening the juvia
shells—cavies **and other small rodent** animals, whose
teeth, formed **for** this very purpose, enable them to
gnaw **a** hole **in** the ligneous pericarps, hard and
thick as they are. Meanwhile the monkeys, squatted around, watch the operation in a careless, non-
chalant sort of way, as if they had no concern whatever in the result; but as soon as they perceive that
an entrance has been effected, big enough to admit
their hand, they **rush** forward, drive off the weaker
creature, who has **been so long and** laboriously at
work, and take possession **of** the prize.

Neither does the Mundrucu nut-gatherer get pos-
session of the juvia fruit without a certain degree
of danger and toil. He has to climb the tallest
trees, to secure the whole crop at one time; and

while engaged in collecting those upon the ground, he is in danger of a blow from odd ones that are constantly falling. To secure his skull against accidents, he wears upon his head a thick wooden cap or helmet—after the fashion of the hats worn by our firemen—and he is always careful to keep his body in an upright attitude, stooping as seldom as he can avoid doing so, lest he might get a thump between the shoulders, or upon the spine of his back, which would be very likely to flatten him out upon the earth. These Brazil nuts furnish the Mundrucu with a portion of his food—as they also do many other tribes of Amazonian Indians—and they are also an item of Indian commerce, being collected from among the different tribes by the Portuguese and Spanish traders.

But the Mundrucu does not depend altogether on the spontaneous productions of the forest, which at best furnish only a precarious supply. He does something in the agricultural line—cultivating a little manioc root, with plantains, yams, and other tropical plants that produce an enormous yield with the very slightest trouble or attention; and this is exactly what suits him. A few days spent by the little community in the yam patch—or rather, by the women and children, for these are the agricultural labourers in Mundrucu land—is sufficient to ensure an abundant supply of breadstuff for the whole year. With regard to flesh-meat he is not so well off, for the domestic animals, and oxen more especially, do not thrive in the Amazon country. In Mundrucu land, the carnivorous jaguar, aided by flies and vampire bats, would soon destroy them, even if the Indian had the inclination to raise them, which he has not.

Instead of beef, therefore, he contents himself with fish, and occasionally a steak from the great tapir, or a griskin of *manati*. Birds, too, furnish him with an occasional meal; but the staple article of his flesh diet is obtained from the *quadrumana* —the numerous species of monkeys with which his forests abound. These he obtains by shooting them down from the trees with his bow and arrows, and also by various other hunting devices.

His mode of cooking them is sufficiently peculiar to be described. A large log-fire is first kindled and permitted to burn until a sufficient quantity of red cinders are produced. Over these cinders a grating is erected with green saplings of wood, laid parallel to each other like the bars of a gridiron, and upon this the "joint" is laid.

Nothing is done to the monkey before its being placed on the gridiron. Its skin is not removed, and even the intestines are not always taken out. The fire will singe off the hair sufficiently to con- tent a Mundrucu stomach, and the hide is broiled and eaten with the flesh. It is thus literally " carne con cuero."

It may be observed that this forest gridiron, or "barbecue," as it is properly termed, is not an idea exclusively confined to South America. It is in use among the Indians of the north, and various unciv- ilized tribes in other parts of the world.

Sometimes the Mundrucu does not take the trou- ble to construct the gridiron. When on the march in some warlike expedition that will not allow time for being particular about the mode of cooking, the joint is broiled upon a spit over the common fire. The spit is simply a stick, sharpened at both ends, one of which impales the monkey, and the other is stuck into the ground. The stick is then set with a lean towards the fire, so as to bring the carcass over the blaze. While on the spit the monkey ap- pears in a sitting position, with its head upward, and its long tail hanging along the sapling—just as if it were still living, and in one of its most natural attitudes, clinging to the branch of a tree! The sight is sufficiently comical; but sometimes a painful spectacle has been witnessed—painful to any one but a savage; when the young of the monkey has been captured along with its dam, and still recognizing the form of its parent—even when all the hair has been singed off, and the skin has become calcined by the fire—is seen rushing forward into the very flames, and with plaintive cry inviting the maternal embrace! Such an affecting incident has been often witnessed amid the forests of Amazonia.

We conclude our sketch of the Mundrucus, by stating that their form of government is despotic, though not to an extreme degree. The "tushao," or chief, has considerable power, though it is not absolute, and does not extend to the taking of life—unless the object of his displeasure be a slave, and many of these are held in abject bondage among the Mundrucus.

The Mundrucu religion resembles that of many other tribes both in North and South America. It consists in absurd ceremonies, and appeals to the good and evil spirits of the other world, and is mixed up with a vast deal of quackery in relation to the ills that afflict the Mundrucu in this life. In other words, it is a combination of the priest and doctor united in one, that arch-charlatan known to the North American Indians as the "Medicine-man," and among the Mundrucus as the "Puge."

THE CENTAURS OF THE "GRAN CHACO."

I HAVE elsewhere stated that a broad band of independent Indian territory—that is, territory never really subdued or possessed by the Spaniards—traverses the interior of South America, extending longitudinally throughout the whole continent. Beginning at Cape Horn, it ends in the peninsula of the free *Goajiros*, which projects into the Caribbean Sea—in other words, it is nearly 5,000 miles in length. In breadth it varies much. In Patagonia and a portion of the Pampas country it extends from the Atlantic to the Pacific, and it is of still wider extent on the latitude of the Amazon river, where the whole country, from the Atlantic to the Peruvian Andes—with the exception of some thinly-placed Brazilian settlements — is occupied by tribes of independent Indians. At either point this territory will appear—upon maps—to be interrupted by tracts of country possessing civilized settlements. The names of towns and villages are set as thickly as if the country were well peopled; and numerous roads are traced, forming a labyrinthine network upon the paper. A broad belt of this kind extends from the Lower Parana (La Plata) to the Andes of Chili, constituting the upper provinces of the "Argentine Confederation;" another apparently joins the settlements of Bolivia and Brazil; and again in the north, the provinces of Venezuela appear to be united to those of New Granada.

All this, however, is more apparent than real. The towns upon the maps are in general mere *rancherias,* or collections of huts; some of them are the names of fortified posts, and a large proportion are but ruins—the ruins of monkish mission settlements long since gone to destruction, and with little else than the name on the map to testify that they ever had an existence. The roads are no roads at all—nothing more than tracings on the chart, showing the general route of travel.

Even across the Argentine provinces—where this nomenclature appears thickest upon the map—the horse-Indian of the Pampas extends his forays at will; his "range" meeting, and, in some cases, "dove-tailing" into that of the tribes dwelling upon the northern side of these settlements. The latter, in their turn, carry their plundering expeditions across to the Campos Parexis, on the head-waters of the Amazon, whence stretches the independent territory, far and wide to the Amazon itself; thence to the Orinoco, and across the *Llanos* to the shores of the Maracaibo Gulf—the free range of the independent Goajiros.

This immense belt of territory, then, is in actual possession of the aborigines. Although occupied at a few points by the white race—Spanish and Portuguese,—the occupation scarce deserves the name. The settlements are sparse and rather *retrograde* than *progressive.* The Indian ranges through and around them, wherever and whenever his inclination leads him; and only when some humiliating treaty has secured him a temporary respite from hostilities does the colonist enjoy tranquillity. At other times he lives in continual dread, scarce daring to trust himself beyond the immediate vicinity of his house or village, both of which he has been under the necessity of fortifying.

It is true that at one period of South American history things were not quite so bad. When the

Spanish nation was at the zenith of its power a different condition existed; but even then, in the territory indicated, there were large tracts circumstanced just as at the present hour—tracts which the Spaniards, with all their boasted warlike strength, were unable even to *explore*, much less to subdue. One of these was that which forms the subject of our sketch, "El Gran Chaco."

Of all the tracts of wild territory existing in South America, and known by the different appellations of *Pampas*, *Paramos*, *Campos Parexis*, the *Puna*, the *Pajonal*, *Llanos*, and *Montañas*, there is none possessed of a greater interest than that of *El Gran Chaco*—perhaps not one that equals it in this respect. It is interesting, not only from having a peculiar soil, climate, and productions, but quite as much from the character and history of its inhabitants—both of which present us with traits and episodes truly romantic.

The "Gran Chaco" is 200,000 square miles in extent, or twice the size of the British isles. Its eastern boundary is well defined, being the Paraguay river, and its continuation the Parana, down to the point where the latter receives one of its great western tributaries—the Salado; and this last is usually regarded as the southern and western boundary of the Chaco. Northward its limits are scarcely so definite; though the highlands of Bolivia and the old missionary province of Chiquitos—forming the water-shed between the rivers of the La Plata and the Amazonian basins—may be geographically regarded as the termination of the Chaco in that direction. North and south it extends through eleven degrees of latitude; east and west it is of unequal breadth—sometimes expanding, sometimes contracting, according to the ability of the white settlers along its borders to maintain their frontier.

On its eastern side, as already stated, the frontier is definite, and terminates on the banks of the Paraguay and Parana. East of this line—coinciding almost with a meridian of longitude—the Indian of the Gran Chaco does not roam, the well-settled province of Corrientes and the dictatorial government of Paraguay presenting a firmer front of resistance; but neither does the colonist of these countries think of crossing to the western bank of the boundary river to form any establishment there. He dares not even set his foot upon the territory of the Chaco. For a thousand miles, up and down, the two races, European and American, hold the opposite banks of this great stream. They gaze across at each other: the one from the portico of his well-built mansion, or perhaps from the street of his town; the other, standing by his humble "toldo," or mat-covered tent—more probably, upon the back of his half-wild horse, reined up for a moment on some projecting promontory that commands a view of the river. And thus have these two races gazed at each other for three centuries, with little other intercourse passing between them than that of a deadly hostility.

The surface of the Gran Chaco is throughout of a champaign character. It may be described as a vast plain. It is not, however, a continuation of the Pampas—since the two are separated by a more broken tract of country, in which lie the sierras of Cordova and San Luis, with the Argentine settlements already mentioned. Besides, these two great plains differ essentially in their character, even to a greater extent than do the Pampas themselves from the desert steppes of Patagonia. Only a few of the animal and vegetable productions of the Gran Chaco are identical with those of the Pampas, and its Indian inhabitants are altogether unlike the sanguin-

K

ary savages of the more southern plain. The Chaco,
approaching **many degrees nearer to the** equator, is
more tropical in **its character; in** fact, the northern
portion of it is truly so—lying **as** it does within the
torrid zone, and presenting the aspect of a tropical
vegetation.   Every **inch** of the Chaco **is** within **the**
palm region; but in **its** northern half these beautiful trees abound in numberless species, **yet** unknown
to the botanist, and forming the characteristic fea-
tures of the landscape. Some grow in forests of
many miles in extent, others only in "clumps," with
open grass-covered plains between, while still other
species mingle their graceful fronds with the leaves
and branches of dicotyledonous trees, or clasped in
the embrace of luxuriant llianas and parasitical
climbers form groves of the most variegated verdure and fantastic outlines. With such groves the
whole surface **of the** Chaco country is **enamelled;**
the intervals **between** being occupied by plains **of**
rich waving grass, now and then tracts of morass
covered with tall and **elegant** reeds, a few arid spots
bristling with singular **forms** of *algarobia* and *cac-*
tus, and, in some **places, isolated** rocky mounds, of
dome or conical shape, rising above **the** general
level of the plains, as if intended to **be** used as
watch-towers for their guardianship and safety.

Such **are** the landscapes which the Gran Chaco
presents **to the** eye—far different from the bald **and**
uniform monotony exhibited in the aspect of either
Prairie **or** Pampa; far grander **and** lovelier than
either—in point of scenic **loveliness,** perhaps, un-
equalled on earth. No **wonder then** that the Indian of South America **esteems** it as an earthly
Elysium; no wonder that the Spaniard dreams of
it as such—though to the Spanish priest and the
Spanish soldier it has ever proved more of a Purga-
tory than a **Paradise.** Both have entered **upon** its

borders, but neither has been **able to dwell** within its domain; **and** the attempts at its conquest, **by** sword and cross, have been alike unsuccessful—equally and fatally repulsed, throughout a period of more than three hundred years. At this hour, as at the time of the Peruvian conquest—as on the day when the ships of Mendoza sailed up the waters of the Parana—the Gran Chaco is an unconquered country, owned by its aboriginal inhabitants, and by them alone. It is true that it is *claimed*, both by Spaniard and Portuguese; and by no less than four separate claimants belonging to these two nationalities. Brazil and Bolivia, Paraguay and the Argentine Confederation, all assert their title to a slice of this earthly paradise: and even quarrel **as** to how their boundary lines should intersect it!

There is something extremely ludicrous **in these** claims—since neither one nor other of the four powers can show the slightest basis for them. Not one of them can pretend to the claim of conquest; and far less can they rest their rights upon the basis of occupation or possession. So far from possessing the land, not one of them dare set foot over its borders; and they are only too well pleased if its present occupants are contented to remain within them. The claim, therefore, of both Spaniard and Portuguese, has no higher title, than that some three hundred and fifty years ago it was given them by the Pope—a title not less ludicrous than their kissing the Pope's toe to obtain it!

In the midst of these four conflicting claimants, there appears a fifth, and that is the real owner—the "red Indian" himself. His claim has "three points of the law" in his favour—possession—and perhaps the fourth, too—the power to keep possession. At all events, he has held it for three hundred years against **all odds and all** comers; and who knows that he may not hold it for three hundred years more?—only, it is to be hoped, for a different use, and under the influence of a more progressive civilization.

The Indian, then, is the undoubted lord of the "Gran Chaco." Let us drop in upon him, and see what sort of an Indian he is, and how he manages this majestic domain.

After having feasted our eyes upon the rich scenery of the land—upon the verdant plains mottled with copses of "quebracho" and clumps of the *Caranday* palm—upon landscapes that resemble the most lordly parks, we look around for the mansions and the owners. The mansion is not there, but the owner stands before us.

We are at once struck by his appearance : his person tall, and straight as a reed—his frame muscular—his limbs round and well-proportioned—piercing coal-black eyes—well-formed features, and slightly aquiline nose,—and perhaps we are a little surprised at the light colour of his skin. In this we note a decided peculiarity which distinguishes him from most other tribes of his race. It is not a *red* Indian we behold, nor yet a *copper-coloured* savage; but a man whose complexion is scarce darker than that of the mulatto, and not at all deeper in hue than many a Spaniard of Andalusian descent, who boasts possession of the purest "sangre azul;" not one shade darker than thousands of Portuguese dwelling upon the other side of the Brazilian frontier.

And remember, that it is the *true* skin of the Chaco Indian we have before our view—and not a *painted* one—for here, almost for the first time, do we encounter the native complexion of the aboriginal, undisfigured by those horrid pigments which in these pages have so often glared before the eyes of our readers.

Of paint the Chaco Indian scarce knows the use; or, at all events, employs it sparingly, and only at intervals, on very particular and ceremonial occasions. We are spared, therefore, the describing his *escutcheon*, and a positive relief it is.

It would be an interesting inquiry to trace out the cause of his thus abstaining from a custom almost universal among his race. Why does he abjure the paint?

Is it because he cannot afford it, or that it is not procurable in his country? No; neither of these can be offered as a reason. The "annotto" bush (*Bixa orellana*), and the wild-indigo, abound in his territory; and he knows how to extract the colours of both—for his women do extract them, and use them in dying the yarn of their webs. Other dye-woods—a multitude of others—he could easily obtain; and even the cochineal cactus, with its gaudy vermilion parasite, is indigenous to his land. It cannot be the scarcity of the material that prevents him from employing it—what then?

The cause is unexplained; but may it not be that this romantic savage, otherwise more highly gifted than the rest of his race, is endowed also with a truer sense of the beautiful and becoming? *Quien sabe?*

Let it not be understood, however, that he is altogether free from the "taint"—for he *does* paint sometimes, as already admitted; and it must be remembered, moreover, that the Chaco Indians are not all of one tribe, nor of one community. There are many associations of them scattered over the face of this vast plain, who are not all alike, either in their habits or customs, but, on the contrary, very unlike; who are not even at all times friendly with each other, but occupied with feuds and *vendettas* of the most deadly description. Some of these

tribes paint most frightfully, while others of them
go still farther, and *scarify* their faces with the in-
delible *tattoo*—a custom that in America is almost
confined to the Indians of the Chaco and a few
tribes on the southern tributaries of the Amazon.
Happily this custom is on the decline; the men
practise it no longer; but, by a singular perversity
of taste, it is still universal among the women, and
no Chaco belle would be esteemed beautiful without a cross of bluish-black dots upon her forehead,
a line of like points extending from the angle of
each eye to the ears, with a variety of similar mark-
ings upon her cheeks, arms, and bosom. All this
is done with the point of a thorn—the spine of a
mimosa, or of the *caraguatay* aloe; and the dark
purple colour is obtained by infusing charcoal into
the fresh and bleeding punctures. It is an operation that requires days to complete, and the pain
from it is of the most acute and prolonged character, enduring until the poisoned wounds become
cicatrized. And yet it is borne without a murmur
—just as people in civilized life bear the painful application of hair-dyes and tweezers.

    I need not say that the hair of the Chaco Indian
does not need to be dyed — that is, unless he were
to fancy having it of a white, or a red, or yellow
colour—not an uncommon fancy among savages.

    His taste, however, does not run that way any
more than among civilized dandies, and he is contented with its natural hue, which is that of the raven's wing. But he is not contented to leave it to
its natural growth. Only a portion of it — that
which covers the upper part of his head—is permitted to retain its full length and flowing glories.
For the remainder, he has a peculiar *tonsure* of his
own; and the hair immediately over the forehead
—and sometimes a stripe running all around above

the ears, to the back of the head—is either close
shaven with a sharp shell, or plucked entirely out
by a pair of horn tweezers of native manufacture.
Were it not for the long and luxuriant tresses that
still remain—covering his crown, as with a crest—
the shorn circle would assimilate him to some orders of friars; but, notwithstanding the similarity
of tonsure, there is not much resemblance between
a Chaco Indian and a brother of the crucifix and
cowl.

This mode of " dressing the hair" is not altogether peculiar to the Indian of the Gran Chaco. It is
also practised by certain prairie tribes—the Osage,
Pawnee, and two or three others; but all these carry the "razor" a little higher up, leaving a mere
patch, or "scalp-lock," upon the crown.

The Chaco tribes are beardless by nature; and if
a few hairs chance to show themselves upon cheek
or chin, they are carefully "wed" out. In a like
fashion both men and women serve their eyebrows
and lashes—sacrificing these undoubted ornaments,
as they say, to a principle of utility, since they allege that they can *see better without them!* They
laugh at white men, who preserve these appendages, calling them " ostrich-eyed"—from a resemblance which they perceive between hairy brows
and the stiff, hair-like feathers that bristle round
the eyes of the rhea, or American ostrich—a well-
known denizen of the Gran Chaco.

The costume of the Chaco Indian is one of exceeding simplicity; and in this again we observe a
peculiar trait of his mind. Instead of the tawdry
and tinsel ornaments, in which most savages delight
to array themselves, he is contented with a single
strip of cloth, folded tightly around his loins. It
is usually either a piece of white cotton, or of wool
woven in a tri-colour of red, white, and blue, and

of hues so **brilliant,** as to produce altogether a pretty effect. The wear **of** the women scarce differs from **that of** the men, and the covering of both, scant as it is, is neither inelegant nor immodest. It is well adapted to their mode of life, and to their climate, which is that of an eternal spring. When cold winds sweep over their grassy plains, they seek protection under the folds of a more ample covering, with which they are provided — a cloak **usually** made **of the** soft fur of the "nutria," or **South** American otter, or a robe of the beautiful spotted skin of the jaguar. They wear neither headdress nor *chaussure* — neither pendants from the nose, nor the hideous lip ornaments seen among other tribes of South America; but many of them pierce the ears; and more especially the women, who split the delicate lobes, and insert into them spiral appendages of rolled palm-leaf, that hang dangling to their very shoulders. It will be observed, therefore, that among the Chaco tribes the women disfigure themselves more than the men, and all, no doubt, in the interest of *fashion.*

It will be seen that the simple dress we have described leaves the limbs and most part of the body bare. To the superficial observer it might be deemed an inelegant costume, and perhaps so it would be among Europeans, or so-called "whites." The deformed figures of European people—deformed by ages of toil and monarchical serfdom—would ill bear exposure to the light, neither would the tripe-coloured skin, of which they are so commonly conceited. A very different impression is produced by the rich brunette hue—bronze, if you will,—especially when, as in the case of the Chaco Indian, it covers a body of proper shape, with arms and limbs in symmetrical proportion. Then, and then only, does costly clothing appear superfluous, and the eye at once admits that there is no fashion on earth equal to that of the human form itself.

Above all does it appear graceful on horseback, and almost universally in this attitude does the Chaco Indian exhibit it. Scarce ever may we meet him afoot, but always on the back of his beautiful horse,—the two together presenting the aspect of the Centaur. And probably in the resemblance he approaches nearer to the true ideal of the Grecian myth than any other horseman in the world; for the Chaco Indians differ not only from other " horse Indians" in their mode of equitation, but also from every other equestrian people. The absurd high-peaked saddles of Tartar and Arab, with their gaudy trappings, are unknown to him,—unknown, too, the ridiculous paraphernalia, half hiding the horse, in use among Mexicans, South American Spaniards, and even the Indians of other tribes,—despised by him the plated bits, the embroidered bridles, and the tinkling spurs, so tickling to the vanity of other New-World equestrians. The Chaco horseman needs no such accessories to his elegance. Saddle he has none, or only the slightest patch of jaguar-skin—spurs and stirrups are alike absent. Naked he sits upon his naked horse, the beautiful curvature of whose form is interrupted by no extraneous trappings—even the thong that guides him scarce observable from its slightness. Who then can deny his resemblance to the centaur?

Thus mounted—with no other saddle than that described—no bridle but a thin strip of raw hide looped around the lower jaw of his horse—he will gallop wildly over the plain, wheel in graceful curves to avoid the burrows of the *viscacha*—pass at full speed through the close-standing and often thorny trunks of the palms, or, if need be, stand erect upon the withers of his horse, like a "star

rider" of the Hippodrome. In this attitude he looks
abroad for his enemies, or the game of which he
may be in search; and, thus elevated above surrounding objects, he discovers the ostrich far off
upon the plain, the large deer (*cervus campestris*),
and the beautiful spotted roebucks that browse in
countless herds upon the grass-covered savannas.

The dwelling of the Chaco Indian is a tent, not
covered with skins, but usually with mats woven
from the epidermis of young leaves of a palm-tree.
It is set up by two long uprights and a ridge-pole,
over which the mat is suspended—very much after
the fashion of the *tente d'abri* used by Zouave soldiers. His bed is a hammock, swung between the
upright poles, or oftener, between two palm-trees
growing near. He only seeks shelter in his tent
when it rains, and he prevents its floor getting wet
by digging a trench around the outside. He cares
little for exposure to the sun; but his wife is more
delicate, and usually carries over her head a large
bunch of *rhea* feathers, *à la parasol*, which protects
her face from the hot scorching beams.

The tent does not stand long in one situation.
Ample as is the supply which Nature affords in the
wilds of the Chaco, it is not all poured out in any
one place. This would be too much convenience,
and would result in an evil consequence. The receiver of such a benefit would soon become indolent
from the absence of all necessity for exertion; and
not only his health, but his moral nature, would suffer from such abundance.

Fortunately no such fate is likely to befall the
Indian of the Chaco. The food upon which he subsists is derived from many varied sources—a few
of which only are to be found in any one particular
place, and each only at its own season of the year.
For instance, upon the dry plains he pursues the

rhea and *viscacha*, the jaguar, puma, and partridges; in woods and marshy places the different species of wild hogs (peccaries). On the banks of rivers he encounters the tapir and capivara, and in their waters, fish, *utrias*, geese, and ducks. In the denser forest-covered tracts he must look for the various kinds of monkeys, which also constitute a portion of his food. When he would gather the legumes of the *algarobias*—of several species—or collect the sugary sap of the *caraguatay*, he must visit the tracts where the *mimosæ* and *bromelias* alone flourish; and then he employs much of his time in searching for the nests of wild bees, from the honey of which and the seeds of the *algarobia* he distils a pleasant but highly intoxicating drink. To his credit, however, he uses this but sparingly, and only upon grand occasions of ceremony—how different from the bestial chicha-drinking revellers of the Pampas!

These numerous journeys, and the avocations connected with them, hinder the Chaco Indian from falling into habits of idleness, and preserve his health to a longevity that is remarkable: so much so, that "to live as long as a Chaco Indian" has become a proverbial expression in the settlements of South America.

The old Styrian monk Dobrezhoffer has chronicled the astounding facts—that among these people a man of eighty is reckoned to be in the prime of manhood; that a hundred years is accounted a common age; and that many of them are still hale and hearty at the age of one hundred and twenty! Allowing for a little exaggeration in the statements of the monk, it is nevertheless certain that the Indians of the Gran Chaco, partly owing to their fine climate, and partly to their mode of life and subsistence, enjoy health and strength to a very old

age, and to a degree unknown in less-favoured regions of the world. Of this there is ample and
trustworthy testimony.

The food of the Chaco Indian is of a simple character, and he makes no use either of salt or spices.
He is usually the owner of a small herd of cattle
and a few sheep—which he has obtained by plundering the neighbouring settlements of the Spaniards.
It is towards those of the south and west that he
generally directs his hostile forays; for he is at
peace with the riverine provinces—Brazilian, Paraguayan, and Correntine.

In these excursions he travels long distances,
crossing many a fordless stream and river, and taking along with him wife, children, tents, and utensils,—in short, everything which he possesses. He
fords the streams by swimming—using one hand to
guide his horse. With this hand he can also pro-
pel himself, while in the other he carries his long
lance, on the top of which he poises any object he
does not wish should be wetted. A "balza," called "pelota," made of bull's hide, and more like a
square box than a boat, carries over the house-
utensils and the puppies—of which there are always a large number. The "precious baby" is also
a passenger by the balza. The *pelota* is propelled,
or rather, pulled over, by means of a tiller-rope,
held in the teeth of a strong swimmer, or tied to
the tail of a horse; and thus the crossing is effected.

Returning with his plunder—with herds of horned cattle or flocks of sheep—not unfrequently with
human captives, women and children,—the crossing
becomes more difficult; but he is certain to effect
it without loss, and almost without danger of being
overtaken in the pursuit.

His freebooting habits should not be censured
too gravely. Many extenuating circumstances must

be taken into consideration,—his wrongs and sanguinary persecutions. It must be remembered that
the hostilities commenced on the opposite side: and
with the Indian the habit is not altogether indigenous, but rather the result of the principle of retaliation. He is near kindred to the *Incas*—in fact,
some of the Chaco tribes are remnants of the scattered Peruvian race—and he still remembers the sanguinary slaughter of his ancestors by the Pizarros
and Almagros. Therefore, using the phraseology
of the French tribunals, we may say there are "extenuating circumstances in his favor." One circumstance undoubtedly speaks trumpet-tongued for the
Chaco Indian; and that is, he does not *torture* his
captives, even when *white* men have fallen into his
hands! As to the captive women and children,
their treatment is rather gentle than otherwise; in
fact, they are adopted into the tribe, and share, alike
with the rest, the pleasures as well as the hardships
of a savage life.

When the Chaco Indian possesses horned cattle
and sheep, he eats mutton and beef; but if these
are wanting, he must resort to the chase. He captures deer and ostriches by running them down
with his swift steed, and piercing them with his
long spear; and occasionally he uses the *bolas*.
For smaller game he employs the bow and arrow,
and fish are also caught by shooting them with arrows.

The Chaco Indian is the owner of a breed of
dogs, and large packs of these animals may be seen
around his camping-ground, or following the caval-
cade in its removal from place to place. They are
small creatures—supposed to be derived from a European stock, but they are wonderfully prolific, the
female often bringing forth twelve puppies at a
birth. They burrow in the ground, and subsist on

the offal of the camp. They **are** used in running
down the spotted roebuck, in hunting the capivara,
the great ant-bear, *viscachas*, and other small animals. The tapir is **taken** in traps, and also speared,
when the opportunity offers. His flesh is relished
by the Chaco Indian, but his hide is of more consequence, **as** from it bags, whips, and various other
articles can be manufactured. The peccary of two
species (*dicotyles torquatus* and *collaris*) is also
pursued by the dogs, and speared by the hunter
while pausing **to** bay the yelping pack; and the
great American **tiger** (jaguar) is killed in a like
manner. The slaying of this fierce and powerful
quadruped is one of the feats of the Chaco hunter,
and both its skin and flesh are articles of eager demand. The latter is particularly sought for; as by
eating the flesh of so strong and courageous a **creat-**
ure the Indian fancies his own strength and courage
will be increased. When a jaguar is killed, its carcass becomes **the** common property of all; and each
individual **of** the tribe **must** have his slice, or " griskin"—however small **the** piece may be after such
multiplied subdivision ! For the same reason, the
flesh of the wild boar **is** relished; also that of the
ant-bear—one of the most courageous of animals,—
and of the tapir, on account of its great strength.

The bread **of the** Chaco Indian is derived as before mentioned, from several species of mimosæ,
called indefinitely *algarobias*, and by the missionary
monks, known **as** " St. **John's** bread." Palms of
various kinds furnish **edible** nuts; **and there** are
many trees in the **Chaco** forests that produce lus-
cious fruits. With **these** the Indian varies his diet,
and **also** with wild honey—a most important article, **for** reasons **already** assigned. In the Chaco
there are stingless bees, of numerous distinct species—a proof of the many blossoms which bloom as

it were "unseen" in that flowery Elysium. The honey of these bees—of some of the species in particular—is known to be of the finest and purest quality. In the Spanish settlements it commands the highest price, and is very difficult to be obtained—for the Chaco Indian is but little given to commerce, and only occasionally brings it to market. He has but few wants to satisfy, and cares not for the tinsel of the trader: hence it is that most of the honey he gathers is reserved for his own use. He searches for the bees' nest by observing the flight of the insect, as it passes back and forward over the wild parterre; and his keenness of sight—far surpassing that of a European—enables him to trace its movements in the air, and follow it to its hoard. He alleges that he could not accomplish this so well were he encumbered with eyebrows and lashes, and offers this as one of his reasons for extracting these hirsute appendages. There may be something in what he says—strange as it sounds to the ear of one who is *not* a bee-hunter. He finds the nest at length—sometimes in a hollow tree, sometimes upon a branch—the latter kind of nest being a large mass, of a substance like blotting-paper, and hanging suspended from the twigs. Sometimes he traces the insect to a subterranean dwelling; but it must be remarked that all these are different species of bees, that build their nests and construct the cells of their honeycombs each in its own favourite place, and according to its own fashion. The bee-hunter cares not how—so long as he can find the nest; though he would prefer being guided to one built upon a species of thick octagonal cactus, known as the habitat of the bee "tosimi." This preference is caused by the simple fact—that of all the honey in the Chaco, that of the bee "tosimi" is the *sweetest*.

It is to be regretted that, with his many virtues, and his fine opportunity of exercising them, the Chaco Indian will not consent to remain in peace and good-will with all men. It seems a necessity of his nature to have an occasional shy at some enemy, whether white or of his own complexion. But, indeed, it would be ridiculous to censure him for this, since it appears also to be a vice universal among mankind; for where is the tribe or nation, savage or civilized, who does not practise it, whenever it feels bold enough or strong enough to do so? The Chaco Indian is not alone in his disregard of the sixth commandment—not the only being on earth who too frequently goes forth to battle.

He has two distinct kinds of enemies—one of European, the other of his own race—almost of his own kindred, you would say. But it must be remembered that there are several distinct tribes dwelling in the Chaco; who, although presenting a certain similitude, are in many respects widely dissimilar; and, so far from forming one nation, or living in harmonious alliance with each other, are more frequently engaged in the most deadly hostilities. Their wars are all conducted on horseback—all cavalry skirmishes—the Chaco Indian disdaining to touch the ground with his foot. Dismounted he would feel himself vanquished—as much out of his element as a fish out of water!

His war weapons are of a primitive kind: they are the bow and lance, and a species of club, known in Spanish phraseology as the "macana." This last weapon is also found in the hands of several of the Amazonian tribes, though differing slightly in its construction. The "macana" of the Chaco Indian is a short, stout piece of heavy iron-wood—usually a species known as the *quebracha*, or "axe-breaker," which grows plentifully throughout the Paraguayan countries. Numerous species are termed "que-bracha" in Spanish American countries, as there are numerous "iron-woods." That of Paraguay, like most others that have obtained this name, is a species of ebony-wood, or lignum vitæ—in short, a true *guaiacum*. The wood is hard, solid, and heavy almost as metal; and therefore just the very stuff for a war-club.

The macana of the Chaco Indian is short—not much over two feet in length, and is used both for striking in the hand and throwing to a distance. It is thicker, and of course heavier, at both extremities; and the mode of grasping it is round the narrow part in the middle. The Indian youths, while training for war, practise throwing the macana, as other people play at skittles or quoits.

The *lazo* and *bolas* are both in the hands of the Chaco tribes, but these contrivances are used sparingly, and more for hunting than war. They rarely trouble themselves with them on a real war expedition.

Their chief weapons against an enemy are their long lances,—for these are far the most effective arms for a man mounted on horseback. Those of the Chaco Indian are of enormous length, their shafts being often 15 feet from butt to barb. They use them also when mounting on horseback, in a fashion peculiar to themselves. They mount by the right side, contrary to our European mode; nor is there the slightest resemblance in any other respect between the two fashions of getting into the saddle. With the Chaco Indian there is no putting toes into stirrups—no tugging at the poor steed's withers— no clinging or climbing into the seat. He places the butt of his lance upon the ground, grasps it a little above his head with the right hand, and then raising his lithe body with an elastic spring, he

L

drops like a cat upon the spine of his well-trained steed. A word—a touch of his knee, or other well-understood signal—and the animal is off like an arrow.

When the Chaco Indian goes to war against the whites, his arms are those already described. He is not yet initiated into the use of guns and gunpowder, though he often experiences their deadly effects. Indeed, the wonder is that he could have maintained his independence so long, with such weapons opposed to him. Gunpowder has often given cowards the victory over brave men; but the Chaco Indian, even without gunpowder, has managed somehow or other to preserve his freedom.

When he makes an expedition against the white settlements, he carries no shield or other defensive armour. He did so at one period of his history; but experience has taught him that these contrivances are of little use against leaden bullets; and he has thrown them away, taking them up again, however, when he goes to war with enemies of his own kind.

In attacking a settlement or village of the whites, one of his favourite strategic plans is to set the houses on fire; and in this he very often succeeds—almost certainly when the thatch chances to be dry. His plan is to project an arrow with a piece of blazing cotton fastened near the head. For this purpose he uses the strongest kind of bow, and lying upon his back, bends it with his feet. By this means a much longer range is obtained, and the aim is of little consequence, so long as the arrow falls upon the roof of a house.

On going to war with a hostile tribe of his own kind and colour, he equips himself in a manner altogether different. His face is then painted most frightfully, and in the most hideous designs that his imagination can suggest, while his body is almost entirely covered by a complete suit of mail. The thick hide of the tapir furnishes him with the materials for helmet, cuirass, cuisses, greaves, everything —and underneath is a lining of jaguar-skin. Thus accoutred he is in little danger from the arrows of the enemy, though he is also sadly encumbered in the management of his horse; and were he upon a plundering expedition against the whites, such an encumbrance would certainly bring him to grief. He knows that very well, and therefore he never goes in such guise upon any foray that is directed towards the settlements.

The Chaco Indian has now been at peace with his eastern neighbours—both Spaniards and Portuguese —for a considerable length of time; but he still keeps up hostility with the settlements on the south —those of Cordova and San Luis—and often returns from these wretched provinces laden with booty. If he should chance to bring away anything that is of no use to him, or that may appear superfluous in his savage home—a harp or guitar, a piece of costly furniture, or even a handsome horse,—he is not required to throw it away: he knows that he can find purchasers on the other side of the river— among the Spanish merchants of Corrientes or Paraguay—who are ready at any time to become the receivers of the property stolen from their kindred of the south!

Such queer three-cornered dealings are also carried on in the northern countries of Spanish America—in the provinces of Chihuahua, New Leon, and New Mexico. They are there called "cosas de Mexico." It appears they are equally "cosas de Paraguay."

THE FEEGEES, OR MAN-EATERS.

HAVE I a reader who has not heard of the "King of the Cannibal Islands?" I think I may take it for granted that there is not one in my large circle of boy-readers who has not heard of that royal anthropophagist, that "mighty king" who,—

> "in one hut,
> Had fifty wives as black as *sut*,
> And fifty of a double smut—
> That King of the Cannibal Islands."

And yet, strange as it may appear, the old song was no exaggeration—neither as regards the number of his wives, nor any other particular relating to King "Musty-fusty-shang." On the contrary, it presents a picture of the life and habits of his polygamous majesty that is, alas! too ludicrously like the truth.

Though the king of the Cannibal Islands has been long known by reputation, people never had any very definite idea in what quarter of the world his majesty's dominions lay. Being, as the name implies, an island-kingdom, it was to be looked for, of course, in some part of the ocean; and the Pacific Ocean or Great South Sea was generally regarded as that in which it was situated; but whether it was the Tonga Islands, or the Marquesas, or the Loo-Choos, or the Soo-loos—or some other group, that was entitled to the distinction of being the man-eating community, with the man-eating king at their head—was not very distinctly ascertained up to a

recent period. On this head there is uncertainty
no longer. Though in several groups of South-Sea
Islands the horrible propensity is known to exist,
yet the man-eaters, *par excellence*, the real *bonâ-fide*
followers of the habit, are the *Feegees.* Beyond
doubt these are the greatest cannibals in all creation, their islands the true " Cannibal Islands," and
their king no other than " Musty-fusty-shang" himself.

Alas! the subject is too serious to jest upon, and
it is not without pain that we employ our pen upon
it. The truth must needs be told; and there is no
reason why the world should not know how des-
perately wicked men may become under the influence of a despotism that leaves the masses in the
power of the irresponsible few, with no law, either
moral or physical, to restrain their unbridled passions.

You will find the Feegee Islands in the Pacific
Ocean, in the latitude of 18° south. This parallel
passes nearly through the centre of the group. Their
longitude is remarkable; it is the complement of the
meridian of Greenwich—the line 180°. Therefore,
when it is noon in London, it is midnight among the
Feegees. Take the intersection of these two lines,
18° latitude and 180° longitude as a centre; describe
an imaginary circle, with a diameter of 300 miles;
its circumference, with the slight exception of a
small outlying group, will enclose, in a "ring fence,"
as it were, the whole Feegee archipelago.

The group numbers, in all, no fewer than 225
islands and islets, of which between 80 and 90 are
at present inhabited—the whole population being
not much under 200,000. The estimates of writers
differ widely on this point; some state 150,000—
others, more than double this amount. There is reason to believe that 150,000 is too low. Say, then,

200,000; since the old adage, "In medias res," is generally true.

Only two of the islands are large,—"Viti," and "Vanua." Viti is 90 miles long, by 50 in breadth, and Vanua 100 by 25. Some are what are known as "coral islands;" others are "volcanic," presenting all varieties of mountain aspect, rugged and sublime. A few of the mountain-peaks attain the elevation of 5,000 feet above sea-level, and every form is known—table-topped, dome-shaped, needle, and conical. . In fact, no group in the Pacific affords so many varieties of form and aspect, as are to be observed in the Feegee archipelago. In sailing through these islands, the most lovely landscapes open out before the eye, the most picturesque groupings of rocks, ridges, and mountain-peaks, ravines filled with luxuriant vegetation, valleys covered with soft verdure, so divinely fair as to appear the abode of angelic beings. "So beautiful was their aspect," writes one who visited them, "that I could scarcely bring my mind to the realizing sense of the well-known fact, that they were the abode of a savage, ferocious, and treacherous race of cannibals." Such, alas! is the fact, well known, as the writer observes.

Perhaps to no part of the world has Nature been more bountiful than to the Feegee Islands. She has here poured out her favours in very profusion; and the *cornucopiæ* might be regarded as an emblem of the land. The richest products of a tropic vegetation flourish in an abundance elsewhere unknown, and the growth of valuable articles of food is almost spontaneous. Many kinds are really of spontaneous production; and those under cultivation are almost endless in numbers and variety. Yams grow to the length of six feet, weighing one hundred pounds each, and several varieties are cultivated. The sweet potato reaches the weight of five or six pounds, and the "taro" (*Arum esculentum*) also produces a root of enormous size, which forms the staple article of the Feegeean's food. Still another great tuber, weighing twenty or thirty pounds, and used as a liquorice, is the produce of the "massawe," or ti-tree (*dracœna terminalis*); and the root of the *piper methisticum* often attains the weight of one hundred and forty pounds! This last is possessed of highly narcotic properties; and is the material universally used in the distillation, or rather brewing, of the native drink called "yaqona"—the "kava" of the South-Sea voyagers. Bread-fruit grows in abundance: there being no less than nine varieties of this celebrated tree upon the different islands of the group, each producing a distinct kind of fruit; and what is equally remarkable, of the *musaceœ*—the plantain and banana—there are in the Feegee isles thirty different kinds, either of spontaneous growth or cultivated! All these are well distinguished from one another, and bear distinct appellations. Three kinds of cocoa-palm add to the extraordinary variety of vegetable food, as well as to the picturesqueness of the scenery; but there is no lack of lovely forms in the vegetation, where the beautiful ti-tree grows,—where the ferns and the screw-pines flourish,—where plantains and bananas unfold their broad bright leaves to the sun; where *arums* spread their huge fronds mingling with the thick succulent blades of the bromelia, and where pawpaws, shaddocks, orange and lime-trees exhibit every hue of foliage, from deep green to the most brilliant golden.

Fruits of a hundred species are grown in the greatest plenty; the orange and the Papuan apple, the shaddock and lemon; in short, almost every species of fruit that will flourish in a tropical clime. In addition, many indigenous and valuable kinds, both of roots and fruits, are peculiar to the Feegee group, yet unknown and uncultivated in any other part of the world. Even the very cloth of the country—and a beautiful fabric it makes—is the product of an indigenous tree, the "malo" or paper-mulberry (*Brousonetia papyrifera*), the "tapa" of voyagers. Not only the material for dresses, but the tapestry for the adornment of their temples, the curtains and hangings of their houses, are all obtained from this valuable tree.

We have not space for a more detailed account of the productions of these isles. It would fill a volume to describe with any degree of minuteness the various genera and species of its plants alone. Enough has been said to show how bountiful, or rather how prodigal nature has been to the islands of the Feegeean Archipelago.

Of the animal kingdom there is not much to be said. Of quadrupeds there is the usual paucity of species that is noticed everywhere throughout the Polynesian islands. Dogs and pigs are kept; the latter in considerable numbers, as the flesh forms an important article of food; but they are not in-digenous to the Feegee group, though the period of their introduction is unknown. Two or three small rodents are the only quadrupeds yet known to be true natives of the soil. Reptiles are alike scarce in species—though the turtle is common upon the coasts, and its fishery forms the regular occupation of a particular class of the inhabitants. The species of birds are more numerous, and there are parrots, peculiar to the islands, of rich and beautiful plumage.

But we are not allowed to dwell upon these subjects. Interesting as may be the zoology and botany of the Feegeean Archipelago, both sink into insignificance when brought into comparison with its ethnology—the natural history of its human inhabitants;—a subject of deep, but alas! of a terribly painful interest. By inquiry into the condition and character of these people, we shall see how little they have deserved the favours which nature has so bounteously bestowed upon them.

In the portrait of the Feegeean you will expect something frightfully hideous—knowing, as you already do, that he is an eater of human flesh—a man of gigantic stature, swarthy skin, bloodshot eyes, gaunt bony jaws, and terrific aspect. You will expect this man to be described as being naked—or only with the skin of a wild beast upon his shoulders—building no house, manufacturing no household or other utensils, and armed with a huge knotted club, which he is ever ready to use;—a man who dwells in a cavern, sleeps indifferently in the open air or under the shelter of a bush; in short, a true savage. That is the sort of creature you expect me to describe, and I confess that just such a physical aspect—just such a condition of personal hideousness—would be exactly in keeping with the moral deformity of the Feegeean. You would furthermore expect this savage to be almost devoid of intellectual power—altogether wanting in moral sense—without knowledge of right and wrong—without knowledge of any kind—without ideas. It seems but natural you should look for such characteristics in a *cannibal.*

The portrait I am about to paint will disappoint you. I do not regret it—since it enables me to bring forward another testimony that man in his original nature is not a being of such desperate wickedness. That simple and primitive state, which men glibly call *savage,* is *not* the condition favourable to cannibalism. I know that it is to such people that the habit is usually ascribed, but quite er-

roneously. The Andaman islander has been blamed
with it simply because he chances to go naked, and
looks as he is, hungry and emaciated. The charge
is proved false. The Bushman of South Africa has
enjoyed a similar reputation. It also turns out to
be a libel. The Carib long lived under the imputa-
tion, simply because he presented a fierce front to
the Spanish tyrant, who would have enslaved him;
and we have heard the same stigma cast upon a
dozen other tribes, the *lowest savages* being usually selected; in other words, those whose condition
appeared the most wretched. In such cases the
accusation has ever been found, upon investigation,
to be erroneous.

In the most primitive state in which man appears
upon the earth, he is either without social organization altogether, or if any do exist, it is either patriarchal or republican. Neither of these conditions
are favourable to the development of vice—much
less the most horrible of all vices.

It will not do to quote the character of the Bushman, or certain other of the low tribes, to refute
this statement. These are not men in their primitive state ascending upward, but a condition altogether the reverse. They are the decaying remnants of some corrupt civilization, sinking back into
the dust out of which they were created.

No—and I am happy to say it,—man, as he originally came from the hands of the Creator, has no
such horrid propensity as cannibalism. In his primitive state he has never been known to practise it
—except when the motives have been such as have
equally tempted men professing the highest civilization—but this cannot be considered cannibalism.
Where that exists in its true unmitigated form—
and unhappily it does so—the early stages of social
organization must have been passed; the republican

and patriarchal forms must both have given place to the absolute and monarchical. This condition of things is absolutely necessary, before **man can** obtain sufficient power to prey upon his fellow-man **to the** extent of eating him. There can **be** no "cannibal" without a "king."

So far from the Feegeean **cannibals** being *savages*—according to the ordinary acceptation of the term—they are in reality the very reverse. If we adhere to the usual meaning of the word civilization, understanding by it a people possessing an intelligent knowledge of arts, living **in** well-built houses, fabricating fine goods, tilling their lands in a scientific and successful manner, practising the little politenesses and accomplishments of social **life**—if these be the *criteria* of civilization, then **it is no** more than the truth to say that the standard possessed by the Feegee islanders **is** incomparably above **that of** the lower **orders** of most European nations.

It is startling to reflect—startling as sad—that a people possessed of such intellectual power, and **who** have ever exercised it to a wonderful extent—in arts, manufactures, and even in the accomplishing of their own persons—should at the same time exhibit moral traits of such **an** opposite character. An atrocious cruelty—an **instinct** for oppression, brutal and ferocious—a heart pitiless as that **of the** fiend himself—a hand ever **ready** to strike the murderous blow, even though the victim be a brother—lips that lie in every word they speak—a tongue **ever bent** on barbaric boasting—a bosom **that** beats only **with** sentiments of treachery and abject cowardice—these are **the** revolting characteristics of the Feegeean. Dark as **is** his skin, his soul is many shades darker.

It is time, however, to descend to a more partic-

ular delineation of this man-eating monster; and
first, we shall give a description of his personal appearance.

The Feegeeans are above the average height of
Europeans, or white men: men of six feet are common among them, though few reach the height of
six feet six. Corpulent persons are not common,
though large and muscular men abound. Their
figure corresponds more nearly to that of the white
man than any other race known. The proportions
of their limbs resemble those of northern Europeans,
though some are narrower across the loins. Their
chests are broad and sinewy, and their stout limbs
and short, well-set necks are conspicuous characters. The outline of the face is a good oval; the
mouth large, with white teeth regularly arranged
—ah! those horrid teeth!—the nose is well shaped,
with full nostrils; yet quite distinct, as are the lips
also, from the type of the African negro. Indeed,
with the exception of their colour, they bear very
little resemblance to the negro—that is, the thick-
lipped, flat-nosed negro of our fancy; for there are
negro tribes in Africa whose features are as fine as
those of the Feegeeans, or even as our own. In
colour of skin the Feegeean is nearly, if not quite,
as dark as the negro; but it may be remarked that
there are different shades, as there are also among
pure Ethiopians. In the Feegee group there are
many men of mulatto colour, but these are not of
the original Feegee stock. They are either a mixed
offspring with the Tonga islander, or pure-bred
Tonga islanders themselves, who for the past 200
years have been insinuating themselves into the social compact of the Feegeeans. These light-colour-
ed people are mostly found on the eastern or windward side of the Feegee group—that is, the side
towards Tonga itself,—and the trade-winds will

account for their immigration, which was at first
purely accidental. They at present play a conspicuous part in the affairs of the Feegeeans—being in
favour with the kings and great chiefs, partly on account of their being better sailors than the native
Feegeeans, and partly on account of other services
which these tyrants require them to perform. In
some arts the Tongans are superior to the Feegeeans, but not in all. In pottery, wood-carving, making of mats or baskets, and the manufacture of the
tapa cloth, the Feegeeans stand unrivalled over all
the Pacific Ocean.

We need say no more of the Tongans here; they
are elsewhere described. Those dwelling in Feegee
are not all fixed there for life. Some are so, and
these are called Tonga-Feegeeans; the others are
only visitors, giving their services temporarily to
the Feegeean chiefs, or occupied in ship-building—
in constructing those great war-canoes that have
been the astonishment of South Sea voyagers, and
which Feegee sends forth from her dockyards in
the greatest perfection. These, when finished by
the Tongan strangers, are used to carry them back
to their own islands, that lie about 300 miles to the
windward (south-east).

But to continue the portrait of the Feegeean.
We have touched almost every part of it except
the hair; but this requires a most elaborate limn-
ing, such as the owner himself gives it. In its natural state, the head of the Feegeean is covered by a
mass of black hair, long, frizzled, and bushy, sometimes encroaching on the forehead, and joined by
whiskers to a thick, round, or pointed beard, to
which mustaches are often added. Black is, of
course, the natural colour of the hair, but it is not
always worn of this hue. Other colours are thought
more becoming; and the hair, both of the men and

women, is dyed in a variety of ways, lime burning
it to a reddish or whity-brown shade. A turmeric
yellow, or even a vermilion red are not uncommon
colours; but all these keep varying, according to
the change of fashions at court!

Commodore Wilkes, who has given a good deal
of his time to an exploration of the Feegee Islands,
states that the Feegee hair, in its natural condition,
is straight, and not "frizzled," as described above;
he says that the frizzling is the work of the barber;
but the commodore is altogether mistaken in this
idea. Thousands of Feegeeans, whose hair was
never touched by a barber, nor dressed even by
themselves, exhibit this peculiarity. We regret to
add that this is only one of a thousand erroneous
statements which the commodore has made during
his gigantic exploration. He may have been excellent at his own speciality of making soundings
and laying down charts; but on all matters per-
taining to natural history or ethnology, the worthy
commodore appears to have been purblind, and, indeed, his extensive staff of naturalists of every kind
have produced far less than might have been expected from such excellent opportunities as they
enjoyed. The observations of the commodore will
not stand the test of time, and can not be depended
upon as safe guides, excepting in those cases where
he was an actual eye-witness. About his truthful
intentions there can be no doubt whatever.

Of one very peculiar performance among the Feegees he appears to have had actual demonstration,
and as he has described this with sufficient minuteness, we shall copy his account; though, after what
we have said, we should apologize largely for the
liberty. The performance referred to is that of
"barberizing" a barbarian monarch, and may be
taken as a proof of high civilization among the Fee-

gees. It will be seen that, with the exception of the tabooed fingers, there is not much difference between a barber of Bond Street and an artist of like calling in the Cannibal Islands.

"The chiefs in particular," writes Commodore Wilkes, "pay great attention to the dressing of their heads, and for this purpose all of them have barbers, whose sole occupation is the care of their masters' heads. These barbers are called *a-vu-ni-ulu*. They are attached to the household of the chiefs in numbers of from two to a dozen. The duty is held to be of so sacred a nature, that their hands are tabooed from all other employment, and they are not even permitted to feed themselves. To dress the head of a chief requires several hours. The hair is made to spread out from the head, on every side, to a distance that is often eight inches. The beard, which is also carefully nursed, often reaches the breast, and when a Feegeean has these important parts of his person well dressed, he exhibits a degree of conceit that is not a little amusing.

"In the process of dressing the hair it is well anointed with oil, mixed with a carbonaceous black, until it is completely saturated. The barber then takes the hair-pin, which is a long and slender rod, made of tortoise-shell or bone, and proceeds to twitch almost every separate hair. This causes it to frizzle and stand erect. The bush of hair is then trimmed smooth by singeing it, until it has the appearance of an immense wig. When this has been finished, a piece of tapa, so fine as to resemble tissue-paper, is wound in light folds around it, to protect the hair from the dew or dust. This covering, which has the look of a turban, is called *sala*, and none but the chiefs are allowed to wear it; any attempt to assume this headdress by a *kai-si*, or com-

mon person, would be immediately punished with
death. The sala, when taken proper care of, will
last three weeks or a month, and the hair is not
dressed except when it is removed; but the high
chiefs and dandies seldom allow a day to pass without changing the sala and having the hair put in
order."

With this account, we conclude our description
of the Feegeean's person. His costume is of the
simplest kind, and easily described. With the men
it is merely a strip of "tapa" or "malo" cloth passed several times round the waist, and the ends left
to hang down in front. The length of the hanging
ends determines the rank of the wearer, and only in
the case of kings or great chiefs are they allowed
to touch the ground. A turban of the finest tapa
cloth among the great mop of hair is another badge
of rank, worn only by kings and chiefs; and this
headdress, which adds greatly to the dignified appearance of the wearer, is not always coifed in the
same fashion, but each chief adapts it to his own or
the prevailing taste of the court. The dress of the
women is a mere waist-belt, with a fringe from six
to ten inches in length. It is worn longer after
they have become wives, sometimes reaching near
the knee, and forming a very picturesque garment.
It is called the "liku," and many of them are manufactured with surprising skill and neatness, the
material being obtained from various climbing plants
of the forest. Under the "liku" the women are tatooed, and there only. Their men, on the contrary,
do not undergo the tatoo; but on grand occasions
paint their faces and bodies in the most fanciful colours and patterns.

The kings and some chiefs suspend from their
necks shell ornaments—often as large as a dining-
plate—that hang down upon the breast. Some, in-

stead of this, wear a necklace of whales' teeth, carved to resemble claws, and bearing a very close resemblance to the necklaces of the Prairie Indians, made of the claws of the grizzly bear. Another kind of necklace — perhaps more appropriate to the Feegee — is a string of human teeth; and this kind is not unfrequently worn by these ferocious dandies.

It must not be supposed that the scantiness of the Feegeean costume arises from poverty or stinginess on the part of the wearer. Nothing of the kind. It is simply because such is the fashion of the time. Were it otherwise, he could easily supply the materials, but he does not wish it otherwise. His climate is an eternal summer, and he has no need to encumber his body with extraneous clothing. With the exception of the turban upon his head, his king is as naked as himself.

You may suppose that the Feegeeans have but little notions of modesty; but, strange as it may appear, this is in reality not one of their failings. They regard the "malo" and "liku" as the most modest of garments; and a man or woman seen in the streets without these scanty coverings would be in danger of being clubbed to death!

It must be acknowledged that they are not *altogether* depraved — for in this respect they present the most astounding anomaly. Certain virtues are ascribed to them, and as I have painted only the dark side of their character, it is but fair to give the other. Indeed, it is a pleasure to do this— though there is not enough of the favourable to make any great alteration in the picture. The whole character is so well described by one of the most acute observers who has yet visited the South Seas —the Wesleyan missionary, Williams—that we borrow the description.

M

"The aspect of the Feegeean," says Mr. Williams, "with reference to his mental character, so far from supporting the decision which would thrust him almost out of mankind, presents many points of great interest, showing that, if an ordinary amount of attention were bestowed on him, he would take no mean rank in the human family, to which, hitherto, he has been a disgrace. Dull barren stupidity forms no part of his character. His feelings are acute, but not lasting; his emotions easily roused, but transient; he can love truly, and hate deeply; he can sympathise with thorough sincerity, and feign with consummate skill; his fidelity and loyalty are strong and enduring, while his revenge never dies, but waits to avail itself of circumstances, or of the blackest treachery, to accomplish its purpose. His senses are keen, and so well employed, that he often excels the white man in ordinary things. Tact has been called 'ready cash,' and of this the native of Fiji has a full share, enabling him to surmount at once many difficulties, and accomplish many tasks, that would have 'fixed' an Englishman. Tools, cord, or packing materials, he finds directly, where the white man would be at a loss for either; and nature seems to him but a general store for his use, where the article he wants is always within reach.

"In social diplomacy the Feegeean is very cautious and clever. That he ever paid a visit merely *en passant*, is hard to be believed. If no request leaves his lips, he has brought the desire, and only waits for a good chance to present it now, or prepare the way for its favourable reception at some other time. His face and voice are all pleasantness; and he has the rare skill of finding out just the subject on which you most like to talk, or sees at once whether you desire silence. Rarely will he fail to read your countenance; and the case must be urgent

indeed which obliges him to ask a favour when he
sees a frown. The more important he feels his
business the more earnestly he protests that he has
none at all; and the subject uppermost in his
thoughts comes last to his lips, or is not even named;
for he will make a second, or even a third visit,
rather than risk a failure through precipitancy. He
seems to read other men by intuition, especially
where selfishness or lust are prominent traits. If
it serves his purpose, he will study difficult and peculiar characters, reserving the results for future
use; if afterwards he wish to please them, he will
know how, and if to annoy them, it will be done
most exactly.

"His sense of hearing is acute, and by a stroke
of his nail he judges of the ripeness of fruits, or
soundness of various substances."

From what source the Feegeean has sprung is
purely matter of conjecture. He has no history,—
not even a tradition of when his ancestors first peopled the Archipelago in which we now find him.
Of his race we have not a much clearer knowledge.
Speculation places him in the same family as the
"Papuan Negro," and he has some points of resemblance to this race, in the colour and frizzled
hair; but there is as much difference between the
wretched native of West Australia and the finely-
developed Feegeean as there is between the stunted
Laplander and the stalwart Norwegian; nor is the
coarse rough skin of the true Papuan to be recognized in the smooth glossy epidermis of the Feegee
islander. This, however, may be the result of better living; and certainly among the mountain-tribes
of the Feegees, who lead lives of greater privation
and hardship, the approach to the Papuan appearance is observable. It is hardly necessary to add
that the Feegeean is of a race quite distinct from

that known as the Polynesian or South-Sea islander.
This last is different not only in form, complexion,
and language, but also in many important mental
characteristics.   It is to this race the Tongans belong,˙and its peculiarities will be sketched in treat-
ing of that people.

Were we to enter upon a minute description of
the manners and customs of the Feegees—of their
mode of house and canoe building—of their arts
and manufactures, for they possess both—of their
implements of agriculture and domestic use—of
their weapons of war—their ceremonies of religion
and court etiquette—our task would require more
space than is here allotted to us: it would in fact
be as much as to describe the complete social economy of a civilized nation; and a whole volume
would scarce suffice to contain such a description.
In a sketch like the present the account of these
people requires to be given in the most condensed
and synoptical form, and only those points can be
touched upon that may appear of the greatest interest.

It must be remembered that the civilization of
the Feegees—of course, I allude to their proficiency
in the industrial arts—is entirely an indigenous
growth.   They have borrowed ideas from the Tongans—as the Tongans have also from them—but
both are native productions of the South Sea, and
not derived from any of the so-called great *centres*
of civilization.   Such as have sprung from these
sources are of modern date, and make but a small
feature in the panorama of Feegeean life.   The
houses they build are substantial, and suitable to
their necessities..   We cannot stay to note the
architecture minutely.   The private dwellings are
usually about twenty-five feet long by fifteen in
breadth, the interior forming one room, but with a

sort of elevated divan at the end, sometimes screen-
ed with beautiful " tapa" curtains, and **serving** as
the dormitory.

The ground-plan of the house is that of **an** oblong square—or, to speak more properly, a parallelogram. The walls are constructed of timber—being straight posts of cocoa-palm, tree-fern, bamboo,
or bread-fruit—the spaces between closely warped
or otherwise filled in with reeds of cane or *calamus.* The thatch is of the leaves of the wild or
cultivated sugar-cane—sometimes of a *pandanus*
—thickly laid on, especially near the eaves, where
it is carefully cropped, exposing an edge of from one
to two feet in thickness. The roof has four faces
—that is, it is a " hip roof." It is made with **a** very
steep pitch, and comes down low, projecting far
over the heads of the upright timbers. This **gives**
a sort of shaded verandah all around the house, **and**
throws the rain quite clear of the walls. The ridge-
pole is a peculiar feature ; it is fastened to the ridge
of the thatch by strong twisted ropes, that give it
an ornamental appearance ; and its carved ends pro-
ject at both gables, or rather, over the " hip roofs,"
to the length **of** a foot, or more ; it is further ornamented by white shells, those of the *cyprea ovu-
la* being most used for the purpose. The Feegee
house presents altogether a picturesque and not inelegant appearance. The worst feature is the low
door. There are usually two of them, neither in
each house being over three feet in height. The
Feegee assigns no reason why his door is made so
low ; **but** as he is frequently in expectation of a
visitor, with a murderous bludgeon in his grasp, it
is possible this may have something to do with his
making the entrance so difficult.

The houses of the chiefs, and the great council-
house, or temple—called the " Bure"—are built pro.

cisely in the same style; only that both are larger,
and the doors, walls, and ridge-poles more elaborately ornamented.   The fashionable style of decoration is a plaiting of cocoa-fibre, or "sinnet," which
is worked and woven around the posts in regular
figures of "relievo."

The house described is not universal throughout
all the group.   There are many "orders" of architecture, and that prevailing in the Windward Islands is different from the style of the Leeward, and
altogether of a better kind.   Different districts have
different forms.   In one you may see a village looking like an assemblage of wicker baskets, while in
another you might fancy it a collection of rustic ar-
bours.   A third seems a collection of oblong hay-
ricks, with holes in their sides; while, in a fourth,
these ricks are conical.

It will be seen that, with this variety in house-
building, it would be a tedious task to illustrate
the complete architecture of the Feegeans.   Even
Master Ruskin himself would surrender it up in
despair.

Equally tedious would it be to describe the various implements or utensils which a Feegee house
contains.   The furniture is simple enough.   There
are neither chairs, tables, nor bedsteads.   The bed
is a beautiful mat spread on the däis, or divan; and
in the houses of the rich the floors are covered with
a similar carpet.   These mats are of the finest texture, far superior to those made elsewhere.   The
materials used are the *Hibiscus tiliaceus, Panda-*
nus odoratissimus, and a species of rush.   They
are in great abundance in every house—even the
poorest person having his mat to sit or lie upon;
and it is they that serve for the broad-spreading
sails of the gigantic canoes.   In addition to the
mats, plenty of tapa-cloth may be seen, and baskets

of every shape and size—the wicker being obtained from the rattan (*flagellaria*), and other sources. One piece of furniture deserves especial mention—this is the pillow upon which the Feegee lord lays his head when he goes to sleep. It presents but little claim to the appellation of a *downy* pillow: since it is a mere cylinder of hard polished wood, with short arched pedestals to it, to keep it firmly in its place. Its object is to keep the great frizzled mop from being tossed or disarranged, during the hours of repose; and Feegeean vanity enables the owner of the mop to endure this flinty bolster with the most uncomplaining equanimity. If he were possessed of the slightest spark of conscience, even this would be soft, compared with any pillow upon which he might rest his guilty head.

In addition to the baskets, other vessels meet the eye. These are of pottery, as varied in shape and size as they are in kind. There are pots and pans, bowls, dishes, cups and saucers, jars and bottles—many of them of rare and curious designs—some red, some ornamented with a glaze obtained from the gum of the *kauri* pine—for this tree is also an indigenous production of the Feejee Islands. Though no potter's wheel is known to the Feegees, the proportions of their vessels are as just and true, and their polish as complete, as if Stafford had produced them. There are cooking-pots to be seen of immense size. These are jars formed with mouths wide enough to admit the largest joint. I dare not mention the kind of joint that is frequently cooked in those great caldrons! Ugh! the horrid pots!

Their implements are equally varied and numerous—some for manufacturing purposes, and others for agriculture. The latter are of the simplest kind. The Feegee plough is merely a pointed stick inserted deeply into the ground, and kept moving about

till a lump of the soil is broken upward. This is
crushed into mould, first by a light club, and afterwards pulverized by the fingers. The process is
slow, but fast enough for the Feegeean, whose farm
is only a garden. He requires no plough, neither
bullocks nor horses. With taro-roots and sweet
potatoes that weigh ten pounds each—yams and
yaqonas over one hundred, and plantains producing
bunches of 150 fruits to the single head, why need
he trouble himself by breaking up more surface?
His **single acre** yields him as much vegetable wealth
as fifty would to an English farmer!

It is not to be supposed that he has it all to himself; no, nor half of it either; nor yet the fifth
part of it. At least four-fifths of his sweat has to
be expended in tax or tithe; and this brings us to
the form of his government. We shall not dwell
long upon this subject. Suffice it to say that the
great body of the people are in a condition of abject serfdom—worse than slavery itself. They own
nothing that they can call their own — not their
wives—not their daughters—not even their lives!
All these may be taken from them at any hour.
There is no law against despoiling them—no check
upon the will and pleasure of their chiefs or supe-
riors; **and, as** these constitute a numerous body,
the poor *canaille* have no end of ruffian despoilers.
It is an **every-day** act for a chief to rob, or *club to
death*, **one of the** common people! and no unfre-
quent occurrence to be himself clubbed to death by
his superior, the king! Of .these *kings* there are
eight in Feegee,—not **one, as the old** song has it;
but the words of the ballad will apply to each of
them with sufficient appropriateness. Any one of
them will answer to the character of " Musty-fusty-
shang!"

These kings have their residences on various islands, and the different parts of the group are distributed somewhat irregularly under their rule. Some islands, or parts of islands, are only tributary to them; others connected by a sort of deferential alliance; and there are communities quite independent, and living under the arbitrary sway of their own chieftains. The kings are not all of equal power or importance; but in this respect there have been many changes, even during the Feegeean historical period — which extends back only to the beginning of the present century. Sometimes one is the most influential, sometimes another; and in most cases the pre-eminence is obtained by him who possesses the greatest amount of truculence and treachery. He who is most successful in murdering his rivals, and ridding himself of opposition, by the simple application of the club, usually succeeds in becoming for the time head "king of the Cannibal Islands." I do not mean that he reigns over the whole archipelago. No king has yet succeeded in uniting all the islands under one government. He only gets so far as to be feared everywhere, and to have tributary presents, and all manner of debasing compliments offered to him. These kings have all their courts and court etiquette, just as their "royal brothers" elsewhere; and the ceremonials observed are quite as complicated and degrading to the dignity of man.

The punishment for neglecting their observance is rather more severe in Feegee than elsewhere. For a decided or wilful non-compliance, the skull of the delinquent is frequently crushed in by the club of his majesty himself—even in presence of a full "drawing-room." Lesser or accidental mistakes, or even the exhibition of an ungraceful *gaucherie*, are punished by the loss of a finger: the consequence of which is, that in Feegee there are many fingers missing! Indeed, a complete set is rather the exception than the rule. If a king or great chief should chance to miss his foot and slip down, it is the true *ton* for all those who are near or around him to fall likewise—the crowd coming down, literally like a "thousand of bricks!"

I might detail a thousand customs to show how far the dignity of the human form is debased and disgraced upon Feegee soil; but the subject could be well illustrated nearer home. Flunkeyism is a fashion unfortunately not confined to the Feegeean archipelago; and though the forms in which it exhibits itself there may be different, the sentiment is still the same. It must ever appear where men are politically unequal—wherever there is a class possessed of hereditary privileges.

I come to the last—the darkest feature in the Feegeean character—the horrid crime and custom of cannibalism. I could paint a picture, and fill up the details with the testimony of scores of eye-witnesses —a picture that would cause your heart to weep. It is too horrid to be given here. My pen declines the office; and, therefore, I must leave the painful story untold.

THE TONGANS, OR FRIENDLY ISLANDERS.

It is a pleasure to pass out of the company of
the ferocious Feegees into that of another people,
which, though near neighbours of the former, are
different from them in almost every respect—I mean
the Tongans, or Friendly Islanders. This appellation scarce requires to be explained. Every one
knows that it was bestowed upon them by the celebrated navigator Cook—who, although not the actual discoverer of the Tonga group, was the first
who thoroughly explored these islands, and gave
any reliable account of them to the civilized world.
Tasman, who might be termed the "Dutch Captain
Cook," is allowed to be their discoverer, so long
ago as 1643 ; though there is reason to believe that
some of the Spanish explorers from Peru may have
touched at these islands before his time. Tasman,
however, has fixed the record of his visit, and is
therefore entitled to the credit of the discovery—as
he is also to that of Australia, New Zealand, Van
Diemen's Land, and other now well-known islands
of the South-western Pacific. Tasman bestowed
upon three of the Tonga group the names—Am-
sterdam, Rotterdam, and Middleburgh ; but, fortunately, geographers have acted in this matter with
better taste than is their wont; and Tasman's Dutch
national titles have fallen into disuse—while the
true native names of the islands have been restored
to the map. This is what should be done with other Pacific islands as well ; for it is difficult to conceive anything in worse taste than such titles as the

Caroline and Loyalty Isles, Prince William's Land,
King George's Island, and the ten thousand Albert
and Victoria Lands which the genius of flattery,
or rather flunkeyism, has so liberally distributed
over the face of the earth. The title of Friendly
Isles, bestowed by Cook upon the Tonga archipelago, deserves to live; since it is not only appropriate, but forms the record of a pleasant fact—the
pacific character of our earliest intercourse with
these interesting people.

It may be here remarked, that Mr. Wylde and
other superficial map-makers have taken a most un-
warrantable liberty with this title. Instead of leaving it as bestowed by the great navigator—applicable to the Tonga archipelago alone—they have
stretched it to include that of the Samoans, and—
would it be believed—that of the *Feegees!* It is
hardly necessary to point out the extreme absurdity of such a classification: since it would be difficult to find two nationalities much more unlike than
those of Tonga and Feegee. That they have many
customs in common, is due (unfortunately for the
Tongans) to the intercourse which proximity has
produced; but in an ethnological sense, white is
not a greater contrast to black, nor good to evil,
than that which exists between a Tongan and a
Feegeean. Cook never visited the Feegee archipelago—he only saw some of these people while at
Tongataboo, and heard of their country as being *a
large island.* Had he visited that island—or rather
that group of over two hundred islands—it is not
at all likely he would have seen reason to extend to
them the title which the map-makers have thought
fit to bestow. Instead of "Friendly Islands," he
might by way of contrast have called them the
"Hostile Isles," or given them that—above all others most appropriate, and which they truly deserve

to bear—that old title celebrated in song! the
"Cannibal Islands." An observer so acute as Cook
could scarce have overlooked the appropriateness
of the appellation.

The situation of the Tonga, or Friendly Isles, is
easily registered in the memory. The parallel of
20° south, and the meridian of 175° west, very nearly intersect each other in Tofoa, which may be regarded as the central island of the group. It will
thus be seen that their central point is 5° east and
2° south of the centre of the Feegeean archipelago,
and the nearest islands of the two groups are about
300 miles apart.

It is worthy of observation, however, that the
Tonga isles have the advantage, as regards the wind.
The *trades* are in their favour; and from Tonga to
Feegee, if we employ a landsman's phraseology, it
is "down hill," while it is all "up hill" in the contrary direction. The consequence is, that many
Tongans are constantly making voyages to the Feegee group—a large number of them having settled
there (as stated elsewhere)—while but a limited
number of Feegeeans find their way to the Friendly Islands. There is another reason for this un-
equally-balanced migration: and that is, that the
Tongans are much bolder and better sailors than
their western neigbours; for although the Feegees
far excel any other South-Sea islanders in the art of
building their canoes (or ships as they might reasonably be called), yet they are as far behind many
others in the art of *sailing* them.

Their superiority in ship-building may be attributed, partly, to the excellent materials which these
islands abundantly afford; though this is not the
sole cause. However much we may deny to the
Feegeeans the possession of moral qualities, we are
at the same time forced to admit their great intel-

lectual capacity—as exhibited in the advanced state of their arts and manufactures. In intellectual capacity, however, the Friendly Islanders are their equals; and the **superiority** of the Feegeeans even in "canoe architecture" is no longer acknowledged. It is true the Tongans go to the Feegee group for most of their large double vessels; but that is for the **reasons** already stated,—the greater abundance and superior quality of the timber and other materials produced there. In the Feegee "dockyards," **the** Tongans build for themselves; and have even improved upon the borrowed pattern.

This intercourse—partaking somewhat of the character of an alliance—although in some respects advantageous to the Friendly Islanders, may be regarded, upon the whole, as unfortunate for them. If it has improved their knowledge in arts **and** manufactures, it **has** far more than counterbalanced this advantage by the damage done to their moral character. It is always much easier to make proselytes **to** vice than to virtue—as is proved in this in**stance**: for his intercourse with the ferocious Feegee **has** done much **to** deteriorate the character of **the Tongan.** From that source he has imbibed a **fondness for** war and other wicked customs; and, **in all** probability, had this influence been permitted to continue uninterrupted for a few years longer, the horrid habit of cannibalism—though entirely repugnant **to** the natural disposition of the Tongans —would have become common among them. Indeed, there can be little doubt that this **would** have been the ultimate consequence of the alliance; for already its precursors—human sacrifices and the vengeful immolation **of** enemies—had made their appearance upon **the** Friendly Islands. Happily for the Tongan, another influence—that of the missionaries—came just in time to avert this dire catastrophe; and, although this missionary interference has not been the best of its kind, it is still preferable to the paganism which it has partially succeeded in subduing.

The Tongan archipelago is much less extensive than that of the Feegees—the islands being of a limited number, and only five or six of them of any considerable size. Tongataboo, the largest, is about ninety miles in circumference. From the most southern of the group Eoo, to Vavau at the other extremity, it stretches, northerly or north-easterly, about two hundred miles, in a nearly direct line. The islands are all, with one or two exceptions, low-lying, their surface being diversified by a few hillocks or mounds, of fifty or sixty feet in height, most of which have the appearance of being artificial. Some of the smaller islets, as Kao, are mountains of some six hundred feet elevation, rising directly out of the sea; while Tofoa, near the eastern edge of the archipelago, presents the appearance of an elevated table-land. The larger number of them are clothed with a rich tropical vegetation, both natural and cultivated, and their botany includes most of the species common to the other islands of the South Sea. We find the cocoa, and three other species of palm, the pandanus, the bread-fruit in varieties, as also the useful musacaæ—the plantain, and banana. The ti-tree (*Dracœna terminalis*), the paper-mulberry (*Broussonetia papyrifera*), the sugar-cane, yams of many kinds, the tree yielding the well-known *turmeric*, the beautiful *casuarina*, and a hundred other sorts of plants, shrubs, or trees, valuable for the product of their roots or fruits, their sap and pith, of their trunks and branches, their leaves and the fibrous material of their bark.

As a scenic decoration to the soil, there is no part of the world where more lovely landscapes are pro-

N

duced by the aid of a luxuriant vegetation. They
are perhaps not equal in picturesque effect to those
of the Feegee group—where mountains form an ad-
junct to the scenery—but in point of soft, quiet
beauty, the landscapes of the Tonga islands are not
surpassed by any others in the tropical world; and
with the climate they enjoy—that of an endless summer—they might well answer to the description of
the "abode of the Blessed." And, indeed, when
Tasman first looked upon these islands, they perhaps merited the title more than any other spot on
the habitable globe; for, if any people on this earth
might be esteemed happy and blessed, surely it was
the inhabitants of these fair isles of the far Southern Sea. Tasman even records the remarkable fact,
that he saw no arms among them—no weapons of
war! and perhaps, at that time, neither the detestable trade nor its implements were known to them.
Alas! in little more than a century afterwards, this
peaceful aspect was no longer presented. When
the great English navigator visited these islands,
he found the war-club and spear in the hands of the
people, both of Feegee pattern, and undoubtedly of
the same ill-omened origin.

The personal appearance of the Friendly Islanders differs not a great deal from that of the other
South-Sea tribes or nations. Of course we speak
only of the true Polynesians of the brown complexion, without reference to the black-skinned islanders—as the Feegees and others of the Papuan stock.
The two have neither resemblance nor relationship
to one another; and it would not be difficult to
show that they are of a totally distinct origin. As
for the blacks, it is not even certain that they are
themselves of one original stock; for the splendid-
ly-developed cannibal of Feegee presents very few
features in common with the wretched kangaroo-

eater of West Australia. Whether the black islanders (or Melanesians as they have been designated) originally came from one source, is still a
question for ethnologists; but there can be no doubt
as to the direction whence they entered upon the col-
onization of the Pacific. That was certainly upon its
western border, beyond which they have not made
much progress: since the Feegeean archipelago is
at the present time their most advanced station to
the eastward. The brown or Polynesian races, on
the contrary, began their migrations from the eastern border of the great ocean—in other words, they
came from America; and the so-called Indians of
America are, in my opinion, the *progenitors*, not the
descendants, of these people of the Ocean world. If
learned ethnologists will give their attention to this
view of the subject, and disembarrass their minds
of that fabulous old fancy, about an original stock
situated somewhere (they know not exactly where)
upon the steppes of Asia, they will perhaps arrive
at a more rational hypothesis about the peopling of
the so-called new worlds, both the American and
Oceanic. They will be able to prove—what might
be here done if space would permit—that the Polynesians are emigrants from tropical America, and
that the Sandwich Islanders came originally from
California, and not the Californians from the island
homes of Hawaii.

It is of slight importance here how this question
may be viewed. Enough to know that the natives
of the Tonga group bear a strong resemblance to
those of the other Polynesian archipelagos—to the
Otaheitans and New Zealanders, but most of all to
the inhabitants of the Samoan or Navigators islands, of whom, indeed, they may be regarded as a
branch, with a separate political and geographical
existence. Their language also confirms the affin-

ity, as it is merely a dialect of the common tongue spoken by all the Polynesians.

Whatever difference exists between the Tongans and other Polynesians in point of personal appearance, is in favour of the former. The men are generally regarded as the best-looking of all South-Sea islanders, and the women among the fairest of their sex. Many of them would be accounted beautiful in any part of the world; and as a general rule, they possess personal beauty in a far higher degree than the much-talked-of Otaheitans.

The Tongans are of tall stature—rather above than under that of European nations. Men of six feet are common enough; though few are seen of what might be termed gigantic proportions. In fact, the true medium size is almost universal, and the excess in either direction forms the exception. The bulk of their bodies is in perfect proportion to their height. Unlike the black Feegeeans—who are often bony and gaunt—the Tongans possess well-rounded arms and limbs; and the hands and feet, especially those of the women, are small and elegantly shaped.

To give a delineation of their features would be a difficult task—since these are so varied in different individuals, that it would be almost impossible to select a good typical face. Indeed the same might be said of nearly every nation on the face of the earth; and the difficulty will be understood by your making an attempt to describe some face that will answer for every set of features in a large town, or even a small village; or still, with greater limitation, for the different individuals of a single family. Just such a variety there will be found among the faces of the Friendly Islanders, as you might note in the inhabitants of an English town or county; and hence the difficulty of making a correct likeness.

A few characteristic points, however, may be given, both as to their features and complexion. Their lips are scarcely ever of a thick or negro form; and although the noses are in general rounded at the end, this rule is not universal;—many have genuine Roman noses, and what may be termed a full set of the best Italian features. There is also less difference between the sexes in regard to their features than is usually seen elsewhere—those of the women being only distinguished by their less size.

The forms of the women constitute a more marked distinction; and among the beauties of Tonga are many that might be termed models in respect to shape and proportions. In colour, the Tongans are lighter than most other South-Sea islanders. Some of the better classes of women—those least exposed to the open air—show skins of a light olive tint; and the children of all are nearly white after birth. They become browner less from age than exposure to the sun; for, as soon as they are able to be abroad, they scarce ever afterwards enter under the shadow of a roof, except during the hours of night.

The Tongans have good eyes and teeth; but in this respect they are not superior to many other Oceanic tribes—even the black Feegeeans possessing both eyes and "ivories" scarce surpassed anywhere. The Tongans, however, have the advantage of their dusky neighbours in the matter of hair—their heads being clothed with a luxuriant growth of true hair. Sometimes it is quite straight, as among the American Indians, but oftener with a slight wave or undulation, or a curl approaching, but never quite arriving at the condition of "crisp."

His hair in its natural colour is jet black; and it is to be regretted that the Tongans have not the good taste to leave it to its natural hue. On the contrary, their fashion is to stain it of a reddish-brown, a purple, or an orange. The brown is obtained by the application of burnt coral, the purple from a vegetable dye applied poultice-fashion to the hair, and the orange is produced by a copious lathering of common turmeric—with which the women also sometimes anoint their bodies, and those of their children. This fashion of hair-dyeing is also common to the Feegees, and whether they obtained it from the Tongans, or the Tongans from them, is an unsettled point. The more probable hypothesis would be, that among many other ugly customs, it had its origin in Feegee-land—where, however, the people assign a reason for practising it very different from the mere motive of ornament. They allege that it also serves a useful purpose, in preventing the too great fructification of a breed of parasitic insects—that would otherwise find the immense mop of the frizzly Feegeean a most convenient dwelling-place, and a secure asylum from danger. This may have had something to do with the origin of the custom; but once established for purposes of utility, it is now confirmed, and kept up by the Tongans as a useless ornament. Their taste in the colour runs exactly counter to that of European fashionables. What a pity it is that the two could not make an exchange of hair! Then both parties, like a pair of advertisements in the "Times," would exactly *fit* each other.

Besides the varied fashion in colours, there is also great variety in the styles in which the Tongans wear their hair. Some cut it short on one side of the head, leaving it at full length on the other; some shave a small patch, or cut off only a single lock; while others—and these certainly display the best taste—leave it to grow out in all its full luxuriance. In this, again, we find the European fashion reversed, for the women are those who wear it shortest. The men, although they are not without beard, usually crop this appendage very close, or shave it off altogether—a piece of shell, or rather a pair of shells serving them for a razor.

The mode is to place the thin edge of one shell underneath the hair — just as a haircutter does his comb — and with the edge of the other applied above, the hairs are rasped through and divided. There are regular barbers for this purpose, who by practice have been rendered exceedingly dexterous in its performance; and the victim of the operation alleges that there is little or no pain produced—at all events, it does not bring the tears to his eyes, as a dull razor often does with us poor thin-skinned Europeans!

The dress of the Tongans is very similar to that of the Otaheitans, so often described and well known; but we cannot pass it here without remarking a notable peculiarity on the part of the Polynesian people, as exhibited in the character of their costume. The native tribes of almost all other warm climates content themselves with the most scant covering—generally with no covering at all, but rarely with anything that may be termed a skirt. In South America most tribes wear the "guayuco,"—a mere strip around the loins, and among the Feegees the "malo" or "masi" of the men, and the scant "liku" of the women are the only excuse for a modest garment. In Africa we find tribes equally destitute of clothing, and the same remark will apply to the tropical countries all around the globe. Here, however, amongst a people dwelling in the middle of a vast ocean,—isolated from the whole civilized world, we find a natural instinct of modesty that does credit to their character, and is even in keeping with that character, as

first observed by voyagers to the South Seas.
Whatever acts of indelicacy may be alleged against
the Otaheitans, this has been much exaggerated by
their intercourse with immoral white men; but
none of such criminal conduct can be charged
against the natives of the Friendly Isles.   On the
contrary, the behaviour of these, both among themselves and in presence of European visitors, has
been ever characterized by a modesty that would
shame either Regent Street or Ratcliffe Highway.

A description of the national costume of the Tongans, though often given, is not unworthy of a place
here; and we shall give it as briefly as a proper understanding of it will allow.   There is but one "garment" to be described, and that is the "pareu,"
which will be better understood, perhaps, by calling
it a "petticoat."   The material is usually of "tapa"
cloth — a fabric of native manufacture, to be described hereafter—and the cutting out is one of the
simplest of performances, requiring neither a tailor
for the men, nor a dressmaker for the other sex, for
every one can make their own pareu.   It needs only
to clip a piece of "tapa" cloth in the form of an
"oblong square"—an ample one, being about two
yards either way.   This is wrapped round the body
—the middle part against the small of the back—
and then both ends brought round to the front are
lapped over each other as far as they will go, producing, of course, a double fold of the cloth.   A
girdle is next tied around the waist—usually a cord
of ornamental plait; and this divides the piece of
tapa into body and skirt.   The latter is of such a
length as to stretch below the calf of the leg—sometimes down to the ankle — and the upper part or
body *would* reach to the shoulders, if the weather
required it, and often does *when the missionaries
require it.*   But not at any other time: such an un-

graceful mode of wearing the pareu was never intended by the simple Tongans, who never dreamt
of there being any immodesty in their fashion until
told of it by their puritanical preceptors!

Tongan-fashion, the pareu is a sort of tunic, and
a most graceful garment to boot; Methodist fashion, it becomes a gown or rather a sleeveless wrapper that resembles a sack. But if the body part is
not to be used in this way, how, you will ask, is it
to be disposed of? Is it allowed to hang down outside, like the gown of a slattern woman, who has
only half got into it? No such thing. The natural
arrangement is both simple and peculiar; and produces, moreover, a costume that is not only characteristic but graceful to the eye that once becomes
used to it. The upper half of the tapa cloth is neatly folded or turned, until it becomes a thick roll;
and this roll, brought round the body, just above
the girdle, is secured in that position. The swell
thus produced causes the waist to appear smaller by
contrast; and the effect of a well-formed bust, rising above the roll of tapa cloth, is undoubtedly
striking and elegant. In cold weather, but more
especially at night, the roll is taken out, and the
shoulders are then covered; for it is to be observed
that the pareu, worn by day as a dress, is also kept
on at night as a sleeping-gown, more especially by
those who possess only a limited wardrobe. It is
not always the cold that requires it to be kept on
at night. It is more used, at this time, as a protection against the musquitoes, that abound amidst
the luxuriant vegetation of the Tongan islands.

The "pareu" is not always made of the "tapa"
cloth. Fine mats, woven from the fibres of the
screw-pine (*pandanus*), are equally in vogue; and,
upon festive occasions, a full-dress pareu is embel-
lished with red feather-work, adding greatly to the

elegance and picturesqueness of its appearance. A coarser and scantier pareu is to be seen among the poorer people, the material of which is a rough tapa, fabricated from the bark of the bread-fruit, and not unfrequently this is only a mere strip wrapped around the loins; in other words, a " malo," " maro," or " maso"—as it is indifferently written in the varied orthography of the voyagers. Having described this only and unique garment, we have finished with the costume of the Tongan islanders, both men and women—for both wear the pareu alike. The head is almost universally uncovered; and no head-dress is ever worn unless a cap of feathers by the great chiefs, and this only upon rare and grand occasions. It is a sort of chaplet encircling the head, and deeper in front than behind. Over the forehead the plumes stand up to the height of twelve or fifteen inches, gradually lowering on each side as the ray extends backward beyond the ears. The main row is made with the beautiful tail-plumes of the tropic bird, *Phaeton æthereus*, while the front or fillet part of the cap is ornamented with the scarlet feathers of a species of parrot.

The head-dress of the women consists simply of fresh flowers: a profusion of which—among others the beautiful blossoms of the orange—is always easily obtained. An ear-pendant is also worn—a piece of ivory of about two inches in length, passed through two holes, pierced in the lobe of the ear, for this purpose. The pendant hangs horizontally, the two holes balancing it, and keeping it in position. A necklace also of pearl-shells, shaped into beads, is worn. Sometimes a string of the seeds of the pandanus is added, and an additional ornament is an armlet of mother-o'-pearl, fashioned into the form of a ring. Only the men tattoo themselves; and the process is confined to that portion of the body from the waist to the thighs, which is always covered with the paren. The practice of tattooing perhaps first originated in the desire to equalize age with youth, and to hide an ugly physiognomy. But the Tongan islander has no ugliness to conceal, and both men and women have had the good taste to refrain from disfiguring the fair features which nature has so bountifully bestowed upon them. The only marks of tattoo to be seen upon the women are a few fine lines upon the palms of their hands; nor do they disfigure their fair skins with the hideous pigments so much in use among other tribes, of what we are in the habit of terming *savages*.

They anoint the body with a fine oil procured from the cocoanut, and which is also perfumed by various kinds of flowers that are allowed to macerate in the oil; but this toilet is somewhat expensive, and is only practised by the better classes of the community. All, however, both rich and poor, are addicted to habits of extreme cleanliness, and bathing in fresh water is a frequent performance. They object to bathing in the sea; and when they do so, always finish the bath by pouring fresh water over their bodies—a practice which they allege prevents the skin from becoming rough, which the sea-water would otherwise make it.

House architecture in the Tongan islands is in rather a backward state. They have produced no Wrens nor Inigo Jones's; but this arises from a natural cause. They have no need for great architects—scarce any need for houses either—and only the richer Tongans erect any dwelling more pretentious than a mere shed. A few posts of palm-trunks are set up, and upon these are placed the cross-beams, rafters, and roof. Pandanus leaves, or

those of the sugar-cane, form the thatch; and the
sides are left open underneath.   In the houses of the
chiefs and more wealthy people there are walls of
pandanus mats, fastened to the uprights; and some
of these houses are of considerable size and neatly
built.   The interiors are kept scrupulously clean—
the floors being covered with beautiful mats woven
in coloured patterns, and presenting all the gay appearance of costly carpeting.   There are neither
chairs nor tables.   The men sit tailor-fashion, and
the women in a reclining posture, with both limbs
turned a little to one side and backwards.   A curious inclosure or partition is formed by setting a
stiff mat, of about two feet width, upon its edge
—the roll at each end steadying it and keeping it
in an upright position.

The utensils to be observed are dishes, bowls,
and cups—usually of calabash or cocoa-shells—and
an endless variety of baskets of the most ingenious
plait and construction.   The "stool-pillow" is also
used; but differing from that of the Feegees in the
horizontal piece having a hollow to receive the
head.   Many kinds of musical instruments may be
seen—the Pandean pipes, the nose-flute, and various
kinds of bamboo drums, all of which have been minutely described by travellers.   I am sorry to add
that war-clubs and spears for a similar purpose are
also to be observed conspicuous among the more
useful implements of peace.   Bows and arrows, too,
are common; but these are only employed for
shooting birds and small rodents, especially rats,
that are very numerous and destructive to the
crops.

For food, the Tongans have the pig—the same
variety as is so generally distributed throughout
the Oceanic Islands.   It is stated that the Feegeeans obtained this animal from the Friendly Isles;

but I am of opinion that in this case the benefit came the other way, as the *Sus Papua* is more likely to have entered the South Sea from its leeward rather than its windward side. In all likelihood the dog may have been derived from the eastern edge; but the pigs and poultry would seem to be of western origin—western as regards the position of the Pacific.

The principal food of the Friendly Islanders, however, is of a vegetable nature, and consists of yams, breadfruit, taro, plantains, sweet potatoes, and, in fact, most of those roots and fruits common to the other islands of the Pacific. Fish also forms an important article of their food. They drink the "kava," or juice of the *Piper methisticum*—or rather of its root chewed to a pulp; but they rarely indulge to that excess observed among the Feegees, and they are not over fond of the drink, except as a means of producing a species of intoxication which gives them a momentary pleasure. Many of them, especially the women, make wry faces while partaking of it; and no wonder they do, for it is at best a disgusting beverage.

The time of the Tongan islanders is passed pleasantly enough, when there is no wicked war upon hand. The men employ themselves in cultivating the ground or fishing; and here the woman is no longer the mere slave and drudge—as almost universally elsewhere among savage or even semi-civilized nations. This is a great fact, which tells a wondrous tale—which speaks trumpet-tongued to the credit of the Tongan islander. Not only do the men share the labour with their more delicate companions, but everything else—their food, conversation, and every enjoyment of life. Both partake alike —eat together, drink together, and join at once in the festive ceremony. In their grand dances—or

balls as they might more properly be termed—the
women play an important part; and these exhibitions, though in the open air, are got up with an elegance and *éclat* that would not disgrace the most fashionable ball-room in Christendom.   Their dances, indeed, are far more graceful than anything ever seen
either at " Almacks" or the " Jardin Mabille."

The principal employment of the men is in the
cultivation of their yam and plantain grounds, many
of which extend to the size of fields, with fences that
would almost appear to have been erected as ornaments.   These are of canes, closely set, raised to the
height of six feet—wide spaces being left between
the fences of different owners to serve as roads for
the whole community.   In the midst of these fields
stand the sheds, or houses, surrounded by splendid
forms of tropic vegetation, and forming pictures of
a softly-beautiful character.

The men also occupy themselves in the construction of their canoes,—to procure the large ones, making a voyage as already stated, to the Feegee Islands, and sometimes remaining absent for several
years.

These, however, are usually professional boat-
builders, and form but a very small proportion of
the 40,000 people who inhabit the different islands
of the Tongan archipelago.

The men also occasionally occupy themselves in
weaving mats and wicker baskets, and carving fancy toys out of wood and shells; but the chief part
of the manufacturing business is in the hands of the
women—more especially the making of the tapa-
cloth, already so often mentioned.   An account of
the manufacture may be here introduced, with the
proviso, that it is carried on not only by the women
of the Feegee group, but by those of nearly all the
other Polynesian islands.   There are slight differ-

ences in the mode of manufacture, as well as in the
quality of the fabric; but the account here given,
both of the making and dyeing, will answer pretty
nearly for all.

The bark of the malo-tree, or " paper-mulberry,"
is taken off in strips, as long as possible, and then
steeped in water, to facilitate the separation of the
epidermis, which is effected by a large volute shell.
In this state it is kept for some time, although fit
for immediate use. A log, flattened on the upper
side, is so fixed as to spring a little, and on this the
strips of bark—or *masi*, as it is called—are beaten
with an *iki*, or mallet, about two inches square, and
grooved longitudinally on three of its sides. Two
lengths of the wet *masi* are generally beaten together, in order to secure greater strength—the
gluten which they contain being sufficient to keep
their fibres united. A two-inch strip can thus be
beaten out to the width of a foot and a half; but
the length is at the same time reduced. The pieces
are neatly lapped together with the starch of the
taro, or arrow-root, boiled whole; and thus reach
a length of many yards. The " widths" are also
joined by the same means laterally, so as to form
pieces of fifteen or thirty feet square; and upon
these the ladies exhaust their ornamenting skill.
The middle of the square is printed with a red
brown, by the following process :—Upon a convex
board, several feet long, are arranged parallel, at
about a finger-width apart, thin straight slips of
bamboo, a quarter of an inch wide. By the side of
these, curved pieces, formed of the mid-rib of cocoanut leaflets, are arranged. On the board thus prepared the cloth is laid, and rubbed over with a dye
obtained from the *lauci* (*Aleurites triloba*). The
cloth, of course, takes the dye upon those parts
which receive pressure, being supported by the slips

beneath; and thus shows the same pattern in the colour employed. A stronger preparation of the same dye, laid on with a sort of brush, is used to divide the square into oblong compartments, with large round or radiated dots in the centre. The *kesa*, or dye, when good, dries bright. Blank borders, two or three feet wide, are still left on two sides of the square; and to elaborate the ornamentation of these, so as to excite applause, is the pride of every lady. There is now an entire change of apparatus. The operator works on a plain board; the red dye gives place to a jet black; the pattern is now formed of a strip of banana-leaf placed on the upper surface of the cloth. Out of the leaf is cut the pattern—not more than an inch long—which the lady wishes to print upon the border, and holds by her first and middle finger, pressing it down with the thumb. Then, taking a soft pad of cloth, steeped in the dye, in her right hand, she rubs it firmly over the stencil, and a fair, sharp figure is made. The practised fingers of the operator move quickly, but it is, after all, a tedious process.

I regret to add, that the men employ themselves in an art of less utility: the manufacture of war weapons—clubs and spears—which the people of the different islands, and even those of the same, too often brandish against one another. This war spirit is entirely owing to their intercourse with the ferocious Feegees, whose boasting and ambitious spirit they are too prone to emulate. In fact, their admiration of the Feegee habits is something surprising; and can only be accounted for by the fact, that while visiting these savages and professed warriors, the Tongans have become imbued with a certain fear of them. They acknowledge the more reckless spirit of their allies, and are also aware that in intellectual capacity the black men are not inferior to themselves. They certainly are inferior in courage, as in every good moral quality; but the Tongans can hardly believe this, since their cruel and ferocious conduct seems to give colour to the contrary idea. In fact, it is this that inspires them with a kind of respect, which has no other foundation than a vague sense of fear. Hence they endeavour to emulate the actions that produce this fear, and this leads them to go to war with one another.

It is to be regretted that the missionaries have supplied them with a motive. Their late wars are solely due to missionary influence—for Methodism upon the Tongan islands has adopted one of the doctrines of Mahomet, and believes in the faith being propagated by the sword! A usurper, who wishes to be king over the whole group, has embraced the Methodist form of Christianity, and linked himself with its teachers—who offer to aid him with all their influence; and these formerly peaceful islands now present the painful spectacle of a divided nationality—the "Christian party," and the "Devil's party." The object of conquest on the part of the former is to place the Devil's party under the absolute sovereignty of a despot, whose laws will be dictated by his missionary ministers. Of the mildness of these laws we have already some specimens, which of course extend only to the "christianized." One of them, which refers to the mode of wearing the pareu, has been already hinted at—and another is a still more off-hand piece of legislation: being an edict that no one hereafter shall be permitted to smoke tobacco, under pain of a most severe punishment.

When it is considered that the Tongan islander enjoys the "weed" (and grows it too) more than almost any other smoker in creation, the severity

O

of the "taboo" may be understood. But it is very certain, if his Methodist majesty were once firmly seated on his throne, *bluer* laws than this would speedily be proclaimed. The American Commodore Wilkes found things in this warlike attitude when he visited the Tongan islands; but perceiving that the right was clearly on the side of the "Devil's party," declined to interfere; or rather, his interference, which would have speedily brought peace, was rejected by the Christian party, instigated by the sanguinary spirit of their "Christian" teachers. Not so, Captain Croker, of Her Britannic Majesty's service, who came shortly after. This unreflecting officer—loath to believe that royalty could be in the wrong—at once took side with the king and Christians, and dashed headlong into the affair. The melancholy result is well known. It ended by Captain Croker leaving his body upon the field, alongside those of many of his brave tars; and a disgraceful retreat of the Christian party beyond the reach of their enemies.

This interference of a British war-vessel in the affairs of the Tongan islanders, offers a strong contrast to our conduct when in presence of the Feegees. There we have the fact recorded of British officers being eye-witnesses of the most horrid scenes —wholesale murder and cannibalism—with full power to stay the crime and full authority to punish it —that authority which would have been freely given them by the accord and acclamation of the whole civilized world—and yet they stood by, in the character of idle spectators, fearful of breaking through the delicate icy line of *non-intervention!*

A strange theory it seems, that murder is no longer murder, when the murderer and his victim chance to be of a different nationality from our own! It is a distinction too delicate to bear the investigation of the philosophic mind; and perhaps will yet yield to a truer appreciation of the principles of justice. There was no such squeamishness displayed when royalty required support upon the Tongan islands; nor ever is there when self-interest demands it otherwise. Mercy and justice may both fail to disarrange the hypocritical fallacy of non-intervention; but the principle always breaks down at the call of political convenience.

THE TURCOMANS.

Asia has been remarkable, from the earliest times, for having a large population without any fixed place of residence, but who lead a *nomade* or wandering life. It is not the only quarter of the globe where this kind of people are found: as there are many *nomade* nations in Africa, especially in the northern division of it; and if we take the Indian race into consideration, we find that both the North and South American continents have their tribes of wandering people. It is in Asia, nevertheless, that we find this unsettled mode of life carried out to its greatest extent—it is there that we find those great pastoral tribes—or " hordes," as they have been termed—who at different historical periods have not only increased to the numerical strength of large nationalities, but have also been powerful enough to overrun adjacent empires, pushing their conquests even into Europe itself. Such were the invasions of the Mongols under Zenghis Khan, the Tartars under Timour, and the Turks, whose degenerate descendants now so feebly hold the vast territory won by their wandering ancestors.

The pastoral life, indeed, has its charms, that render it attractive to the natural disposition of man, and wherever the opportunity offers of following it, this life will be preferred to any other. It affords to man an abundant supply of all his most prominent wants, without requiring from him any very severe exertion, either of mind or body; and, considering the natural indolence of Asiatic people, it

is not to be wondered at that so many of them betake themselves to this mode of existence. Their
country, moreover, is peculiarly favourable to the
development of a pastoral race. Perhaps not one-
third of the surface of the Asiatic continent is adapted to agriculture. At least one-half of it is occupied by treeless, waterless plains, many of which
have all the characters of a desert, where an agricultural people could not exist, or, at all events,
where their labor would be rewarded by only the
most scant and precarious returns.

Even a pastoral people in these regions would
find but a sorry subsistence, were they confined to
one spot; for the luxurious herbage which, for the
most part, characterizes the great savanna plains of
America, is either altogether wanting upon the
steppes of Asia, or at best very meagre and incon-
stant. A fixed abode is therefore impossible, except
in the most fertile tracts or *oäses:* elsewhere, the
nomad life is a necessity arising from the circumstances of the soil.

It would be difficult to define exactly the limits
of the territory occupied by the wandering races in
Asia; but in a general way it may be said that the
whole central portion of the continent is thus peopled: indeed, much more than the central portion
—for, if we except the rich agricultural countries
of Hindostan and China, with a small portion of
Persia, Arabia, and Turkey, the whole of Asia is of
this character. The countries known as Balk and
Bokara, Yarkand and Khiva, with several others of
equal note, are merely the central points of oäses—
large towns, supported rather by commerce than by
the produce of agriculture, and having nomad tribes
dwelling within sight of their walls. Even the present boundaries of Asiatic Turkey, Arabia, and Persia, contain within them a large proportion of no-

madic population; and the same is true of Eastern Poland and Russia in Europe. A portion of the Affghan and Belochee country **is** also inhabited by nomad people.

These wandering people are of many different types and races of men; but there is a certain similarity in the habits and customs of all: as might be expected from the similar circumstances in which they are placed.

It is always the more sterile steppes that are thus **occupied**; and **this** is easily accounted for: where **fertile** districts occur, the nomad life is no longer necessary. Even a wandering tribe, entering upon such a tract, would no longer have a motive for leaving it, and would soon become attached to the soil—in other words, would cease to be wanderers; and whether they turned their attention to the pursuit of agriculture, or not, they would be certain to give up their tent-life, and fix themselves in a permanent abode. This has been the history of many Asiatic tribes; but **there** are many others, again, who from time immemorial, have shown a repugnance to the idea of fixing themselves to the soil. They prefer the free roving life which the desert enables them to indulge in; and wandering from place to place as the choice of pasture guides them, occupy themselves entirely in feeding their flocks and herds—the sole means of their subsistence. These never have been, and never could be, induced to reside in towns or villages.

Nor is it that they have been driven into these desert tracts to seek shelter from political oppression—as is the case with some of the native tribes of Africa and America. On the contrary, these Asiatic nomads are more often the aggressors than the objects of aggression. It is rather a matter of choice and propensity with them: as with those tribes of the Arabian race—known as "Bedouins."

The proportion of the Asiatic wandering population to those who dwell in towns, or fixed habitations, varies according to the nature of the country. In many extensive tracts, the former greatly exceed the latter; and the more sterile steppes are almost exclusively occupied by them. In general, they acknowledge the sovereignty of some of the great powers—such as the empires of China, Russia, and Turkey, the kingdom of Persia, or that of several powerful khans, as those of Khiva and Bokara; but this sovereignty is, for the most part, little more than nominal, and their allegiance is readily thrown off, whenever they desire it. It is rarely so strong, as to enable any of the aforesaid powers to draw a heavy tribute from them; and some of the more warlike of the wandering tribes are much courted and caressed—especially when their war services are required. In general they claim an hereditary right to the territories over which they roam, and pay but little heed to the orders of either king, khan, or emperor.

As already stated, these wandering people are of different races; in fact they are of nearly all the varieties indigenous to the Asiatic continent; and a whole catalogue of names might be given, of which Mongols, Tartars, Turcomans, Usbecks, Kirghees, and Calmucks, are perhaps the most generally known. It has been also stated that in many points they are alike; but there are also many important particulars in which they differ—physical, moral, and intellectual. Some of the "hordes," or tribes, are purely pastoral in their mode of life, and of mild and hospitable dispositions, exceedingly fond of strangers, and kind to such as come among them. Others again are averse to all intercourse with oth-

ers, than those **of their** own race and religion, and
are shy, if not inhospitable, when visited by strangers.   But there is a class of a still less creditable
character—a large **number of tribes that** are not
only inhospitable, and hostile to strangers, but as
ferocious and bloodthirsty as any savages in Africa,
America, or the South-Sea Islands.

As a fair specimen of this class we select the Turcoman**s; in** fact, they may be regarded as its *type;*
and **our** description henceforward may be regarded
as applying particularly to these people.

The country of the Turcomans will be found upon
the map without difficulty; but to define its exact
boundary would be an impossibility, since none such
exists.   Were you to travel along the whole northern frontier of Persia, almost from the gates of Teheran to the eastern frontier of the kingdom—or
even farther towards Balk—you would be pretty
sure of hearing of Turcoman robbers, and in very
great danger of being plundered by them—which
last misfortune would be of less importance, as it
would only be the prelude to your being either murdered on the spot, **or** carried off by them into captivity.   In making this journey along the northern
frontier of Persia, you would become acquainted
with the whereabouts of the Turcoman hordes; or
rather you would discover that the whole north part
of Persia—a good broad band of it extending hundreds of miles into its interior,—if not absolutely in
possession of the Turcomans, **is overrun** and plundered by them **at will.**   This, however, **is** not their
home—it is **only their** " stamping-ground"—the
home of their victims.   Their place of habitual resi-
dence lies further **to** the north, and is defined with
tolerable accuracy by its having the whole eastern
shore of the Caspian Sea for its western border,
while the Amou river (the ancient Oxus) may be

generally regarded as the limit of their range towards the east. Some tribes go still further east than the Amou; but those, more particularly distinguished for their plundering habits, dwell within the limits described—north of the Elburz mountains, and on the great steppe of Kaurezm, where they are contiguous to the Usbeck community of Khiva.

The whole of this immense territory, stretching from the eastern shore of the Caspian to the Amou and Aral Sea, may be characterized as a true desert. Here and there oäses exist, but none of any importance, save the country of Khiva itself: and even that is but a mere irrigated strip, lying on both banks of the Oxus. Indeed, it is difficult to believe that this territory of Khiva, so insignificant in superficial extent, could have been the seat of a powerful empire, as it once was.

The desert, then, between the Caspian Sea and the Oxus river may be regarded as the true land of the Turcomans, and is usually known as Turcomania. It is to be remembered, however, that there are some kindred tribes not included within the boundaries of Turcomania—for the Turkistan of the geographers is a country of much larger extent; besides, an important division of the Turcoman races are settlers, or rather wanderers in Armenia. To Turcomania proper, then, and its inhabitants, we shall confine our remarks.

We shall not stay to inquire into the origin of the people now called Turcomans. Were we to speculate upon that point, we should make but little progress in an account of their habits and mode of living. They are usually regarded as of Tartar origin, or of Usbeck origin, or of Mongolian race; and in giving this account of them, I am certain that I add very little to your knowledge of what they really are. The truth is, that the words Tar-

tar and Mongol and some half-dozen other titles,
used in relation to the Asiatic races, are without
any very definite signification—simply because the
relative distinctions of the different nations of that
continent are very imperfectly known; and learned
ethnologists are ever loth to a confession of limited
knowledge. One of this class, Mr. Latham—who
requires only a few words of their language to de-
cide categorically to what variety of the human
race **a people** belongs—has unfortunately added to
this confusion by pronouncing nearly everybody
Mongolian: placing the proud turbaned Turk in
juxtaposition with the squat and stunted Laplander ! Of course this is only bringing us back to the
old idea, that all men are sprung from a single pair
of first parents—a doctrine, which, though popular,
is difficult to reconcile with the rational knowledge
derived from ethnological investigation.

It matters little to our present purpose from
what original race the Turcoman has descended :
whether he be a true Turk, as some regard him, or
whether he is a descendant of the followers of the
Great Khan of the Tartars. He possesses the Tartar physiognomy to a considerable extent—some
of the tribes more than others being thus distinguished,—and high cheek-bones, flat noses, small
oblique eyes, and scanty beards, are all characteristics that are very generally observed. Some of
these peculiarities are more common among the
women than the men—many **of the latter** being
tall, stout, and well-made, **while a** large number
may be seen who have **the** regular features of a
Persian. Perhaps it would be safest to consider the
present Turcoman tribes as not belonging to a pure
stock, but rather an admixture of several ; and their
habit of taking slaves from other nations, which has
for **a** long time existed among them, would give

probability to this idea. At all events, without
some such hypothesis, it is difficult to account for
the wonderful variety, both in feature and form,
that is found among them. Their complexion is
swarthy, in some cases almost brown as that of an
American Indian; but constant exposure to the
open air, in all sorts of weather, has much to do in
darkening the hue of their skin. The newborn
children are nearly as white as those of the Persians; and their young girls exhibit a ruddy brunette tint, which some consider even more pleasing
than a perfectly white complexion.

The costume of the Turcoman, like that of most
Oriental nations, is rich and picturesque. The dress
of the men varies according to rank. Some of the
very poorer people wear nothing but a short woollen tunic or shirt, with a pair of coarse woollen
drawers. Others, in place of this shirt, are clad in
a longer garment, a sort of robe or wrapper, like a
gentleman's dressing-gown, made of camel's-hair
cloth, or some coarse brown woollen stuff. But the
true Turcoman costume, and that worn by all who
can afford it, consists of a garment of mixed silk
and cotton—the *baronnee*,—which descends below
the knee, and though open in front, is made to button over the breast quite up to the neck. A gay
sash around the waist adds to the effect; and below
the skirt are seen trowsers of cotton or even silk.
Cloth wrappers around the legs serve in the place
of boots or gaiters; and on the feet are worn slippers of Persian fashion, with socks of soft Koordish
leather.

As the material of which the baronnee is made is
of good quality—a mixture of silk and cotton—and
as the fabric is always striped or chequered in colours of red, blue, purple, and green, the effect produced is that of a certain picturesqueness. The

head-dress adds to this appearance—being a high
fur cap, with truncated top, the fur being that beautiful kind obtained from the skins of the Astracan
lamb, well known in commerce. These caps are of
different colours, either black, red, or grey. Another style of head-dress much worn is a round-
topped or helmet-shaped cap, made of quilted cotton stuff; but this kind, although in use among the
Turcomans, is a more characteristic costume of their
enemies, the "Koords," who wear it universally.

The "jubba" is a kind of robe generally intended
to go over the other garments, and is usually of
woollen or camel's-hair cloth. It is also made like
a dressing-gown, with wide sleeves—tight, however, around the wrist. It is of ample dimensions,
and one side is lapped over the other across the
front, like a double-breasted coat. The "jubba" is
essentially a national garment.

The dress of the women is exceedingly picturesque. It is thus minutely described by a traveller :—

"The head-dress of these women is singular
enough: most of them wear a lofty cap, with a
broad crown, resembling that of a soldier's cap
called a shako. This is stuck upon the back of the
head; and over it is thrown a silk handkerchief of
very brilliant colours, which covers the top, and
falls down on each side like a veil. The front of
this is covered with ornaments of silver and gold,
in various shapes; more frequently gold coins,
mohrs, or tomauns, strung in rows, with silver bells
or buttons, and chains depending from them; hearts
and other fanciful forms, with stones set in them.
The whole gives rather the idea of gorgeous trappings for a horse, than ornaments for a female.

"The frames of these monstrous caps are made
of light chips of wood, or split reeds, covered with

cloth; and when they do not wear these, they wrap
a cloth around their heads in the same form; and
carelessly throw another, like a veil over it. The
veil or curtain above spoken of, covers the mouth;
descending to the breast. Earrings are worn in the
ears; and their long hair is divided, and plaited
into four parts, disposed two on each side; one of
which falls down behind the shoulders and one before, and both are strung with a profusion of gold
ornaments, agates, cornelians, and other stones, according to the means and quality of the wearer.
The rest of their dress consists of a long loose vest
or shirt, with sleeves, which covers the whole person down to the feet, and is open at the breast, in
front, but buttons or ties close up to the neck: this
is made of silk or cotton-stuff, red, blue, green,
striped red, and yellow, checked, or various-coloured: underneath this, are the zere-jameh, or drawers, also of silk or cotton; and some wear a short
peerahn or shirt of the same. This, I believe is
all; but in the cold weather, they wear in addition,
jubbas, or coats like those of the men, of striped
stuff made of silk and cotton; on their feet they
generally wear slippers like those of the Persian
women."

The tents, or "portable houses" of the Turcomans—as their movable dwellings rather deserve
to be called—differ from most structures of the
kind in use elsewhere. They are thus described by
the same intelligent traveller:—

"The portable wooden houses of the Turcomans
have been referred to by several writers; but I am
not aware that any exact description of their structure has been given. The frame is curiously constructed of light wood, disposed in laths of about
an inch broad by three-quarters thick, crossing one
another diagonally, but at right angles, about a foot

asunder, and pinned at each crossing with thongs of raw hide, so as to be movable; and the whole framework may be closed up or opened in the manner of those toys for children that represent a company of soldiers, and close or expand at will, so as to form open or close column.

"One or more pieces thus constructed being stretched out, surround a circular space of from fifteen to twenty feet diameter; and form the skeleton of the walls—which are made firm by bands of hair or woollen ropes, hitched round the end of each rod, to secure it in its position. From the upper ends of these, rods of a similar kind, bent near the wall end into somewhat less than a right angle, are so disposed that the longer portions slope to the centre, and being tied with ropes, form the framework of a roof. Over this is thrown a covering of black *numud*, leaving in the centre a large hole to give vent to the smoke, and light to the dwelling. Similar numuds are wrapped round the walls; and outside of these, to keep all tight, is bound another frame, formed of split reeds or cane, or of very light and tough wood, tied together with strong twine, the pieces being perpendicular. This is itself secured by a strong broad band of woven hair-stuff, which firmly unites. The large round opening at top is covered, as occasion requires, by a piece of numud, which is drawn off or on by a strong cord, like a curtain. If the wind be powerful, a stick is placed to leeward, which supports the fabric.

"In most of these houses they do not keep a carpet or numud constantly spread; but the better classes use a carpet shaped somewhat in the form of a horse-shoe, having the centre cut out for the fire-place, and the ends truncated, that those of inferior condition, or who do not choose to take off their boots, may sit down upon the ground. Upon this carpet they place one or two other numuds, as may be required, for guests of distinction. When they have women in the tent, a division of split reeds is made for their convenience; but the richer people have a separate tent for their private apartments.

"The furniture consists of little more than that of the camels and horses; *joals*, or bags in which their goods are packed, and which are often made of a very handsome species of worsted velvet carpet, of rich patterns; the swords, guns, spears, bows and arrows, and other implements of the family, with odds and ends of every description, may be seen hung on the ends of the wooden rods, which form very convenient pins for the purpose. Among some tribes all the domestic utensils are made of wood—calleeoons, trays for presenting food, milk-vessels, &c.: among others, all these things are formed of clay or metal. Upon the black tops of the tents may frequently be seen large white masses of sour curd, expressed from butter-milk, and set to dry as future store; this, broken down and mixed with water, forms a very pleasant acidulous drink, and is used as the basis of that intoxicating beverage called *kimmiz*. The most common and most refreshing drink which they offer to the weary and over-heated traveller in the forenoon is butter-milk, or sour curds and water; and, indeed, a modification of this, with some other simple sherbets, are the only liquors presented at their meals.

"Such are the wooden houses of the Turcomans, one of which just makes a camel's load. There are poorer ones, of a less artificial construction, the framework of which is formed of reeds.

"The encampment is generally square, inclosing an open space, or forming a broad street, the houses

P

being ranged on either side, with their doors towards each other. At these may always be seen
the most picturesque groups, occupied with their
various domestic duties, or smoking their simple
wooden *calleeoons*. The more important encamp-
ments are often surrounded by a fence of reeds,
which serves to protect the flocks from petty
thefts."

It is now our place to inquire how the Turcomans occupy their time. We have already described them as a pastoral and nomadic people;
and, under ordinary circumstances, their employment consists in looking after their flocks. In a
few of the more fertile oäses they have habitations,
or rather camps, of a more permanent character,
where they cultivate a little corn or barley, to supply them with the material for bread; but these settlements, if they deserve the name, are only exceptional; and are used chiefly as a kind of head-quar-
ters where the women and property are kept, while
the men themselves are absent on their thieving expeditions. More generally their herds are kept on
the move, and are driven from place to place at
short intervals of a few weeks or even days. The
striking and pitching of their tents gives them employment; to which is added that of milking the
cattle, and making the cheese and butter. The
women, moreover, fill up their idle hours in weaving the coarse blankets, or "numuds," in plaiting
mats, and manufacturing various articles of dress
or household use. The more costly parts of their
costume, however, are not of native manufacture:
these are obtained by trade. The men alone look
after the camels and horses, taking special care of
the latter.

Their flocks present a considerable variety of species. Besides horses, cattle, and sheep, they own

many camels, and they have no less than three distinct varieties of this valuable animal in their possession—the dromedary with two humps, and the common camel. The third sort is a cross breed— or " mule"—between these two. The dromedary is slightly made, and swifter than either of the others, but it is not so powerful as either; and being inferior as a beast of burden, is least cared for by the Turcomans. The one-humped camel is in more general use, and a good one will carry a load of 600 or 700 lbs. with ease. The mule camel is more powerful than either of its parents, and also more docile and capable of greater endurance. It grows to a very large size, but is low in proportion to its bulk, with stout bony legs, and a large quantity of coarse shaggy hair on its haunch, shoulders, neck, and even on the crown of its head, which gives it a strange, somewhat fantastic appearance. Its colour varies from light grey to brown, though it is as often nearly black. This kind of camel will carry a load of from 800 to 1,000 lbs.!

The Turcoman sheep are of the large-tailed breed —their tails often attaining enormous dimensions. This variety of sheep is a true denizen of the desert, the fat tail being unquestionably a provision of nature against seasons of hunger—just as is the single protuberance, or "hump," upon the camel.

The horse of the Turcoman is the animal upon which he sets most value. The breed possessed by him is celebrated over all Eastern Asia, as that of the Arab is in the West. They cannot be regarded, however, as handsome horses, according to the true standard of "horse beauty;" but the Turcoman cares less for this than for other good qualities. In point of speed and endurance they are not excelled, if equalled, by the horses of any other country.

Their size is that of the common English horse, but they are very different in make. Their bodies are long in proportion to the bulk of carcase; and they do not **appear to possess** sufficient compactness of frame. **Their** legs are **also** long, generally falling off in muscular development below the knee-joint; and they would appear to an **English jockey** too narrow in the counter. They have also long necks, with large heavy heads. These are the points which **are** generally observed in the Turcoman **horses**; but it is to be remarked, that it is only when **in an under-condition they look so** ungraceful; and **in this condition their owners** are accustomed to keep them, especially when **they** have any very heavy service to perform. Feeding produces a better shape, and brings them much nearer to the look of a well-bred English horse.

Their powers of endurance are, indeed, almost **incredible**: when trained for a chappow, or plundering expedition, they will carry their rider and provisions for seven or eight days together, at the rate of twenty or even thirty fursungs—that is, from eighty to **one** hundred **miles—a** day. Their mode of training is more like that of our pugilistic and pedestrian performers, than that adopted for race-horses. When any expedition of great length, and requiring **the** exertion of much speed, is in contemplation, they commence by running their horses every day for many miles together; they feed them sparingly on barley alone, and pile numuds upon them at night to **sweat** them, until **every** particle of fat has been **removed,** and the flesh becomes hard **and** tendonous. **Of this** they judge by the feel of the muscles, particularly on the crest, at the back **of** the neck, and on the haunches; and when these are sufficiently firm and hard, they say in praise of the animal, that " his flesh is marble." After this sort of training, the horse will proceed with expedition and perseverance, for almost any length of time, without either falling off in condition or **knocking up, while** horses that **set out fat seldom survive.** They are taught a quick walk, a light trot, or a sort of amble, which carries the rider on easily, at the rate of six miles an hour; **but they** will also go **at** a round canter, or gallop, **for** forty or fifty miles, without ever drawing bridle **or** showing the least symptom of fatigue. Their *yaboos*, or galloways, and large ponies are fully as remarkable, if not superior, to their horses, in their power of sustaining fatigue; they are stout, compact, spirited beasts, without the fine blood of the larger breeds, but more within the reach of the poorer **classes, and** consequently used in by far greater numbers **than** the superior and more expensive horses.

"It is a common practice of the **Turcomans to** teach their horses to fight with their heels, **and thus** assist their masters in the time of action. At the will of their riders they will run at and lay hold with their teeth of whatever man or animal may be before them. This acquirement is useful in the day of battle and plunder, for catching prisoners and stray cattle, but it at the same time renders them vicious and dangerous to be handled."

In addition **to the flocks and** herds, the Turcomans possess a **breed of very** large fierce dogs, to assist them in keeping their cattle. These are **also** necessary as watch-dogs, to protect the camp from thieves as well as more dangerous enemies to their peace; and so well trained are those faithful creatures, that it would be impossible for either friend or enemy to approach a Turcoman camp without the inmates being forewarned in time. Two or three of these dogs may always be seen lying by the entrance of each tent; and throughout the night

several others keep sentry at the approaches to the
camp.

Other breeds of dogs owned by them are used
for hunting—for **these wild** wanderers sometimes
devote their hours to the chace. They have two
sorts—a smooth-skinned dog, half hound half point-
er, that hunts chiefly by the scent; and **a** grey-
hound, of great swiftness, with a coat of long silky
hair, which they make use of in coursing—hares and
antelopes being their game.

They have a mode of hunting—also practised by
the Persians—which is peculiar. It should rather
be termed hawking than hunting, as **a hawk** is employed for the purpose. It is a species of falcon denominated "goork," and is trained not only to dash
at small game, such as partridges and bustards, but
upon antelopes and even the wild ass that is found
in plenty upon the plains of Turcomania. **You will**
wonder how a bird, not larger than the common
falcon, could capture such game as this; but it will
appear simple enough when the method has been
explained. The "goork" is trained to fly at the
quadruped, and fix its claws in one particular place
—that is, upon the frontlet, just between the eyes.
When thus attached, the bird, instead of closing its
wings and remaining at rest, keeps them constantly
in motion, flapping them over the eyes of the quadruped. This it does, no doubt, to enable it to retain its perch; while the unfortunate animal, thus
assailed, knows not in what direction to run, and is
soon overtaken by the pursuing sportsmen, and either speared or shot with the bow-and-arrow.

Wild boars are frequently hunted by the Turcomans; and this, like everything else with these rude
centaurs, is performed on horseback. The bow-and-
arrow is but a poor weapon when employed against
the thick tough hide of the Hyrcanian boar (for he

is literally the Hyrcanian boar), and of course the
matchlock would be equally ineffective. How, then,
does the Turcoman sportsman manage to bag this
bristly game? With all the ease in the world. It
costs him only the effort of galloping his horse close
up to the side of the boar after he has been brought-
to by the dogs, and then suddenly wheeling the
steed. The latter, well trained to the task, without
farther prompting, goes through the rest of the performance, which consists in administering to the
boar such a slap with his iron-shod heel, as to pros-
trate the porcine quadruped, often killing it on the
instant!

Such employments and such diversions occupy
only a small portion of the Turcoman's time. He
follows another calling of a far less creditable character, which unfortunately he regards as the most
honourable occupation of his life. This is the calling of the robber. His pastoral pursuits are matters of only secondary consideration. He only looks
to them as a means of supplying his daily wants—
his food and the more necessary portion of his clothing; but he has other wants that may be deemed
luxuries. He requires to keep up his stock of horses
and camels, and wishes to increase them. He needs
costly gear for his horses, and costly garments for
himself—and he is desirous of being possessed of
fine weapons, such as spears, swords, bows, matchlocks, daggers, and pistols. His most effective
weapons are the spear and sword, and these are the
kinds he chiefly uses.

His spear consists of a steel head with four flutes,
and edges very sharp, fixed upon a slender shaft
of from eight to ten feet in length. In using it he
couches it under the left arm, and directs it with
the right hand, either straightforward, or to the
right or left; if to the right, the butt of the shaft

lies across the hinder part of the saddle; if to the left, the forepart of the **spear** rests on the horse's neck. The Turcomans manage their horses with the left hand, but most of **these are so** well broken **as** to obey the movement of **the knee, or** the impulse of the body. When close to **their object,** they frequently grasp the spear with both **hands, to** give greater effect to the thrust. The horse, spurred to the full speed of a charge, in this way, offers an **attack no** doubt very formidable in appearance, but **perhaps** less really dangerous than the other, in **which** success depends so greatly on skill and address. The Turcomans are all sufficiently dexterous with the sword, which **is** almost universally formed in the curved Persian fashion, and very sharp; they also wear a dagger at the waist-belt. Firearms are as yet little in use among them; they possess a few, taken from the travellers they have plundered, and procure a few more occasionally from the Russians by the way of Bokara. Some **use** bows and arrows, but they are by no means so dexterous as their ancestors were in the handling **of** those weapons.

Mounted, then, upon his matchless steed, and armed **with spear** and sword, the Turcoman goes forth to practise his favourite profession—that of plunder. He does not go alone, nor with a small number of his comrades, either. The number depends altogether **on** the distance or danger of the expedition; and where these are considered great, a troop of 500, or even 1,000, usually **proceed together** upon their errand.

You will be inquiring **to** what point they direct themselves — east, **west,** north, or south? That altogether depends upon who may be their enemies for the time, for along with their desire for booty, there is also mixed **up** something like a sentiment of hostility. In this respect, however, the Turcoman is a true Ishmaelite, and in lack of other victim he will not hesitate to plunder the people of a kindred race. Indeed, several of the Turcoman tribes have long been at war with one another; and their animosity is quite as deadly among themselves as when directed against strangers to their race. The *butt*, however, of most of the Turcoman expeditions is the northern part of Persia—Korassan in particular. It is into this province that most of their great forays are directed, either against the peaceful citizens of the Persian towns and villages, or as often against the merchant caravans that are constantly passing between Teheran and the cities of the east — Mushed, Balkh, Bokara, Herat, and Kelat. I have already stated that these forays are pushed far into the interior of Persia; and the fact of Persia permitting such a state of things to continue will perhaps surprise you; but you would not be surprised were you better acquainted with the condition of that kingdom. From historic associations, you believe Persia to be a powerful nation; and so it once was, both powerful and prosperous. That day is past; and at the present hour, this decaying monarchy is not only powerless to maintain order within its own borders, but is even threatened with annihilation from those very nomad races that have so often given laws to the great empires of Asia. Even at this moment, the more powerful Tartar Khans turn a longing look towards the tottering throne of Nadir Shah; and he of Khiva has more than once made a feint at invasion. But the subject is too extensive to be discussed here. It is only introduced to explain with what facility a few hundreds of Turcoman robbers can enter and harass the land. We find a parallel in many other parts of the world—old as well as new. In the latter,

the northern provinces of Mexico, and the southern
countries of La Plata and Paraguay, are in just such
a condition : the weak, worn-out descendants of the
Spanish conquerors on one side, well representing
the remnants of the race of Nadir Shah ; while, on
the other, the Turcoman is type enough of the Red
Indian. The comparison, however, is not just to
the latter. He, at least, is possessed of courage and
prowess ; while the Turcoman, notwithstanding his
propensities for plunder, and the bloodthirsty ferocity of his character, is as arrant a coward as ever
carried lance. Even the Persian can cope with him,
when fairly matched ; and the merchant-caravans
—which are usually made up of true Turks, and
other races possessing a little "pluck," are never
attacked, unless when outnumbered in the ratio of
three to one.

For all this, the whole northern portion of the
Persian kingdom is left to the mercy of these des-
ert-robbers. The towns and villages have each their
large fortress, into which the people retire whenever the plunderers make their appearance, and
there dwell till the latter have ridden away—driving off their flocks and herds to the desert fastness-
es. Even the poor farmer is obliged to build a fortress in the middle of his fields, to which he may retire upon the occasion of any sudden alarm, and his
labourers till the ground with their swords by their
sides, and their matchlocks lying near !

These field fortresses of Korassan are altogether
so curious, both as to construction and purpose,
that we cannot pass them without a word of description. They are usually placed in some conspicuous place, at a convenient distance from all
parts of the cultivated tract. They are built of
mud, and raised to a height of fifteen or twenty
feet, of a circular form—bearing some resemblance

to the well-known round towers of Ireland. **A**
small aperture is left open at the bottom, through
which those seeking shelter may just squeeze their
bodies, and this being barricaded inside, the defence
is complete. From the top—which can be reached
easily on the inside—the farmer and his labourers
can use their matchlocks with effect; but they are
never called upon to **do** so—as the cowardly free-
booter takes good **care to give** the mud tower a
wide berth. He has no weapons by which he might
assail it; and, moreover, he has no time for sieges:
since an hour's delay might bring him into danger
from the force that is fast approaching. His only
thought is to keep on his course, and sweep off such
cattle, or make prisoners of such people as he may
chance to find, unwarned and unarmed. Now and
then he ventures upon an attack—where **there is**
much booty to tempt him, and but a weak force **to**
defend it. His enemies—the hated "Kuzzilbashes,"
as he calls the Persians,—if defeated, have no mercy
to expect from him. All who resist are killed upon
the spot, and often torture is the mode of their
death; but if they can be made prisoners, the des-
ert-robber prefers letting them live, as **a** captive is
to him a more valuable consideration than the death
of an enemy. **His prisoner, once** secured, knows
tolerably well **what is to follow.** The first thing
the Turcoman does **is to** bind the victim's hands securely behind his back; he then puts a long halter
around his neck, attaching the other end of **it to**
the tail of his horse, and in this fashion the homeward march commences. If the poor pedestrian
does **not keep** pace with the horse, he knows what
he may expect—to be dragged at intervals along
the ground, **and perhaps** torn to pieces upon the
rocks. With this **horrid fate** before his fancy, he
makes efforts almost superhuman to keep pace with

the troop of his inhuman captors: though well aware that they are leading him off into a hopeless bondage.

At night, his feet are also tied; and, thrown down upon the earth, he is covered with a coarse "numud." Do not fancy that this is done to screen him from the cold: the object is very different indeed. The numud is placed over him in order that two of his captors may sleep upon its edges —one on each side of him—thus holding him down, and frustrating any chance of escape.

On arriving at the robber-camp, the captive is not kept long in suspense as to his future fate. His owner—for he is now in reality a slave—wants a new sword, or a piece of silken cloth, or a camel, or some other article of luxury. That he can obtain either at Khiva or Bokara, in exchange for his slave; and therefore the new captive—or captives, as the chance may be—is marched off to the ready market. This is no isolated nor rare incident. It is one of everyday occurrence; and it is a noted fact, that of the 300,000 people who constitute the subjects of the Khivan Khan, nearly one-half are Persian slaves obtained from the robbers of Turcomania!

The political organization of the Turcomans is of the patriarchal character. From necessity they dwell in small communities that are termed "teers," the literal signification of which is "arrows"— though for what reason they are so styled does not appear. Perhaps it is on account of the rapidity of their movements: for, in hostile excursions, or moving from place to place, they proceed with a celerity that may be compared to arrows.

Over each tribe or teer there is a chief, similar to the "sheik" of the Arab tribes—and indeed, many of their customs offer a close analogy to those of the wandering Bedouins of Arabia and Egypt, and the Kabyles of Morocco and the Algerine provinces. The circumstances of life—almost alike to both—could not fail to produce many striking resemblances.

The Turcoman tribes, as already observed, frequently go to war with each other, but they oftener unite to rob the common enemy—the caravan or the Persian village. In these mere plundering expeditions they go in such numbers as the case may require; but when called forth to take side in anything like a national war, they can muster to the strength of many thousands; and then indeed, they become terrible—even to the most potent sovereigns of Central Asia, by whom much diplomacy is employed to enlist them on one side or the other. It matters little to them what the cause be—he who can promise them the largest booty in cattle or slaves is sure to have the help of their spears and swords.

The Turcomans are not Pagans—that is, they are not professedly so, — though, for all the regard which they pay to religious observances, they might as well be termed true infidels. They profess a religion, however, and that is Mahometanism in its worst and most bigoted form — the "Sunnite." The Persians, as is well known, hold the milder Sheean doctrines; and as the votaries of the two, in most countries where both are practised, cordially hate each other, so it is between Turcomans and Persians. The former even scorn the Persian creed, calling its followers "infidel" dogs, or *Kuzzilbashes;* and this bigoted rancour gives them a sort of plausible excuse for the hostile attitude which they hold towards them.

Taking them upon the whole, the Turcomans may be looked upon as true savages—savages dressed in *silk* instead of in *skins.*

THE OTTOMACS, OR DIRT-EATERS.

On the banks of the Orinoco, a short distance above the point where that mighty river makes its second great sweep to the eastward, dwells a remarkable people—a tribe of savages that, even among savages, are remarkable for many peculiar and singular customs. These are the *Ottomacs*.

They have been long known—and by the narratives of the early Spanish missionaries, rendered notorious—on account of some curious habits; but although the missionaries have resided among them, and endeavoured to bring them within " sound of the bell," their efforts have met with a very partial and temporary success; and at this present hour, the Ottomacs are as savage in their habits, and as singular in their customs, as they were in the days of Columbus.

The Ottomacs are neither a stunted nor yet a weak race of men. Their bodies are strong, and their arms and limbs stout and muscular; but they are remarkably ill-featured, with an expression of countenance habitually stern and vindictive.

Their costume is easily described, or rather cannot be described at all, since they have *none*. Both sexes go entirely naked—if we except a little belt of three or four inches in width, made from cotton or the bark of trees, and called the *guayuco*, which they wear around the waist—but even this is worn from no motives of modesty.

What they regard in the light of a costume is a coat of paint, and about this they are as nice and particular as a Parisian dandy. Talk about "blooming-up" a faded *belle* for the ball-room, or the time spent by an exquisite in adjusting the tie of his cravat! these are trifles when compared with the lengthy and elaborate toilette of an Ottomac lady or gentleman.

The greater part of a day is often spent by them in a single dressing, with one or two helpers to assist in the operation; and this is not a *tatooing* process, intended to last for a lifetime, but a costume certain to be disfigured, or entirely washed off, at the first exposure to a heavy shower of rain. Add to this, that the pigments which are used for the purpose are by no means easily obtained : the vegetable substances which furnish them are scarce in the Ottomac country; and it costs one of these Indians the produce of several days of his labour to purchase sufficient paint to give his whole skin a single "coat." For this reason the Ottomac paints his body only on grand occasions—contenting himself at ordinary times with merely staining his face and hair.

When an Ottomac wishes to appear in "full dress" he first gives himself a "priming" of red. This consists of the dye called " annotto," which is obtained from the fruit pulp of the *Bixa orellana*, and which the Indians knew how to prepare previous to their intercourse with Europeans. Over this red ground is then formed a lattice-work of lines of black, with a dot in the centre of every little square or diamond. The black dye is the " caruto," also a vegetable pigment, obtained from the *Genipa Americana*. If the gentleman be rich enough to possess a little " chica," which is a beautiful lake-coloured red—also the produce of a plant —the *Bignonia chica*, he will then feel all the ecstatic delight of a fashionable dandy who possesses a good wardrobe; and, with half a pound of turtle-oil rubbed into his long black tresses, he will regard himself as dressed " within an inch of his life." It is not always, however, that he can afford the *chica* —for it is one of the costliest materials of which a South American savage can manufacture his suit.

The Ottomac takes far less trouble in the building of his house. Very often he builds none; but when he wishes to guard his body from the rays of the sun, or the periodical rains, he constructs him a slight edifice—a mere hut—out of saplings or bamboos, with a thatch of palm-leaves.

His arms consist of the universal bow-and-arrows, which he manages with much dexterity; and he has also a harpoon which he employs in killing the manatee and the alligator. He has, besides, several other weapons, to aid him in the chase and fishing—the latter of which forms his principal employment as well as his chief source of subsistence.

The Ottomac belongs to one of those tribes of Indians termed by the Spanish missionaries *Indios andantes*, that is " wandering," or " vagabond Indians," who, instead of remaining in fixed and permanent villages, roam about from place to place, as necessity or inclination dictates. Perhaps this arises from the peculiarity of the country which they inhabit: for the *Indios andantes* do not live in the thick forests, but upon vast treeless savannas, which stretch along the Orinoco above its great bend. In these tracts the "juvia" trees (*bertholletia* and *lecythys*), which produce the delicious " Brazil nuts"— and other plants that supply the savage spontaneously with food, are sparsely found; and as the savannas are annually inundated for several months, the Ottomac is forced, whether he will or no, to shift his quarters and try for subsistence elsewhere. When the inundations have subsided and the waters become settled enough to permit of fishing, the Otto-

mac "winter" is over, and he can obtain food in
plenty from the alligators, the manatees, the turtles,
the *toninas* or dolphins, and other large fish that
frequent the great stream upon which he dwells.
Of these the *manatee* is the most important in the
eyes of the Ottomac—as it is the largest in size,
and consequently furnishes him with the greatest
amount of meat.

This singular semi-cetaceous creature is almost too
well known to require description. It is found in
nearly all the large rivers of tropical America, where
it feeds upon the grass and aquatic plants growing
along their banks. It is known by various names,
according to the place and people. The Spaniards
call it *vaca marina*, or "sea-cow," and the Portuguese *peixe boi*, or "fish-ox"—both being appellations equally inappropriate, and having their origin
in a slight resemblance which there exists between
the animal's "countenance" and that of an ox.

The West Indian name is the one we have given,
though the true orthography is *manati*, not *manatee*, since the word is of Indian origin. Some writers deny this, alleging that it is a derivative from
the Spanish word "mano," a hand, signifying,
therefore, the fish with hands—in allusion to the
rudimentary hands which form one of its distin-
guishing characteristics. This is the account of the
historian Oviedo, but another Spanish missionary,
Father Gili, offers a more correct explanation of the
name—in fact, he proves what is neither more nor
less than the simple truth, that "manati" was the
name given to this animal by the natives of Hayti
and Cuba—where a species is also found—and the
word has no reference whatever to the "hands" of
the creature. The resemblance to the Spanish word
which should signify "handed," is merely an accidental circumstance; and, as the acute Humboldt

Q

very justly remarks, according to the genius of the Spanish language, the word thus applied would have been written *manudo*, or *manon*, and not *manati*.

The Indians have almost as many different names for this creature as there are rivers in which it is found; but its appellation in the "lingo ageral" of the great Amazon valley, is "juarua." Among the Ottomacs it is called the "apoia." It may be safely affirmed that there are several species of this amphibious animal in the rivers of tropical America; and possibly no one of them is identical with that of the West Indies. All have hitherto been regarded as belonging to the same species, and described under the scientific title of *Manatus Americanus*— a name given to the American manati, to distinguish it from the "lamantin" of Africa, and the "dugong" of the East Indian seas. But the West Indian species appears to have certain characteristic differences, which shows that it is a separate one, or, at all events, a variety. It is of much larger size than those of the South American rivers generally are—though there also a large variety is found, but much rarer than those commonly captured by the fishermen. The West Indian manati has nails well developed upon the outer edge of its fins, or fore-arms; while those on the other kinds are either not seen at all, or only in a very rudimentary state. That there are different species, may be deduced from the accounts of the natives, who employ themselves in its capture: and the observations of such people are usually more trustworthy than the speculations of learned anatomists. The Amazon fishermen all agree in the belief that there are three kinds of manati in the Amazon and its numerous tributaries, that not only differ greatly in size—from seven to twenty feet long—and in weight, from 400 to 2,000 lbs.—but also in the color of their skin, and

the shape of their tails and fins. The species found
in the Orinoco, and called "apoia" by the Ottomacs, is usually about twelve feet in length, and
weighs from 500 to 800 lbs.; but now and then a
much larger individual is captured, perhaps owing
to a greater age, or other accidental circumstance.
Humboldt heard of one that weighed 8,000 lbs.;
and the French naturalist D'Orbigny speaks of one
killed in the Bolivian waters of the Amazon that
was twenty feet in length. This size is often attained by the *Manatus Americanus* of Cuba and
Hayti.

The manati is shaped somewhat like a huge seal,
and has certain resemblances to a fish. Its body is
of an oval oblong, with a large flat rounded tail, set
horizontally, and which serves as a rudder to direct
its course in the water. Just behind its shoulders
appear, instead of fins, a pair of flippers, which have
a certain resemblance to hands set on to the body
without arms. Of these it avails itself, when creeping against the bank, and the female also uses them
in carrying her young. The mammæ (for it must
be remembered that this creature is a mammiferous
animal) are placed just below and behind the flippers. The muzzle is blunt, with thick lips—the upper projecting several inches beyond the lower, and
covered with a delicate epidermis: showing evidently that it avails itself of this prominence—which
possesses a keen sense of touch—just as the elephant of his proboscis. The lips are covered with
bristles, or beard, which impart a kind of human-
like expression to the animal's countenance—a circumstance more observable in the "dugongs" of
the Oriental waters. "Woman-fish," too, these
have been called, and no doubt such creatures, along
with the seals and walruses, have given rise to many
a story of sirens and mermaids. The "cow-face,"

however, from which the **manati** obtains its Spanish
and Portuguese epithets, **is the most** characteristic;
and **in** its food **we find a still** greater analogy to the
bovine quadruped **with** which **it is** brought in comparison.   **Beyond this the resemblance ceases.**   The
body is **that of a seal; but** instead **of being** covered with **hair,** as the cetaceous animal, **the** manati
has **a smooth** skin that resembles india-rubber more
than **anything** else.   A few short hairs are set here
and there, but they are scarce observable.   The
colour of the manati **is** that of lead, with a few mot-
tlings of a pinkish-**white** hue upon the belly; but in
this respect there **is no** uniformity.   **Some** are seen
with the whole under-parts of a uniform cream-col-
our.

The lungs of **this** animal present a peculiarity
worthy of being **noted.**   They are very voluminous
—being sometimes three feet in length, and **of such**
a porous **and elastic** nature **as to** be capable of immense extension.   **When blown** out, they present
the appearance of great swimming bladders; and
it is by means of this capacity for containing air
that the manati is enabled to remain so long under
water—though, like the true *cetaceæ*, it requires to
come at intervals **to** the surface to obtain breath.

The **flesh** of the manati is eaten by all the tribes
of Indians **who** can procure it—though by some it
is more highly esteemed than by others.   It was
once **much** relished in the colonial settlements of
Guiana and the West Indies, and form**ed** a considerable article **of commerce; but in these** quarters
manatis have **grown scarce—**from the incessant
persecution **of the fishermen.**   The flesh has been
deemed unwholesome by some, and apt to produce
fevers; **but** this is **not** the general opinion.   It has
a greater resemblance to pork than beef—though it
be the flesh of a cow—and is very savoury when

fresh, though neither is it bad eating when salted
or dried in the sun. In this way it will keep for
several months; and it has always been a stock article with the monks of the South American missions
—who, in spite of its mammiferous character, find
it convenient, during the days of Lent, to regard it
as a *fish!* The skin of the manati is of exceeding
thickness—on the back an inch and a half at least,
though it becomes thinner as it approaches the
under-parts of the body. It is cut into slips which
serve various purposes, as for shields, cordage, and
whips. "These whips of manati leather," says
Humboldt, "are a cruel instrument of punishment
for the unhappy slaves, and even for the Indians of
the missions, though, according to the laws, the latter ought to be treated as freemen."

Another valuable commodity obtained from this
animal is oil, known in the missions as manati-butter
(*manteca de manati*). This is produced by the
layer of pure fat, of an inch and a half in thickness,
which, lying immediately under the skin, envelops
the whole body of the animal. The oil is used for
lamps in the mission churches; but among the Indians themselves it is also employed in the *cuisine*
—as it has not that fetid smell peculiar to the oil
of whales and salt-water cetaceæ.

The food of the manati is grass exclusively, which
it finds on the banks of the lakes and rivers it fre-
quents. Of this it will eat an enormous quantity;
and its usual time of browsing is at night—though
this habit may have arisen from its observance of
the fact, that night is the safest time to approach
the shore. In those places, where it has been left
undisturbed, it may be often seen browsing by day.

I have been thus particular in my account of this
animal, because it is more nearly connected with
the history of Ottomac habits than perhaps that of

any other tribe of South American Indians—the
Guamos alone excepted, who may themselves be regarded as merely a branch of the Ottomac family.
Though, as already remarked, all the tribes who
dwell upon manati rivers pursue this creature and
feed upon its flesh, yet in no other part of South
America is this species of fishery so extensively or
so dexterously carried on as among the Ottomacs
and Guamos—the reason being, that, amidst the
great grassy savannas which characterize the Ottomac country, there are numerous streams and lagoons that are the favourite haunts of this herbiv-
orous animal.   In one river in particular, so great a
number are found that it has been distinguished by
the appellation of the *Rio de Manatis* (river of
manatis).   The manati, when undisturbed, is gregarious in its habits, going in troops (or "herds," if
we preserve the analogy) of greater or less numbers, and keeping the young "calves" in the centre,
which the mothers guard with the tenderest affection.   So attached are the parents to their young,
that if the calf be taken, the mother can be easily
approached; and the devotion is reciprocated on
the filial side; since in cases where the mother has
been captured and dragged ashore, the young one
has often been known to follow the lifeless body up
to the very bank!

As the manati plays such an important part in
the domestic economy of the Ottomacs, of course
the capturing of this animal is carried on upon the
grandest scale among these people, and, like the
"harvest of turtle eggs," hereafter to be described,
the manati fishery has its particular *season*.   Some
writers have erroneously stated this season as being
the period of inundation, and when the water is at
its maximum height.   This is quite contrary to the
truth; since that period, both on the Amazon and

Orinoco rivers, is just the time when all **kinds** of fishing is difficult and precarious. Then is the true winter—the "blue months" of the South American river Indians; and it is then, as will presently be seen, that the Ottomac comes nearest the point **of** starvation—which he approaches every year of **his** life.

There are manati **and** other kinds of fish taken at all times **of the** year; **but** the true season of the manati-fishing is when the waters of the great flood have considerably subsided, and are still continuing to diminish rapidly. When the inundation is at its height the manati passes out of the channel current of the great river, and in search of grass it finds its way into the lakes and surrounding marshes, remaining there to browse along their banks. When the flood is rapidly passing away from it, it begins to find itself a "little out of its element," and just then is the time when it is most easily captured.

Sometimes the Indians assemble in a body with their canoes, forming a large fleet; and, proceeding to the best haunts of the "cow-fish," carry on the fishery in a wholesale manner. The monks of the missions also head the *tame* tribes on these expeditions—as they **do** when collecting the eggs of the turtle—and a **regular** systematic course is carried **on** under the eye **of** discipline and authority. A camp **is** formed **at some convenient** place **on the** shore. Scaffolds **are** erected for sun-drying **the** flesh and skins; and vessels and other utensils brought upon the ground to render the fat into oil. The manatis that have been captured are all brought in **the** canoes to this central point, and delivered up to be "*flensed*," cured, and cooked. There is the usual assemblage of small traders from Angostura and other ports on the lower Orinoco, who come to barter their Indian trinkets for the *manteca de ma-*

nati in the same manner as it will presently be seen they trade for the *manteca de tortugas.* I need not add that this is a season of joy and festivity, like the wine-gatherings and harvest-homes of the European peasantry.

The mode of capturing the manati is very similar to that employed by the Esquimaux in taking the seal, and which has been elsewhere described. There is not much danger in the fishery, for no creature could be more harmless and inoffensive than this. It makes not the slightest attempt either at defence or retaliation—though the accident sometimes occurs of a canoe being swamped or drawn under water—but this is nothing to the Ottomac Indian, who is almost as amphibious as the manati itself.

At the proper hour the fisherman starts off in search of the manati. His fishing-boat is a canoe hollowed from a single trunk, of that kind usually styled a "dugout." On perceiving the cow-fish resting upon the surface of the water, the Ottomac paddles towards it, observing the greatest caution; for although the organs of sight and hearing in this animal are, externally, but very little developed, it both hears and sees well; and the slightest suspicious noise would be a signal for it to dive under, and of course escape.

When near enough to insure a good aim, the Ottomac hurls his harpoon into the animal's body; which, after piercing the thick hide, sticks fast. To this harpoon a cord is attached, with a float, and the float remaining above water indicates the direction in which the wounded animal now endeavours to get off. When it is tired of struggling, the Indian regains the cord; and taking it in, hand over hand, draws up his canoe to the side of the fish. If it be still too lively, he repeatedly strikes it with a spear; but he does not aim to kill it outright until he has got it "aboard." Once there, he ends the creature's existence by driving a wooden plug into its nostrils, which in a moment deprives it of life.

The Ottomac now prepares himself to transport the carcase to his home; or, if fishing in company, to the common rendezvous. Perhaps he has some distance to take it, and against a current; and he finds it inconvenient to tow such a heavy and cumbrous article. To remedy this inconvenience, he adopts the expedient already mentioned, of placing the carcase in his canoe. But how does he get it there? How can a single Indian of ordinary strength raise a weight of a thousand pounds out of the water, and lift it over the gunwale of his unsteady craft? It is in this that he exhibits great cunning and address: for instead of raising the carcase above the canoe, he sinks the canoe below the carcase, by first filling the vessel nearly full of water; and then, after he has got his freight aboard, he bales out the water with his gourd-shell. He at length succeeds in adjusting his load, and then paddles homeward with his prize.

On arriving at his village—if it be to the village he takes it—he is assisted in transporting the load by others of his tribe; but he does not carry it to his own house—for the Ottomacs are true socialists, and the produce of both the chase and the fishery is the common property of all. The chief of the village, seated in front of his hut, receives all that is brought home, and distributes it out to the various heads of families—giving to each in proportion to the number of mouths that are to be fed.

The manati is flayed—its thick hide, as already observed, serving for many useful purposes; the strata of fat, or "blubber," which lies beneath is removed, to be converted into oil; and finally, the flesh, which is esteemed equal to pork, both in delicacy and flavour, is cut into thin slices, either to be broiled or eaten **at the time, or** to be preserved for **a** future occasion, **not by salt, of which** the Ottomac is entirely ignorant, but by drying **in the** sun and smoking over a slow fire.   Fish and the flesh of the alligator are similarly "cured;" and when **the process is carefully** done, both will keep for months.

The alligator is captured in various ways: some-**times** by a baited hook with a strong cord attached —sometimes he is killed by a stab of the harpoon-**spear,** and not unfrequently is he taken by a noose slipped over his paw, the Ottomac diving fearlessly under him **and** adjusting the snare.

Some of the Indian tribes will not eat the musky flesh of the alligator; but the Ottomacs are not thus particular.   Indeed, these people refuse scarce any article of food, however nasty or disagreeable; and it is a saying among their neighbours—the Indians of other tribes—that "nothing is too loathsome for the stomach of an Ottomac."

Perhaps the saying will be considered as perfect-**ly true** when we come to describe a species of food which these people eat, and which, for a long time, has rendered them famous—or rather infamous—under the appellation of "dirt-eaters."   Of them it may literally be said that they "eat dirt," for such, in reality, is one of their customs.

This singular practice is chiefly resorted to dur-ing those months in the **year when the rivers** swell to their greatest height, **and continue full.**   At this time all fishing ceases, **and the** Ottomac finds it dif-**ficult** to obtain a sufficiency **of** food.   To make up **for** the deficiency, **he** fills his stomach with a kind **of** unctuous clay, which he has already stored up **for** the emergency, and of which he eats about a **pound per** diem!   It does not constitute his sole diet, but often for several days together it is the only food which passes his lips! There is nothing nourishing in it—that has been proved by analysis. It merely *fills* the belly—producing a satiety, or, at least, giving some sort of relief from the pangs of hunger. Nor has it been observed that the Ottomac grows thin or unhealthy on this unnatural viand: on the contrary, he is one of the most robust and healthy of American Indians.

The earth which the Ottomac eats goes by the name of *poya*. He does not eat clay of every kind: only a peculiar sort which he finds upon the banks of streams. It is soft and smooth to the touch, and unctuous, like putty. In its natural state it is of a yellowish-grey colour; but, when hardened before the fire, it assumes a tinge of red, owing to the oxide of iron which is in it.

It was for a long time believed that the Ottomac mixed this clay with cassava and turtle oil, or some other sort of nutritive substance. Even Father Gumilla—who was credulous enough to believe almost anything—could not "swallow" the story of the clay in its natural state, but believed that it was prepared with some combination of farinha or fat. This, however, is not the case. It is a pure earth, containing (according to the analysis of Vauquelin) silex and alumina, with three or four per cent. of lime!

This clay the Ottomac stores up, forming it into balls of several inches in diameter; which, being slightly hardened before the fire, he builds into little pyramids, just as cannon-balls are piled in an arsenal or fortress. When the Ottomac wishes to eat of the *poya*, he softens one of the balls by wetting it; and then, scraping off as much as he may require for his meal, returns the *poya* to its place on the pyramid.

The dirt-eating does not entirely end with the falling of the waters. This practice has begot a craving for it; and the Ottomac is not contented without a little *poya*, even when more nutritious food may be obtained in abundance.

This habit of eating earth is not exclusively Otto-mac. Other kindred tribes indulge in it, though not to so great an extent; and we find the same unnatural practice among the savages of New Caledonia and the Indian archipelago. It is also common on the west coast of Africa. Humboldt believed it to be exclusively a tropical habit. In this the great philosopher was in error, since it is known to be practised by some tribes of northern Indians on the frigid banks of the Mackenzie River.

When the floods subside, as already stated, the Ottomac lives better. Then he can obtain both fish and turtles in abundance. The former he captures, both with hooks and nets, or shoots with his arrows, when they rise near the surface.

The turtles of the Ottomac rivers are of two kinds: the *arau* and *terecay*. The former is the one most sought after, as being by far the largest. It is nearly a yard across the back, and weighs from fifty to a hundred pounds. It is a shy creature, and would be difficult to capture, were it not for a habit it has of raising its head above the surface of the water, and thus exposing the soft part of its throat to the Indian's arrow. Even then an arrow might fail to kill it; but the Ottomac takes care to have the point well coated with *curare* poison, which in a few seconds does its work, and secures the death of the victim.

The *terecay* is taken in a different and still more ingenious manner. This species, floating along the surface, or even when lying still, presents no mark at which a shaft can be aimed with the slightest chance of success. The sharpest arrow would glance off its flat shelly back as from a surface of steel. In order, therefore, to reach the vitals of his victim, the Indian adopts an expedient, in which he exhibits a dexterity and skill that are truly remarkable.

He aims his shaft, not at the turtle, but up into the air, describing by its course a parabolic curve, and so calculating its velocity and direction that it will drop perpendicularly, point foremost, upon the back of the unsuspecting swimmer, and pierce through the shell right into the vital veins of its body!

It is rare that an Indian will fail in hitting such a mark; and, both on the Orinoco and Amazon, thousands of turtles are obtained in this manner.

The great season of Ottomac festivity and rejoicing, however, is that of the *cosecha detortugas*, or "turtle crop." As has been already observed, in relation to the manati fishery, it is to him what the harvest-home is to the nations of northern Europe, or the wine-gathering to those of the south; for this is more truly the character of the *cosecha*. It is then that he is enabled, not only to procure a supply of turtle-oil with which to lubricate his hair and skin, but he obtains enough of this delicious grease wherewith to fry his dried slices of manati, and a surplus for sale to the turtle-traders from the Lower Orinoco. In this petty commerce no coin is required; harpoon-spears, and arrow-heads of iron, rude knives, and hatchets; but, above all, a few cakes of *annotto*, *chica*, and *caruto*, are bartered in exchange for the turtle-oil. The thick hide of the manati—for making slave-whips—the spotted skin of the jaguar, and some other pelts which the chase produces, are also items of his export trade.

The pigments above mentioned have already

been procured by the trader, as the *export* articles of commerce of some other tribe.

The turtle oil is the product of the eggs of the larger species—the *arau*—known simply by the name *tortuga*, or turtle. The eggs of the *terecay* would serve equally as well; but, from a difference in the habit of this animal, its eggs cannot be obtained in sufficient quantity for oil-making. There is no such thing as a grand "cosecha" or crop of them—for the creature is not gregarious, like its congener, but each female makes her nest apart from the others, in some solitary place, and there brings forth her young brood. Not but that the nests of the *terecay* are also found and despoiled of their eggs—but this only occurs at intervals; and as the contents of a single nest would not be sufficient for a "churning," no "butter" can be made of them. They are, therefore, gathered to be used only as *eggs*, and not as *butter*.

The *arau*, on the other hand, although not gregarious under ordinary circumstances, becomes pre-eminently so during the "laying season." Then all the turtles in the Orinoco and its tributaries collect into three or four vast gangs—numbering in all over a million of individuals—and proceed to certain points of rendezvous which they have been in the habit of visiting from time immemorial. These common breeding-places are situated between the cataracts of the river and the great bend, where it meets the Apure; and are simply broad beaches of sand, rising with a gentle slope from the edge of the water, and extending for miles along the bank. There are some small rookeries on tributary streams, but the three most noted are upon the shores of the main river, between the points already indicated. That frequented by the Ottomacs is upon an island, at the mouth of the Uruana river, upon which these people principally dwell.

The laying season of the *arau* turtle varies in the different rivers of tropical America—occurring in the Amazon and its tributaries at a different period from that of the Orinoco. It is regulated by the rise, or rather the fall of the inundations; and takes place when the waters, at their lowest stage, have laid bare the low sand-banks upon the shores. This occurs (in the Orinoco) in March, and early in this month the great assemblages are complete. For weeks before, the turtles are seen, in all parts of the river near the intended breeding-places, swimming about on the surface, or basking along the banks. As the sun grows stronger, the desire of depositing their eggs increases—as though the heat had something to do with their fecundation. For some time before the final action, the creatures may be seen ranged in a long line in front of the breeding-place, with their heads and necks held high above the water, as if contemplating their intended nursery, and calculating the dangers to which they may be exposed. It is not without reason that they may dwell upon these. Along the beach stalks the lordly jaguar, waiting to make a meal of the first that may set his foot on terra firma, or to fill his stomach with the delicious "new-laid" eggs. The ugly alligator, too, is equally *friand* of a gigantic omelette; and not less so the "garzas" (white cranes), and the "zamuros" (black vultures), who hover in hundreds in the air. Here and there, too, may be observed an Indian sentinel, keeping as much as possible out of sight of the turtles themselves, but endeavouring to drive off all other enemies whose presence may give them fear. Should a canoe or boat appear upon the river, it is warned by these sentinels to keep well off from the phalanx of the turtles—lest these should be disturbed or alarmed—for the Indian well knows that if anything should occur to produce a panic among the araus, his *cosecha* would be very much shortened thereby.

When at length the turtles have had sun enough to warm them to the work, they crawl out upon the dry sand-beach, and the laying commences. It is at night that the operation is carried on: for then their numerous enemies—especially the vultures—are less active. Each turtle scoops out a hole, of nearly a yard in diameter and depth; and having therein deposited from fifty to one hundred eggs, it covers them up with the sand, smoothing the surface, and treading it firmly down. Sometimes the individuals are so crowded as to lay in one another's nests, breaking many of the eggs, and causing an inextricable confusion; while the creaking noise of their shells rubbing against each other may be heard afar off, like the rushing of a cataract. Sometimes a number that have arrived late, or have been slow at their work, continue engaged in it till after daybreak, and even after the Indians have come upon the ground—whose presence they no longer regard. Impelled by the instinct of philoprogenitiveness, these "mad turtles," as the Indians call them, appear utterly regardless of danger, and make no effort to escape from it; but are turned over on their backs, or killed upon the spot without difficulty.

The beach being now deserted by the turtles, the egg-gatherers proceed to their work. As there are usually several tribes who claim a share in the *cosecha*, the ground is measured out, and partitioned among them. The regularity with which the nests are placed, and the number of eggs in each being pretty nearly the same, an average estimate of the quantity under a given surface is easily made. By means of a pointed stick thrust into the sand, the outline of the deposit is ascertained—usually running along the beach in a strip of about thirty yards in breadth.

When the allotments are determined, the work of oil-making begins—each tribe working by itself, and upon the social system. The covering of sand is removed, and the eggs placed in baskets, which are then emptied into large wooden troughs, as a common receptacle. The canoes, drawn up on the sand, are frequently made to do duty as troughs. When a sufficient number of eggs have been thrown in, they are broken and pounded together, and whipped about, as if intended for a gigantic omelette. Water is added, and then the mixture is put into large caldrons, and boiled until the oil comes to the top; after which it is carefully skimmed off and poured into earthen jars ("botigas"), provided by the traders.

It takes about two weeks to complete the operations, during which time many curious scenes occur. The sand swarms with young turtles about as big as a dollar, which have been prematurely hatched; and have contrived to crawl out of the shell. These are chased in all directions, and captured by the little naked Ottomacs, who devour them "body, bones, and all," with as much gusto as if they were gooseberries. The cranes and vultures, and young alligators too, take a part in this by-play—for the offspring of the poor arau has no end of enemies.

When the oil is all boiled and bottled, the trader displays his tempting wares, and makes the best market he can; and the savage returns to his palm-hut village—taking with him the articles of exchange and a few baskets of eggs, which he has reserved for his own eating; and so ends the *cosecha de tortugas*.

·R

It is in this season that the Ottomac indulges most in good living, and eats the smallest quantity of dirt. The waters afford him abundance of fish and turtle-flesh, beef from the sea-cow, and steaks from the tail of the alligator. He has his turtle and manati butter, in which to fry all these dainties, and also to lubricate his hair and skin.

He can dress too, " within an inch of his life," having obtained for his oil a fresh supply of the precious pigments. He indulges, moreover, in fits of intoxication, caused by a beverage made from maize or manioc root; but oftener produced by a species of snuff which he inhales into his nostrils. This is the *niopo*, manufactured from the leaves of a *mimosa*, and mixed with a kind of lime, which last is obtained by burning a shell of the genus *helix*, that is found in the waters of the Orinoco. The effect of the *niopo* resembles that produced by chewing *betel*, tobacco, opium, or the narcotic *coca* of Peru. When freely taken, a species of intoxication or rather mania is produced; but this snuff and its effects are more minutely described elsewhere. It is here introduced because, in the case of the Ottomac, the drug often produces most baneful consequences. During the continuance of his intoxication the Ottomac is quarrelsome and disorderly. He picks a hole in the coat of his neighbour; but if there chance to be any " old sore" between him and a rival, the vindictive feeling is sure to exhibit itself on these occasions; and not unfrequently ends in an encounter, causing the death of one or both of the combatants. These duels are not fought either with swords or pistols, knives, clubs, nor any similar weapons. The destruction of the victim is brought about in a very different manner; and is the result of a very slight scratch which he has received during the fight from the *nail* of his antagonist. That a wound of so trifling a nature should prove mortal would be **something very** mysterious, did we not know that **the nail which** inflicted that scratch **has been already enfiltrated with** *curare*— one of the deadliest of vegetable poisons, **which the** Ottomac understands how to prepare in its **most** potent and virulent form.

Should it ever be your unfortunate fate, therefore, **to** get into **a** " scrimmage" with an Ottomac Indian, you must remember to keep clear of his " claws !"

THE COMANCHES, OR PRAIRIE INDIANS.

YOUNG reader, I need scarce tell you that the noblest of animals—the horse—is not indigenous to America. You already know that when Columbus discovered the New World, no animal of the horse kind was found there; and yet the geologist has proved incontestably that at one time horses existed in the New World—at a period too, geologically speaking, not very remote. The fossilized bones examined by one of the most accomplished of modern travellers—Dr. Darwin—establish this truth beyond a doubt.

The horse that at present inhabits America, though not indigenous, has proved a flourishing exotic. Not only in a domestic state has he increased in numbers, but he has in many places escaped from the control of man, and now runs wild upon the great plains both of North and South America. Although you may find in America almost every "breed" of horses known in Europe, yet the great majority belong to two very distinct kinds. The first of these is the large English horse, in his different varieties, imported by the Anglo-Americans, and existing almost exclusively in the woodland territory of the United States. The second kind is the Andalusian-Arab—the horse of the Spanish conquerors,—a much smaller breed than the English-Arabian, but quite equal to him in mettle and beauty of form. It is the Andalusian horse that is found throughout all Spanish America,—it is he that has

multiplied to such a wonderful extent,—it is he that has " run wild."

That the horse in his normal state is a dweller upon open plains, is proved by his habits in America—for in no part where the forest predominates is he found wild — only upon the prairies of the north, and the llanos and pampas of the south, where a timbered tract forms the exception.

He must have found these great steppes congenial to his natural disposition — since, only a very short time after the arrival of the Spaniards in the New World, we find the horse a runaway from civilization—not only existing in a wild state upon the prairies, but in possession of many of the Indian tribes.

It would be an interesting inquiry to trace the change of habits which the possession of the horse must have occasioned among these Arabs of the Western world. However hostile they may have been to his European rider, they must have welcomed the horse as a friend. No doubt they admired the bold, free spirit of the noble animal, so analogous to their own nature. He and they soon became inseparable companions; and have continued so from that time to the present hour. Certain it is that the prairie, or " horse-Indians" of the present day, are in many respects essentially different from the staid and stoical sons of the forest so often depicted in romances; and almost equally certain is it, that the possession of the horse has contributed much to bring about this dissimilarity. It could not be otherwise. With the horse new habits were introduced—new manners and customs—new modes of thought and action. Not only the chase, but war itself, became a changed game—to be played in an entirely different manner.

We shall not go back to inquire what these Indians *were* when afoot. It is our purpose only to describe what they *are* now that they are on horseback. Literally, may we say *on horseback ;* for, unless at this present writing they are asleep, we may safely take it for granted they are upon the backs of their horses—young and old of them, rich and poor—for there is none of them so poor as not to be the master of a "mustang" steed.

In "Prairie-land" every tribe of Indians is in possession of the horse. On the north the Crees, Crows, and Blackfeet, the Sioux, Cheyennes, and Arapahoes; on the plains of the Platte, the Kansas, and Osage, we find the Pawnees, the Kansas, and Osages—all horse-Indians. West of the great mountain-range, the Apache is mounted: so likewise the Utah, the Navajo, and the Snake, or Shoshonee — the latter rather sparingly. Other tribes, to a greater or less degree, possess this valuable animal; but the true type of the "horse-Indian is to be found in the Comanche, the lord of that wide domain that extends from the Arkansas to the Rio Grande. He it is who gives trouble to the frontier colonists of Texas, and equally harasses the Spanish settlements of New Mexico; he it is who carries his forays almost into the heart of New Spain—even to the gates of the populous Durango.

Regarding the Comanche, then, as the type of the horse-Indians, we shall speak more particularly of him. Allowing for some slight difference in the character of his climate and country, his habits and customs will be found not very dissimilar to those of the other tribes who make the prairie their home.

To say that the Comanche is the finest horseman in the world would be to state what is not the fact. He is not more excellent in this accomplishment than his neighbour and bitter foeman, the Pawnee —no better than the "vaquero" of California, the

" ranchero" of Mexico, the "llanero" of Venezuela, the "gaucho" of Buenos Ayres, and the horse-Indians of the "Gran Chaco" of Paraguay, of the Pampas, and Patagonia. He is *equal*, however, to any of these, and that is saying enough—in a word, that he takes rank among the finest horsemen in the world.

The Comanche is on horseback almost from the hour of infancy—transferred, as it were, from his mother's arms to the withers of a mustang. When able to walk, he is scarce allowed to practise this natural mode of progression, but performs all his movements on the back of a horse. A Comanche would no more think of making a journey afoot—even if it were only to the distance of a few hundred yards—than he would of crawling upon his hands and knees. The horse, ready saddled and bridled, stands ever near—it differs little whether there is either saddle or bridle—and flinging himself on the animal's back, or his neck, or his croup, or hanging suspended along his side, the Indian guides him to the destined spot, usually at a rapid gallop. It is of no consequence to the rider how fast the horse may be going: it will not hinder him from mounting or dismounting at will. At any time, by clutching the mane, he can spring upon the horse's shoulders—just as may be often seen in the arena of a circus.

The horse-Indian is a true type of the *nomadic* races—a dweller in tents, which his four-footed associate enables him to transport from place to place with the utmost facility. Some of the tribes, however, and even some of the Comanches, have fixed residences, or "villages," where at a certain season of the year they—or rather their women—cultivate the maize, the pumpkin, the melon, the calabash, and a few other species of plants—all being vegetable products indigenous to their country. No doubt, before the arrival of Europeans, this cultivation was carried on more extensively than at present; but the possession of the horse has enabled the prairie tribes to dispense with a calling which they cordially contemn : the calling of the husbandman.

These misguided savages, one and all, regard agricultural pursuits as unworthy of men ; and wherever necessity compels them to practise them, the work falls to the lot of the women and slaves—for be it known that the Comanche is a slave-owner ; and holds in bondage not only Indians of other tribes, but also a large number of mestizoes and whites of the Spanish race, captured during many a sanguinary raid into the settlements of Mexico ! It would be easy to show that it is this false pride of being hunters and warriors, with its associated aversion for an agricultural life, that has thinned the numbers of the Indian race—far more than any persecutions they have endured at the hands of the white man. This it is that starves them, that makes unendurable neighbours of them, and has rendered it necessary in some instances to " civilize them off the face of the earth."

But they are not yet all civilized from off the face of the earth ; nor is it their destiny to disappear so readily as short-seeing prophets have declared. Their idle habits and internecine wars have done much to thin their numbers—far more than the white man's hostility—but wherever the white man has stepped in and put a stop to their tribal contentions—wherever he has succeeded in conquering their aversion to industrial pursuits—the Indian is found not only to hold his ground, but to increase rapidly in numbers. This is the case with many tribes—Creeks, Choctaws, and Cherokees—so that I can promise you, young reader, that by the time you get to be an old man, there will be as many Indians in the world as upon that day when Columbus first set his foot upon " Cat" Island.

You will be inquiring how the horse could render the prairie Indian more independent of agriculture? The answer is simple. With this valuable auxiliary a new mode of subsistence was placed within his reach. An article of food, which he had hitherto been able to obtain only in a limited quantity, was now procurable in abundance—the flesh of the buffalo.

The prairies of North America have their own peculiarities. They are not stocked with large droves of ruminant animals, as the plains of Southern Africa—where the simplest savage may easily obtain a dinner of flesh-meat. A few species of deer, thinly distributed—all swift, shy animals—the pronghorn antelope, still swifter and shier—and the " bighorn," shiest of all—were the only ruminants of prairie-land, with the exception of the great bison, or buffalo, as he is generally called. But even this last was not so easily captured in those days. The bison, though not a swift runner, is yet more than a match for the biped man; and though the Indian might steal upon the great drove, and succeed in bringing down a few with his arrows, it was not always a sure game. Moreover, afoot, the hunter could not follow the buffalo in its grand migrations —often extending for hundreds of miles across plains, rivers, and ravines. Once mounted, the circumstances became changed. The Indian hunter could not only overtake the buffalo, but ride round him at will, and pursue him, if need be, to the most distant parts of prairie-land. The result, therefore, of the introduction of the horse was a plentiful supply of buffalo-meat, or, when that failed, the flesh of the horse himself—upon which two articles of diet the prairie Indian has almost exclusively subsisted ever since.

The Comanche **has several modes of** hunting the buffalo. If alone, and he wishes to make a grand *coup*, he will leave his horse at a distance—the animal being trained to remain where his master has left him. The hunter then approaches the herd with great caution, keeping to leeward—lest he might be "winded" by the old sentinel bulls who keep watch. Should there be no cover to shelter the approach of the hunter, the result would be that the bulls would discover him; and, giving out their bellow of alarm, cause the others to scamper off.

To guard against this, the Indian has already prepared himself by adopting a *ruse*—which consists in disguising himself in the skin of a buffalo, horns and all complete, and approaching the herd, as if he were some stray individual that had been left behind, and was just on the way to join its fellows. Even the motions of the buffalo, when browsing, are closely imitated by the red hunter; and, unless the wind be in favour of his being scented by the bulls, this device will insure the success of a shot. Sometimes the skin of the large whitish-grey wolf is used in this masquerade with equal success. This may appear singular, since the animal itself is one of the deadliest enemies of the buffalo: a large pack of them hanging on the skirts of every herd, and patiently waiting for an opportunity to attack it. But as this attack is only directed against the younger calves—or some disabled or decrepit individual who may lag behind—the strong and healthy ones have no fear of the wolves, and permit them to squat upon the prairie within a few feet of where they are browsing! Indeed, they could not hinder them, even if they wished: as the long-legged wolf in a few springs can easily get out of the way of the more clumsy ruminant; and therefore does not dread the lowering frontlet of the most shaggy and ill-tempered bull in the herd.

Of course the hunter, in the guise of a wolf, obtains the like privilege of close quarters; and, when he has arrived at the proper distance for his purpose, he prepares himself for the work of destruction. The bow is the weapon he uses—though the rifle is now a common weapon in the hands of many of the horse-Indians. But the bow is preferred for the species of "still hunting" here described. The first crack of a rifle would scatter the gang, leaving the hunter perhaps only an empty gun for his pains; while an arrow at such close quarters is equally as deadly in its effect; and, being a *silent* weapon, no alarm is given to any of the buffaloes, except that one which has felt the deadly shaft passing through its vitals.

Often the animal thus shot—even when the wound is a mortal one—does not immediately fall; but sinks gradually to the earth, as if lying down for a rest. Sometimes it gets only to its knees, and dies in this attitude; at other times it remains a long while upon its legs, spreading its feet widely apart, as if to prop itself up, and then rocking from side to side like a ship in a ground-swell, till at last, weakened by loss of blood, it yields its body to the earth. Sometimes the struggles of a wounded individual cause the herd to "stampede," and then the hunter has to content himself with what he may already have shot; but not unfrequently the unsuspicious gang keeps the ground, till the Indian has emptied his quiver. Nay, longer than that: for it often occurs that the disguised buffalo or wolf (as the case may be) approaches the bodies of those that have fallen, recovers some of his arrows, and uses them

a second time with like deadly effect; for this purpose it is his practice, if the aim and distance favour
him, to send his **shaft clear** through the body of the
bison, in order that the barb may not hinder it from
being extracted on the other side! This feat is by
no means of uncommon occurrence among the buf-
falo-hunters of the prairies.

Of course, a grand wholesale slaughter of the
kind just described is not an every-day matter;
and can only be accomplished when the buffaloes
are in a state of comparative rest, or browsing
slowly. More generally they detect the dangerous
counterfeit in time to save their skins; or else keep
moving too rapidly for the hunter to follow them
on foot. His only resource, then, is to ride rapidly
up on horseback, fire his arrows without dismounting, or strike the victim with his long lance while
galloping side by side with it. If in this way he
can obtain two or three fat cows, before his horse
becomes *blown*, or the herd scatters beyond his
reach, he considers that he has had good success.

But in this kind of chase the hunter is rarely
alone: the whole tribe takes part in it; and, mounted on their well-trained mustangs, often pursue the
buffalo gangs for an hour or more, before the latter
can get off and hide themselves in the distance, or
behind the swells of the prairie. The clouds of dust
raised in a *mêlée* of this kind often afford the buffalo
a chance of escaping—especially when they are running *with* the wind.

A "buffalo surround" is effected by a large party
of hunters riding to a great distance; deploying
themselves into a circle around the herd; and then
galloping inward with loud yells. The buffaloes
thus attacked on all sides, become frightened and
confused, and are easily driven into a close-packed
mass—around the edges of which the mounted

hunters wheel and deliver their arrows, or strike those that try to escape, with their long spears. Sometimes the infuriated bulls rush upon the horses, and gore them to death; and the hunters, thus dismounted, often run a narrow risk of meeting with the same fate—more than a risk, for not unfrequently they are killed outright. Often are they obliged to leap up on the croup of a companion's horse, to get out of the way of danger; and many instances are recorded where a horseman, by the stumbling of his horse, has been pitched right into the thick of the herd, and has made his escape by mounting on the backs of the bulls themselves, and leaping from one to another until he has reached clear ground again.

The buffalo is never captured in a " pound," as large mammalia are in many countries. He is too powerful a creature to be imprisoned by anything but the strongest stockade fence; and for this the prairie country does not afford materials. A contrivance, however, of a somewhat similar character is occasionally resorted to by various tribes of Indians. When it is known that the buffaloes have become habituated to range in any part of the country, where the plain is intersected by deep ravines —*cañons*, or *barrancas*, as they are called,—then a grand *battue* is got up by driving the animals pell-mell over the precipitous bluffs, which universally form the sides of these singular ravines. To guide the herd to the point where it is intended they should take the fatal leap, a singular contrivance is resorted to. This consists in placing two rows of objects—which appear to the buffalo to be human beings—in such a manner that one end of each row abuts upon the edge of the precipice, not very distant from the other, while the lines extend far out into the plain, until they have diverged into a wide and extensive funnel. **It is** simply the contrivance used for guiding **animals into a** pound ; but, instead of a pair of close log **fences,** the objects forming these rows **stand at a considerable** distance apart ; and, as already **stated, appear to the not** very discrimating **eye of the buffalo to be human** beings. They are in reality designed to resemble **the human form in a** rude fashion ; and the material **out of** which they are constructed is neither more **nor less than** the dung of the buffaloes themselves—the *bois de vache,* as it is called by the Canadian trappers, who often warm their shins, and roast their buffalo ribs over a fire **of this same** material.

The decoy **being thus set, the** mounted hunters next make a wide sweep around the prairie—including in their deployment such gangs of buffaloes as may be browsing between their line **and the** mouth of the funnel. **At first** the buffaloes **are** merely **guided** forward, or driven slowly **and with** caution—as **boys in snow-time often** drive larks toward **their snares. When the animals,** however, **have** entered between **the** converging lines of mock men, a rush, accompanied by hideous yells, is made upon **them** from behind : the result of which is, that they **are** impelled forward in a headlong course towards the precipice.

The buffalo is, at best, but a half-blind creature. Through the long shaggy locks hanging **over** his frontlet he sees objects in a dubious light, **or not at** all. He depends more **on** his **scent** than his sight, but though he may scent **a living enemy, the** keenness of his organ does **not warn him** of the yawning **chasm** that **opens before** him—not till **it** is too late **to retire :** for **although he** may perceive the fearful leap **before** taking it, and would willingly turn on his track, and refuse it, he finds it no longer possible to do so. In fact, he is not allowed time for reflection. The dense crowd presses from behind, and he is left no choice, except that of springing forward or suffering himself to be tumbled over upon his head. In either case it is his last leap; and, frequently, the last of a whole crowd of his companions.

With such persecutions, I need hardly say that the buffaloes are becoming scarcer every year; and it is predicted that at no distant period this really valuable mammal will be altogether extinct. At present their range is greatly contracted within the wide boundaries which it formerly occupied. Going west from the Mississippi—at any point below the mouth of the Missouri—you will not meet with buffalo for the first three hundred miles; and, though the herds formerly ranged to the south and west of the Rio Grande, the Comanches on the banks of that river no longer know the buffalo, except by their excursions to the grand prairie far to the north of their country. The Great Slave Lake is the northern terminus of the buffalo range; and westward the chain of the Rocky Mountains; but of late years stray herds have been observed at some points west of these—impelled through the passes by the hunter-pressure of the horse-Indians from the eastward. Speculators have adopted several ingenious and plausible reasons to account for the diminution of the numbers of the buffalo. There is but one cause worth assigning—a very simple one too—the horse.

With the disappearance of the buffalo—or perhaps with the thinning of their numbers,—the prairie Indians may be induced to throw aside their roving habits. This would be a happy result, both for them and their neighbours; though it is even doubtful whether it might follow from such a circumstance. No doubt some change would be effected in their mode of life; but unfortunately these Bedouins of

S

the Western world can live upon the horse, even if the buffalo were entirely extirpated. Even as it is, whole tribes of them subsist almost exclusively upon horse-flesh, which they esteem and relish more than any other food. But this resource would, in time, also fail them; for they have not the economy to raise a sufficient supply for the demand that would occur were the buffaloes once out of the way: since the *caballadas* of wild mustangs are by no means so easy to capture as the "gangs" of unwieldy and lumbering buffaloes.

It is to be hoped, however, that before the horse-Indians have been put to this trial, the strong arm of civilization shall be extended over them, and, withholding them from those predatory incursions, which they annually make into the Mexican settlements, will induce them to *dismount*, and turn peaceably to the tillage of the soil—now so successfully practised by numerous tribes of their race, who dwell in fixed and flourishing homes upon the eastern border of the prairies.

At this moment, however, the Comanches are in open hostility with the settlers of the Texan frontier. The *lex talionis* is in active operation while we write, and every mail brings the account of some sanguinary massacre, or some act of terrible retaliation. The deeds of blood and savage cruelty practised alike by both sides—whites as well as Indians—have had their parallel, it is true, but they are not the less revolting to read about. The colonists have suffered much from these Ishmaelites of the West—these lordly savages, who regard industry as a dishonourable calling; and who fancy that their vast territory should remain an idle hunting-ground, or rather a fortress, to which they might betake themselves during their intervals of war and plundering. The colonists have a clear title to the land—that title acknowledged by all right-thinking men, who believe the good of the majority must not be sacrificed to the obstinacy of the individual, or the minority—that title which gives the right to remove the dwelling of the citizen—his very castle —rather than that the public way be impeded. All admit this right; and just such a title has the Texan colonist to the soil of the Comanche. There may be guilt in the *mode* of establishing the claim,— there may have been scenes of cruelty, and blood unnecessarily spilt—but it is some consolation to know that there has occurred nothing yet to parallel in cold-blooded atrocity the annals of Algiers, or the similar acts committed in Southern Africa. The crime of *smoke-murder* is yet peculiar to Pellisier and Potgieter.

In their present outbreak, the Comanches have exhibited but a poor short-sighted policy. They will find they have committed a grand error in mistaking the courageous colonists of Texas for the weak Mexicans—with whom they have long been at war, and whom they have almost invariably conquered. The result is easily told: much blood may be shed on both sides, but it is sure to end as all such contests do; and the Comanche, like the Caffre, must " go to the wall." Perhaps it is better that things should be brought to a climax—it will certainly be better for the wretched remnant of the Spano - Americans dwelling along the Comanche frontiers—a race who for a hundred years have not known peace.

As this long-standing hostility with the Mexican nation has been a predominant feature in the history of the Comanche Indian, it is necessary to give some account of how it is usually carried on. There was a time when the Spanish nation entertained the hope of *Christianizing* these rude savages—that is, taming and training them to something of the condition to which they have brought the Aztec descendants of Montezuma—a condition scarce differing from slavery itself. As no gold or silver mines had been discovered in Texas, it was not their intention to make mine-labourers of them; but rather *peons*, or field-labourers, and tenders of cattle — precisely as they had done, and were still doing, with the tribes of California. The soldier and the sword had proved a failure—as in many other parts of Spanish America — in fact, everywhere, except among the degenerated remnants of monarchical misrule found in Mexico, Bogota, and Peru. In these countries was encountered the *débris* of a declining civilization, and not, as is generally believed, the children of a progressive development; and of course they gave way—as the people of all corrupted monarchies must in the end.

It was different with the "Indios bravos," or warrior tribes, still free and independent—the so-called *savages*. Against these the soldier and the sword proved a complete failure; and it therefore became necessary to use the other kind of conquering power—the monk and his cross. Among the Comanches this kind of conquest had attained a certain amount of success. Mission-houses sprung up through the whole province of Texas,—the Comanche country—though the new neophytes were not altogether Comanches, but rather Indians of other tribes who were less warlike. Many Comanches, however, became converts; and some of the "missiones" became establishments on a grand scale—each having, according to Spanish missionary-fashion, its "presidio," or garrison of troops, to keep the new believers within sound of the bell, and to hunt and bring them back, whenever they endeavoured to escape from that Christian vassalage for which they had too rashly exchanged their pagan freedom.

All went well, so long as Spain was a power upon the earth, and the Mexican viceroyalty was rich enough to keep the presidios stocked with troopers. The monks led as jolly a life as their prototypes of " Bolton Abbey in the olden time." The neophytes were simply their slaves, receiving, in exchange for the sweat of their brow, baptism, absolution, little pewter crucifixes, and various like valuable commodities.

But there came a time when they grew tired of the exchange, and longed for their old life of roving freedom. Their brethren had obtained the horse; and this was an additional attraction which a prairie life presented. They grew tired of the petty tricks of the Christian superstition—to their view less rational than their own—they grew tired of the toil of constant work, the childlike chastisements inflicted, and sick of the sound of that ever-clanging clapper—the bell. In fine, they made one desperate effort, and freed themselves for ever.

The grand establishment of San Saba, on the river of the same name, fell first. The troops were abroad on some convert-hunting expedition. The Comanches entered the fort—their tomahawks and war-clubs hidden under their great robes of buffalo-hide: the attack commenced, and ended only with the annihilation of the settlement.

One monk alone escaped the slaughter—a man renowned for his holy zeal. He fled towards San Antonio, pursued by a savage band. A large river coursed across the route it was necessary for him to take; but this did not intercept him: its waters opened for a moment, till the bottom was bare from bank to bank. He crossed without wetting his feet. The waves closed immediately behind him, offering an impassable barrier to his pursuers, who could only **vent** their fury in idle curses! But the monk could curse too, He had, perhaps, taken **some** lessons at the Vatican; and, turning round, he anathematized every "mother's **son**" of the red-skinned savages. The wholesale **excomm**unication produced a wonderful effect. Every one of the accursed fell back where he stood, and lay face upward upon the plain, dead as a post! The monk, after baptizing the river "Brazos de Dios" (arm of **God**), continued his flight, and reached San Antonio in safety—where he duly detailed his miraculous adventure to the credulous converts of Bejar, and the other **missions**.

Such is the supposed origin of the name Brazos de Dios, which the second river in Texas bears to this day. It is to be remarked, however, that the **river** crossed by the monk was the present Colorado, not the Brazos: for, by a curious error of the colonists, the two rivers have made an exchange of titles!

The Comanches, freed from missionary rule—and **now** equal to their adversaries by possession of the horse—forthwith commenced their plundering expeditions; and, with short intervals of truce—periods *en paz*—have continued them to the present hour. All northern and western Texas they soon recovered; but they were not content with territory; they wanted horses and cattle and chattels, and white wives and slaves; and it would scarce be credited, were I to state the number of these they have taken within the last half-century. Nearly every year they **have been in the** habit of making an expedition to the Mexican settlements of the provinces Tamaulipas, New Leon, and Chihuahua—every expedition a fresh conquest over their feeble and corrupt adversaries. On every occasion they have returned with booty, consisting of horses, cattle, sheep, household utensils, and, sad to relate, human captives. Women and children only **do** they bring back—the men they kill upon sight. The children may be either male or female—it matters not which, **as these** are to be adopted into their tribe, to become future warriors; and, strange to relate, many of these, when grown up, not only refuse to return to the land of their birth, but prove the most bitter and dangerous foes to the people from whom they have sprung! Even the girls and women, after a period, become reconciled to their new home, and no longer desire to leave it. Some, **when** afterwards discovered and ransomed by their kindred, have refused to accept the conditions, but prefer to continue the savage career into which misfortune has introduced them! Many a heart-rending scene has been the consequence of such **apparently** unnatural predilections.

You would wonder why such a state of things has been so long submitted to by a civilized people; but it is not so much to be wondered at. The selfishness that springs from constant revolutions **has** destroyed almost every sentiment of patriotism **in** the Mexican national heart; and, indeed, many **of** these captives are perhaps not much worse off under the guardianship of the brave Comanches than they would have been, exposed to the petty tyranny and robber rule that has so long existed in Mexico. Besides, it is doubtful whether the Mexican government, with all her united strength, could retake them. The Comanche country is as inaccessible to a regular army as the territory of Timbuctoo; and it will give even the powerful republic of the north no small trouble to reduce these red freebooters **to subjection.** Mexico had quite despaired of being able to make **an effort**; and in the last treaty made between her and the United States, one of the articles **was** a special agreement on the part of the latter to **restrain** the Comanches from future forays **into the Mexican** states, and also cause them to deliver up the Mexican captives then in the hands of the Indians!

It was computed that their **number at the** time amounted to 4,000! It is with regret **I** have to add, that these unfortunates are still held in **bondage.** The great republic, too busy with its own **concerns,** has not carried out the stipulations of the **treaty; and** the present Comanche war is but the **result of** this criminal negligence. Had energetic **measures been** adopted **at the close of** the Mexico-American war, **the** Comanche would not now be harrying the settlers of Texas.

To prove the incapacity of **the** Mexicans to deal with this warlike race, it only needs to consider the present condition **of** the northern Mexican states. One half **the** territory in that extensive region has returned **to the condition of a** desert. The isolated " ranchos" have been long since abandoned—the **fields are** overgrown **with** weeds—and the cattle **have** run wild, or been carried off by the Comanches. Only **the** stronger settlements and large fortified haciendas any longer exist; and many of these, too, have been deserted. Where children once played in the security of innocence—where gaily-dressed cavaliers and elegant ladies amused themselves in the pleasant *dia de campo*, such scenes are **no** longer witnessed. The rancho **is in ruins—the door** hangs upon its hinge, **broken and** battered, or has been torn off to feed **the camp-fire** of the savage; the dwelling **is empty and** silent, except when the howling wolf **or coyote** wakes up the echoes of its walls.

About ten years ago, the proud governor of the **state of** Chihuahua—one of the most energetic soldiers of the Mexican republic—had a son taken captive by the Comanches. Powerful though this man was, he knew it was idle to appeal to arms; and was only too contented to recover his child by paying a large ransom! This fact, more than a volume of words, will illustrate the condition of unhappy Mexico.

The Comanche leads a gay, merry life—he is far from being the Indian of Cooper's description. In scarcely any respect does he resemble the sombre son of the forest. He is lively, talkative, and ever ready for a laugh. His butt is the Mexican presidio soldier, whom he holds in too just contempt. He is rarely without a meal. If the buffalo fails him, he can draw a steak from his spare horses, of which he possesses a large herd: besides, there are the wild mustangs, which he can capture on occasions. He has no work to do except war and hunting: at all other times he has slaves to wait upon him, and perform the domestic drudgery. When idle, he sometimes bestows great pains upon his dress—which is the usual deer-skin tunic of the prairie Indian, with moccasins and fringed leggins. Sometimes a head-dress of plumes is worn; sometimes one of the skin of the buffalo's skull, with the horns left on! The robe of buffalo pelt hangs from his shoulders, with all the grandeur of a toga; but when he proceeds on a plundering expedition, all these fripperies are thrown aside, and his body appears naked from the waist to the ears. Then only the breech-clout is worn, with leggins and moccasins on his legs and feet. A coat of scarlet paint takes the place of the hunting-shirt—in order to render his presence more terrific in the eyes of his enemy. It needs not this. Without any disguise, the sight of him is sufficiently horrifying—sufficiently suggestive of "blood and murder."

THE PEHUENCHES, OR PAMPAS INDIANS.

THE vast plain known as the "Pampas" is one of the largest tracts of level country upon the face of the earth. East and west it stretches from the mouth of the Rio de la Plata to the foot-hills of the Andes mountains. It is interrupted on the north by a series of mountains and hill country, that cross from the Andes to the Paraguay river, forming the Sierras of Mendoza, San Luis, and Cordova; while its southern boundary is not so definitely marked, though it may be regarded as ending at the Rio Negro, where it meets, coming up from the south, the desert plains of Patagonia.

Geologically, the Pampas (or plains, as the word signifies, in the language of the Peruvian Indians) is an alluvial formation—the bed of an ancient sea—upheaved by some unknown cause to its present elevation, which is not much above the ocean-level. It is not, therefore, a *plateau* or "table-land," but a vast natural meadow. The soil is in general of a red colour, argillaceous in character, and at all points filled with marine shells and other testimonies that the sea once rolled over it. It is in the Pampas formation that many of the fossil monsters have been found—the gigantic *megatherium*, the colossal *mylodon*, and the giant armadillo (*glyptodon*), with many other creatures, of such dimensions, as to make it a subject of speculation how the earth could have produced food enough for their maintenance.

In giving to the Pampas the designation of a

vast meadow, do not suffer yourself to be misled by this phrase—which is here and elsewhere used in rather a loose and indefinite manner. Many large tracts in the Pampas country would correspond well enough to this definition—both as regards their appearance and the character of the herbage which covers them; but there are other parts which bear not the slightest resemblance to a meadow. There are vast tracts thickly covered with tall thistles—so tall as to reach to the head of a man mounted on horseback, and so thickly set, that neither man nor horse could enter them without a path being first cleared for them.

Other extensive tracts are grown over with tall grass so rank as to resemble reeds or rushes more than grass; and an equally extensive surface is timbered with small trees, standing thinly and without underwood, like the fruit-trees in an orchard. Again, there are wide morasses and extensive lakes, many of them brackish, and some as salt as the sea itself. In addition to these, there are "salinas," or plains of salt—the produce of salt lakes, whose waters have evaporated, leaving a stratum of pure salt often over a foot in thickness, and covering their beds to an extent of many square leagues. There are some parts, too, where the Pampas country assumes a sterile and stony character—corresponding to that of the great desert of Patagonia. It is not correct, therefore, to regard the Pampas as one unbroken tract of *meadow*. In one character alone is it uniform: in being a country without mountains—or any considerable elevations in the way of ridges or hills—though a few scattered sierras are found both on its northern and southern edges.

The *Thistle Pampas*, as we take the liberty of naming them, constitute perhaps the most curious section of this great plain; and not the less so that

the "weed" which covers them is supposed not to
be an indigenous production, but to have been carried there by the early colonists. About this, however, there is a difference of opinion. No matter
whence sprung, the thistles have flourished luxuriantly, and at this day constitute a marked feature
in the scenery of the Pampas. Their position is
upon the eastern edge of the great plain, contiguous to the banks of the La Plata; but from this
river they extend backwards into the interior, at
some points to the distance of nearly two hundred
miles. Over this vast surface they grow so thickly
that, as already mentioned, it is not possible for
either man or horse to make way through them.
They can only be traversed by devious paths—already formed by constant use, and leading through
narrow lanes or glades, where, for some reason, the
thistles do not choose to grow. Otherwise they
cannot be entered even by cattle. These will not,
unless compelled, attempt penetrating such an im-
pervious thicket; and if a herd driven along the
paths should chance to be "stampeded" by any object of terror, and driven to take to the thistles,
scarce a head of the whole flock can ever afterwards be recovered. Even the instincts of the
dumb animals do not enable them to find their way
out again; and they usually perish, either from
thirst, or by the claws of the fierce pumas and jaguars, which alone find themselves at home in the
labyrinthine "*cardonales*." The little *viscacha* contrives to make its burrow among them, and must
find subsistence by feeding upon their leaves and
seed, since there is no other herbage upon the
ground—the well-armed thistle usurping the soil,
and hindering the growth of any other plants. It
may be proper to remark, however, that there are
two kinds of these plants, both of which cover large

tracts of the plain. One is a true thistle, while the other is a weed of the artichoke family, called by the Spanish Americans "cardoon." It is a species of *Cardunculus.* The two do not mingle their stalks, though both form thickets in a similar manner and often in the same tract of country. The cardoon is not so tall as the thistle; and, being without spines, its "beds" are more easily penetrated; though even among these, it would be easy enough to get entangled and lost.

It is proper to remark here, that these thistle-thickets do not shut up the country all the year round. Only for a season—from the time they have grown up and "shoot," till their tall ripened stalks wither and fall back to the earth, where they soon moulder into decay. The plains are then open and free to all creatures—man among the rest—and the Gaucho, with his herds of horses, horned cattle, and sheep, or the troops of roving Indians, spread over and take possession of them.

The young thistles now present the appearance of a vast field of turnips; and their leaves, still tender, are greedily devoured by both cattle and sheep. In this condition the Pampas thistles remain during their short winter; but as spring returns, they once more "bristle" up, till, growing taller and stouter, they present a *chevaux-de-frise* that at length expels all intruders from their domain.

On the western selvage of this thistle tract lies the grass-covered section of the Pampas. It is much more extensive than that of the "cardonales" —having an average width of three hundred miles, and running longitudinally throughout the whole northern and southern extension of the Pampas. Its chief characteristic is a covering of coarse grass —which at different seasons of the year is short or tall, green, brown, or yellowish, according to the

different degrees of ripeness. When dry, it is sometimes fired—either by design or accident—as are
also the withered stems of the thistles; and on these
occasions a conflagration occurs, stupendous in its
effects—often extending over vast tracts, and re-
ducing everything to black ashes. Nothing can be
more melancholy to the eye than the aspect of a
burnt pampa.

The grass section is succeeded by that of the
"openings," or scanty forests, already mentioned;
but the trees in many places are more closely set;
assuming the character of thickets, or "jungles."
These tracts end among the spurs of the Andes—
which, at some points, are thrown out into the plain,
but generally rise up from it abruptly and by a
well-defined border.

The marshes and bitter lakes above mentioned
are the produce of numerous streams, which have
their rise in the Great Cordillera of the Andes, and
run eastward across the Pampas. A few of these,
that trend in a southerly direction, reach the Atlantic by means of the two great outlets—the "Colorado" and "Negro." All the others—and "their
name is legion"—empty their waters into the morasses and lakes, or sink into the soil of the plains,
at a greater or less distance from the Cordillera,
according to the body of water they may carry
down. Evaporation keeps up the equilibrium.

Who are the dwellers upon the Pampas? To
whom does this vast pasture-ground belong?
Whose flocks and herds are they that browse upon
it?

You will be told that the Pampas belong to the
republic of Buenos Ayres, or rather to the "States
of the Argentine Confederation,"—that they are inhabited by a class of citizens called "Gauchos,"
who are of Spanish race, and whose sole occupa-

tion is that of herdsmen, breeders **of cattle** and horses—men famed for their skill as horsemen, and **for** their dexterity in the use of the **"lazo" and** "bolas"—two weapons borrowed from **the aborig-**inal races.

All this is but partially true. The proprietorship of this great plain **was** never actually in the hands of the Buenos-Ayrean government, nor in those **of** their predecessors — the Spaniards. Neither **has** ever owned it—either by conquest or otherwise—**no** farther than an empty boast of ownership; for, from **the** day when they first set foot upon its borders to the present hour, neither has ever **been** able to cross it, or penetrate any great distance **into** it, without a grand army to back their progress. But their possession virtually ceased, at the termination of each melancholy excursion; and the land **re-**lapsed to its original owners. With the exception of some scanty strips along its borders, and some wider ranges, thinly occupied by the half-nomade Gauchos, the Pampas are in reality an Indian territory, as they have always been; and the claim of the white man is no more than nominal—a mere title upon the map. It is not the only vast expanse of Spanish American soil that *never was Spanish.*

The true owners of **the** Pampas, then, are **the red** aborigines—the Pampas Indians; and to give some account of these is now our purpose.

Forming so large an extent, it is not **likely it** should all belong to one united **tribe—that would** at once elevate them into the character of **a** nation. **But they are not** united. On the contrary, they **form several** distinct associations, with an endless number **of smaller** subdivisions or communities—just in **the same** way as it is among their prairie cousins of the north. They may all, however, be

referred to four grand tribal associations or nationalities — the *Pehuenches*, *Puelches*, *Picunches*, and
Ranqueles.

Some add the **Puilliches,** who dwell on the southern rim of the Pampas; but these, although they
extend their excursions over a portion of the great
plain, are different from the other Pampas Indians
in many respects—altogether a braver and better
race of men, and partaking more of the character
of the Patagonians—both in point of *physique* and
morale,—of which tribes, indeed, they are evidently
only a branch.   In their dealings with white men,
when fairly treated, these have exhibited the same
noble bearing which characterizes the true Patagonian.   I shall not, therefore, lower the standard—
neither of their bodies nor their minds—by classing
them among " Pampas Indians."

Of these tribes—one and all of them—we have,
unfortunately, a much less favourable impression ;
and shall therefore be able to say but little to their
credit.

The different names are all native.   *Puelches*
means the people living to the east, from "*puel*,"
east and *che*, people.   The *Picunches* derive this
appellation, in a similar fashion, from "*picun*," signifying the north.   The *Pehuenches* are the people
of the pine-tree country, from "*pehuen*," the name
for the celebrated " Chili pine" (*Araucaria*) ; and
the *Ranqueles* are the men who dwell among the
thistles, from *ranquel*, a thistle.

These national appellations will give some idea
of the locality which each tribe inhabits.   The *Ranqueles* dwell, not among the thistles—for that would
be an unpleasant residence, even to a red-skin ; but
along the western border of this tract.   To the
westward of them, and up into the clefts of the Cordilleras extends the country of the Pehuenches ; and

northward of both lies the land of the Picunches. Their boundary in that direction *should be* the front-iers of the *quasi-civilized* provinces of San Luis and Cordova, but they are *not;* for the Picunche can at will extend his plundering forays as far north as he pleases; even to *dovetailing* them into the similar excursions of his *Guaycuru* kinsman from the "Gran Chaco" on the north.

The Puelche territory is on the eastern side of the Pampas, and south from Buenos Ayres. At one time these people occupied the country to the banks of the La Plata; and no doubt it was they who first met the Spaniards in hostile array. Even up to a late period their forays extended almost to Buenos Ayres itself; but Rosas, tyrant as he may have been, was nevertheless a true soldier, and in a grand military expedition against them swept their coun-try, and inflicted such a terrible chastisement upon both them and the neighbouring tribes, as they had not suffered since the days of Mendoza. The re-sult has been a retirement of the Puelche frontier to a much greater distance from Buenos Ayres; but how long it may continue stationary is a ques-tion — no longer than some strong arm — such as that of Rosas—is held threateningly over them.

It is usual to inquire whence come a people; and the question has been asked of the Pampas Indians. It is not difficult to answer. They came from the land of Arauco. Yes, they are the kindred of that famed people whom the Spaniards could never sub-due—even with all their strength put forth in the effort. They are near kindred too—the Puenches especially—whose country is only separated from that of the Araucanians by the Great Cordillera of Chili; and with whom, as well as the Spaniards on the Chilian side, they have constant and friendly in-tercourse.

T

But it must be admitted, that the Araucanians have had far more than their just meed of praise. The romantic stories, in that endless epic of the rhymer Ercilla, have crept into history; and the credulous Molina has endorsed them: so that the true character of the Araucanian Indian has never been understood. Brave he has shown himself, beyond doubt, in defending his country against Spanish aggression; but so, too, has the Carib and Guaraon—so, too, has the Comanche and Apache, the Yaqui of Sonora, the savage of the Mosquito shore, the Guaycuru of the Gran Chaco, and a score of other Indian tribes — in whose territory the Spaniard has never dared to fix a settlement. Brave is the Araucanian; but, beyond this, he has few virtues indeed. He is cruel in the extreme — uncivil and selfish — filthy and indolent — a polygamist in the most approved fashion—a very tyrant over his own — in short, taking rank among the beastliest of semi-civilized savages — for it may be here observed, that he is not exactly what is termed a *savage:* that is, he does not go naked, and sleep in the open air. On the contrary, he clothes himself in stuff of his own weaving — or rather that of his slave-wives — and lives in a hut which they build for him. He owns land, too—beautiful fields—of which he makes no use: except to browse a few horses, and sheep, and cattle. For the rest, he is too indolent to pursue agriculture; and spends most of his time in drinking *chicha*, or tyrannizing over his wives. This is the heroic Araucanian who inhabits the plains and valleys of Southern Chili.

Unfortunately, by passing to the other side of the Andes he has not improved his manners. The air of the Pampas does not appear to be conducive to virtue; and upon that side of the mountains it can scarce be said to exist—even in the shape of per-

sonal courage. The men of the pines and thistles
seem to have lost this quality, while passing through
the snows of the Cordilleras, or left it behind them,
as they have also left the incipient civilization of
their race. On the Pampas we find them once more
in the character of the true savage: living by the
chase or by plunder; and bartering the produce of
the latter for the trappings and trinkets of personal
adornment, supplied them by the unprincipled white
trader. Puelches and Picunches, Pehuenches and
Ranqueles, all share this character alike—all are
treacherous, quarrelsome, and cowardly.

But we shall now speak more particularly of their
customs and modes of life, and we may take the
" pine people" as our text—since these are supposed
to be most nearly related to the true Araucanians
—and, indeed, many of their "ways" are exactly
the same as those of that "heroic nation."

The "people of the pines" are of the ordinary
stature of North-American Indians, or of Europeans; and their natural color is a dark coppery hue.
But it is not often you can see them in their natural
color: for the Pampas Indians, like nearly all the
aboriginal tribes, are " painters." They have pigments of black and white, blue, red, and yellow—
all of which they obtain from different coloured
stones, found in the streams of the Cordilleras.
"Yama," they call the black stone; "colo," the
red; "palan," the white; and " codin," the blue;
the yellow they obtain from a sort of argillaceous
earth. The stones of each colour they submit to a
rubbing or grinding process, until a quantity of dust
is produced; which, being mixed with suet, constitutes the paint, ready for being laid on.

The Pampas Indians do not confine themselves to
any particular " escutcheon." In this respect their
fancy is allowed a wide scope, and their fashions

change. A face quite black, or red, is a common countenance among them; and often may be seen a single band, of about two inches in width, extending from ear to ear across the eyes and nose. On war excursions they paint hideous figures: not only on their own faces and bodies, but on their trappings, and even upon the bodies of their horses— aiming to render themselves as appalling as possible in the sight of their enemies. The same trick is employed by the warriors of the prairies, as well as in many other parts of the world. Under ordinary circumstances, the **Pampas** Indian is not a *naked* savage. On the contrary he is well-clad; and, so far from obtaining the material of his garments from the looms of civilized nations, he weaves it for himself—that is, his wives weave it; and in such quantity that he has not only enough for his own "wear," · but more than enough—a surplus for trade. The cloth is usually a stuff spun and woven from sheep's wool. It is coarse, but durable; and in the shape of blankets or "ponchos," is eagerly purchased by the Spanish traders. Silver spurs, long pointed knives, lance-heads, and a few other iron commodities, constitute the articles of exchange, with various ornamental articles, as beads, rings, bracelets, and large-headed silver bodkins to fasten their cloaks around the shoulders of his "ladies." Nor is he contented with mere tinsel, as other savages are—he can tell the difference between the real metal and the counterfeit, as well as the most expert assayer; and if he should fancy to have a pair of silver spurs, not even a Jew peddler could put off upon him the plated "article." In this respect the Araucanian Indian has been distinguished, since his earliest intercourse with Europeans; and his Pampas kindred are equally subtle in their appreciation.

The Pampas Indian, when well-dressed, has a cloak upon his shoulders of the thick woollen stuff already described. It is usually woven in colours; and is not unlike the " poncho" worn by the " gauchos" of Buenos Ayres, or the " serape" of the Mexicans. Besides the cloak, his dress consists of a mere skirt—also of coloured woollen stuff, being an oblong piece swathed around his loins, and reaching to the knee. A sash or belt—sometimes elaborately ornamented—binds the cloth around the waist. Boots of a peculiar construction complete the costume. These are manufactured in a very simple manner. The fresh skin taken from a horse's hind leg is drawn on—just as if it were a stocking —until the heel rests in that part which covered the hock-joint of the original wearer. The superfluous portion is then trimmed to accommodate itself as a covering for the foot; and the boot is not only finished, but put on—there to remain until it is worn out, and a new one required! If it should be a little loose at first, that does not matter. The hot sun, combined with the warmth of the wearer's leg, soon contracts the hide, and brings it to "fit like a glove." The head is often left uncovered; but as often a sort of skull cap or helmet of horseskin is worn; and not unfrequently a high conical hat of palm-fibre. This last is not a native production, but an importation of the traders. So also is a pair of enormous rings of brass, which are worn in the ears; and are as bulky as a pair of padlocks. In this costume, mounted on horseback with his long lance in hand, the Pampas Indian would be a picturesque object; and really is so, when *clean ;* but that is only on the very rarest occasions—only when he has donned a new suit. At all other times, not only his face and the skin of his body, but every rag upon his back, are covered with grease and filth

—so as to produce an effect rather "tatterdemalion" than picturesque.

The "squaw" is costumed somewhat differently. First, she has a long "robe," which covers her from neck to heels, leaving only her neck and arms bare. The robe is of red or blue woollen stuff of her own weaving. The garment is the "quedeto." A belt, embroidered with beads, called "quepique," holds it around the waist, by means of a large silver buckle. This belt is an article of first fashion. Over the shoulders hangs the "iquilla," which is a square piece of similar stuff—but usually of a different dye; and which is fastened in front by a pin with a large silver head, called the "tupo." The shock of thick black hair—after having received the usual anointment of mare's tallow—the fashionable hair-oil of the Pampas Indians—is kept in its place by a sort of cap or *coiffure*, like a shallow dish inverted, and bristling all over with trader's beads. To this a little bell is fastened; or sometimes a brace of them are worn as ear-rings. These tinkle so agreeably in the ears of the wearer, that she can scarce for a moment hold her head at rest, but keeps rocking it from side to side, as a Spanish coquette would play with her fan.

In addition to this varied wardrobe the Pampas belle carries a large stock of bijouterie—such as beads and bangles upon her neck, rings and circlets upon her arms, ankles, and fingers; and, to set her snaky locks in order, she separates them by means of a stiff brush, made from the fibrous roots of a reed. *She* is *picturesque* enough, but never *pretty*. Nature has given the Araucanian woman a plain face; and all the adornment in the world cannot hide its homeliness.

The Pehuenche builds no house. He is a true nomade, and dwells in a tent, though one of the rudest construction. As it differs entirely from the tent of the prairie Indians, it may be worth while describing it.

Its frame-work is of reeds—of the same kind as are used for the long lances so often mentioned; and which resemble *bambusa* canes. They grow in plenty throughout the Pampas, especially near the mountains—where they form impenetrable thickets on the borders of the marshy lakes. Any other flexible poles will serve as well, when the canes are not "handy."

The poles being procured, one is first bent into a semicircle, and in this shape both ends are stuck into the ground, so as to form an arch about three feet in height. This arch afterwards becomes the doorway or entrance to the tent. The remaining poles are attached to this first one at one end, and at right angles; and being carried backward with a slight bend, their other ends are inserted into the turf. This forms the skeleton of the tent; and its covering is a horse-skin, or rather a number of horse-skins stitched together, making a sort of large tarpaulin. The skins are sewed with the sinews of the horse or ox—which are first chewed by the women, until their fibres become separated like hemp, and are afterwards spun by them into twine.

The tent is not tall enough to admit of a man standing erect; and in it the Pehuenche crouches, whenever it snows, rains, or blows cold. He has sheep-skins spread to sleep upon, and other skins to serve as bed-clothes—all in so filthy a condition, that but for the cold, he might find it far more comfortable to sleep in the open air. He never attempts to sweep out this miserable lair; but when the spot becomes *very* filthy, he "takes up his sticks" and shifts his *penates* to a fresh "location." He is generally, however, too indolent to make a "remove,"

until the **dirt** has accumulated so as to "be in **the**
way."

The **Pampas** Indian **is less of** a hunter than most
other tribes of savages.   **He** has less need to be—
at least, in modern days; **for he is in** possession of
three kinds of valuable domestic animals, upon which
he can subsist without hunting—horses, horned cattle, and sheep.   Of course, these are of colonial origin.   **He** hunts, nevertheless, for amusement, and
to vary his food.   The larger ostrich (*rhea Americana*), **the guanaco,** and the great "gama" stag of
the Pampas (*cervus campestris*) are his usual game.
These **he** captures with the *bolas* — which is his
chief implement **for the chase.   In the** flesh of the
stag he may find a variety, but not a delicacy.   Its
venison would scarce tempt a Lucullian palate—
since even the hungriest Gaucho will not eat it.   **It**
is a large beast, often weighing above three hundred pounds, and infecting the air with such a rank
odour that dogs decline to **follo**w it in the chase.
This odour is generated in a pair of glands situated
near the eyes; and **it has** the power of projecting
it at will—just as skunks and pole-cats when closely chased by an enemy.   If these glands are cut out
immediately after the animal is killed, the flesh
tastes well enough: otherwise it is too rank to be
eatable.   **The** Indians cure it of the "bad smell" by
burying **it for** several days in the ground; **which**
has the effect of "sweetening" it, while at **the same**
time it makes it more **tender.**   ᴬ

But the Pampas **Indian does not** rely upon the
chase for his subsistence.   **He is a** small grazier in
his way; and is usually accompanied in his wanderings by a herd of horned cattle and sheep.   He has
also his stud **of horses;** which furnish the *staple*
of his food—for whenever he hungers, a horse is
"slaughtered."   Strictly speaking, it is not a horse,

for it is the mare that is used for this purpose. In no part of the Pampas region—not even in the white settlement—are the mares used for riding. It would be considered derogatory to the character of either Gaucho or Indian, to mount a mare; and these are kept only for breeding purposes. Not that the Indian is much of a horse-breeder. He keeps up his stock in quite another way—by stealing. The same remark will apply to the mode by which he recruits his herds of horned cattle, and his flocks of sheep. The last he values only for their wool, out of which his garments are woven; and which has replaced the scantier fleece of the vicuna and guanaco—the material used by him in days gone by.

From whom does he steal these valuable animals —and in such numbers as almost to subsist upon them? That is a question that can be easily answered; though it is not exact language to say that he steals them. Rather say he *takes* them, by main force and in open daylight—takes them from the creole Spaniard—the Gaucho and *estanciero*. Nay, he does not content himself always with four-footed plunder; but often returns from his forays with a crowd of captives—women and children, with white skins and ruddy cheeks—afterwards to be converted into his drudges and slaves. Not alone to the frontier does he extend these plundering expeditions; but even into the heart of the Spanish settlements—to the estancias of grandees, and the gates of fortified towns; and, strange as it may read, this condition of things has been in existence, not for years, but, at intervals, extending over a century.

But what may read stranger still—and I can vouch for it as true—is, that *white men* actually purchase this plunder from him—not the human part of it, but the four-footed and the *furniture—*

for this, too, sometimes **forms** part of his booty. Yes, the surplus, **of which** the Indian can make no use or cares nothing about—more especially the large droves of fine horses, taken from the Spaniards of Buenos Ayres—are driven through the passes of the Cordilleras, and sold to the Spaniards of Chili! the people of one province actually encouraging the robbery of their kindred race in another! The very same condition of things exists in North America. The Comanche steals, or rather takes, from the white settler of Tamaulipas and New Leon—the Apache rieves from the white settler of Chihuahua and Sonora: both sell to the **white** settlers, who dwell along the banks of the Rio del Norte! And all these settlers are of one race—one country—one kindred! These things have hitherto been styled *cosas de Mexico*. Their signification may be extended **to South America:** since they are equally *cosas de las Pampas.*

We **are** not permitted to doubt the truth of these appalling facts—neither as regards the nefarious traffic, nor the captive women and children. **At** this very hour, not less than four thousand individuals of Spanish-Mexican race are held captives by the prairie tribes; and when Rosas swept the Pampas, he released fifteen hundred of similar unfortunates from their worse than Egyptian taskmasters—the Puelches!

With such facts as these before our eyes, who can doubt the decline of the Spanish power? the utter enfeeblement of that once **noble race?** Who can contradict the hypothetical prophecy—more than **once** offered **in** these pages—that if the two races be left to themselves, the aboriginal, before the lapse of **a** single century, will once more recover the soil; and his haughty victor be swept from the face of the American continent?

Nor need such a change be too keenly regretted. The Spanish occupation of America has been an utter failure. It has served no high human purpose, but the contrary. It has only corrupted and encowardiced a once brave and noble race; and, savage as may be the character of that which would supplant it, still that savage has within him the elements of a future civilization.

Not so the Spaniard. The fire of his civilization has blazed up with a high but fitful gleam. It has passed like the lightning's flash. Its sparks have fallen and died out—never to be rekindled again.

THE YAMPARICOS, OR ROOT-DIGGERS.

It is now pretty generally known that there are many *deserts* in North America—as wild, waste, and inhospitable as the famed Säara of Africa. These deserts occupy a large portion of the central regions of that great continent—extending, north and south, from Mexico to the shores of the Arctic Sea; and east and west for several hundred miles, on each side of the great vertebral chain of the Rocky Mountains. It is true that in the vast territory thus indicated, the desert is not continuous; but it is equally true that the fertile stripes or valleys that intersect it, bear but a very small proportion to the whole surface. Many tracts are there, of larger area than all the British islands, where the desert is scarce varied by an oäsis, and where the very rivers pursue their course amidst rocks and barren sands, without a blade of vegetation on their banks. Usually, however, a narrow selvage of green—caused by the growth of cottonwoods, willows, and a few humbler plants—denotes the course of a stream—a glad sight at all times to the weary and thirsting traveller.

These desert wastes are not all alike, but differ much in character. In one point only do they agree —they are all *deserts*. Otherwise they exhibit many varieties—both of aspect and nature. Some of them are level plains, with scarce a hill to break the monotony of the view: and of this character is the greater portion of the desert country extending eastward from the Rocky Mountains to about 100°

of west longitude. At this point the soil gradually becomes more fertile—assuming the character of timbered tracts, with prairie openings between—at length terminating in the vast unbroken forests of the Mississippi.

This eastern desert extends parallel with the Rocky Mountains—throughout nearly the whole of their length—from the Rio Grande in Mexico, northward to the Mackenzie River. One tract of it deserves particular mention. It is that known as the *Llano estacado,* or " staked plain." It lies in northwestern Texas, and consists of a barren plateau of several thousand square miles in extent, the surface of which is raised nearly a thousand feet above the level of the surrounding plains. Geologists have endeavoured to account for this singular formation, but in vain. The table-like elevation of the Llano estacado still remains a puzzle. Its name, however, is easier of explanation. In the days of Spanish supremacy over this part of prairie-land, caravans frequently journeyed from Santa Fé in New Mexico, to San Antonio in Texas. The most direct route between these two provincial capitals lay across the Llano estacado ; but as there were neither mountains nor other landmarks to guide the traveller, he often wandered from the right path—a mistake that frequently ended in the most terrible suffering from thirst, and very often in the loss of life. To prevent such catastrophes, *stakes* were set up at such intervals as to be seen from one another, like so many "telegraph posts;" and although these have long since disappeared, the great plain still bears the name, given to it from this circumstance.

Besides the contour of surface, there are other respects in which the desert tracts of North America differ from one another. In their vegetation— if it deserves the name—they are unlike. Some

have no vegetation whatever; but exhibit a surface
of pure sand, or sand and pebbles; others are covered with a stratum of soda of snow-white colour,
and still others with a layer of common salt equally
white and pure. Many **of these salt** and soda
"prairies"—as the trappers term them—are hundreds of square miles in extent. Again, there are
deserts of scoria, of lava, and pumice-stone—the
"cut-rock prairies" of the trappers—a perfect contrast in colour to the above-mentioned. All these
are absolutely without vegetation of any sort.

On some of the wastes—those of southern latitudes—the **cactus appears of several** species, and
also the wild agave, or "pita" plant; but these
plants are in reality but emblems of the desert itself. So, also, is the *yucca*, which thinly stands
over many of the great plains, in the south-western
part of the desert region—its stiff shaggy foliage **in**
no way relieving the sterile landscape, but rather
rendering **its** aspect more horrid and austere.

Again, there are the deserts known as "chap-
parals,"—extensive jungles of brush and low trees,
all of a thorny character; among **which the** "mezquite" **of** several species (*mimosas* **and** *acacias*),
the "stink-wood" or creosote plant (*kœberlinia*), the
"grease-bush" (*obione canescens*), several kinds of
prosopis, and now and then, as if to gratify the eye
of the tired traveller, the tall flowering spike of the
scarlet *fouquiera*. Further to the north—especially throughout the upper section **of the** Great **Salt**
Lake territory—are vast tracts, **upon which scarce**
any vegetation appears, **except the** *artemisia* **plant,**
and other kindred products **of a** sterile soil.

Of all the desert tracts upon the North-American
continent, perhaps none possesses greater interest
for the student of cosmography than that known as
the "Great Basin." It has been so styled from the

fact of its possessing a hydrographic system of its own—lakes and rivers that have no communication with the sea; but whose waters spend themselves within the limits of the desert itself, and are kept in equilibrium by evaporation—as is the case with many water systems of the continents of the old world, both in Asia and Africa.

The largest lake of the "Basin" is the "Great Salt Lake,"—of late so celebrated in Mormon story: since near its southern shore the chief city of the "Latter-day Saints" is situated. But there are other large lakes within the limits of the Great Basin, both fresh and saline—most of them entirely unconnected with the Great Salt Lake, and some of them having a complete system of waters of their own. There are "Utah" and "Humboldt," "Walker's" and "Pyramid" lakes, with a long list of others, whose names have been but recently entered upon the map, by the numerous very intelligent explorers employed by the government of the United States.

Large rivers, too, run in all directions through this central desert, some of them falling into the Great Salt Lake, as the "Bear" river, the "Weber," the "Utah," from Utah lake—upon which the Mormon metropolis stands—and which stream has been absurdly baptized by these free-living fanatics as the "Jordan!" Other rivers are the "Timpanogos," emptying into Lake Utah; the "Humboldt," that runs to the lake of that name; the "Carson" river; besides many of lesser note.

The limits assigned to the Great Basin are tolerably well defined. Its western rim is the *Sierra Nevada*, or "snowy range" of California; while the Rocky and Wahsatch mountains are its boundaries on the east. Several cross-ranges, and spurs of ranges separate it from the system of waters, that empty northward into the Columbia river of Ore-

gon ; while upon its southern edge there is a more
indefinite "divide" between it and the great desert
region of the western "Colorado." Strictly speaking, the desert of the Great Basin might be regarded as only a portion of that vast tract of sterile, and
almost treeless soil, which stretches from the Mexican state of Sonora to the upper waters of Oregon;
but the deserts of the Colorado on the south, and
those of the "forks" of the Columbia on the north,
are generally treated as distinct territories; and the
Great Basin, with the limits already assigned, is suffered to stand by itself. As a separate country,
then, we shall here consider it.

From its name, you might fancy that the Great
Basin was a low-lying tract of country. This, however, is far from being the case. On the contrary,
nearly all of it is of the nature of an elevated table-
land: even its lakes lying several thousand feet
above the level of the sea. It is only by its "rim,"
of still more elevated mountain ridges, that it can
lay claim to be considered as a "basin;" but, indeed, the name—given by the somewhat specula-
tive explorer, Fremont—is not very appropriate:
since later investigations show that this rim is in
many places neither definite nor regular—especially
on its northern and southern sides, where the "Great
Basin" may be said to be badly cracked, and even
to have some pieces chipped out of its edge.

Besides the mountain chains that surround it,
many others run into and intersect it in all directions. Some are spurs of the main ranges; while
others form "sierras"—as the Spaniards term them
—distinct in themselves. These sierras are of all
shapes and of every altitude—from the low-lying
ridge scarce rising above the plain, to peaks and
summits of over ten thousand feet in elevation.
Their forms are as varied as their height. Some

are round or dome-shaped; others shoot up little
turrets or " needles;" and still others mount into
the sky in shapeless masses—as if they had been
flung upon the earth, and upon one another, in some
struggle of Titans, who have left them lying in chaotic confusion. A very singular mountain form is
here observed—though it is not peculiar to this region, since it is found elsewhere, beyond the limits
of the Great Basin, and is also common in many
parts of Africa. This is the formation known among
the Spaniards as *mesas*, or " table-mountains," and
by this very name it is distinguished among the
colonists of the Cape.

The *Llano estacado*, already mentioned, is often
styled a " mesa," but its elevation is inconsiderable
when compared with the *mesa* mountains that occur
in the regions west of the great Rocky chain—
both in the Basin and on the deserts of the Colorado.
Many of these are of great height—rising several
thousand feet above the general level; and, with
their square truncated *table-like* tops, lend a peculiar character to the landscape.

The characteristic vegetation of the Great Basin
is very similar to that of the other central regions
of the North-American continent. Only near the
banks of the rivers and some of the fresh-water lakes,
is there any evidence of a fertile soil; and, even in
these situations, the timber is usually scarce and
stunted. Of course, there are tracts that are exceptional—oäses as they are geographically styled. Of
this character is the country of the Mormons on the
Jordan, their settlements on the Utah and Bear
rivers, in Tuilla and Ogden valleys, and elsewhere
at more remote points. There are also isolated
tracts on the banks of the smaller streams and the
shores of lakes not yet " located" by the colonist;
and only frequented by the original dwellers of the

U

desert, the red aborigines. In these oäses are usually found cottonwood trees, of several distinct species—one or other of which is the characteristic vegetation on nearly every stream from the Mississippi to the mountains of California.

Willows of many species also appear; and now and then, in stunted forms, the oak, the elm, maples, and sycamores. But all these last are very rarely encountered within the limits of the desert region. On the mountains, and more frequently in the mountain ravines, pines of many species—some of which produce edible cones—grow in such numbers as to merit the name of forests, of greater or less extent. Among these, or apart from them, may be distinguished the darker foliage of the cedar (*juniperus*) of several varieties, distinct from the *juniperus virginiana* of the States.

The arid plains are generally without the semblance of vegetation. When any appears upon them, it is of the character of the "chapparal," already described; its principal growth being "tornilla," or "screw-wood," and other varieties of *mezquite*; all of them species of the extensive order of the *leguminosæ*, and belonging to the several genera of *acacias*, *mimosas*, and *robinias*. In many places *cactaceæ* appear of an endless variety of forms; and some—as the "pitahaya" (*cereus giganteus*), and the "tree" and "cochineal" cacti (*opuntias*)—of gigantesque proportions. These, however, are only developed to their full size in the regions further south—on the deserts of the Colorado and Gila— where also the "tree yuccas" abound, covering tracts of large extent, and presenting the appearance of forests of palms.

Perhaps the most characteristic vegetation of the Great Basin—that is, if it deserve the name of a vegetation—is the wild sage, or *artemisia*. With this plant vast plains are covered, as far as the eye can reach; not presenting a hue of green, as the grass prairies do, but a uniform aspect of greyish white, as monotonous as if the earth were without a leaf to cover it. Instead of relieving the eye of the traveller, the artemisia rather adds to the dreariness of a desert landscape—for its presence promises food neither to man nor horse, nor water for them to drink, but indicates the absence of both. Upon the hill-sides also is it seen, along the sloping declivities of the sierras, marbling the dark volcanic rocks with its hoary frondage.

More than one species of this wild sage occurs throughout the American desert: there are four or five kinds differing very considerably from each other, and known to the trappers by such names as "wormwood," "grease-bush," "stink-plant," and "rabbit-bush." Some of the species attain to a considerable height—their tops often rising above the head of the traveller on horseback—while another kind scarce reaches the knee of the pedestrian.

In some places the plains are so thickly covered with this vegetation, that it is difficult for either man or horse to make way through them—the gnarled and crooked branches twisting into each other and forming an impenetrable wattle. At other places, and especially where the larger species grow, the plants stand apart like apple-trees in an orchard, and bear a considerable resemblance to shrubs or small trees.

Both man and horse refuse the artemisia as food; and so, too, the less fastidious mule. Even a donkey will not eat it. There are animals, however—both birds and beasts, as will be seen hereafter—that relish the sage-plant; and not only eat of it, but subsist almost exclusively on its stalks, leaves, and berries.

The denizens of the Great Basin desert—I mean its human denizens—are comprehended in two great families of the aboriginal race—the *Utahs* and *Snakes*, or **Shoshonees**. Of the white inhabitants—the Mormons and trapper-settlers—we have nothing to say here. Nor yet much respecting the above-mentioned Indians, the Utahs and Snakes. It will be enough for our purpose to make known: that these two tribes are distinct from each other—that there are many communities or sub-tribes of both—that each claims ownership of a large tract of the central region, lying between the Rocky Mountains and the Sierra Nevada; and that their limits are not coterminal with those of the Great Basin: since the range of the Snakes extends into Oregon upon the north; while that of the Utahs runs down into the valley of the Rio del Norte upon the south. Furthermore, that both are in possession of the horse—the Utahs owning large numbers—that both are of roving and predatory habits, and quite as wicked and warlike as the generality of their red brethren.

They are also as well to do in the world as most Indians; but there are many degrees in their "civilization," or rather in the comforts of their life, depending upon the situation in which they may be placed. When dwelling upon a good "salmon stream," or among the rocky mountain "parks," that abound in game, they manage to pass a portion of the year in luxuriant abundance. In other places, however, and at other times, their existence is irksome enough—often bordering upon actual starvation.

It may be further observed, that the Utahs and Snakes usually occupy the larger and more fertile oäses of the desert—wherever a tract is found of sufficient size to subsist a community. With this observation I shall dismiss both these tribes; for it is not of them that our present sketch is intended to treat.

This is specially designed for a far *odder* people than either—for the *Yamparicos*, or "Root Diggers;" and having described their country, I shall now proceed to give some account of themselves.

It may be necessary here to remark that the name "Diggers" has of late been very improperly applied —not only by the settlers of California, but by some of the exploring officers of the United States government. Every tribe or community throughout the desert, found existing in a state of special wretchedness, has been so styled; and a learned ethnologist (!), writing in the "Examiner," newspaper, gravely explains the name, by deriving it from the gold-diggers of California! This "conceit" of the London editor is a palpable absurdity—since the Digger Indians were so designated long before the first gold-digger of California put spade into its soil. The name is of "trapper" origin; bestowed upon these people from the observation of one of their most common practices—viz., the *digging for roots*, which form an essential portion of their subsistence. The term "yamparico" is from a Spanish source, and has a very similar meaning to that of "Root-digger." It is literally "Yampa-rooter," or "Yampa-root-eater," the root of the "yampah" (*anethum graviolens*) being their favourite food. The true "Diggers" are not found in California west of the Sierra Nevada; though certain tribes of ill-used Indians in that quarter are called by the name. The great deserts extending between the Nevada and the Rocky Mountains are their locality; and their limits are more or less cotemporaneous with those of the Shoshonees or Snakes, and the Utahs—of both of which tribes they are supposed to be a sort of outcast kindred. This hypothesis, **however, rests only on a** slight foundation : that of some resemblance in habits and language, which are **very** uncertain *criteria* where two people dwell **within** the same boundaries—as, for instance, the whites and blacks **in Virginia.** In fact, the language of the Diggers can scarce **be** called **a** language at all: being a sort of gibberish **like** the growling of a dog, eked out by a copious vocabulary of signs; and perhaps, here and there, by an odd word from the Shoshonee or Utah—not unlikely, introduced by the association of the Diggers with **these** last-mentioned tribes.

In the western **and** southern division of the Great Basin, the Digger exists under **the** name of *Paiute*, or more properly *Pah-Utah*—so called from his supposed relationship with the tribe of the Utahs. In some respects the Pah-Utahs differ from **the** Shoshokee, or Snake Diggers ; though in most of their characteristic habits they are very similar to **each other.** There might be no anomaly committed **by** considering them as one people ; for, in personal appearance and habits of life, the Pah-Utah **and the** " Shoshokee"—this last is the national appellation of the yampah-eater—are as like each other as *eggs.* We shall here speak, however, principally **of the** Shoshokees ; leaving it to be understood, **that** their neighbours the " Paiutes" will equally answer the description.

Although the Shoshokees, **as already** observed, **dwell** within the same **limits as their** supposed kindred the Shoshonees, **they rarely or** never associate **with** the latter. **On the** contrary, they keep well out of their way—inhabiting only those districts of country **where** the larger Shoshonee communities could not dwell. The very smallest oäsis, or the tiniest stream, affords all the fertility that is re-

quired for the support of a Digger family; and
rarely are these people found living more than one,
or at most, two or three families together. The
very necessity of their circumstances precludes the
possibility of a more extensive association; for, on
the deserts where they dwell, neither the earth nor
the air, nor yet the water, affords a sufficient supply of food to support even the smallest "tribe."
Not in tribes, then, but in single families, or little
groups of two or three, do the Digger Indians
dwell—not in the larger and more fertile valleys,
but in those small and secluded; in the midst of
the sage-plains, or more frequently in the rocky defiles of the mountains that stand thickly over the
"Basin."

The Shoshokee is no *nomade*, but the very reverse. A single and isolated mountain is often the
abode of his group or family; and beyond this his
wanderings extend not. There he is at home,
knowing every nook and rat-hole in his own neighbourhood; but as ignorant of the world beyond as
the "sand-rats" themselves—whose pursuit occupies the greater portion of his time.

In respect to his "settled" mode of life, the *Shoshokee* offers a striking contrast to the *Shoshonee*.
Many of the latter are Indians of noble type—warriors who have tamed the horse, and who extend
their incursions, both hunting and hostile, into the
very heart of the Rocky Mountains—up their fertile valleys, and across their splendid "parks," often
bringing back with them the scalps of the savage
and redoubtable Black-feet.

Far different is the character of the wretched
Shoshokee—the mere semblance of a human being
—who rarely strays out of the ravine in which he
was brought forth; and who, at sight of a human
face—be it of friend or enemy—flies to his crag or
cave like a hunted beast!

The Pah-Utah Diggers, however, are of a more warlike disposition; or rather a more wicked and hostile one—hostile to whites, or even to such other Indians as may have occasion to travel through the deserts they inhabit. These people are found scattered throughout the whole southern and south-western portion of the Great Basin—and also in the north-western part of the Colorado desert—especially about the Sevier river, and on several of the tributaries of the great Colorado itself of the west. It was through this part of the country that the caravans from California to New Mexico used to make their annual "trips,"—long before Alta California became a possession of the United States—and the route by which they travelled is known as the *Spanish trail*. The object of these caravans was the import of horses, mules, and other animals —from the fertile valleys of the San Joaquin and Sacramento rivers, to the more sterile settlements of New Mexico. Several kinds of goods were also carried into these interior countries.

This Spanish trail was far from running in a direct line. The sandy waterless plain—known more particularly as the Colorado desert—could not be crossed with safety, and the caravan-route was forced far to the north; and entered within the limits of the Great Basin—thus bringing it through the country inhabited by the Pah-Utah Diggers. The consequence was, that these savages looked out annually for its arrival; and, whenever an opportunity offered, stole the animals that accompanied it, or murdered any of the men who might be found straggling from the main body. When bent on such purposes, these Diggers for a time threw aside their solitary habits—assembling in large bands of several hundred each, and following the caravan travellers, like wolves upon the track of a gang of

buffaloes.   They never made their attacks upon the
main body, or when the white men were in any
considerable force.   Only small groups who had
lagged behind, or gone too rashly in advance, had
to fear from these merciless marauders—who never
thought of such a thing as making captives, but
murdered indiscriminately all who fell into their
hands.   When horses or mules were captured, it
was never done with the intention of keeping them
to ride upon.   Scarcely ever do the Pah-Utahs
make such a use of the horse.   Only for food were
these stolen or plundered from their owners; and
when a booty of this kind was obtained, the animals were driven to some remote defile among the
mountains, and there slaughtered outright.   So long
as a morsel of horse or mule flesh remained upon
the bones, the Diggers kept up a scene of feasting
and merriment—precisely similar to the *carnivals*
of the African Bushmen, after a successful foray
upon the cattle of the Dutch settlers near the Cape.
Indeed, there is such a very striking resemblance
between the Bushmen of Africa and these Digger
Indians of North America; that, were it not for
the distinction of race, and some slight differences
in personal appearance, they might pass as one people.   In nearly every habit and custom, the two
people resemble each other; and in many mental
characteristics they appear truly identical.

The Pah-Utah Diggers have not yet laid aside
their hostile and predatory habits.   They are at
the present hour engaged in plundering forays—
acting towards the emigrant trains of Californian
adventurers, just as they did towards the Spanish
caravans.   But they usually meet with a very different reception from the more daring Saxon travellers, who constitute the "trains" now crossing
their country; and not unfrequently a terrible pun-

ishment is the reward of their audacity. For all that, many of the **emigrants**, who have been so imprudent as to travel **in** small parties, have suffered at their hands, losing not only their property, but their lives: since hundreds of the bravest men have fallen by the arrows of these insignificant savages! Even the exploring parties of the United **States** government, accompanied by troops, **have been attacked** by them; and more than one officer has fallen a victim to their Ishmaelitish propensities.

It is not in open warfare that there is any dread **of** them. The smallest party of whites need not fear to encounter a hundred of them at once; but their attacks are made by stealth, and under cover **of** the night; and, as soon as they have succeeded in separating the horses or other animals from the travellers' camp, they drive them off so adroitly that pursuit is impossible. Whenever a grand blow has been struck—that is, a traveller has been murdered—they all disappear as if by magic; and for several **days after** not one is to be seen, upon whom revenge might be taken. The numerous "**smokes,**" rising up out of the rocky defiles of the mountains, are then the only evidence that human **beings** are in the neighbourhood of the travellers' camp.

The Digger is different from other North-American Indians—both in physical organization and intellectual character. So low is he in the scale of both, as to dispute with the African Bushman, the Andaman islander, and **the starving** savage of Tierra del Fuego, the claim **to that** point in the transition, which is supposed to separate the monkey **from the man.** It has **been** variously awarded by ethnologists, and I as one have had my doubts, as to which of the three is deserving of the distinction. Upon mature consideration, however, I have come to the conclusion that the Digger is entitled to it.

This miserable creature is of a dark-brown or copper colour—the hue so generally known as characteristic of the American aborigines. He stands about five feet in height—often under but rarely over this standard—and his body is thin and meagre, resembling that of a frog stretched upon a fishhook. The skin that covers it—especially that of an old Digger—is wrinkled and corrugated like the hide of an Asiatic rhinoceros—with a surface as dry as parched buckskin. His feet, turned in at the toes—as with all the aborigines of America—have some resemblance to human feet; but in the legs this resemblance ends. The lower limbs are almost destitute of calves, and the knee-pans are of immense size—resembling a pair of pads or callosities, like those upon goats and antelopes. The face is broad and angular, with high cheek-bones; the eyes small, black, and sunken, and sparkle in their hollow sockets, not with true intelligence, but that sort of vivacity which may often be observed in the lower animals, especially in several species of monkeys. Throughout the whole physical composition of the Digger, there is only one thing that appears luxuriant—and that is his hair. Like all Indians he is amply endowed in this respect, and long black tresses—sometimes embrowned by the sun, and matted together with mud or other filth—hang over his naked shoulders. Generally he crops them.

In the summer months, the Digger's costume is extremely simple—after the fashion of that worn by our common parents, Adam and Eve. In winter, however, the climate of his desert home is rigorous in the extreme—the mountains over his head, and the plains under his feet, being often covered

with snow.   At this season he requires a garment
to shelter his body from the piercing blast; and this
he obtains by stitching together a few skins of the
sage-hare, so as to form a kind of shirt or body coat.
He is not always rich enough to have even a good
coat of this simple material; and its scanty skirt too
often exposes his wrinkled limbs to the biting frost.

Between the Digger and his wife, or "squaw,"
there is not much difference either in costume or
character.   The latter may be distinguished, by being of less stature, rather than by any feminine
graces in her physical or intellectual conformation.
She might be recognized, too, by watching the employment of the family ; for it is she who does nearly all the work, stitches the rabbit-skin shirt, digs
the "yampa" and "kamas" roots, gathers the "mezquite" pods, and gets together the larder of "prairie
crickets."   Though lowest of all American Indians
in the scale of civilization, the Digger resembles
them all in this—he regards himself as lord and master, and the woman as his slave.

As already observed, there is no such thing as a
tribe of Diggers—nothing of the nature of a political
organization ; and the chief of their miserable little
community—for sometimes there is a head man—is
only he who is most regarded for his strength.   Indeed, the nature of their country would not admit
of a large number of them living together.   The
little valleys or "oäses"—that occur at intervals
along the banks of some lone desert stream—would
not, any one of them, furnish subsistence to more
than a few individuals—especially to savages ignorant of agriculture—that is, not knowing how to
plant or *sow*.   The Diggers, however, if they know
not how to *sow*, may be said to understand something about how to *reap*, since *root-digging* is one
of their most essential employments—that occupa-

tion from which they have obtained their distinctive appellation, in the language of the trappers.

Not being agriculturists, you will naturally conclude that they are either a pastoral people, or else a nation of hunters. But in truth they are neither one nor the other. They have no domestic animal —many of them not even the universal dog; and as to hunting, there is no large game in their country. The buffalo does not range so far west; and if he did, it is not likely they could either kill or capture so formidable a creature; while the pronghorned antelope, which does inhabit their plains, is altogether too swift a creature, to be taken by any wiles a Digger might invent. The " big-horn," and the black and white-tailed species of deer, are also too shy and too fleet for their puny weapons; and as to the grizzly bear, the very sight of one is enough to give a Digger Indian the " chills."

If, then, they do not cultivate the ground, nor rear some kind of animals, nor yet live by the chase, how do these people manage to obtain subsistence? The answer to this question appears a dilemma— since it has been already stated, that, their country produces little else than the wild and worthless sage plant.

Were we speaking of an Indian of tropical America, or a native of the lovely islands of the great South Sea, there would be no difficulty whatever in accounting for his subsistence—even though he neither planted or sowed, tended cattle, nor yet followed the chase. In these regions of luxuriant vegetation, nature has been bountiful to her children; and, it may be almost literally alleged, that the loaf of bread grows spontaneously on the tree. But the very reverse is the case in the country of the Digger Indian. Even the hand of cultivation could scarce wring a crop from the sterile soil; and

Nature has provided **hardly one** article, that **de-** serves the name of food.

Perhaps you may **fancy that the** Digger is a fisherman; and obtains **his living from** the stream, by the side of which **he makes his** dwelling. Not even this **is** permitted **to** him. It **is** true that his supposed kindred, the Shoshonees, occasionally follow the **occuption** of fishermen upon the banks **of** the Great **Snake** River—which at certain seasons of the year **swarms** with the finest salmon; but the poor Digger has no share **in** the finny spoil. The streams, **that** traverse **his desert** home, empty their waters **into** the briny **bosom of the** Great Salt Lake—a true *Dead Sea*, **where neither salmon,** nor any other fish could live **for an instant.**

How then does the Digger **obtain** his food? Is he a manufacturer—and perforce **a** merchant—who exchanges with **some** other tribe **his** manufactured goods for provisions **and "raw** material?" **Noth**ing **of the** sort. **Least of all is** he a manufacturer. The **hare-skin shirt is his highest effort, in** the line of textile **fabrics; and his** poor **weak bow, and** flint**tipped** arrows, **are the** only tools he is capable of **making.** Sometimes he is even without these weapons; **and** may be **seen** with another—a long stick, with a hook at **one** end—the hook itself being the stump **of a** lopped branch, with its natural inclination to **that** which forms the stick. The object and purpose **of** this simple weapon we shall presently describe.

The Digger's wife **may be seen with a weapon** equally simple **in its construction.** This is also a stick—but a **much shorter** one—pointed at one end, and bearing some resemblance **to** a gardener's "dibble." **Sometimes** it is tipped with horn—when this **can** be procured—but otherwise the hard point is produced by calcining it in the fire. This tool is essentially an implement of husbandry—as will presently appear.

Let us now clear up the mystery, and explain how the Digger maintains himself. There is not much mystery after all. Although, as already stated, his country produces nothing that could fairly be termed *food*, yet there are a few articles within his reach upon which a human being *might* subsist—that is, might just keep body and soul together. One of these articles is the bean, or legume of the "mezquite" tree, of which there are many kinds throughout the desert region. They are known to Spanish Americans as *algarobia* trees; and, in the southern parts of the desert, grow to a considerable size—often attaining the dimension of twenty to twenty-five feet in height.

They produce a large legume, filled with seeds and a pulp of sweetish-acid taste—similar to that of the "honey locust." These beans are collected in large quantities, by the squaw of the Digger, stowed away in grass-woven baskets, or sometimes only in heaps in a corner of his cave, or hovel, if he chance to have one. If so, it is a mere wattle of artemisia, thatched and "chinked" with grass.

The mezquite seeds, then, are the *bread* of the Digger; but, bad as is the quality, the supply is often far behind the demands of his hungry stomach. For vegetables, he has the "yampah" root, an umbelliferous plant, which grows along the banks of the streams. This, with another kind, known as "kamas" or "quamash" (*Camassia esculenta*), is a spontaneous production; and the digging for these roots forms, at a certain season of the year, the principal occupation of the women. The "dibble"-like instrument already described is the *root-digger*. The roots here mentioned, before being eaten, have to undergo a process of cooking. The yampah is

boiled in a very ingenious manner; but this piece
of ingenuity is not native to the Shoshokees, and
has been obtained from their more clever kindred,
the Snakes. The pot is a *wooden one ;* and yet
they can boil meat in it, or make soup if they wish!
Moreover, it is only a basket, a mere vessel of wick-
er-work! How, then, can water be boiled in it?
If you had not been already told how it is done, it
would no doubt puzzle you to find out.

But most likely you have read of a somewhat
similar vessel among the Chippewa Indians — especially the tribe known as the " Assineboins," or
" stone-boilers" — who cook their fish or flesh in
pots made of birch-bark. The phrase *stone-boilers*
will suggest to you how the difficulty is got over.
The birch-bark pot is not set over fire; but stones
are heated and thrown into it—of course already
filled with water. The hot stones soon cause the
water to simmer, and fresh ones are added until it
boils, and the meat is sufficiently cooked. By just
such a process the "Snakes" cook their salmon and
deer's flesh—their wicker pots being woven of so
close a texture that not even water can pass through
the interstices.

It is not often, however, that the Digger is rich
enough to have one of these wicker pots—and when
he has, he is often without anything to put into it.

The *kamas* roots are usually baked in a hole dug
in the earth, and heated by stones taken from the
fire. It requires nearly two days to bake them
properly ; and then, when taken out of the " oven,"
the mass bears a strong resemblance to soft glue or
size, and has a sweet and rather agreeable taste—
likened to that of baked pears or quinces.

I have not yet specified the whole of the Digger's
larder. Were he to depend altogether on the roots
and seeds already mentioned, he would often have

to starve—and in reality he often *does* starve—for,
even with the additional supplies which his sterile
soil scantily furnishes him, he is frequently the victim of famine.

There may be a bad season of the mezquite-crop,
and the bears—who are as cunning "diggers" as
he—sometimes destroy his "plantations" of yampah
and kamas. He finds a resource, however, in the
prairie-cricket, an insect—or reptile, you may call
it—of the *gryllus* tribe, of a dark-brown colour, and
more like a bug than any other crawler. These, at
certain seasons of the year, make their appearance
upon the desert-plains, and in such numbers that
the ground appears to be alive with them. An allied species has of late years become celebrated: on
account of a visit paid by vast numbers of them to
the Mormon plantations; where, as may be remembered, they devastated the crops—just as the locusts do in Africa—causing a very severe season
of famine among these isolated people. It may be
remembered also, that flocks of white birds followed
the movements of these American locusts—preying
upon them, and thinning their multitudinous hosts.

These birds were of the gull genus (*Larus*), and
one of the most beautiful of the species. They frequent the shores and islands of the rivers of *Prairie-land*, living chiefly upon such insects as are
found in the neighbourhood of their waters. It
was but natural, therefore, they should follow the
locusts, or "grasshoppers," as the Mormons termed them; but the *pseudo-prophet* of these deluded
people could not suffer to pass such a fine opportunity of proving his divine inspiration: which he did
by audaciously declaring that the birds were "heav-
en-born," and had been sent by the Almighty (in
obedience to a prayer from him, the prophet) to rid
the country of the pest of the grasshoppers!

X

These prairie-crickets are of a dark-brown colour
—not unlike the *gryllus migratorius* of Africa, and
with very similar habits.   When settled thickly
upon the ground, the whole surface assumes a dark-
ish hue, as if covered with crape; and when they
are all in motion—creeping to and fro in search of
their food—a very singular effect is produced.   At
this time they do not take to wing; though they
attempt to get out of the way, by making short
hops from place to place, and crawling with great
rapidity.   Notwithstanding their efforts to escape,
hundreds of them are "squashed" beneath the foot
of the pedestrian, or hoofs of the traveller's horse.

These crickets, with several bug-like insects of
different species, furnish the Digger with an important article of food.   It may appear a strange
provender for a human stomach; but there is nothing unnatural about it—any more than about the
eating of shrimps or prawns; and it will be remembered that the Bushmen, and many other tribes of
South Africa eat the *gryllus migratorius ;* while, in
the northern part of that same continent, many nations regard them as a proper article of food.
Though some writers have asserted, that it was the
legume of the locust-tree (an acacia) which was
eaten by St. John the Baptist in the wilderness, it
is easily proved that such was not the case.   That
his food was the locust (*gryllus migratorius*) and
wild honey, is strictly and literally true; and at the
present day, were you to visit the "wilderness"
mentioned by the Apostle, you might see people
living upon "locusts and wild honey," just as they
did eighteen hundred years ago.

The Diggers *cook* their crickets sometimes by
boiling them in the pots afore-mentioned, and sometimes by "roasting."   They also mix them with
the mezquite seeds and pulp—the whole forming a

kind of plum-pudding, or "cricket-pasty,"—or, as it is jocosely termed by the trappers, "cricket-cake."

Their mode of collecting the grasshoppers is not without some display of ingenuity. When the insects are in abundance, there is not much difficulty in obtaining a sufficient supply; but this is not always the case. Sometimes they appear very sparsely upon the plains; and, being nimble in their movements, are not easily laid hold of. Only one could be taken at a time; and, by gleaning in this way, a very limited supply would be obtained. To remedy this, the Diggers have invented a somewhat ingenious contrivance for capturing them wholesale—which is effected in the following manner:—When the whereabouts of the grasshoppers has been discovered, a round hole—of three or four feet in diameter, and of about equal depth—is scooped out in the centre of the plain. It is shaped somewhat after the fashion of a kiln; and the earth, that has been taken out, is carried out of the way.

The Digger community then all turn out—men, women, and children—and deploy themselves into a wide circle, enclosing as large a tract as their numbers will permit. Each individual is armed with a stick, with which he beats the sage bushes, and makes other violent demonstrations: the object being to frighten the grasshoppers, and cause them to move inward towards the pit that has been dug. The insects, thus beset, move as directed—gradually approaching the centre—while the "beaters" follow in a circle constantly lessening in circumference. After a time the crickets, before only thinly scattered over the plain—grow more crowded as the space becomes contracted; until at length the surface is covered with a black moving swarm; and the beaters, still pressing upon them, and driving

them onward, force the whole body pell-mell over
the edges of the pit.

Bunches of grass, already provided, are now flung
over them, and upon that a few shovelfuls of earth
or sand; and then—horrible to relate!—a large pile
of artemisia-stalks is heaped upon the top and set
on fire! The result is that, in a few minutes, the
poor grasshoppers are smoked to death, and parched at the same time—so as to be ready for eating,
whenever the *débris* of the fire has been removed.

The prairie cricket is not the only article of the
flesh-meat kind, found in the larder of the Digger.
Another animal furnishes him with an occasional
meal. This is the "sage-hare," known to hunters
as the "sage-rabbit," but to naturalists as the *lepus
artemisia*. It is a very small animal—less in size
than the common rabbit—though it is in reality a
true hare. It is of a silvery, or whitish-grey colour
—which adapts it to the hue of the *artemisia* bushes on the stalks and berries of which it feeds.

It is from the skins of this animal, that the Digger women manufacture the rabbit-skin shirts, already described. Its flesh would not be very agreeable to a European palate—even with the addition
of an onion—for it has the sage flavour to such a
degree, as to be as bitter as wormwood itself. An
onion with it would not be tasted! But tastes differ, and by the Digger the flesh of the sage-hare is
esteemed one of the nicest delicacies. He hunts it,
therefore, with the greatest assiduity; and the
chase of this insignificant animal is to the Digger,
what the hunt of the stag, the elephant, or the wild
boar, is to hunters of a more pretentious ambition.

With his bow and arrows he frequently succeeds
in killing a single hare; but this is not always so
easy—since the sage-hare, like all of its kind, is shy,
swift, and cunning. Its colour, closely resembling

the hue of the artemisia foliage, is a considerable protection to it; and it can hide among these bushes, where they grow thickly—as they generally do —over the surface of the ground.

But the Digger is not satisfied with the scanty and uncertain supply, which his weak bow and arrows would enable him to obtain. As in the case of the grasshoppers, he has contrived a plan for capturing the sage-hares by wholesale.

This he accomplishes by making a "surround," and driving the animals, not into a *pit*, but into a *pound*. The pound is constructed something after the same fashion as that used by the Chippewas, and other northern Indians, for capturing the herds of reindeer; in other words, it is an enclosure, entered by a narrow mouth — from the *jaws* of which mouth, two fences are carried far out into the plain, in a gradually diverging direction. For the deer and other large animals, the fences of the pound— as also those of the funnel that conducts to it, require to be made of strong stakes, stockaded side by side; but this work, as well as the timber with which to construct it, is far beyond the reach of the Digger. His enclosure consists of a mere wattle of artemisia stalks and branches, woven into a row of those already standing — with here and there a patching of rude nets, made of roots and grass. The height is not over three feet; and the sage-hare might easily spring over it; but the stupid creature, when once "in the pound," never thinks of looking upward; but continues to dash its little skull against the wattle, until it is either "clubbed" by the Digger, or impaled upon one of his obsidian arrows.

Other quadrupeds, constituting a portion of the Digger's food, are several species of "gophers," or sand-rats, ground-squirrels, and marmots. In many parts of the Great Basin, these small rodents abound: dwelling between the **crevices of** rocks, or honeycombing the dry **plains** with **their** countless burrows. The Digger captures them by various wiles. One method is by shooting them with blunt arrows; but the more successful plan is, by setting **a trap** at the entrance to their earthern caves. It is the "figure **of 4** trap," which the Digger employs for **this** purpose, and which he constructs with ingenuity—placing a great many around a " warren," and often **taking** as many as fifty or sixty " rats" in a single day!

In weather too cold for the gophers to come out of their caves, the Digger then "digs" for them: thus further entitling him to his special appellation.

That magnificent bird, the " cock of the plains," sometimes furnishes the Digger with "fowl" for his dinner. This is a bird of the grouse family (*tetrao urophasianus*), and the largest species that is known —exceeding in size the famed " cock of the woods" of northern Europe. A full-fledged cock of the plains is as large as an eagle; and, unlike most of **the** grouse kind, has a long narrow body. His plumage is of a silvery grey colour—produced by a mottle **of** black and white—no doubt, given him by nature to assimilate him to the hue of the artemisia —amidst which he habitually dwells, and the berries of which furnish him with most of his food.

He is remarkable for two large *goitre-like* swellings on the breast, covered with a sort of hair instead of feathers; but, though a fine-looking large bird, and a grouse too, his flesh is bitter and unpalatable—even more so than that of the sage-hare. **For all** that, **it is** a delicacy to the Digger, and a **rare one; for the** cock of the plains is neither plentiful, nor easily captured when seen.

There are several other small animals—both quad-

rupeds and birds—inhabiting Digger-land, upon
which an occasional meal is made. Indeed, the food
of the Digger is sufficiently varied. It is not in the
quality but the quantity he finds most cause of complaint: for with all his energies he never gets
enough. In the summer season, however, he is less
stinted. Then the berries of the buffalo-bush are
ripe; and these, resembling currants, he collects in
large quantities—placing his rabbit-skin wrapper
under the bush, and shaking down the ripe fruit in
showers. A *mélange* of prairie crickets and buffa-
lo-berries is esteemed by the Digger, as much as
would be the best specimen of a "currant-cake" in
any nursery in Christendom!

The Digger finds a very curious species of edible
bug, which builds its nest on the ledges of the cliffs
—especially those that overhang a stream. These
nests are of a conical or pine-apple shape, and about
the size of this fruit.

This bug—not yet classified or described by en-
tomologists—is of a dark-brown colour, about the
size of the ordinary cockroach; and when boiled is
considered a proper article of food—not only by
the unfastidious Diggers, but by Indians of a more
epicurean *goût*.

Besides the yampah and kamas, there are several
other edible roots found in the Digger country.
Among others may be mentioned a species of thistle (*circium virginiarum*)—the root of which grows
to the size of an ordinary carrot, and is almost as
well flavoured. It requires a great deal of roasting, or boiling, before it is sufficiently cooked to
be eaten.

The *kooyah* is another article of food still more
popular among Digger gourmands. This is the
root of the *valeriana edulis*. It is of a bright-yel-
low colour, and grows to a considerable size. It

has the characteristic odor of the well-known plant; but not so strong as in the prepared substance of *valerian*. The plant itself does not grow in the arid soil of the desert, but rather in the rich fertile bottoms of the streams, or along the shores of marshy lakes—in company with the kamas and yampah. It is when these roots are in season, that the Shoshokees most frequent such localities; and, indeed, this same season is the time when all other articles of Digger food are plenteous enough—the summer. The winter months are to him the "tight times."

In some parts of the desert country, as already observed, grow species of pines, with edible cones —or rather edible seeds which the cones contain. These seeds resemble nuts, and are about the size of the common filberts.

More than one species of pine produces this sort of food; but, in the language of the Spanish Californians and New-Mexicans, they are all indifferently termed *piñon*, and the seeds simply *piñones*, or "piñons." Where these are within the reach of the Digger—as they are in some districts—he is then well provided for; since the piñons, when roasted, not only form an agreeable and nutritious article of food, but can be stored up as a winter stock—that will keep for a considerable time, without danger of spoiling, or growing too stale.

Such is the *commissariat* of the Digger Indian; and, poor in quality though it be, there are times when he cannot obtain a sufficient supply of it. At such times he has recourse to food of a still meaner kind—to roots, scarce eatable, and even to the seeds of several species of grass! Worms, grubs, the *agama cornuta*, or "horned-frog of the prairies," with other species of lizards, become his sole resource; and in the search and capture of these he occupies himself from morning to night.

It is ín this employment that he finds use for the long sapling, with the hooked end upon it—the hook being used for dragging the lizards out of clefts in the rocks, within which they have sought shelter. In the accomplishment of this, the Digger displays an adroitness that astonishes the traveller: often "jerking" the reptile out of some dark crevice within which it might be supposed to have found a retreat secure from all intruders.

Many other curious habits might be related of this abject and miserable race of human beings; but, perhaps enough has been detailed, to secure them a place in the list of our "odd people."

THE GUARAONS, OR PALM-DWELLERS.

Young reader, I may take it for granted that you have heard of the great river Orinoco—one of the largest rivers not only of South America, but in the world. By entering at its mouth, and ascending to its source, you would have to make a journey of about 1,500 miles; but this journey, so far from being direct, or in a straight line, would carry you in a kind of spiral curve—very much like the figure 6, the apex of the figure representing the mouth of the river. In other words, the Orinoco, rising in the unexplored mountains of Spanish Guiana, first runs eastward; and then, having turned gradually to every point of the compass, resumes its easterly course, continuing in this direction till it empties its mighty flood into the Atlantic Ocean.

Not by one mouth, however. On the contrary, long before the Orinoco approaches the sea, its channel separates into a great many branches (or "caños," as they are called in the language of the country), each of which slowly meandering in its own course, reaches the coast by a separate mouth, or "boca." Of these caños there are about fifty, embracing within their ramifications a "delta" nearly half as large as England! Though they have all been distinguished by separate names, only three or four of them are navigable by ships of any considerable size; and, except to the few pilots whose duty it is to conduct vessels into that main channel of the river, the whole delta of the Orinoco may be regarded as a country still unexplored, and almost

THE GUARAONS, OR PALM-DWELLERS.

unknown. Indeed, the same remark might be made
of the whole river, were it not for the magnificent
monument left by the great traveller Von Humboldt—whose narrative of the exploration of the
Orinoco is, beyond all comparison, the finest book
of travels yet given to the world. To him are we
chiefly indebted for our knowledge of the Orinoco;
since the Spanish nation, who, for more than three
centuries, have held undisputed possession of this
mighty stream, have left us scarce a line about it
worth either credit or record.

It is now more than half a century, since the
date of Humboldt's " Personal Narrative;" and yet,
strange to say, during all that period, scarce an item
has been added to our knowledge of the Orinoco,
beyond what this scientific traveller had already
told us. Indeed, there is not much to say : for there
has been little change in the river since then—either
in the aspect of nature, or the condition of man.
What change there has been, possesses rather a retrograde, than a progressive character. Still, now,
as then, on the banks of the Orinoco, we behold a
languid commerce—characteristic of the decaying
Spano-American race—and the declining efforts of
a selfish and bigoted missionary zeal, whose boasted aim of " christianizing and civilizing" has ended
only in producing a greater *brutalization*. After
three centuries of *paternosters* and bell-ringing, the
red savage of the Orinoco returns to the worship
of his ancestral gods—or to no worship at all—and
for this backsliding he can, perhaps, give a sufficient
reason.

Pardon me, young reader, for this digression. It
is not my purpose to discuss the polemical relations
of those who inhabit the banks of the Orinoco; but
to give you some account of a very singular people
who dwell near its mouth—upon the numerous

caños, already mentioned as constituting its delta. These are the "Guaraons,"—a tribe of Indians— usually considered as a branch of the Great Carib family, but forming a community among themselves of seven or eight thousand souls; and differing so much from most other savages in their habits and mode of life, as fairly to entitle them to the appellation of an "Odd People."

The Orinoco, like many other large rivers, is subject to a periodical rise and fall; that is, once every year, the river swells to a great height above its ordinary level. The swelling or "flood" was for a long time supposed to proceed from the melting of snow upon the cordilleras of the Andes—in which mountains several of the tributaries of the Orinoco have their rise. This hypothesis, however, has been shown to be an incorrect one; since the main stream of the Orinoco does not proceed from the Andes, nor from any other snow-capped mountains; but has its origin, as already stated, in the *sierras* of Guiana. The true cause of its periodical rising, therefore, is the vast amount of rain which falls within the tropics; and this is itself occasioned by the sun's course across the torrid zone, which is also the cause of its being periodical or "annual." So exact is the time at which these rains fall, and produce the floods of the Orinoco, that the inhabitants of the river can tell, within a few days, when the rising will commence, and when the waters will reach their lowest!

The flood season very nearly corresponds to our own summer—the rise commencing in April, and the river being at its maximum height in August —while the minimum is again reached in December. The height to which the Orinoco rises has been variously estimated by travellers: some alleging it to be nearly one hundred feet; while others

estimate it to be only fifty, or even less! The reason of this discrepancy may be, that the measurements have been made at different points—at each
of which, the actual height to which the flood attains, may be greater or less than at the others.
At any one place, however, the rise is the same—or
very nearly so—in successive years. This is proved
by observations made at the town of Angostura—
the lowest Spanish settlement of any importance
upon the Orinoco. There, nearly in front of the
town, a little rocky islet towers up in the middle
of the river; the top of which is just fifty feet above
the bed of the stream, when the volume of water is
at its minimum. A solitary tree stands upon the
pinnacle of this rock; and each year, when the water is in full flood, the tree alone is visible—the islet
being entirely submerged. From this peculiar circumstance, the little islet has obtained the name of
" Orinocometer," or measurer of the Orinoco.

The rise, here indicated, is about fifty feet; but it
does not follow from this, that throughout its whole
course the river should annually rise to so great a
height. In reality it does not.

At Angostura, as the name imports, the river is
narrowed to less than half its usual width—being
there confined between high banks that impinge
upon its channel. Above and below, it widens
again; and, no doubt, in proportion to this widening will the annual rise be greater or less. In fact,
at many places, the width of the stream is no longer
that of its ordinary channel; but, on the contrary,
a vast "freshet" or inundation, covering the country
for hundreds of miles—here flooding over immense
marshes or grassy plains, and hiding them altogether—there flowing among forests of tall trees,
the tops of which alone project above the tumult
of waters! These inundations are peculiarly ob-

servable in the *delta* of the Orinoco—where every
year, in the months of July and August, the whole
surface of the country becomes changed into a grand
fresh-water **sea**: the tops of the trees alone rising
above the flood, and proclaiming that there is *land*
at the bottom.

At this season the ordinary channels, or *caños*,
would be obliterated; and navigation through them
become difficult or impossible, but for the tree-tops;
which, after the manner of "buoys" and signal-
marks, serve to guide the pilots through the intricate mazes of the "**bocas** del Orinoco."

Now it is this annual inundation, and the semi-
submergence of these trees under the flood, that
has given origin to the peculiar people of whom we
are about to speak—the Guaraons; or, perhaps, we
should rather say: from these causes have arisen
their strange habits and modes of life, which entitle
them to be considered an "odd people."

During the period of the inundation, if you should
sail up the southern or principal caño of the Orinoco—known as the "boca de navios," or "ships'
mouth"—and keep your face to the northward, you
would behold the singular spectacle of a forest growing out of the water! In some places you would
perceive single trees, with the upper portion of their
straight branchless trunks rising vertically above
the surface, and crowned by about a dozen great
fan-shaped leaves, radiating outwards from their
summits. At other places, you would see many
crowded together, their huge fronds meeting, and
forming close clumps, or "water groves," whose
deep-green colour contrasts finely as it flings its reflection on the glistening surface below.

Were it night—and your course led you through
one of the smaller caños in the northern part of the
delta—you would behold a spectacle yet more sin-

gular, and more difficult to be explained; a spectacle that astounded and almost terrified the bold navigators who first ventured to explore these intricate
coasts. You would not only perceive a forest growing out of the water; but, high up among the tops
of the trees, you would behold blazing fires—not
the conflagration of the trees themselves, as if the
forest were in flames — but fires regularly built,
glowing as from so many furnaces, and casting their
red glare upwards upon the broad green leaves, and
downwards upon the silvery surface of the water!

If you should chance to be near enough to these
fires, you would see cooking utensils suspended over
them; human forms, both of men and women, seated or squatting around them; other human forms,
flitting like shadows among the tops of the trees;
and down below, upon the surface of the water, a
fleet of canoes (*periaguas*), fastened with their
mooring-ropes to the trunks. All this would surprise you—as it did the early navigators—and, very
naturally, you would inquire what it could mean.
Fires apparently suspended in the air! human beings moving about among the tops of the trees,
talking, laughing, and gesticulating! in a word, acting just as any other savages would do—for these
human beings *are* savages—amidst the tents of their
encampment, or the houses of their village. In reality it is a village upon which you are gazing—a
village suspended in the air—a village of the Guaraon Indians!

Let us approach nearer; let us steal into this wa-
ter-village—for it would not be always safe to enter
it, except by stealth—and see how its singular habitations are constructed, as also in what way their
occupants manage to get their living. The village
under our observation is now—at the period of inundation—nearly a hundred miles from shore, or

Y

from any dry land: it will be months before the
waters can subside; and, even then, the country
around will partake more of the nature of a quagmire, than of firm soil; impassable to any human being—though *not* to a Guaraon, as we shall presently see.   It is true, the canoes, already mentioned,
might enable their owners to reach the firm shores
beyond the delta; and so they do at times; but it
would be a voyage too long and too arduous to be
made often—as for the supply of food and other
daily wants—and it is not for this purpose the canoes are kept.   No: these Guaraons visit terra firma
only at intervals; and then for purposes of trade,
with a portion of their own and other tribes who
dwell there; but they permanently reside within
the area of the inundated forests; where they are
independent, not only of foreign aggression, but also
for their supply of all the necessaries of life.   In
these forests, whether flooded or not, they procure
everything of which they stand in need—they there
find, to use an old-fashioned phrase, "meat, drink,
washing, and lodging."   In other words: were the
inundation to continue for ever, and were the Guaraons entirely prohibited from intercourse with the
dry land, they could still find subsistence in this,
their home upon the waters.

Whence comes their subsistence?   No doubt
you will say that fish is their food; and drink, of
course, they have in abundance; but this would not
be the true explanation.   It is true they eat fish,
and turtle, and the flesh of the *manatee*, or "fish-
cow"—since the capturing of these aquatic creatures is one of the chief occupations of the Guaraons—but they are ofttimes entirely without such
food; for, it is to be observed, that, during the period of the inundations fish are not easily caught—
sometimes not at all.   At these times the Guaraons

would starve—since like all other savages, they are
improvident—were it not that the singular region
they inhabit supplies them with another **article** of
food—one that is inexhaustible.

What is this food, and from whence derived? **It**
will scarce surprise you **to** hear **that** it is the produce of the trees **already** mentioned; but, perhaps,
you *will* deem **it singular** when I tell you that the
trees of this great *water forest* are all of one kind—
all of the same species—so that here we have the
remarkable fact of a single species of vegetable,
growing without **care** or cultivation, and supplying
all the wants of man—his food, clothing, fuel, utensils, ropes, houses, and boats—not **even** drink excepted, as will presently be seen.

The name of this wonderful tree? "Itá," the
Guaraons call it; though it is **more generally known**
as "morichi" among the Spanish **inhabitants of the**
Orinoco; but I shall here give my young **reader an**
account of it, from which he will learn something
more than its name.

The *itá* is a true palm-tree, belonging to the genus
mauritia; and, I may remark, that notwithstanding the resemblance **in** sound, the name of the genus
is not derived from **the** words "morichi," "murichi," or "muriti," all of which are different Indian
appellations **of this tree.** *Mauritia* is simply **a**
Latinized **designation borrowed** from the name of
Prince Maurice **of Nassau, in** whose honour **the**
genus was named. The resemblance, therefore, is
merely accidental. I may add, too, that there are
many species of *mauritia* growing in different parts
of tropical America—some of them palms of large
size, and towering height, with straight smooth
trunks; while others are only tiny little trees, scarce
taller than **a man,** and with their trunks thickly
covered with conical protuberances or spines.

Some of them, moreover, affect a high dry soil, beyond the reach of floods; while others do not prosper, except on tracts habitually marshy, or annually covered with inundations. Of these latter, the *itá* is perhaps the most conspicuous: since we have already stated, that for nearly six months of the year it grows literally out of the water.

Like all its congeners, the itá is a "fan-palm;" that is, its leaves, instead of being *pinnately* divided as in most species of palms, or altogether *entire* as in some few, radiate from the midrib of the leaf-stalk, into a broad palmated shape, bearing considerable resemblance to a fan when opened to its full extent. At the tips these leaflets droop slightly, but at that end where they spring out of the midrib, they are stiff and rigid. The petiole, or leaf-stalk itself, is long, straight, and thick; and where it clasps the stem or trunk, is swollen out to a foot in width, hollowed, or concave on the upper side. A full-grown leaf, with its petiole, is a wonderful object to look upon. The stalk is a solid beam full twelve feet in length, and the leaf has a diameter of nearly as much. Leaf and stalk together make a load, just as much as one man can carry upon his shoulders!

Set about a dozen of these enormous leaves on the summit of a tall cylindrical column of five feet in circumference, and about one hundred in height—place them with their stalks clasping or sheathing its top—so that the spreading fans will point, in every direction outwards, inclining slightly upwards; do this, and you will have the great *morichi* palm. Perhaps, you may see the trunk swollen at its middle or near the top—so that its lower part is thinner than above—but more often the huge stem is a perfect cylinder. Perhaps, you may see several of the leaves drooping downward, as if threatening to fall from the tree; you may even see them upon the ground where they have fallen, and a splendid ruin they appear. You may see again rising upward out of the very centre of the crown of foliage, a straight thick-pointed column. This is the young leaf in process of development—its tender leaflets yet unopened, and closely clasped together. But the fervid tropical sun soon produces expansion; and a new fan takes the place of the one that has served its time and fallen to the earth —there to decay, or to be swept off by the flood of waters.

Still more may be noticed, while regarding this noble palm. Out of that part of the trunk—where it is embraced by the sheathing bases of the petioles—at a certain season of the year, a large spathe will be seen to protrude itself, until it has attained a length of several feet. This spathe is a bract-like sheath, of an imperfect tubular form. It bursts open; and then appears the huge spadix of flowers, of a whitish-green colour, arranged along the flower-stalk in rows—*pinnately*. It will be observed, moreover, that these spadices are different upon different trees; for it must be remembered that the mauritia palm is *diœcious*—that is having the female flowers on one tree, and the male or staminiferous flowers upon another. After the former have glowed for a time in the heat of the sun, and received the fertilizing pollen wafted to them by the breeze—carried by bee or bird, or transported by some unknown and mysterious agency of nature— the fruits take form and ripen. These, when fully ripe, have attained to the size of a small apple, and are of a very similar form. They are covered with small brown smooth scales—giving them somewhat the appearance of fir-cones, except that they are roundish instead of being cone-shaped. Under-

neath the scales there is a thinnish layer of pulp,
and then the stone or *nut*. A single spadix will
carry several hundreds—thousands, I might say—
of these nuts; and the whole bunch is a load equal
to the strength of two ordinary men!

Such is the itá palm. Now for its uses—the uses
to which it is put by the Guaraons.

When the Guaraon wishes to build himself a habitation, he does not begin by digging a foundation
in the earth. In the spongy soil on which he stands,
that would be absurd. At a few inches below the
surface, he would reach water; and he might dig to
a vast depth without finding firm ground. But he
has no idea of laying a foundation upon the ground,
or of building a house there. He knows that in a
few weeks the river will be rising; and would over-
top his roof, however high he might make it. His
foundation, therefore, instead of being laid in the
ground, is placed far above it—just so far, that
when the inundation is at its height the floor of his
dwelling will be a foot or two above it. He does
not take this height from guess work. That would
be a perilous speculation. He is guided by certain
marks upon the trunks of palm-trees—notches
which he has himself made on the preceding year,
or the natural watermark, which he is able to distinguish by certain appearances on the trees. This
point once determined, he proceeds to the building
of his house.

A few trunks are selected, cut down, and then
split into beams of sufficient length. Four fine
trees, standing in a quadrangle, have already been
selected to form the corner posts. In each of these,
just above the watermark, is cut a deep notch with
a horizontal base to serve as a rest for the cross-
beams that are to form the foundation of the structure. Into these notches the beams are hoisted—

by means of ropes—and there **securely tied.** To
reach the point where the platform **is to be** erected
— sometimes a very high elevation — ladders are
necessary; and these are of native manufacture —
being simply the trunk of a palm-tree, with **notches**
cut in it for the toes of the climber. These afterwards serve **as a means of** ascending and descending to the surface **of the** water—during the period
of its rise and fall. **The** main timbers having been
firmly secured in their places, cross-beams are laid
upon them, the latter being either pieces of the split
trunks, or, what is usually easier **to** obtain, the petioles **of** the great leaves — each of which, as already stated, forms of itself a large beam, twelve
feet in length and from **six** to twelve inches in
breadth. These **are** next secured at both **ends** by
ropes of the palm-fibre.

Next comes a layer of palm-leaves, **the strong,**
tough leaflets serving admirably as laths to uphold
the coating of mud, which is laid thickly over them.
The mud is obtained from below, without difficulty,
and in any quantity required; and when trowelled
smooth and dry—which it soon becomes under the
hot sun—constitutes an excellent floor, where a fire
may be kindled without danger of burning either
the laths or **joists** underneath.

As yet the **Guaraon** has completed only the **floor**
of his dwelling, **but that is** his principal labour. He
cares not **for walls** — neither sides nor **gables.**
There is no cold frosty weather to chill him **in** his
tropical home—no snow to **be** kept **out.** The rain
alone, usually falling in a vertical **direction,** has to
be guarded against; and from this **he** secures himself by a second platform of lighter materials, covered with mats, **which** he has already woven for the
purpose, and with palm-leaflets, so placed as to cast
off the heaviest shower. This also shelters **him**

against the **burning sun—an enemy which** he dreads
even more **than the rain.**

His home **is now finished; and,** with the exception
of the **mud floor, is all of itá** palm — beams, cross-
timbers, **laths,** ropes, and mats.   The ropes he has
obtained, by stripping off the epidermis of the full-
grown leaflets, and then twisting it into cordage of
any thickness required.   For this purpose it is equal
to hemp.   The mats he has made from the same
material—and well does he, or rather his wife—for
this **is** usually the work of the females—know how
to plait and weave them.

Having completed the building of his aërial dwelling, the Guaraon would eat.   He has fish, which
has been caught in the neighbouring caño—perhaps
turtle—perhaps the flesh of the manatee, or the alligator—for his palate is by no means of a delicate
fineness, and will not refuse a steak from the tail of
the American crocodile.   But when the flood time
is on, fish become scarce, or cannot be had at all—
no more can turtles, or sea-cows, or alligators.   Besides, scarce or plenty, something else is wanted to
vary the diet.   Bread is wanted; and for this the
Guaraon has not far to go.   The itá again befriends
him for he finds, upon splitting open its trunk, a
large deposit of medullary pith or fecula; which,
when submitted to the process of bruising or grating, and afterwards stirred in water, forms a sediment at the bottom of the vessel, a substance not
only eatable, but equal in excellence to the well-
known produce of the *sago* palm.

This farinaceous pith, formed into cakes and roasted over the fire—the fuel being supplied by leaves
and leaf-stalks—constitutes the *yuruma*—the daily
bread of the Guaraon.

The yuruma, or rather the sago out of which it is
made, is not obtainable at all times.   It is the male

palm which produces it; and it must be extracted just as the tree is about to expand its spadix of flowers. The same curious fact is observed with regard to the *maguey*, or great American aloe, which produces the drink called "pulque." To procure the sap in any considerable quantity, the maguey must be tapped, just on that day when the flower-stalk is about to shoot upward from among the leaves.

The Guaraon, having eaten his yuruma, would drink. Does he have recourse to the water which flows in abundance beneath his dwelling? No. On ordinary occasions he may quench his thirst in that way; but he wishes for some beverage more cheering. Again the itá yields it without stint, and even gives him a choice. He may tap the trunk, and draw forth the sap; which, after being submitted to a process of fermentation, becomes a wine— "murichi wine," a beverage which, if the Guaraon be so inclined, and drink to excess, will make him "as drunk as a lord!"

But he may indulge in a less dangerous, and more delicate drink, also furnished by his favourite itá. This he obtains by flinging a few of the nuts into a vessel of water, and leaving them awhile to ferment; then beating them with a pestle, until the scales and pulp are detached; and, lastly, passing the water through a sieve of palm fibre. This done, the drink is ready to be quaffed. For all these purposes tools and utensils are required, but the itá also furnishes them. The trunk can be scooped out into dishes; or cut into spoons, ladles, and trenchers. The flower "spathe," also gives him cups and saucers. Iron tools, such as hatchets and knives, he has obtained from commerce with Europeans; but, before their arrival in the New World, the Guaraon had his hatchet of flint, and his knife-blade of obsidian : and even now, if necessary, ho could manage without metal of any kind.

The bow and arrows which he uses are obtained from the tough, sinewy petiole of the leaf; so is the harpoon-spear with which he strikes the great manatee, the porpoise, and the alligator; the canoe light as cork, which carries him through the intricate channels of the delta, is the hollow trunk of a morichi palm. His nets and lines, and the cloth which he wears around his loins, are all plaited or woven from the young leaflets before they have expanded into the fan-like leaf.

Like other beings, the Guaraon must at times sleep. Where does he stretch his body—on the floor?—on a mat? No. He has already provided himself with a more luxurious couch—the "rede," or hammock, which he suspends between two trees; and in this he reclines—not only during the night, but by day, when the sun is too hot to admit of violent exertion. His wife has woven the hammock most ingeniously. She has cut off the column of young leaves, that projects above the crown of the morichi. This she has shaken, until the tender leaflets become detached from each other and fall apart. Each she now strips of its outer covering—a thin riband-like pellicle of a pale yellow colour—which shrivels up almost like a thread. These she ties into bundles, leaving them to dry awhile; after which she spins them into strings, or, if need be, twists them into larger cords. She then places two horizontal rods or poles about six feet apart, and doubles the string over them some forty or fifty times. This constitutes the *woof;* and the *warp* is obtained by cross-strings twisted or tied to each of the longitudinal ones, at intervals of seven or eight inches. A strong cord, made from the epidermis of the full-grown leaves, is now passed

through the loop of all the strings, drawn together
at both ends, and the poles are then pulled out.
The hammock, being finished and hung up between
two trees, provides the naked Indian with a couch,
upon which he may repose as luxuriantly as a monarch on his bed of down. Thus, then, does a single
tree furnish everything which man, in his primitive
simplicity, may require. No wonder that the enthusiastic missionaries have given to the morichi-
palm the designation of "arbol de vida" (tree of
life).

It may be asked why does the Guaraon live in
such a strange fashion—especially when on all sides
around him there are vast tracts of *terra firma*
upon which he might make his dwelling, and where
he could, with far less difficulty, procure all the
necessaries, and many of the luxuries of life? The
question is easily answered; and this answer will
be best given by asking others in return. Why do
the Esquimaux and Laplanders cling to their inhospitable home upon the icy coasts of the Arctic Sea?
Why do tribes of men take to the cold barren
mountains, and dwell there, within sight of lovely
and fertile plains? Why do others betake themselves to the arid steppes and dreary recesses of the
desert?

No doubt the Guaraon, by powerful enemies
forced from his aboriginal home upon the firm soil,
first sought refuge in the marshy flats where we
now encounter him: there he found security from
pursuit and oppression; there—even at the expense
of other luxuries—he was enabled to enjoy the
sweetest of all—the luxury of liberty.

What was only a necessity at first, soon became
a habit; and that habit is now an essential part of
his nature. Indeed, it is not so long since the necessity itself has been removed.

Even at the present hour, the Guaraon would not be secure, were he to stray too far from his sheltering marshes—for, **sad** though it be to say so, the poor Indian, **when beyond** the protection of his tribe, is in many parts of South America **still** treated as a slave. In the *delta* **he** feels secure. **No** slave-hunter — no enemy can follow him th**ere**. Even the foemen of his own race cannot compete with him in crossing the wide flats of spongy quagmire—over which, from long habit, he is enabled **to** glide with the lightness and fleetness of a bird. During the **season** of overflow, **or** when the waters have fallen to their lowest, he is equally secure from aggression or pursuit; and, no doubt, in spite of missionary zeal—in spite of the general progress of civilization—in this savage security he will long remain.

THE LAPLANDERS.

ONE of the oldest "odd" people with which we are acquainted are the Laps or Laplanders. For many centuries the more civilized nations of Europe have listened to strange accounts, told by travellers of these strange people; many of these accounts being exaggerated, and others totally untrue. Some of the old travellers, being misled by the deerskin dresses worn by the Laps, believed, or endeavoured to make others believe, that they were born with hairy skins like wild beasts; and one traveller represented that they had only a single eye, and that in the middle of the breast! This very absurd conception about a one-eyed people gained credit, even so late as the time of Sir Walter Raleigh—with this difference, that the locality of these gentry with the odd "optic" was South America instead of Northern Europe.

In the case of the poor Laplander, not the slightest exaggeration is needed to render him an interesting study, either to the student of ethnology, or to the merely curious reader. He needs neither the odd eye, nor the hairy pelt. In his personal appearance, dress, dwelling, mode of occupation, and subsistence, he is so different from almost every other tribe or nation of people, as to furnish ample matter for a monograph at once unique and amusing.

I shall not stay to inquire whence originated this odd specimen of humanity. Such speculations are more suited to those so-called *learned* ethnologists,

who, resembling the anatomists in other branches
of natural history, delight to deal in the mere ped-
antry of science—who, from the mere coincidence
of a few words, can prove that two peoples utterly
unlike have sprung from a common source; precisely as Monsieur Cuvier, by the examination of a
single tooth, has proved that a rabbit was a rhinoceros!

I shall not, therefore, waste time in this way, in
hunting up the origin of the miserable Laplander;
nor does it matter much where he sprang from.
He either came from somewhere else, or was created in Lapland—one of the two; and I defy all
the philosophers in creation to say which: since
there is no account extant of when he first arrived
in that cold northern land—not a word to contradict the idea of his having been there since the first
creation of the human race. We find him there
now; and that is all that we have to do with his
origin at present. Were we to speculate, as to
what races are kindred to him, and to which he
bears the greatest resemblance, we should say that
he was of either the same or similar origin with
the Esquimaux of North America, the Greenlanders of Greenland, and the Samoeids, Tuski, and other tribes dwelling along the northern shores of Asia.
Among all these nations of little men, there is a
very great similarity, both in personal appearance
and habits of life; but it would not be safe to say
that they all came from one common stock. The
resemblances may be the result of a similarity in
the circumstances, by which they are surrounded.
As for language—so much relied upon by the *scientific* ethnologist—there could scarce be a more
unreliable guide. The black negro of Carolina, the
fair blue-eyed Saxon, and the red-skinned, red-poll-
ed Hibernian, all speak one language; the descend-

ants of all three, thousands of years hence, will
speak the same—perhaps when they are widely
scattered apart—and the superficial philosopher of
those future times will, no doubt, ascribe to them
all one common origin!

Language, of itself, is no *proof* of the natural af-
finities of two peoples. It is evidence of their once
having been in juxtaposition—not much more. Of
course when other points correspond, similarity of
speech becomes a valuable corroboration. It is not
our purpose, then, to inquire whence the Laplander
came—only *where* he is now, and *what* he is now.
Where is he now?

If you take your map of Europe, and draw a line
from the Gulf of Kandalax in the White Sea to the
middle of the Loffoden Isles on the Norwegian
coast you will cut off the country which is now
properly called Lapland. The country at present
inhabited by the people called Laplanders, will be
found north of this line. It is a boundary more
imaginary than real: for in truth there is no political division known as Lapland, nor has there been
for hundreds of years. It is said there once was a
kingdom of Lapland, and a nation of Laplanders;
but there is no proof that either one or the other
ever existed. There was a peculiar people, whom
we now style Laplanders, scattered over the whole
northern part of the Scandinavian peninsula, and
wandering as far south as the shores of the Gulf of
Bothnia; but, that this people had ever any general compact, or union, deserving the name of government or nation, there is no proof. There is no
evidence that they ever enjoyed a higher degree of
civilization than they do at present; and that is not
one iota higher than exists among the Esquimaux
of North America—notwithstanding the advantage
which the Laplander has, in the domestication of a

ruminating quadruped, and a knowledge of the Christian religion.

The tract of country which I have above assigned to the modern Laplander, is to be regarded rather as meaning that portion of northern Europe, which can scarcely be said to be in the occupation of any other people. True Laplanders may be found dwelling, or rather wandering, much to the south of the line here indicated—almost to the head of the Bothnian gulf—but in these southern districts, he no longer has the range clear to himself. The Finn—a creature of a very different kind—here meets him; constantly encroaching as a *colonist* on that territory, which once belonged to the Laplander alone.

It becomes necessary to say a few words about the names we are using: since a perfect chaos of confusion has arisen among travellers and writers, in relation to the nomenclature of these two people —the Finns and the Laplanders.

In the first place, then, there is in reality no such a people as Laplanders in northern Europe. The word is a mere geographical invention, or "synonyme," if you wish. The people to whom we apply the name, call themselves "*Samlash ;*" the Danes and Norwegians term them "*Finns ;*" and the Swedes and Russians style them "*Laps.*" The people whom *we* know as Finns—and who are not Laplanders in any sense—have received the appellation of Finns erroneously. These Finns have for a long period been making progress, as colonists, in the territory once occupied by the true Finns, or Laplanders; and have nothing in common with these last people. They are agriculturists, and dwell in fixed settlements; not pastoral and nomadic, as the Laplanders eminently are. Besides, there are many other essential points of difference

between the two—in mind, in personal appearance,
in habits, in almost everything. I am particular
upon this point—because the wrong application of
the name *Finns*, to this last-mentioned race, has
led writers into a world of error; and descriptions
given of them and their habits have been applied
to the people who are the subjects of the present
chapter—leading, of course, to the most erroneous
conclusions. It would be like exhibiting the picture of a Caffre as the likeness of a Hottentot or
Bushman!

The Finns, as geography now designates them—
and which also assigns to them a country called
Finland—are, therefore, not Finns at all. Where
they are found in the old Lapland territory as colonists, they are called *Qüans;* and this name is
given them alike by Russians, Swedes, Danes, and
Norwegians.

To return to our Laplanders, who are the true
Finns. I have said that they are called by different names; by the Danes and Norwegians "Finns,"
and by the Russians and Swedes simply "Laps."
No known meaning is attached to either name;
nor can it be discovered at what period either came
into use. Enough to know that these are the des-
ignations by which they are now known to those
four nations, who have had chiefly to deal with
them.

Since these people have received so many appellations—and especially one that leads to much confusion—perhaps it is better, for geography's sake,
to accept the error: to leave the *new* Finns to their
usurped title, and to give the old Finns that distinctive name, by which they are best known to the
world, viz. *Laplanders.* So long as it is remembered, that this is merely a geographical title, no
harm can result from employing it; and should the

Z

word *Finns* occur hereafter, it is to be considered as meaning not the Finns of Norwegian Finmark, but the Qüans of Finland, on the Gulf of Bothnia.

I have spoken of the country of the Laplanders, as if they *had* a country. They have not. There is a territory in which they dwell; but it is not theirs. Long, long ago the lordship of the soil was taken from them; and divided between three powerful neighbours. Russia took her largest slice from the east; Sweden fell in for its southern part; and Norway claimed that northern and western portion, lying along the Atlantic and Arctic Oceans. This afterwards became the property of Denmark: when Norway herself ceased to be independent.

The country, therefore, which I have defined as Lapland, in modern times is so styled merely because it is almost exclusively occupied by these people: it not being worth the while of their Danish, Swedish, or Russian masters to colonize it. All three, however, claim their share of it—have their regular boundary lines—and each mulcts the miserable Laplander of an annual tribute, in the shape of a small poll-tax. Each, too, has *forced* his own peculiar views of Christianity on those within his borders—the Russian has shaped the Lap into a Greek Christian; while, under Swedish influence, he is a disciple of Martin Luther. His faith, however, is not very rational, one way or the other; and, in out-of-the-way corners of his chaotic country, he still adheres to some of his old mythic customs of sorcery and witchcraft: in other words, he is a " pagan."

Before proceeding to describe the Laplander, either personally or intellectually, a word about the country in which he dwells. I have called it a *chaotic* land. It has been described as a " huge congeries of frightful rocks and stupendous mountains, with many pleasant valleys, watered by an infinite number of rivulets, that run into the rivers and lakes." Some of the lakes are of large extent, containing a countless number of islands; one alone —the Lake Enaro—having so many, that it has been said no Laplander has lived long enough to visit each particular island. There is a great variety in the surface of the land. In some parts of the country, the eye rests only on peaks and ridges of bleak barren mountains—on summits covered with never-melting snow—on bold rocky cliffs or wooded slopes, where only the firs and birches can flourish. In other parts there are dusky forests of pines, intersected here and there by wide morasses or bogs. Elsewhere, are extensive tracts of treeless champaign, covered with the white reindeer lichen, as if they were under a fall of snow!

During summer there are many green and beautiful spots, where even the rose sheds its fragrance around, and many berry-bearing bushes blossom brightly; but the summer is of short duration, and in those parts where it is most attractive, the pest of gnats, musquitoes, and gad-flies, renders the country uninhabitable to the Laplander. We shall see presently, that, in the summer months, he flees from such lowland scenes as from a pestilence, and betakes himself and his herd to the bleak barren mountains.

Having given this short sketch of the country inhabited by the Laplander, we proceed to a description of himself.

He is short—not more than five feet five inches, average height—squat and stoutish—rarely corpulent; though there is a difference, in all these respects, between those who inhabit different parts of the country. The Laps of Norwegian Lapland are taller than those in the Russian and Swedish territory.

His features are small, **his eyes** elongated, or slit-like, as among the Mongolian tribes; his cheek-bones prominent, **his mouth** large and wide, and his chin sharply pointed. **His** hair is black, or sometimes brownish; though among some tribes settled **along** the coasts, light hair is not uncommon. **It is** probable that this may have originated **in some** admixture of blood with Norwegian, Russian, and other fishermen who frequent these coasts.

The Laplander **has** little or no beard; and in this respect he resembles the **Greenlander** and Esquimaux. His body is ill made, bony and muscular, and stronger than would be expected from his pigmy stature. He is active, and capable of enduring extreme fatigue and privation; though it is a mistake to suppose that he is the agile creature **he has** been represented—this error arising no doubt from the surprising speed with which habit has enabled him **to** skate over the frozen snow; and which, **to a person** unused to it, would appear to prove an extraordinary degree of agility. The hands and **feet** are small—another point in common with the Esquimaux. The Laplander's voice is far from being a manly one. On the contrary, it is of small compass, weak, and of a squeaking tone. The complexion of the Laplander is generally regarded as *dark*. Its natural hue is perhaps not much darker than that of the Norwegian. Certainly not darker than many Portuguese **or Spaniards**; but, **as he is** seen, he appears **as swarth as an** Indian. This, however, arises from **the long and** almost constant exposure to smoke, **in the midst of** which the miserable creature spends more than half of his time.

It may again be observed, that those dwelling on the sea-shore are of lighter complexion; but, perhaps, that is also due to a foreign admixture.

We have given a picture of the **Laplander's** person; now a word or two about his **mind**.

Both his intellectual and moral man **are** peculiar —even more so than his physical—differing essentially from **that** of all the other nationalities **with** which he is brought in contact. He is cold-hearted, selfish, and morose. **To love** he is almost **a** stranger; and when **such a feeling** does exist within his bosom, it **is rather as a spark** than a passion. His courtship **and marriage are** pure matters of business, rarely **having** any other motive than self-interest. One woman will do for his wife as well **as** another; and better, if she be richer by half a dozen reindeer!

Hospitality is a virtue equally **unknown to** him. He wishes to see no stranger; and **even wonders** why a stranger should stray into **his wild** bleak country. He is ever suspicious **of** the **traveller** through his land, unless that traveller chance to come in the guise of a Russian or Norwegian merchant, **to** exchange strong brandy for his reindeerskins, or the furs of the animals he may have trapped. In his dealings, he exhibits a sufficient degree of cunning—much more than might be expected from the low standard of his intellect; and he will take no **paper-money or** any kind of "scrip" in exchange. This caution, however, he has acquired from **a terrible experience, which** he once had in dealing with paper-money, **and he** is determined that the folly shall never again be repeated. Even in *his* out-of-the-way corner of the globe, there was at one time a bank speculation of the "Anglo-Bengalee" character, of which the poor **Lap was** made an especial **victim.**

He has no courage whatever. He will not resist oppression. The stranger—Russ or Norwegian— may strike, **kick, or** cuff him; he will not return the blow. Belike he will **burst into** tears!

And yet, under some circumstances, he shows a feeling akin to courage. He is cool in moments of danger from the elements, or when opposed to fierce animals, as the wolf or the bear. He is also capable of enduring fatigue to an extreme degree; and it is known historically that he was once warlike— at least much more so than at present. *Now*, there is not a drop of warrior blood in his veins. On the contrary, he is timid and pacific, and rarely quarrels. He carries constantly upon his person a long ugly knife, of Norwegian manufacture; but he has never been known to draw it—never known to commit murder with it.

These are certainly virtues; but it is to be feared that with him they owe their origin to timidity and the dread of consequences. Now and then he has a quarrel with one of his fellows; but the knife is never used; and the "punishment" consists in giving and receiving various kicks, scratches, pullings of the hair and ears; genuine blows, however, are not attempted, and the long knife never leaves its sheath.

In the olden time he was a great believer in witches; in fact, noted for his faith in sorcery. Christianity, such as it is, has done much to eradicate this belief; but he is still troubled with a host of superstitions.

Of filial and parental affection his stock is but scanty. The son shifts for himself, as soon as he is able to do so; and but little anxiety is exhibited about him afterwards. The daughter goes to the highest bidder—to him who is most liberal in presents of brandy to the parent. Jealousy is little known. How could it be felt, where there is no love?

One of the worst vices of the Laplander is his fondness for drink—amounting almost to a passion.

It is one of his costliest, too: since he often con-
sumes the produce of his industry in its indulgence.
His favourite beverage is strong bad brandy—a
staple article kept by the traders, to exchange for
the commodities which the country affords. As
these men care little for the result, and have a far
greater influence over the Laplander than either
the government officials or the lazy, time-serving
missionaries, it is not probable that temperance
will ever be introduced among these wretched people. Fortunately, only the coast Laplanders are at
all times subject to this influence. The mountain
people, or those who dwell most of their time in
the interior, are too distant from the "tap" to be
so grievously affected by it. It is only on their
short annual visits to the merchant stations on the
coast, that they fall extensively into the jaws of
this degrading vice.

The dress of the Laplander is now to be described.

The men wear on their heads tall caps, of a conical form, usually of a cloth called *wadmal*, or some
species of kersey furnished by the merchants. This
cap has a tassel at top, and around the bottom is
turned up several inches—where it is strengthened
by a band of reindeer skin, or the fur of the otter.
The coat is a loose garment or frock: made of the
skin of the reindeer, with the hairy side out, and
fastened around the waist with a broad leathern
belt.

In this belt is stuck the pointed knife, and a pouch
or two, for pipe, tobacco, and spoon, are also suspended from it. Breeches of reindeer-skin—the hide
of the young fawns—reach to the ankles; and bus-
kins, or rather stockings, of the same material, cover the feet. These are gartered over the ends of
the breeches, in such a way that no snow can get
in; and since there is neither shirt nor drawers

worn, we have **given every** article of a Laplander's
dress. No. There are **the** gloves or mittens, which
must not be forgotten—as they are one of the things
most essential to his **comfort.** These are also of the
universal deer hide.

Simple as is this dress of the Lapland **men, it is**
not more **simple** than that of the Lapland **women,**
since **both one** and the other are exactly alike. A
slight difference is observable in the shape of the
bonnet; but for the rest, the lady wears the deer-
skin frock, the breeches, and boots—and, like her
liege lord, she scorns to include linen in her wardrobe. This plain dress, however, is the every-day
winter costume. The summer one, and especially
upon grand occasions, **is** somewhat different, and
altogether gayer. The shape is much the same;
but the tunic or frock is of cloth, sometimes plain
coarse *wadmal;* but in **the case** of the richer proprietors, of fine **coloured cloth—even** scarlet being
sometimes **worn. No** matter what **the** quality of
the cloth, **however, the** trimmings **are** always of
rich, bright-coloured stuffs ; **and** consist of bands or
cords around the **skirt,** sleeves, and collar, elabo-
rately stitched by the females—who are in all cases
the tailors. The leathern belt, worn with this dress,
is loaded with ornaments—little square and trian-
gular **plates** of brass or white metal, and often of
heavy **solid** silver. The belt is an esteemed article
—as **much so as** his wampum to a North-American
savage—and it requires a large sum to tempt a Laplander to part with the **precious** equipment. A finer
cap is also worn, **on** these summer and holiday occasions. Not unfrequently, **however,** the Laplander—especially the mountain Lap—sticks to his deer-
skin coat, the *paesk,* through all weathers, and
throughout all seasons—when it is too hot simply
taking off the belt, and leaving the flaps loose and

open. In cold weather, and especially when riding in his sledge, an additional garment is worn. This is a fur "tippet," which covers his shoulders down to the elbows. It is made from the shaggy skin of the brown bear—with the claws left on and hanging down in front of the breast.

Before proceeding to describe the mode of life and occupation of the Laplander, it is necessary to state that all of the people known as Laplanders are not occupied alike. On the contrary, they may be separated into three distinct classes, according to the lives which they lead ; and it is absolutely necessary to make this classification in the illustration of their habits. They are all alike in race and national characteristics—all Laplanders—and they differ but little in their style of dressing ; but, in other respects, what might be said of one would not be true of the other two. I proceed, therefore, to point out the distinction.

The first to be noticed are those we have already mentioned under the title of "Coast," or "Shore Laplanders." The name will give an idea of their *habitat*—as also of their mode of life and subsistence. They dwell along the Norwegian coasts, round to the North Cape, and even beyond it. They build their *gammes*, or sod-thatched dwellings, in little villages around the numerous creeks and "fiords" that intersect this rock-bound shore.

Their calling is that of fishermen. They subsist almost entirely upon fish ; and live by selling their surplus to the merchants and Russian traders. They keep a few sheep, sometimes a poor cow, but rarely own the reindeer. The life they lead is entirely different from that of their kindred, who dwell habitually in the interior. As it differs little from that of poor fishermen elsewhere, I shall dismiss the coast Laplander without another word.

The second kind of Lap, who merits our consideration is that known as the "Wood Laplander," or, more commonly, "Wood Lap." He is less known than either of the two other varieties; but, as already stated, he differs from them principally on account of his occupation. His home is to be found upon the extensive plain country of Russian Lapland, and not near the sea. He is a dweller in the pine and fir-forests; and builds him a rude hut, very similar to the gamme of the coast Lap; but he is in possession of some reindeer—not enough, however, to support him—and he ekes out a subsistence by fishing in the rivers and fresh-water lakes of the interior, by shooting the elk and wild reindeer, and trapping the fur-bearing animals—the ermine, the sable, the miniver-squirrel, the badger, glutton, foxes, and wolves.

As his calling is chiefly that of a hunter and trapper, and therefore very similar to like occupations in many other parts of the world, we need not enter into details of it here. For the present, therefore, we must *shelve* the *Wood Lap* along with his kinsman of the coast.

This brings us to the third class—the "Mountain," or, as he is often called, the "Reindeer Laplander;" since it is the possession of this animal that chiefly distinguishes him from the other two classes of his countrymen.

His mode of life is altogether different from either —in fact, resembling theirs in but few particulars. True, he fishes a little, and occasionally does a bit of amateur hunting; but these are mere adjuncts or pastimes. His main support is his antlered flock: it would be more truthful to call it his *sole* support. By the reindeer he lives, by the reindeer he *moves*, by the reindeer he has his being.

His life is purely pastoral; he is a nomade—a

wanderer. All the world knows this; but all the
world does not know *why* he wanders. Writers
have asserted that it was to seek new pasture for
his flocks—the old ground having been eaten bare.
Nothing of the sort. He leaves the fertile plains,
just as the willows are putting forth their succulent shoots—just as the rich grass begins to spring
fresh and green—and betakes himself to the bleak
sides of the mountains. That does not look like
seeking for a better pasture. It has nothing to do
with it.

Let us follow him, however, throughout his wanderings—through the circuit of a single year—and,
perhaps, we shall find out the motive that inducts
him into the roving habit.

First, then, to be a "Reindeer Laplander," he
must be the owner of one hundred head of deer;
fewer than that will be of no use. If he have **only**
fifty he must sell out, and betake himself to some
settlement of Qüans or Norwegians—there to give
his service for hire—or else turn coast Laplander
and fisherman—a calling which he despises. This
would be a sinking in the social scale; but, if he
has been imprudent or unfortunate, and his flock
has got reduced to fifty head, there is no help for
it. If he have one hundred, however, he may manage with great economy to rub on; and keep **up**
his character as a *free reindeer Lap*. With three
hundred he can live comfortably; better with five
hundred; but a thousand would render him afflu-
ent. With fifteen hundred he would be a grandee;
and two thousand would give him the **rank** of a
millionaire! There are very few millionaires in
Lapland, and not many grandees. Proprietors of
even a thousand head are scarce; there are more
whose herds number from three hundred to five
hundred each.

And here, I may remark, that there is no government—no tribal organization. The owner of each herd is the head of **a family**; **over** them he is patriarch, but his power extends **no** further. It is not even great so far, if there **chance to be grown-up** unruly sons sharing the common tent.

I have used the word tent. That is the reindeer Laplander's home—winter and summer alike. **N**otwithstanding the severity of his clime, he builds no **house**; and even his tent is of the very rudest kind kno**wn** among tenting tribes. It consists of some birch saplings set up in the snow, bent towards each other, and then covered over with a piece of coarse cloth—the *wadmal*. This he prefers to a covering **of** skins; and obtains it from the Norwegian or Russ trader in exchange for the latter. The tent, when standing, is only six feet high, and not much more in diameter. In this circumscribed space his whole family, wife, daughters, sons, often a retainer or **two**, and about a dozen dogs find shelter **from** the piercing blast—seated, **or** lying beside, or on **top** of one another, higgledy-piggledy, any way they **can**. There is room found besides for a large iron **or** brass cooking-pot, some dishes and **bowls of birch, a** rude stone furnace, and a fire in the middle of the floor. **Above** the fire, a rack forms a shelf for countless tough cheeses, pieces of reindeers' flesh, bowls of milk, bladders of deers' blood, and a multiplicity of like objects.

The spring is just opening; the frost has thawed from the trees—for the **winter home is** in the midst of a forest—the ground **is bare of** snow, and already smiling with a carpet **of** green, enamelled by many brilliant flowers. It is time, therefore, for the reindeer Laplander **to** decamp from the spot, and seek some other scene less inviting to the eye. You will naturally inquire why he does this? and perhaps you will express some surprise, at a man showing so little judgment as to take leave of the fertile plain—just now promising to yield him a rich pasture for his herds—and transport his whole stock to the cold declivity of a bleak mountain? Yes, it is natural this should astonish you—not, however, when you have heard the explanation.

Were he to stay in that plain—in that wood where he has wintered—a month longer, he would run the risk of losing half of his precious herd: perhaps in one season find himself reduced to the necessity of becoming a *coast Lap.* The reason is simple—the great gad-fly (*Œstrus tarandi*), with numerous other tormentors, are about to spring forth from the morass; and, as soon as the hot sun has blown them into full strength and vitality, commence their work of desolation upon the deer. In a few short days or hours, their eggs would be deposited in the skin—even in the nostrils of the antlered creature—there to germinate and produce disease and death. Indeed, the torment of biting gnats and other insects would of itself materially injure the health and condition of the animals; and if not driven to the mountains, they would "stampede," and go there of their own accord. It becomes a necessity, then, for the reindeer Lap to remove his habitation; and, having gathered a few necessary utensils, and packed them on his stoutest bucks, he is off to the mountains.

He does not take the whole of his *penates* along with him. That would be difficult, for the snow is now gone, and he cannot use his proper mode of travelling—the sledge. This he leaves behind him; as well as all other implements and articles of household use, which he can do without in his summer quarters. The cooking-pot, and a few bowls and dishes, go along with him—also the tent-cloth, and some skins for bedding. The smaller articles are deposited in panniers of wicker, which are slung over the backs of a number of pack-deer; and, if a balance be required, the infant Lap, in its little boat-like cradle, forms the adjusting medium.

The journey is often of immense length. There may be highlands near, but these are not to the Laplander's liking. Nothing will satisfy him but the bold mountain range that overlooks the sea, trending along the whole Norwegian coast: only on the declivities of this, or on one of the thousand elevated rocky isles that guard this extensive sea-board, does the Laplander believe that his deer will enjoy proper health. He has a belief, moreover, that at least once every year, the reindeer should drink sea-water to keep them in condition. Certain it is, that on reaching the sea, these animals rush eagerly into the water, and drink the briny fluid; and yet ever after, during that same season, they refuse to taste it! It is the general opinion that the solitary draught thus taken has the effect of destroying such larvæ, as may have already formed in their skins.

This journey often costs the Laplander great fatigue and trouble. It is not uncommon for him to go two hundred miles to the Norwegian coast; for although his habitual home may lie much nearer to the shores of the Bothnian gulf, it would not serve his purpose to take his flock there. The forest on that side grows to the water's edge; and the gad-fly is as abundant there, as in the wooded districts of the interior.

On reaching his destination, the Laplander chooses his grazing-ground, sometimes on the mountains of the main land; but he prefers one of the elevated islets so numerous along the shore. This ensures him against all danger from the flies, and also saves him much trouble in herding his deer. The islet may be two miles from the main, or any other land. That does not signify. The reindeer can swim like ducks, and the herd is soon driven over. The wadmal tent is then pitched, and the work of the summer begins. This consists in milking, cheese-making, and looking after the young deer; and a little fishing adds to the keep of the family: for it is at this time that foreign support is most required. The season of summer is with the mountain Lap his season of scarcity! He does not dream of killing his deer at this season—that would be sheer waste —nor does he drink their milk, only in very little quantity. It goes to the making of cheese, and the owner of the herd contents himself with the whey. Butter is not made at all by the reindeer Lap, though the Qüans and Norwegians make some. The Lap would have no use for it—since he eats no bread—and it would not keep so well, nor yet be so safe an article of merchandise as the cheese. The latter he regards as his staple article of profit. He sells it to the coast-merchant: receiving in exchange his favourite dram-stuff, and a few pieces of coarse cloth, or utensils. The merchant is near at hand: for just for this very purpose are several small ports and settlements kept in existence along the otherwise desert shores of Norway. Deer-skins and dried fish, oils of the seal, furs and pelts of various kinds, have drawn these little settlements to the coast. Otherwise they would not be there.

When the heat of the summer is over, the reindeer Laplander commences his return to his winter abode—back to the place whence he came. The gad-flies are now gone, and he can drive his deer back with safety; and just as he travelled to the coast, he wends his way home again: for it is to be observed that he regards the winter residence as

the real home, and the summer one only as a place
of temporary sojourn.   He does not look upon it, as
we at such a season.   To him it is no pleasant excursion: rather is it his period of toil and dearth—
his *tightest* time.

Once home again, he has nothing to do but erect
his wadmal tent and look after his deer—that now
find food upon their favourite lichen.   It is buried
inches deep under the snow.   They care not for
that.   They can soon uncover the pasture with their
broad hoofs; and their keen scent never allows
them to scrape up the snow without finding the
lichen underneath.   Upon it they thrive, and at this
season are in the best condition for the knife.

The Laplander now also enjoys life.   If rich, he
has fresh venison every day; but even if only mod-
erately well off, he "kills" two or three times a
week.   His mode of slaughtering is original.   He
sticks his long knife-blade into the throat of the animal, leaving it there till the creature is dead!   This
precaution he takes to prevent waste.   Were he to
pull out the blade, the blood would flow and be
lost.   The knife acts as a stopper to the wound it
has made.   The blood is preserved and carefully
put away—the bladder being used as the vessel to
contain it.

You must not imagine that the reindeer Lap remains all the winter in one place; on the contrary,
he moves repeatedly, always taking his tent and
tent-utensils along with him.   The tent is as easily
set up as taken down.   The ground in all sheltered
places is, at this season, covered with snow.   It is
only necessary to shovel it off, clearing a circular
space about the size of the ground-plan of the tent.
The snow, thus removed, produces a sort of elevated
ring or snow-dyke all round the bare spot; and into
this the tent-poles are hammered.   They are then

bent inward, tied near the tops, and the *wadmal* being laid on as before, the tent is ready for use.

Fresh branches of evergreen pines, and other trees, are strewed over the floor; and on top of these are laid the deer-skins that serve for beds, chairs, tables, and blankets. These, with the iron cooking pot, a large iron or brass pail to hold melted snow-water for drinking, and a few other utensils, are the only furniture of the dwelling. I have already stated that the fire is built in the centre of the tent—on some large stones, forming a rudely-constructed hearth. A hole in the roof is intended for a chimney; but its draught is so bad, that the tent is almost always filled with a cloud of bitter smoke—so thick as to render objects invisible. In this atmosphere no other European, excepting a Lap, could possibly exist; and travellers, passing through the Lapland country, have often preferred braving the cold frost of the night air, to being half smothered by the smoke; and have consequently taken shelter under a neighbouring tree. The Laplander himself feels but little inconvenienced by the very thickest smoke.

Habit is everything, and to this habit has he been used from his infancy. His eyes, however, are not so indifferent to the annoyance. These suffer from it; and the consequence is that the eyes of the Laplanders are almost universally sore and watery. This is a notable characteristic of the race. Smoke, however, is not the sole cause of it. The Esquimaux equally suffer from sore eyes; and these, burning oil in their houses instead of wood, are seldom troubled with smoke. More likely it is the snow-glare to which the Laplander, as well as the Esquimaux, is much exposed, that brings about this copious *watering* of the eyes.

The Laplander cooks the reindeer flesh by boil-

A A

ing. A large piece is put into the great family pot, and nothing added but a quantity of water. In this the meat boils and simmers till it is done tender. The oily fat is then skimmed off, and put into a separate vessel; and the meat is "dished" in a large tray or bowl of birch-bark.

A piece is then cut off, for each individual of the family; and handed around the circle. It is eaten without bread, and even salt is dispensed with. A dip in the bowl of skim-fat is all the seasoning it gets; and it is washed down with the "liquor" in which it has been boiled, and which is nothing but greasy water, without vegetables or any other "lining." It has the flavour of the fat venison, however; and is by no means ill-tasted. The *angelica* flourishes in the country of the Laplander; and of this vegetable he makes occasional use, not eating the roots, but the stalks and leaves, usually raw and without any preparation. Perhaps he is led to use it, by a knowledge of the antiscorbutic properties of the plant.

Several species of berry-producing bushes also furnish him with an occasional meal of fruit. There are wild currants, the cranberry, whortle, and bilberries. The fruits of these trees do not fall in the autumn, as with us; but remain all winter upon the branches. Buried under the snow, they are preserved in perfect condition, until the thaw of the following spring once more brings them into view. At this time they are sweet and mellow; and are gathered in large quantities by the Lap women. Sometimes they are eaten, as they come from the tree; but it is more usual to make them into a "plum-pudding:" that is, they are mixed with a kind of curdled milk, and stored away in bladders. When wanted, a slice is cut from the mass—including a piece of the bladder, within which they have

now attained to the stiffness and consistence of a
" cream-cheese."

Another great luxury of the Laplander, is the
reindeer's milk frozen into an " ice." This is easily
obtained ; and the process consists simply in filling
a birchen bowl with milk, and exposing it to the
open air during frost. It is soon converted into
solid ice; and in this condition will keep perfectly
sweet throughout the whole of the winter. As the
reindeer are never milked in the depth of the winter season, the Laplander takes care, before that
period approaches, to lay in a stock of ice-milk : so
that he may have a drink of it at all times, by simply setting one of his birchen bowls within reach
of the fire. He even makes a merchandise of this
article : for the frozen reindeer milk is highly prized
by the foreign merchants ; who are ready, at any
time, to exchange for the delicious article a dram
of their devilish fire-water.

It is at this season that the Laplander moves
about, both on foot and in his sledge. He not only
travels from place to place, in a circuit of twenty
miles—round the little solitary church which the
Swedish missionary has built for him—but he makes
an occasional journey to the distant coast.

In his sledge, or even afoot, a hundred miles are
to him as nothing : for the frozen snow enables him
to perform such a distance in an incredibly short
time. On his " skies," or snow-skates he could do
a hundred miles in a couple of days ; even though
the paths led him over hills, mountains, lakes, and
rivers. All are now alike—all concealed under the
common covering of a deep snow. The lakes and
rivers are frozen and bridged for him ; and the
mountain declivities are rendered smooth and easily
traversed — either by the sledge or the " skies."
With the former he would think little of a hundred

miles in a single day; and if the occasion were a
"killing" one, and relays could be had upon the
route, twice that enormous distance he could easily
accomplish.

The mode of sleigh-travelling by the reindeer
Laplander, as also his snow-skimming, or skating,
have been both often and elaborately described. I
have only space here to present the more salient
points of the picture.

This sleigh or sledge is termed by him "pulka;"
but he has three varieties of this article—two for
travelling, and the third for carrying luggage. The
two first kinds are nearly alike; and, in fact, differ
only in a little extra "furniture," which one of
them has upon it—that is, a covering over the top,
to keep more comfortable the feet and legs of the
traveller. In other respects it is only the common
pulk, being similar to the latter in shape, size, *ate-
lage* and everything.

To get an idea of the Laplander's sledge, you
must fancy a little boat, about six feet long and
sixteen inches in breadth of beam. This is the
width at the stern, where it is broadest; but from
the stern it narrows all the way forward, until, on
reaching the stem, it has tapered almost to a point.
Its sides are exactly like those of a boat; and it
rests upon a "keel" of about four inches breadth,
which keel is the one and only "runner." A strong
board boxes up the stern end, in front of which is
the seat; and the board itself serves to support the
back of the rider. His legs and feet are stretched
out longitudinally; filling up the space between the
quarter-deck and the "for'ard" part of the little
craft; and, thus fixed, the Laplander is ready for
the road.

In the best class of "pulk"—that used by the
Russ and Swedish traders and travellers—the for-

ward part is covered with a sort of half-deck of
skins or leather; but the Laplander does not often
fancy this. It gives him too much trouble to get
out and in; as he is often compelled to do to look
after his train of deer. His pulk, therefore, is open
from stem to stern; and his deer-skin coverings
keep his legs warm enough.

Only one deer is used; and the mode of harness-
ing is of primitive simplicity. A band of skin acts
as a collar round the neck of the animal; and from
the lowest point of this, a piece falls downwards
below the animal's breast—striking it on the counter like the pendants of a martingale. To this piece
is attached the trace—there is but one—which,
passing between the forelegs, and afterwards the
hind ones, is looped into an iron ring upon the stem
of the sledge. Upon this trace, which is a strong
strap of raw hide or leather, the whole draught-
power is exerted. A broad surcingle—usually of
cloth, neatly stitched and ornamented—passes round
the deer's body. Its use is to hold up the trace
underneath the belly, and prevent it from dragging
the ground, or getting among the animal's feet. A
similar band of cloth passes round its neck, giving
a fine appearance to the noble creature. A single
rein attached to the left horn, or fixed halter-fash-
ion around the deer's head, is all that is necessary
to guide it along; the movements of this, aided by
the accents of its master's voice, are understood by
this well-trained animal.

For all that, the deer does not *always* travel
kindly. Frequently he takes a fit of obstinacy or
anger; and will then turn upon his trainer—presenting his antlered front in an attitude of attack.
On such occasions the Lap takes shelter behind his
"pulk," raising it in his arms, and holding it as a
shield wherewith to defend himself; until he can
pacify, or otherwise subdue, the irritated buck.

The tumbling of the sledge, and consequent spilling of its load, is a thing of frequent occurrence: owing to the narrow base upon which the vehicle is supported; but the Laplander thinks nothing of a trifling mishap of this nature. In a trice the "snow-boat" is righted, the voyager in his seat again, and off over the frozen snow with the speed of lightning.

The reindeer can travel nearly twenty English miles an hour! This rate of speed has been proved and tested; and with fresh relays along the route, over 400 miles might be made in a day. But the same thing could be done with horses—that is, upon a desperate emergency.

The luggage "pulk" of the Laplander differs only from the other kinds of sledges in being longer, broader, deeper, and consequently of more capacity to carry goods. It is used for transporting the skins, and other merchantable commodities, from the interior to the trading depôts on the coast.

The *skies* or snow-skates require very little description. They are on the same principle as the snow-shoes in use among the North-American Indians; though from these they differ materially in construction. They are merely two long pieces of smooth board, a few inches in breadth, and slightly turned up at the ends. One is full six feet—the right one; the left is about twelve inches shorter. Near the middle they are lashed firmly to the feet, by strong pieces of hide; and by means of these curious appendages, when the snow is crusted over, the Laplander can skim over its surface with great rapidity. He uses a long pole to guide and assist him in his movements; and this pole has a piece of circular board, or a round ball, near its point—to prevent it from sinking too deeply in the snow. Going *up hill* upon the skies is not so easy; but the practised skater can ascend even the steep acclivities of the mountains with less difficulty than might be imagined. This is accomplished in zigzag lines —each leading to a higher elevation. Down hill, the course upon *skies* is rapid almost as the flight of an arrow; and, by means of the long pole, rocks, ravines, and precipices, are shunned with a dexterity that is quite surprising. Altogether a Laplander, either in his reindeer sledge, or upon his long wooden "skies," is as interesting a sight as may be seen anywhere.

After all that has been said, it will appear pretty clearly, that the Laplander, though dwelling so very near to civilized lands, is still very far distant from *true civilization.*

THE ANDAMANERS, OR MUD-BEDAUBERS.

ON the eastern side of the Bay of Bengal lies a cluster, or archipelago, of islands known as the "Andamans." They form a long string running nearly northward and southward; and with the Nicobar group, still further to the south, they appear like a series of stepping-stones connecting Cape Negrais, in the Burmese country, with the island of Sumatra. Independent of the Nicobar Islands, the Andamans themselves have an extent of several hundred miles in length; while their breadth is nowhere over about twenty miles. Until of late the greater portion of the group was supposed to form only one island—known as the "Great Andaman;" but, in the year 1792, this was discovered to have a channel across it that divided it into two distinct parts.

The discovery of this channel was accidental; and the accident was attended with melancholy consequences. A vessel from Madras had entered between the Great Andaman and the opposite coast of Burmah. This vessel was laden with provisions, intended for the supply of Port Cornwallis—a convict settlement, which the British had formed the preceding year on the eastern side of the island. The master of the vessel, not knowing the position of Port Cornwallis, sent a boat to explore an opening which he saw in the land—fancying that it might be the entrance to the harbour. It was not this, however; but the mouth of the channel above mentioned. The crew of the boat consisted of two Europeans and six Lascars. It was late in the aft-

ernoon when they stood into the entrance; and, as it
soon fell dark upon them, they lost their way, and
found themselves carried along by a rapid current
that set towards the Bay of Bengal. The **north-
east** monsoon was blowing at the time with great
violence; and this, together with the rapid current,
soon carried the boat through **the** channel; and, in
spite of their efforts, they were driven out into the
Indian Ocean, far beyond sight of land! Here, for
eighteen days the unfortunate crew were buffeted
about; until they were picked up by a French ship,
almost under the equinoctial line, many hundreds
of miles from the channel they had thus involuntari-
ly discovered! The sad part of the story remains
to be told. When relieved by the French vessel,
the two Europeans and three of the Lascars were
still living; the other three Lascars had disappeared. Shocking to relate, they had been killed, and
eaten by their companions!

The convict settlement above mentioned was carried on only for a few years, and then abandoned—
in consequence of the unhealthiness of the climate,
by which the Sepoy guards of the establishment
perished in great numbers.

Notwithstanding this, the Andaman Islands present a very attractive aspect. A ridge of mountains runs nearly throughout their whole extent, rising in some places to a height of between two and
three thousand feet. These mountains are covered
to their tops by dense forests, that might be called
primeval—since no trace of clearing or cultivation
is to be found on the whole surface of the islands;
nor has any ever existed within the memory of
man, excepting that of the convict settlement referred to. Some of the forest trees are of great
size and height; and numerous species are inter-
mixed. Mangroves line the shores; and prickly

ferns and wild rattans form an impenetrable brake on the sides of the hills; bamboos are also common, and the "gambier" or "cutch" tree (*Agathis*), from which is extracted the *Terra Japonica* of commerce. There are others that yield dyes, and a curious species of screw-pine (*pandanus*)—known as the "Nicobar bread-fruit."

Notwithstanding their favourable situation, the zoology of these islands is extremely limited in species. The only quadrupeds known to exist upon them are wild hogs, dogs, and rats; and a variety of the monkey tribe inhabits the forests of the interior. The land birds are few—consisting of pigeons, doves, small parrots, and the Indian crow; while hawks are seen occasionally hovering over the trees; and a species of humming-bird flies about at night, uttering a soft cry that resembles the cooing of doves. There are owls of several species; and the cliffs that front the coast are frequented by a singular swallow—the *hirundo esculenta*, whose nests are eaten by the wealthy mandarins of China. Along the shores there are gulls, kingfishers, and other aquatic birds. A large lizard of the *guana* species is common, with several others; and a green snake, of the most venomous description, renders it dangerous to penetrate the jungle thickets that cover the whole surface of the country.

In all these matters there is not much that is remarkable—if we except the extreme paucity of the zoology; and this is really a peculiarity—considering that the Andaman Islands lie within less than eighty leagues of the Burman territory, a country so rich in mammalia; considering, too, that they are covered with immense forests, almost impenetrable to human beings, on account of their thick intertwining of underwood and parasitical plants—the very home, one would suppose, for wild beasts

of **many** kinds! **And withal** we find **only** three
species of quadrupeds, and these small **ones,** thinly
distributed along the skirts of the forest. **In** truth,
the Andaman Islands and their *fauna* have long
been a puzzle to the zoologist.

But longer still, and to a far greater extent, have
their human inhabitants perplexed the ethnologist;
and here **we arrive at** the **true** peculiarity of **the**
Andaman **Islands—that is to say,** the *people* who
inhabit them. **W**ith perhaps no exception, these
people are the most truly savage of any on the face
of the globe; and this has been their character from
the earliest times: for they have been known to the
ancients as far back as the time **of** Ptolemy. Ptol-
emy mentions them under the title of *anthropophagi*
(man-eaters); and the Arabs of the **ninth century,**
who navigated the Indian Ocean, have **given a sim-**
ilar account of them. Marco Polo adopts **this state-**
ment, and what is still more surprising, **one of** the
most noted ethnologists of our own time—Dr. Latham—has given way to a like credulity, and puts
the poor Andamaners down as "pagan cannibals."
It **is an** error: they **are** not cannibals in any sense
of **the word; and** if they have ever eaten human
flesh—**of which there is no** proof—it has been when
impelled **by famine.** Under like circumstances,
some **of** every **nation on earth** have done the **same**
—Englishmen, Germans, Frenchmen, Americans—
of late years frequently—**in the mountains** of New
Mexico and California.

The charge of cannibalism, against **these** miserable beings, rests on no other foundation than the
allegations of Chinese sailors, and the vague statements of Ptolemy and the Arabs above mentioned.

The Chinese have occasion now and then to visit
the Andaman **Islands in** their junks, to collect the
edible nests of the swallow (*hirundo esculenta*)—

which birds have **extensive** breeding-places on the cliffs that overhang the **coast** of the Great Andaman. The "trepang," or sea-slug, is also found in large quantities upon the **rocks near the shore;** and this is equally an object of **commerce, and** esteemed an article of the greatest luxury, **among** the mandarins, **and** other rich celestials who can afford to indulge **in it.**

Now and then, a junk has been wrecked among these rocks; and its miserable crew have fallen a victim to the hostility of **the** natives: just as they might have done **on more** civilized coasts, where no cannibalism was **ever** suspected **to exist.** Crews of junks have been totally destroyed—murdered, if you please—but it would not be difficult to show, that this **was done** more from motives of revenge, than from a mere sanguinary instinct or disposition; but there is no proof whatever of, **even a single** case, of true cannibalism. **Indeed,** there are strong reasons for our disbelief in this horrid custom—so far as regards **the poor** savages of the Andamans. An incident, that seems to give a flat contradiction to it, occurred during the occupancy of the island **by the** East-**India** Company in the year 1793; and **other** proofs **of** non-cannibalism have been obtained at a still more recent period, to which we shall presently allude.

The incident of 1793 was as follows:—A party of fishers belonging to the settlement enticed an Andaman woman to **come near, by holding out** presents of food. The **woman was** made captive by these treacherous **men; who,** instead of relieving her hunger, proceeded to behave to her in the most brutal and unfeeling manner. The cries of the poor creature brought a numerous troop of her people to the spot; who, rushing out of the thickets from every side, collected around the fishermen; and,

having attacked them with spears and arrows, succeeded in killing two of their number. The rest
with difficulty escaped to the settlement; and, having obtained assistance, a large party set out to
search for the bodies of their companions. There
was but little expectation that these would be recovered: as all were under the belief that the savages must have carried them away for the purpose
of making a cannibal feast upon them. There had
been ample time for the removing of them: since
the scene of the struggle was at a considerable distance from the fort.

The searchers, therefore, were somewhat astonished, at finding both bodies on the spot where they
had fallen, and the enemy entirely gone from the
ground! The bodies were disfigured in the most
shocking manner. The flesh was pierced in every
part—by spears, no doubt—and the bones had been
pounded with heavy stones, until they were mash-
ed into fragments; but not a bit of flesh was removed, not even an arm or limb had been sev-
ered!

The other instance to which we have promised
to allude occurred at a much more recent period—
so late, in fact, as the period of the King of Delhi's
imprisonment. It will be fresh in the memory of
my readers, that his Hindoo majesty was carried to
the island of Great Andaman, along with a number
of "Sepoy" rebels, who had been taken prisoner
during the late Indian revolt. The convict settlement was restored, especially for this purpose; and
a detachment of "East-India Company's troops"
was sent along with the rebel sepoys to guard them.
It was supposed that the troops would have great
difficulty in the performance of their duty; since
the number of their prisoners was larger than could
be fairly looked after; and, it was well known,

that, if a prisoner could once get clear of the walls
of the fort, it would be altogether idle to pursue
him. The chase after a fugitive through the tangled forests of the Andamans would be emphatically a "wild-goose" chase; and there would be ten
chances to one against his being recaptured.

Such, in reality, did it appear, for the first week
or two, after the settlement was re-established.
Numerous prisoners escaped into the woods, and
as it was deemed idle to follow them, they were
given up as "lost birds."

In the end, however, it proved that they were
not all lost—though some of them were. After a
week or two had expired, they began to straggle
back to the fort, and voluntarily deliver themselves
up to their old guards—now one, now another, or
two or three at a time—but all of them in the most
forlorn and deplorable condition. They had enjoyed a little liberty on the Andaman isles; but a taste
of it had proved sufficient to satisfy them, that captivity in a well-rationed guard-house was even preferable to freedom with a hungry stomach, added
to the risk which they ran every hour of the day
of being impaled upon the spears of the savages.
Many of them actually met with this fate; and others only escaped half dead from the hostile treatment they had received at the hands of the islanders. There was no account, however, that any of
them had been *eaten*—no evidence that their im-
placable enemies were cannibals.

Such are a few arguments that seem to contro-
vert the accusation of Ptolemy and the two Arab
merchants—in whose travels the statement is found,
and afterwards copied by the famous Marco Polo.
Probably the Arabs obtained their idea from Ptolemy, Marco Polo from the Arabs, and Dr. Latham
from Marco Polo. Indeed it is by no means cer-

tain that Ptolemy meant the Andaman Islands by
his *Islæ bonæ Fortunæ*, or " Good-luck Isles"—certainly a most inappropriate appellation. He may
have referred to Sumatra and its Battas—who *are*
cannibals beyond a doubt. And, after all, what
could Ptolemy know about the matter except from
vague report, or, more likely still, more vague *speculation*,—a process of reasoning practised in Ptolemy's time, just as at the present day. We are
too ready to adopt the errors of the ancient writers
—as if men were more infallible then than they are
now; and, on the other hand, we are equally prone
to incredulity—often rejecting their testimony when
it would conduct to truth.

I believe there is no historic testimony—ancient
or modern—before us, to prove that the Andaman
islanders are cannibals; and yet, with all the testimony to the contrary, there is one fact, or rather a
hypothesis, which shall be presently adduced, that
would point to the *probability* of their being so.

If they are not cannibals, however, they are not
the less unmitigated *savages*, of the very lowest
grade and degree. They are unacquainted with almost the very humblest arts of social life; and are
not even so far advanced in the scale as to have an
organization. In this respect they are upon a par
with the Bushmen of Africa and the Diggers of
North America: still more do they resemble the
wretched starvelings of Tierra del Fuego. They
have no tribal tie; but dwell in scattered groups or
gangs—just as monkeys or other animals of a gregarious nature.

In person, the Andaman is one of the very " ugliest" of known savages. He is of short stature,
attaining to the height of only five feet: and his
wife is a head shorter than himself. Both are as
black as pitch, could their natural colour be discov-

ered; but the skin is usually hidden under a mask
of rare material, which we shall presently have occasion to describe.

The upper half of the **Andamaner's body** is strongly and compactly built, and **his arms are** muscular
enough. It is below, in the limbs, where he is most
lacking in development. His legs are osseous and
thin; and, only when he is in fine condition, is there
the slightest swell on them that would indicate the
presence of a **calf**. His feet are of monstrous length,
and without any symmetry—the heel projecting far
backwards, in the fashion usually styled "lark-heel-
ed." It is just possible that a good deal of practice,
by running over mud-banks and quick-sands in
search of his shell-fish subsistence, may have added
to the natural development of his pedal extremities;
for there can be no longer any doubt that like effects have been produced by such causes—effects
that are indeed, after all, more *natural* than *artificial.*

The Andamaner exhibits the protuberance of belly noticed among other savages who lead a starving life; and his countenance is usually marked
with an expression, that betrays a mixture of ferocity and famine.

It is worthy of remark, however, that though these
stunted proportions are generally observable among
the natives of the Andaman Islands, they do not appear to be universal. It is chiefly on the island of
the Great Andaman that the most wretched of these
savages are found. The Little Andaman seems to
produce a better breed: since parties have been
met with on this last-named island, in which many
individuals were observed nearly six feet in height,
and stout in proportion. One of these parties, and
the incident of meeting with it, are thus described
by an officer who was present:—

" We had not gone far, when at an angle of the
jungle, which covers the island to within a few
yards of the water's edge, we came suddenly upon
a party of the natives, lying upon their bellies behind the bushes, armed with spears, arrows, and
long-bows, which they bent at us in a threatening
manner. Our Lascars, as soon as they saw them,
fell back in great consternation, levelling their muskets and running into the sea towards the boats.
It was with great difficulty we could prevent our
cowardly rascals from firing; the tyndal was the
only one who stood by the chief mate and myself.
We advanced within a few paces of the natives,
and made signs of drinking, to intimate the purpose
of our visit. The tyndal salaamed to them, according to the different oriental modes of salutation—
he spoke to them in Malay, and other languages;
but they returned no answer, and continued in their
crouching attitude, pointing their weapons at us
whenever we turned. I held out my handkerchief,
but they would not come from behind the bushes
to take it. I placed it upon the ground; and we
retired in order to allow them an opportunity of
picking it up: still they would not move.

"I counted sixteen strong and able-bodied men
opposite to us, many of them very lusty; and farther on, six more. They were very different in appearance from what the natives of the Great Andaman are represented to be—that is of a puny
race. The whole party was completely naked, with
the exception of one—a stout man nearly six feet
in height, who was standing up along with two or
three women in the rear. He wore on his head a
red cloth with white spots.

"They were the most ferocious and wild-looking
beings I ever beheld. Those parts of their bodies
that were not besmeared with mud, were of a sooty

black colour. Their faces seemed to be painted
with a red ochre."

Notwithstanding the difference in stature and
other respects—the result no doubt of a better condition of existence—the inhabitants of both islands,
Great and Little Andaman, are the same race of
people; and in the portrait, the faces of both may
be considered as one and the same. This brings us
to the strangest fact in the whole history of the
Andaman islander. Instead of a Hindoo face, or a
Chinese Mongolian face, or that of a Malay—any
of which we might reasonably expect to find in an
aboriginal of the Bay of Bengal—we trace in the
Andaman islander the true physiognomy of a negro. Not only have we the flat nose and thick
lips, but the curly hair, the sooty complexion, and
all the other negro characteristics. And the most
ill-favoured variety at that; for, in addition to the
ungraceful features already mentioned, we find a
head large beyond all proportion, and a pair of small
red eyes deeply sunken in their sockets. Truly the
Andaman islander has few pretensions to being a
beauty!

Wretched, however, as the Andaman islander
may appear, and of little importance as he certainly
is in the great social family of the human race, he
is, ethnologically speaking, one of its most interesting varieties. From the earliest times, he has been
a subject of speculation, or rather his presence in
that particular part of the world where he is now
found: for, since it is the general belief that he is
entirely isolated from the two acknowledged negro
races, and surrounded by other types of the human
family, far different from either, the wonder is how
he came to be there.

Perhaps no other two thousand people on earth
—for that is about the number of the Andaman isl-

anders—have been honoured with a greater amount
of speculation in regard to their origin. Some ethnologists assign to them an African origin, and account for their presence upon the Andaman islands
by a singular story: that a Portuguese ship laden
with African slaves, and proceeding to the Indian
colonies, was wrecked in the Bay of Bengal, and,
of course, off the coast of the Andamans: that the
crew were murdered by the slaves; who, set free
by this circumstance, became the inhabitants of the
island. This story is supported by the argument,
that the hostility which the natives now so notoriously exhibit, had its origin in a spirit of revenge:
that still remembering the cruel treatment received
on the "middle passage" at the hands of their Portuguese masters, they have resolved never to be enslaved again; but to retaliate upon the white man,
whenever he may fall into their power!

Certainly the circumstances would seem to give
some colour to the tale, if it had any foundation;
but it has none. Were we to credit it, it would be
necessary to throw Ptolemy and the Arab merchants overboard, and Marco Polo to boot. All
these have recorded the existence of the Andaman
islanders, long before ever a Portuguese keel cleft
the waters of the Indian Ocean—long even before
Di Gama doubled the Cape!

But without either the aid of Ptolemy or the testimony of the Arabian explorers, it can be established that the Andaman Islands were inhabited before the era of the Portuguese in India; and by the
same race of savages as now dwell upon them.

Another theory is: that it was an *Arabian* slave-
ship that was wrecked, and not a Portuguese; and
this would place the peopling of the islands at a
much earlier period. There is no positive fact,
however, to support this theory—which, like the
other, rests only on mere speculation.

The error of these hypotheses lies in their mistaken *data;* for, although we have stated that the Andaman islanders are undoubtedly a negro race, they are not that negro race to which the speculation points—in other words, they are not *African* negroes. Beyond certain marked features, as the flat nose and thick lips, they have nothing in common with these last. Their hair is more of the kind called "frizzly," than of the "woolly" texture of that of the Ethiopian negro; and in this respect they assimilate closely to the "Papuan," or New Guinea "negrillo," which every one knows is a very different being from the *African* negro.

Their moral characteristics—such as there has been an opportunity of observing among them—are also an additional proof that they are not of African origin; while these point unmistakeably to a kinship with the other side of the Indian Ocean. Even some of their fashions, as we shall presently have occasion to notice, have a like tendency to confirm the belief that the Andaman is a "negrillo," and not a "negro." The only obstacle to this belief has hitherto been the fact of their isolated situation: since it is alleged—rather hastily as we shall see—that the whole of the opposite continent of the Burmese and other empires, is peopled by races entirely distinct: that none of the adjacent islands —the Nicobars and Sumatra—have any negro or negrillo inhabitants: and that the Andamaners are thus cut off, as it were, from any possible line of migration which they could have followed in entering the Bay of Bengal. Ethnologists, however, seem to have overlooked the circumstance that this allegation is not strictly true. The *Sámangs*—a tribe inhabiting the mountainous parts of the Malayan peninsula—are also a negro or negrillo race; a fact which at once establishes a link in the chain of a supposed migration from the great Indian archipelago.

This lets the Andaman islander into the Great China Sea; or, rather, coming from that sea, it forms the stepping stone to his present residence in the Bay of Bengal. Who can say that he was not at one time the owner of the Malayan peninsula? How can we account for the strange fact, that figures of Boodh—the Guadma of the Burmese and Siamese—are often seen in India beyond the Ganges, delineated with the curly hair and other characteristic features of the negro?

The theory that the Samang and Andaman islander once ruled the Malay peninsula; that they themselves came from the eastward—from the great islands of the Melanesian group, the centre and source of the negrillo race—will in some measure account for this singular monumental testimony. The probability, moreover, is always in favour of a migration *westward within the tropics*. Beyond the tropics, the rule is sometimes reversed.

A coincidence of personal habit, between the Andaman islander and the Melanesian, is also observed. The former dyes his head of a brown or reddish colour—the very fashion of the Feegee!

Suppose, then, that the Samang and Andaman islander came down the trades, at a period too remote for even tradition to deal with it: suppose they occupied the Malay peninsula, no matter how long; and that at a much more recent period, they were pushed out of place—the one returning to the Andaman Islands, the other to the mountains of the Quedah: suppose also that the party pushing them off were Malays—who had themselves been drifted for hundreds of years down the trades from the far shores of America (for this is *our* "speculation"): suppose all these circumstances to have taken place,

and you will be **able to account for** two facts, that
have for a long **time puzzled the** ethnologist.   One
is the presence **of negroes on the** islands of Andaman—and the other of Malays in the south-eastern
corner of Asia.   We might bring forward many
arguments to uphold the probability of these hypotheses, had we space and time.   Both, however,
compel us to return to the more particular subject
of **our** sketch; **and** we shall do so after having
made a remark, promised above, and which relates
to the *probability* of the Andaman islander being a
cannibal.   This, then, *would lie* in *the fact of his
being a Papuan negro.*   And yet, again, it is only
a seeming; for it might be shown that with the
Papuan cannibalism is not a natural instinct.   It is
only where he has reached a high degree of *civilization*, as in the case of the Feegee islander.   **Call**
the latter a monster if you will; but, as may **be**
learnt from our account of him, **he** is anything but
a *savage,* **in** the usual acceptation of the term.   In
fact, language has no epithet sufficiently vile to
characterize such an anomalous animal as he.

   I have endeavoured to clear the Andaman islander **of the** charge of this guilt; and, since appearances are so much against him, he ought to feel
grateful.   It is doubtful whether he would, should
this fall into his hands, and he be able to read it.
The portrait of his face without that stain upon it,
he might regard as ugly enough; and **that of** his
habits, which now follows, is **not much more** flatter-
ing.

   His house is little **better** than the den of a wild
beast; **and** far inferior in ingenuity of construction
to those which beavers build.   A few poles stuck
in the ground **are leant** towards each other, and tied
together at the top.   Over these a wattle of reeds
and rattan-leaves forms the roof; and on the floor

a "shake-down" of withered leaves makes his bed,
or, perhaps, it should rather be called his "lair."
This, it will be perceived, is just the house built by
Diggers, Bushmen, and Fuegians. There are no
culinary utensils—only a drinking-cup of the *nau-
tilus* shell; but implements of war and the chase in
plenty: for such are found even amongst the lowest of savages. They consist of bows, arrows, and
a species of javelin or dart. The bows are very
long, and made of the bamboo cane—as are also the
darts. The arrows are usually pointed with the
tusks of the small wild hogs which inhabit the islands. These they occasionally capture in the chase,
hanging up the skulls in their huts as trophies and
ornaments. With strings of the hog's teeth also
they sometimes ornament their bodies; but they
are not very vain in this respect. Sometimes pieces
of iron are found among them—nails flattened to
form the blades of knives, or to make an edge for
their adzes, the heads of which are of hard wood.
These pieces of iron they have no doubt obtained
from wrecked vessels, or in the occasional intercourse which they have had with the convict establishment; but there is no regular commerce with
them—in fact, no commerce whatever—as even the
Malay traders, that go everywhere, do not visit the
Andamaners, from dread of their well-known Ishmaelitish character. Some of the communities,
more forward in civilization, possess articles of more
ingenious construction—such as baskets to hold
fruits and shell-fish, well-made bows, and arrows
with several heads, for shooting fish. The only other article they possess of their own manufacture, is
a rude kind of canoe, hollowed out of the trunk of
a tree, by means of fire and their poor adze. A
bamboo raft, of still ruder structure, enables them
to cross the narrow bays and creeks by which their
coast is indented.

Their habitual dwelling-place is upon the shore. They rarely penetrate the thick forests of the interior, where there is nothing to tempt them: for the wild hog, to which they sometimes give chase, is found only along the coasts where the forest is thinner and more straggling, or among the mangrove-bushes—on the fruits of which these animals feed. Strange to say, the forest, though luxuriant in species, affords but few trees that bear edible fruits. The cocoa-palm—abundant in all other parts of the East-Indian territories, and even upon the Cocos Islands, that lie a little north of the Andamans—does not grow upon these mountain islands. Since the savages know nothing of cultivation, of course their dependence upon vegetable diet would be exceedingly precarious. A few fruits and roots are eaten by them. The pandanus, above mentioned, bears a fine cone-shaped fruit, often weighing between thirty and forty pounds; and this, under the name of *mellori*, or "Nicobar bread-fruit," forms part of their food. But it requires a process of cooking, which, being quite unknown to the Andamaners, must make it to them a "bitter fruit" even when roasted in the ashes of their fires, which is their mode of preparing it. They eat also the fruit of the mangrove, and of some other trees; but these are not obtainable at all seasons, or in such quantity as to afford them a subsistence. They depend principally upon fish, which they broil in a primitive manner over a gridiron of bamboos, sometimes not waiting till they are half done. They especially subsist upon shell-fish, several kinds abounding on their coasts, which they obtain among the rocks after the tide has gone out. To gather these is the work of the women, while the men employ themselves in fishing or in the chase of the wild hog. The species of shell-fish most common are the

Murex tribulus, Trochus telescopium, Cyprœ acaurica, and mussels. They are dexterous in capturing other fish with their darts, which they strike down upon the finny prey, either from their rafts, or by wading up to their knees in the water. They also take fish by torchlight — that is, by kindling dry grass, the blaze of which attracts certain species into the shallow water, where the fishers stand in wait for them.

When the fishery fails them, and the oysters and mussels become scarce, they are often driven to sad extremities, and will then eat anything that will sustain life—lizards, insects, worms—perhaps even *human flesh*. They are not unfrequently in such straits; and instances are recorded, where they have been found lying upon the shore in the last stages of starvation.

An instance of this kind is related in connection with the convict settlement of 1793. A coasting-party one day discovered two Andamaners lying upon the beach. They were at first believed to be dead, but as it proved, they were only debilitated from hunger: being then in the very last stages of famine. They were an old man and a boy; and having been carried at once to the fort, every means that humanity could suggest was used to recover them. With the boy this result was accomplished; but the old man could not be restored: his strength was too far gone; and he died, shortly after being brought to the settlement.

Two women or young girls were also found far gone with hunger; so far, that a piece of fish held out was sufficient to allure them into the presence of a boat's crew that had landed on the shore. They were taken on board the ship, and treated with the utmost humanity. In a short time they got rid of all fears of violence being offered them; but

seemed, at the same time, to be sensible of modesty
to a great degree. They had a small apartment
allotted to them; and though they could hardly
have had any real cause for apprehension, yet it was
remarked that the two never went to sleep at the
same time: one always kept watch while the other
slept! When time made them more familiar with
the good intentions towards them, they became exceedingly cheerful, chatted with freedom, and were
amused above all things at the sight of their own
persons in a **mirror**. They allowed clothes to be
put on them; but took them off again, whenever
they thought they were not watched, and threw
them away as a useless encumbrance! They were
fond of singing; sometimes in a melancholy recita-
tive, and sometimes in a lively key; and they often
gave exhibitions of dancing around the deck, in the
fashion peculiar to the Andamans. They would not
drink either wine, or any spirituous liquor; but
were immoderately fond of fish and sugar. They
also ate rice when it was offered to them. They
remained, or rather were retained, several weeks on
board the ship; and had become so smooth and
plump, under the liberal diet they indulged in, that
they were scarce recognizable as the half-starved
creatures that had been brought aboard so recently. It was evident, however, that they were not
contented. Liberty, even with starvation allied to
it, appeared sweeter to them than captivity in the
midst of luxury and ease. The result proved that
this sentiment was **no stranger to** them: for one
night, when all but **the** watchman were asleep, they
stole silently through the captain's cabin, jumped
out of the stern windows into the sea, and swam to
an island full half a mile distant from the ship! It
was thought idle to pursue them; but, indeed, there
was no intention of doing so. The object was to

retain them by kindness, and try what effect might thus be produced on their wild companions, when they should return to them. Strange to say, this mode of dealing with the Andaman islanders has been made repeatedly, and always with the same fruitless result. Whatever may have been the original cause that interrupted their intercourse with the rest of mankind, they seem determined that this intercourse shall never be renewed.

When plenty reigns among them, and there has been a good take of fish, they act like other starved wretches; and yield themselves up to feasting and gorging, till not a morsel remains. At such times they give way to excessive mirth—dancing for hours together, and chattering all the while like as many apes.

They are extremely fond of "tripping it on the light fantastic toe;" and their dance is peculiar. It is carried on by the dancers forming a ring, and leaping about, each at intervals saluting his own posteriors with a slap from his foot—a feat which both the men and women perform with great dexterity. Not unfrequently this mode of salutation is passed from one to the other, around the whole ring—causing unbounded merriment among the spectators.

Their fashion of dress is, perhaps, the most peculiar of all known costumes. As to clothing, they care nothing about it—the females only wearing a sort of narrow fringe around the waist—not from motives of modesty, but simply as an ornament; and in this scant garment we have a resemblance to the *liku* of the Feegeeans. It can hardly be said, however, that either men or women go entirely naked; for each morning, after rising from his couch of leaves, the Andamaner plasters the whole of his body with a thick coat of mud, which he

wears throughout **the day. Wherever** this cracks
from getting dry by **the sun, the** place is patched
or mended up with **a fresh layer.** The black mop
upon his head **is not permitted to wear its** natural hue; **but,** as already mentioned, **is** coloured **by**
means **of a** red ochreous earth, which is found **in**
plenty **upon** the islands. This reddening **of his poll**
is the **only** attempt which the Andamaner makes **at .**
personal adornment; for his livery of mud is as-
sumed for a purpose of utility—to protect his body
from the numerous musquitoes, and other biting insects, whose myriads infest the lowland **coast** upon
which he dwells.

A startling peculiarity **of these** islanders is the
unmitigated hostility which they exhibit, and have
always exhibited, towards every people with whom
they have come in **contact. It** is not the white **man**
alone whom they hate **and harass;** but they **also**
murder the Malay, **whose skin is** almost as dark **as**
their **own. This would seem to** contradict the hypothesis **of a** tradition **of hostility** preserved among
them, and directed against **white men** who **enslaved**
their ancestors; but, indeed, that story has been
sufficiently refuted. A far more probable cause of
their universal hatred is : that, at some period of
their history, they have been grossly abused ; so
much so, **as** to render suspicion and treachery almost an instinct of their nature.

In these very characteristic **moral** features, we
find another of those **striking** analogies that would
seem to connect them **with the** negrillo races of the
Eastern Archipelago ; **but,** whether they are or are
not connected with them, their appearance upon the
Andamans **is** no greater mystery than the solitary
"fox-wolf" **on** the Falkland Islands, or the smallest
wingless insect in some lone islet of the Ocean !

THE PATAGONIAN GIANTS.

Who has not heard of the *giants* of Patagonia?
From the days of Magellan, when they **were first**
seen, many a tale has been told, and many a speculation indulged in about these colossal men: some
representing them **as** very Titans of **twelve** feet in
height, and stout **in** proportion: that, **when** standing a little astride, an ordinary-sized man could pass
between their legs without even stooping his head!
So talked the early navigators of the Great South
Sea.

Since **the** time when these people were first **seen**
by Europeans, up to the present hour—in all, three
hundred and thirty years ago—it is astonishing how
little has been added to our knowledge of them;
the more so, that almost every voyager who has
since passed through the Straits of Magellan, has
had **some** intercourse with them;—the more so, that
Spanish people have had settlements on the confines
of their country; **and one — an** unsuccessful **one,**
however—in the **very heart of it!** But these Spanish **settlements have all decayed, or** are fast decaying; and when **the Spanish race** disappears from
America—which sooner **or** later it will most certainly do,—it will leave behind it a greater paucity
of monumental record, than perhaps any civilized
nation ever before transmitted to posterity.

Little, however, as we have learnt about the cus-
toms of the Patagonian people, we have at least obtained a more definite idea of their height. *They
have been measured.* The **12-feet** giants can no

longer be found ; they never existed, except in the fertile imaginations of some of the old *navigators* —whose embodied testimony, nevertheless, it is difficult to disbelieve.   Other and more reliable witnesses have done away with the Titans; but still we are unable to reduce the stature of the Patagonians to that of ordinary men.   If not actual *giants*, they are, at all events, very tall men—many of them standing seven feet in their boots of guanaco-leather, few less than six, and a like few rising nearly. to eight!   These measurements are definite and certain; and although the whole number of the Indians that inhabit the plains of Patagonia may not reach the above standard—there are tribes of smaller men called by the common name Patagonians—yet many individuals certainly exist who come up to it.

If not positive giants, then, it is safe enough to consider the Patagonians as among the "tallest" of human beings—perhaps the very tallest, that exist, or ever existed, upon the face of the earth; and for this reason, if for no other, they are entitled to be regarded as an "odd people."   But they have other claims to this distinction; for their habits and customs, although in general corresponding to those of other tribes of American Indians, present us with many points that are peculiar.

It may be remarked that the Patagonian women, although not so tall as the men, are in the usual proportion observable between the sexes.   Many of them are more corpulent than the men; and if the latter be called *giants*, the former have every claim to the appellation of *giantesses !*

We have observed, elsewhere, the very remarkable difference between the two territories lying respectively north and south of the Magellan Straits —the Patagonian on the north, and the Fuegian on the south. No two lands could exhibit a greater contrast than these—the former with its dry sterile treeless plains, the latter almost entirely without plains ; and, excepting a portion of its eastern end, without one level spot of an acre in breadth, but a grand chaos of humid forest-clad ravines and snow-covered mountains. Yet these two dissimilar regions are only separated by a narrow sea-channel—deep, it is true; but so narrow, that a cannon-shot may be projected from one shore to the other. Not less dissimilar are the people who inhabit these opposite shores; and one might fancy a strange picture of contrast presented in the Straits of Magellan : on some projecting bluff on the northern shore, a stalwart Patagonian, eight feet in height, with his ample guanaco-skin floating from his shoulders, and his long spear towering ten feet above his head;—on the southern promontory, the dwarfed and shrivelled figure of a Fuegian—scarce five feet tall—with tiny bow and arrows in hand, and shivering under his patch of greasy seal-skin!—and yet so near each other, that the stentorian voice of the giant may thunder in the ears of the dwarf, while the hen-like cackle of the latter may even reach those of his colossal *vis-à-vis !*

Notwithstanding this proximity, there is no converse between them; for, unlike as are their persons, they are not more dissimilar than their thoughts, habits, and actions. The one is an aquatic animal, the other essentially terrestrial ; and, strange to say, in this peculiarity the weaker creature has the advantage, since the Fuegian can cross in his bark canoe to the territory of his gigantic neighbour, while the latter has no canoe nor water-craft of any kind, and therefore never thinks of extending his excursions to the " land of fire," excepting at one very narrow place, where he has effected a cross-

ing. In many other respects, more particularly detailed elsewhere—in their natural dispositions and
modes of life, these two **peoples are** equally dissimilar; and although learned craniologists may prove
from their skulls that both belong **to** one division
of the **human** family, this fact prove salso that crani-
ology, **like** anatomy, is but a blind guide in the illustration **of** scientific truth, whether the subject be
the **skull of a** man or an animal. Despite all the
revelations of craniologic skill, an Indian of Patago-
nia bears about the same resemblance to an Indian
of Tierra del Fuego, as may be found **between a
bull** and a bluebottle!

Before proceeding to describe the modes of life
practised by the Patagonian giants, a word or two
about the country they inhabit.

It may be generally described as occupying **the**
whole southern part of South America—from **the**
frontier of the Spanish settlements to the Straits of
Magellan—and bounded east and west by the two
great oceans. Now, the most Southern Spanish
(Buenos Ayrean) settlement is at the mouth **of** Rio
Negro; therefore, the Rio Negro—which **is** the
largest river south of the La Plata—may be taken
as the northern boundary of Patagonia. Not that
the weak vitiated Spanish-American extends his
sway **from** the Atlantic to the Andes; on the contrary, **the** Indian aborigines, under one name **or**
another, are masters of the whole interior—not
only to the north of the Rio **Negro, but** to the very
shores of the Caribbean **Sea!** Yes, the broad in-
land of South America, from Cape Horn to the **Sea**
of the Antilles, is now, **as it** always has been, the
domain of the red Indian, who, so far from having
ever been reduced by conquest, has not only resist-
ed the power **of** the Spanish sword, and the blandishments of **the** Spanish cross, but at this hour is

encroaching, with constant and rapid strides, upon the blood-stained territory wrested from him by that *Christian conquest!*

And this is the man who is so rapidly to disappear from the face of the earth! If so, it is not the puny Spaniard who is destined to push him off. If he is to disappear, it will be at such a time, that no Spaniard will be living to witness his extermination.

Let us take Patagonia proper, then, as bordered upon the north by the Rio Negro, and extending from the Atlantic to the Pacific. In that case it is a country of 800 miles in length, with a breadth of at least 200,—a country larger than either France or Spain. Patagonia is usually described as a continuation of the great plains, known as the "Pampas," which extend from the La Plata river to the eastern slope of the Andes. This idea is altogether erroneous. It is true that Patagonia is a country of plains—excepting that portion of it occupied by the Andes, which is, of course, a mountain-tract, much of it resembling Tierra del Fuego in character more than Patagonia. Indeed, Patagonia proper can hardly be regarded as including this mountain strip: since the Patagonian Indians only inhabit the plains properly so called. These plains differ essentially from those of the Pampas. The latter are based upon a calcareous formation: and produce a rank rich herbage—here of gigantic thistles and wild artichokes — there of tall grasses; and, still nearer the mountains, they are thinly covered with copses of low trees. The plains of Patagonia, on the other hand, are of tertiary formation, covered all over with a shingly pebble of porphyry and basalt, and almost destitute of vegetation. Here and there are some tufts of scanty grass with a few stunted bushes in the valleys of the streams, but nothing that can be called a tree. A surface drear

C c

and arid, in places mottled with "salinas" or salt-
lakes; with fresh **water** only found **at** long intervals, and, when **found, of** scanty supply. There are
many hilly tracts, but nothing that can be called
mountains—excepting the snow-covered Cordilleras
in the west. The Patagonian plain is not everywhere of equal elevation: it rises by steps, as you
follow it westward, beginning from the sea-level of
the Atlantic shore; until, having reached the *pied-
mont* of the Andes, you still find yourself on a plain,
but one which is elevated 3,000 feet above the point
from which you started. At all elevations, however, it presents the same sterile aspect; and you
perceive that Patagonia is a true desert—as much
so as Atacama, in Peru, the desert of the Colorado
in the north, the "barren grounds" of Hudson's
Bay, the Säara and Kalahari, Gobi, or the steppe of
Kaurezm. To the South-African deserts it bears a
more striking resemblance than to any of the others—a resemblance heightened by the presence of
that most remarkable of birds—the ostrich. Two
species stalk over the plains of Patagonia,—the
Struthio rhea and *Struthio Darwinii*. The former
extends northward over the Pampas, but not southward **to** the Straits of Magellan; the latter reaches
the Straits, but is never seen upon the Pampas.
The ranges of both meet and overlap, near the middle of the Patagonian plain.

In addition to the ostrich, there are other large
birds that frequent the steppes of Patagonia. The
great condor here crosses the continent, and appears
upon the Atlantic shores. He perches upon the
cliffs of the sea—as well as those that overhang the
inland streams—and builds his nest upon the bare
rock. Two species of *polyborus*, or vulture-eagles,
—the "carrancha" and "chiniango,"—fly side by
side with the condor; and the black turkey-vultures

are also denizens of this desert land. **The** red puma, too, has his home here; the fox **of Azara**; and
several species of hawks and eagles.

With the exception of the first-mentioned — the
ostrich — all these beasts and birds are predatory
creatures; and require flesh for their subsistence.
Where **do** they **get** it? Upon what do they all
prey? Surely **not** upon the ostrich: since this bird
is bigger **than any** of the birds of prey, and able to
defend itself even against the great condor. There
are only one or two other species of birds upon
which the eagles might subsist — a partridge and
two kinds of plover; but the vultures could not get
a living out of partridges and plovers. Small quadrupeds are alike scarce. There are only two or
three species; and very small creatures they are—
one a sort of mole "terutero," and several kinds of
mice. The latter are, indeed, numerous enough in
some places—swarming over the ground in tracts
so sterile, that it is difficult to understand upon
what they subsist. But vultures do not relish food
which they require to kill for themselves. They are
too indolent for that; and wherever they are found,
there must be some source of supply,—some large
quadrupeds to provide them with their favourite
food—carrion. Otherwise, in this desert land, how
should the ravenous puma maintain himself?—how
the vultures and vulture-eagles? and, above all,
upon what does the Patagonian himself subsist—a
man of such great bulk as naturally to require more
than the ordinary amount of food? The answer to
all these questions, then, is, that a quadruped *does*
exist in the deserts of Patagonia; which, if it furnish not all these creatures with their full diet, supplies a very large proportion of it. This quadruped
is the *guanaco*.

Before proceeding **to** give an account of the

guanaco, let us paint the portrait of the Patagonian himself.

As already observed, he is nearly seven feet in height, without any exaggeration in the way of a hat. He wears none, but suffers his long black hair to hang loosely over his shoulders, or, more frequently, gathers it into a knot or club upon the crown of his head. To keep it from straggling into his eyes, he usually wears a narrow strap of guanaco-skin around his forehead, or a plaited band of the hair of the same animal; but, although possessing ostrich-feathers at discretion, he rarely indulges in the fashion of wearing a plume—he knows he is tall enough without one. Over his shoulders, and hanging nearly to his heels, he wears a loose mantle of guanaco-skins; which is of sufficient width to wrap round his body, and meet over his breast— should he feel cold enough to require it. But he is not of a chilly nature; and he often throws this mantle entirely aside to give him the freedom of his arms; or more generally ties a girdle round it, and leaves the upper part to fall back from his shoulders, and hang down over the girdle. This mantle—with the exception of a small pouch-like apron in front—is the only "garment" the Pata-gonian wears upon his body; but his lower limbs have a covering of their own. These are encased in a sort of boots or mocassins—but differing from all other boots and mocassins, in the fact of their being without *soles!* They are made of the same material as the mantle—that is, of the skin of the *guanaco* — but sometimes also of the skin of a horse's shank—for the Patagonian, like the Pampas Indians, is in possession of this valuable animal.

This soleless boot covers the leg all round from below the knee, passing over the top of the foot like a gaiter; it extends also around the heel, and a little under it, but not so far as the instep, thus leaving the greater part of the sole bare, and the toes peeping out in front! They are, in reality, nothing more or less than gaiters, but gaiters of *guanaco*-skin, with the hair turned outward, and worn, not over a pair of boots or shoes as gaiters usually are, but upon the naked shanks.

I have been thus particular in my description of the Patagonian *chaussure;* but you will understand my reasons, when I tell you that, from this trifling circumstance, not only has a vast territory of country, but the people who inhabit it, obtained the appellation by which both have long been known to the civilized world, that is *Patagonian.*

When the sailors who accompanied Magellan first saw these colossal men, they noticed a peculiar circumstance in relation to their feet. The flaps, or "uppers" of the gaiters extending loosely across the tops of their feet, and exaggerated in breadth by the long hair that fringed out from their edges, gave to these Indians the appearance of having paws or "patas;" and the name *patagones,* or "duck-feet," was given them by the sailors—ever prone to the bestowal of a ludicrous epithet. This name, in a slightly altered form, they have borne ever since—so that Patagonia means the country of the *duck-footed* men.

The gaiters of the Patagonians have their peculiar purpose. They are not worn merely for the sake of keeping the legs warm, but also as a protection against the thorny shrubs which in Patagonia, as in all desert lands, are exceedingly abundant.

The mantle and mocassins, then, constitute the Patagonian's sole costume; and it does not differ so widely from that of his neighbour the Fuegian —the chief points of difference being in the size and material.

Of course the guanaco-skin is much larger than that of the common seal; and a good Patagonian cloak would furnish "doublets" for a whole tribe of the diminutive Fuegians. Perhaps this ample garment has something to do, in producing the exaggerated accounts that have been given of the stature of the Patagonians. Certain it is, that a man thus apparelled, looks larger than he otherwise would do; and presents altogether a more imposing appearance. The Caffre, in his civet-cat "kaross," and the Pawnee Indian, in his robe of shaggy buffalo hide, loom very large upon karroo and prairie—much larger in appearance than they really are. It is but natural, therefore, to suppose, that the Patagonian attired in his guanaco mantle, and seen against the sky, standing upon the summit of a conspicuous cliff, would present a truly gigantic appearance.

When first seen in this position, he was on foot. It was in the year 1520—before the Spaniards had set foot upon South-American soil—and of course before the horse became naturalized to that continent. In less than thirty years afterward, he appeared upon these same cliffs bestriding a steed: for this noble animal had extended his range over the plains of America—even at an earlier period than his European owner. When the Spaniards, in their after-attempts at conquering the Indians of the Pampas and those of the northern prairies, entered upon these great plains, they encountered, to their great astonishment, their red enemies upon horseback, brandishing long lances, and managing fiery chargers with a skill equal to their own!

Among the earliest tribes that obtained possession of the horse, were those of the Pampas: since the first of these animals that ran wild on the plains of America were those landed in the La Plata ex-

pedition of Mendoza—whence they **became** scattered over the adjacent pampas of Buenos **Ayres.**

From the banks of the La Plata, the **horse** passed
rapidly southward to the Straits of Magellan ; and
from that hour the Patagonian walked no **more.**
With the exception of a spur—usually a sharp **stick**
of wood, upon his heel—the only additional article
of his " wear"—the horse **has** made no change **in**
his costume, nor **in** the fashion of his toilette. He
still paints his face, **as** Magellan first saw it—with a
white ring encircling one eye, and a black or red
one around the other; with one half of his body
coloured black, and a white sun delineated upon it,
while the other half is white, forming the "ground"
for a black moon! Scarce two individuals, however, wear the same escutcheon; for the fashion of
having eyes, arms, and legs of two different colours
—just as our ancestors used to wear their **doublets**
and hose—is that followed by the Patagonians.

Notwithstanding this queer custom—usually regarded as savage—it would be unjust to call the
Patagonian a *savage.* If we overlook the circum-
stance of his painting himself—which, after all, is
scarce more absurd than numberless practices of
civilized life—if we excuse him for too scantily covering the nakedness of his person, and relishing his
food a little " underdone," **we** find little else, either
in his habits or his moral nature that would **entitle**
him to be termed a savage. **On** the contrary, from
all the testimony that can be obtained—in all the
intercourse which white men have had with him—
there is scarce an act recorded, that would hinder
his claim **to** being considered as civilized as they.
Honourable and amiable, brave and generous, he
has ever proved himself; and never has he exhibited those traits of vindictive ferocity supposed to be
characteristic of **the untutored man.** He has not

even harboured malice for the wrongs done him, by
the unprincipled adventurer Magellan: who, in his
treatment of these people, proved himself more of
a savage than they. But the Patagonian restrain-
ed his vengeance; and apparently, burying the out-
rage in oblivion, has ever since that time treated
the white man with a generous and dignified friendship. Those who have been shipwrecked upon his
solitary shores, have had no reason to complain of
the treatment they have received at his hands. He
is neither cannibal nor yet barbarian—but in truth
a gentleman—or, if you prefer it, a *gentleman savage.*

But how does this gentleman maintain himself?
We have already seen that he is not a fisherman—
for he owns no species of boat; and without that
his chances of capturing fish would be slight and
uncertain. We have stated, moreover, that his
country is a sterile desert; and so it is—producing
only the scantiest of herbage; neither plant, nor
tree, that would furnish food; and incapable of being cultivated with any success. But he does not
attempt cultivation—he has no knowledge of it;
nor is it likely he would feel the inclination, even if
tempted by the most fertile soil. Neither is he pastoral in his habits: he has no flocks nor herds.
The horse and dog are his only domestic animals;
and these he requires for other purposes than food.
The former enables him to pass easily over the wide
tracts of his sterile land, and both assist him in the
chase—which is his true and only calling. One of
the chief objects of his pursuit is the ostrich; and
he eats the flesh of this fine desert bird. He eats
it, whenever he can procure it; but he could not
live solely upon such food: since he could not obtain
it in sufficient quantity; and were this bird the
only means he had for supplying his larder, he

would soon be in danger of starvation. True, the ostrich lays a great many eggs, and brings forth a large brood of young; but there are a great many hungry mouths, and a great many large stomachs among the Patagonian people. The ostrich could never supply them all; and were it their only resource, the bird would soon disappear from the plains of Patagonia, and, perhaps, the race of Patagonian giants along with it.

Fortunately for the Patagonian, his country furnishes him with another kind of game, from which he obtains a more sufficient supply; and that is the guanaco. Behold yonder herd of stately creatures! There are several hundreds of them in all. Their bodies are covered with long woolly hair of a reddish brown colour. If they had antlers upon their heads, you might mistake them for stags—for they are just about the size of the male of the red deer. But they have no horns; and otherwise they are unlike these animals—in their long slender necks, and coat of woolly hair. They are not deer of any kind—they are *guanacos*. These, then, are the herds of the Patagonian Indian; they are the game he chiefly pursues; and their flesh the food upon which he is mainly subsisted.

I need not here give the natural history of the guanaco. Suffice it to say that it is one of the four (perhaps five) species of *llamas* or "camel-sheep" peculiar to the continent of South America—the other three of which are the *vicuña*, the true *llama*, and the *paco*, or *alpaca*. The llama and alpaca are domesticated; but the vicuña, the most graceful of all, exists only in a wild state, like the guanaco. The four kinds inhabit the table-lands of the Andes, from Colombia to Chili; but the guanaco has extended its range across to the Atlantic side of the continent: this only in the territory south of the

La Plata river. On the plains of Patagonia it is
the characteristic quadruped: rarely out of sight,
and usually seen in herds of twenty or thirty individuals; but sometimes in large droves numbering
as many as five hundred. There the puma—after
the Indian of course—is its greatest enemy—and
the *debris* of *his* feast constitutes the food of the
vultures and vulture-eagles—thus accounting for
the presence of these great birds in such a desert
land.

The guanaco is among the shiest of quadrupeds;
and its capture would be difficult to any one unacquainted with its habits. But these betray them to
the skilled Patagonian hunter—who is well acquainted with every fact in the natural history of
the animal.

The Patagonian mode of capturing these creatures is not without many peculiarities in hunting
practice. His first care is to find out their whereabouts: for the haunts which the guanacos most affect are not the level plains, where they might be
seen from afar, but rather those places where the
ground is hilly or rolling. There they are to be
met with, ranged in extended lines along the sides
of the hills, with an old male keeping watch upon
the summit of some eminence that overlooks the
flock. Should the sentinel espy any danger, or
even suspect it, he gives the alarm by uttering a
shrill whistling cry, somewhat resembling a neigh.
On hearing this well-known signal, the others at
once take to flight, and gallop straight for the side
of some other hill—where they all halt in line, and
stand waiting to see if they are followed. Very
often the first intimation which the hunter has of
their presence, is by hearing their strange signal of
flight—which may be described as a sort of trian-
gular cross, between squealing, neighing, and whistling.

Shy as they are, and difficult to be approached, they have the strange peculiarity of losing all their senses when put into confusion. On these occasions they behave exactly like a flock of sheep: not knowing which way to run; now dashing to one side, then to the other, and often rushing into the very teeth of that danger from which they are trying to escape!

Knowing their stupidity in this respect the Patagonian hunter acts accordingly. He does not go out to hunt the guanacos alone, but in company with others of his tribe, the hunting party often comprising the whole tribe. Armed with their "chuzos"—light cane spears of eighteen feet in length—and mounted on their well-trained steeds, they sally forth from their encampment, and proceed to the favourite pasturing-ground of the guanacos. Their purpose is, if possible, to effect the "surround" of a whole herd; and to accomplish this, it is necessary to proceed with great skill and caution. The animals are found at length; and, by means of a deployment of dogs and horsemen, are driven towards some hill which may be convenient to the pasture. The instinct of the animal guiding it thither, renders this part of the performance easy enough. On reaching the hill, the guanacos dash onward, up to its summit; and there, halting in a compact crowd, make front towards their pursuers. These meanwhile have galloped into a circle—surrounding the eminence on all sides; and, advancing upwards amidst loud yells and the yelping of their dogs, close finally around the herd, and rush forward to the attack.

The long chuzos do their work with rapidity; and, in a few minutes, numbers of the guanacos lie lifeless among the rocks. The dogs, with some men, form an outer circle of assailants; and should any guanacos escape through the line of horsemen, they are seized upon by the dogs, and pinned to the spot—for it is another sheep-like trait in the character of this animal, that the moment a dog—even though he be the merest cur—seizes hold of it, it neither attempts further flight nor resistance, but remains "pinned" to the spot as if under a paralysis of terror! They sometimes give battle, however, though never to a dog; and their mode of assault is by kicking behind them—not with their hoofs as horses do, but with the knee-joints, the hind legs being both raised at once. Among themselves the males fight terrible battles: biting each other with their teeth, and often inflicting cruel lacerations.

Strange to say, when the guanacos are found solitary, or only two or three together, they are far less shy than when assembled in large herds. At such times, the feeling of curiosity seems stronger than that of fear within them; and the hunter can easily approach within a dozen paces of one, by simply cutting a few capers, or holding up something that may be new to it—such as a strip of coloured rag, or some showy article of any kind. It was by such devices that the Patagonian captured these creatures before possession of the horse enabled him to effect their destruction in the more wholesale fashion of the " surround."

By tumbling about over the ground, he was enabled to bring the game within reach—not of his bow and arrows; nor yet of his long spear—for he did not use it for such a purpose—and, of course, not of a gun, for he never had heard of such a weapon. Within reach of what then? Of a weapon peculiarly his own—a weapon of singular construction and deadly effect; which he knew how to employ before ever the white man came upon his shores, and which the Spaniards who dwell in the Pampas country have found both pride and profit in adopting. This weapon is the "bolas."

It is simple and easily described. Two round stones—the women make them round by grinding the one against the other—two round stones are covered with a piece of guanaco raw hide, presenting very much the appearance of cricket-balls, though of unequal size—one being considerably smaller than the other. Two thongs are cut; and one end of each is firmly attached to one of the balls.

The other ends of the thongs are knotted to each other; and when the strings are at full stretch, the balls will then be about eight feet apart—in other words, each thong should be four feet in length. The bolas are now made, and ready for use. The chief difficulty in their manufacture lies in the rounding of the stones; which, as above observed, is the work of the women; and at least two days are required to grind a pair of bola-stones to the proper spherical shape. To handle them requires long practice; and this the Patagonian has had: for, ever since the young giant was able to stand upon his feet, he has been in the habit of playing with the bolas. They have been the toy of his childhood; and to display skill in their management has been the pride of his boyish days; therefore, on arriving at full maturity, no wonder he exhibits great dexterity in their use. He can then project them to a distance of fifty yards—with such precision as to strike the legs of either man or quadruped, and with such force, that the thong not only whips itself around the object struck, but often leaves a deep weal in the skin and flesh. The mode of throwing them is well known. The right hand only is used; and this grasps the thongs at their point of union, about halfway between the ends. The balls are then whirled in a circular motion around the head; and, when sufficient centrifugal power has been obtained, the weapon is launched at the object to be captured. The aim is a matter of nice calculation—in which arm, eye, and mind all bear a part—and so true is this aim, in Patagonian practice, that the hunter seldom fails to bring down or otherwise cripple his game—be it ostrich, cavy, or guanaco.

By these bolas, then, did the Patagonian hunter capture the guanaco and ostrich in times past; and by the same weapon does he still capture them: for he can use it even better on horseback than on foot.   Either the bird or the quadruped, within fifty yards, has no chance of escape from his unerring aim.

The bolas, in some districts, have been improved upon by the introduction of a third ball; but this the Patagonian does not consider an *improvement*. Wooden balls are sometimes employed; and iron ones, where they can be had—the last sort can be projected to the greatest distance.

The Patagonian takes the young guanacos alive; and brings them up in a state of domestication. The little creatures may often be observed, standing outside the tents of a Patagonian encampment—either tied by a string, or held in hand by some "infant giant" of the tribe. It is not solely for the pleasure of making pets of them, that the young guanacos are thus cherished; nor yet to raise them for food. The object aimed at has a very different signification. These young guanacos are intended to be used as *decoys:* for the purpose of attracting their own relatives—fathers, mothers, sisters, brothers, uncles, and aunts, even to the most distant thirty-second cousinship—within reach of the terrible bolas!

This is effected by tying the innocent little creature to some bush—behind which the hunter conceals himself—and then imitating the mother's call; which the Indian hunter can do with all the skill of a ventriloquist. The young captive responds with the plaintive cry of captivity—the parents are soon attracted to the spot, and fall victims to their instinct of natural affection. Were it not for this, and similar stratagems adopted by the Patagonian hunter, he would pursue the guanaco in vain. Even with the help of his pack of dogs, and mounted upon the fleet Spanish horse, the guanaco cannot be hunted with success. Nature, in denying to these animals almost every means of defence, has also bestowed upon them a gift which enables them to escape from many kinds of danger. Of mild and inoffensive habits—defenceless as the hare—they are also possessed of a like swiftness. Indeed, there is perhaps no quadruped—not even the antelope—can get over the ground as speedily as the guanaco or its kindred species the vicuña. Both are swift as the wind; and the eye, following either in its retreat over the level plain, or up the declivity of a hill, is deluded into the fancy that it is watching some great bird upon the wing.

There are certain seasons, during which the guanaco is much more difficult to approach, than at other times; but this is true of almost every species of animal—whether bird or quadruped. Of course, the tame season is that of sexual intercourse, when even the wild beasts become reckless under the influence of passion. At other times the guanacos are generally very shy; and sometimes extremely so. It is not uncommon for a herd of them to take the alarm, and scamper off from the hunter, even before the latter has approached near enough to be himself within sight of them! They possess great keenness of scent; **but it is the** eye which usually proves their friend, **warning them** of the approach of an enemy—especially **if that** enemy be a man upon horseback—before **the latter is** aware of their proximity.   Often **a** cloud **of dust, rising afar** off over **the plain, is** the only proof **the hunter can obtain, that there was** game within the **range of his** vision.   It is a curious circumstance connected with hunting **on these** great plains—both on the Pampas and in Patagonia—that a man on foot can approach **much** nearer to **any** game, **than** if he were mounted **upon a** horse.   **This** is **true not** only in relation to **the guanaco and ostrich, but also** of the large Pampas deer (*Cervus campestris*) ; and indeed of almost every animal **that inhabits these regions.**   The reason is simple enough.   **All** these creatures are accustomed to seeing **their** human enemy only on horseback : for " still **hunting,"** or hunting **afoot, is** rarely **or never practised** upon the plains.   **Not** only that, **but a man on foot,** would be a rare sight either **to an** ostrich **or guanaco;** and they would **scarce** recognize **him as an enemy!**   Curiosity would be their **leading** sentiment; **and,** being influenced **by this,** the hunter *on foot* can often approach **them** without difficulty.   The Patagonian, knowing this peculiarity, not unfrequently takes advantage **of it,** to kill or capture both the bird and the quadruped.

   This sentiment of the brute creation, on **the** plains **of Patagonia, is directly the reverse** of what may be observed in our **own** fields.   **The sly** crow shows **but** little of this shyness, so long as you approach it **on a horse's back;** but only attempt to steal up to it on foot—**even** with **a** thick hawthorn hedge to screen you—and **every fowler** knows how wary the bird can **prove itself.**   Some people pronounce this *instinct.*   If so, instinct and reason must be one and the same thing.

Besides hunting the guanaco, much of the Patagonian's time is spent in the chase of the ostrich; and, to circumvent this shy creature, he adopts various *ruses*. The American ostrich, or more properly *rhea*, has many habits in common with its African congener. One of these is, when pursued it runs in a straight track, and, if possible, *against* the wind. Aware of this habit, the Patagonians pursue it on horseback—taking the precaution to place some of their party in ambush in the direction which the bird is most likely to run. They then gallop hastily up to the line of flight, and either intercept the *rhea* altogether, or succeed in "hoppling" it with the bolas. The moment these touch its long legs, both are drawn suddenly together; and the bird goes down as if shot!

Drake and other voyagers have recorded the statement that the Patagonians attract the rhea within reach, by disguising themselves in a skin of this bird. This is evidently an untruth; and the error, whether wilful or otherwise, derives its origin from the fact, that a stratagem of this kind is adopted by the Bushmen of Africa to deceive the ostrich. But what is practicable and possible between a pigmy Bushman and a gigantic African ostrich, becomes altogether impracticable and improbable, when the *dramatis personæ* are a gigantic Patagonian and an American *rhea*. Moreover, it is also worthy of remark, that the *rhea* of the Patagonian plains is not the larger of the two species of American ostrich, but the smaller one (*Rhea Darwinii*), which has been lately specifically named after the celebrated naturalist. And justly does Mr. Darwin merit the honour: since he was the first to give a scientific description of the bird. He was not the first, however—as he appears himself to believe—to discover its existence, or to give a record of it in writing.

D D

The old Styrian monk, Dobrizhoffer, two centuries before Mr. Darwin was born, in his " History of the Abipones" clearly points to the fact that there were two distinct species of the " avestruz," or South-American ostrich.

Mr. Darwin, however, has confirmed Dobrizhoffer's account; and brought both birds home with him; and he, who chooses to reflect upon the subject, will easily perceive how impossible it would be for a Patagonian to conceal his bulky *corpus* under the skin of a *Rhea Darwinii*, or even that of its larger congener, the *Rhea americana*. The skin of either would be little more than large enough to form a cap for the *colossus* of the Patagonian plains.

In the more fertile parts of Patagonia, the large deer (*Cervus campestris*) is found. These are also hunted by the Patagonian, and their flesh is esteemed excellent food; not, however, until it has lain several days buried underground—for it requires this funereal process, to rid it of the rank goat-like smell, so peculiar to the species. The mode of hunting this deer—at least that most likely to ensure success—is by stealing forward to it on foot.

Sometimes a man may approach it, within the distance of a few yards—even when there is no cover to shelter him—by walking gently up to it. Of all the other quadrupeds of the Pampas—and these plains are its favourite *habitat*,—the *Cervus campestris* most dreads the horseman:—since its enemy always appears in that guise; and it has learnt the destructive power of both lazo and bolas, by having witnessed their effects upon its comrades. The hunter dismounted has no terrors for it; and if he will only keep lazo and bolas out of sight—for these it can distinguish, as our crow does the gun, —he may get near enough, to fling either one or the other with a fatal precision.

The "agouti" (*Cavia patagonica*) frequently furnishes the Patagonian with a meal. This species is a true denizen of the desert plains of Patagonia; and forms one of the characteristic features of their landscape. I need not describe its generic characters; and specifically it has been long known as the "Patagonian cavy." Its habits differ very little from the other South American animals of this rodent genus—except that, unlike the great capivare, it does not affect to dwell near the water. It is altogether a denizen of dry plains, in which it burrows, and upon which it may be seen browsing, or hopping at intervals from one point to another, like a gigantic rabbit or hare. In fact, the cavies appear to be the South American representatives of the hare family—taking their place upon all occasions: and, though of many different species—according to climate, soil, and other circumstances—yet agreeing with the hares in most of their characteristic habits. So much do some of the species assimilate to these last, that colonial sportsmen are accustomed to give them the Old-World appellation of the celebrated swift-footed rodent. The Patagonian cavies are much larger than English hares—one of them will weigh twenty-five pounds—but, in other respects, there is a great deal of resemblance. On a fine evening, three or four cavies may be seen squatted near each other, or hopping about over the plains, one following the other in a direct line, as if they were all proceeding on the same errand! Just such a habit is frequently observed among hares and rabbits in a field of young corn or fallow.

The Patagonian boys and women often employ themselves in seeking out the ostriches' nests, and robbing them of their eggs—which last they find good eating. In the nests of the smaller species—

which we have already stated to be the most common in the Patagonian country—they are not rewarded so liberally for their trouble. Only from
sixteen to twenty eggs are hatched by the *Rhea
Darwinii*, and about twenty-five to thirty by the
Rhea americana. It will be seen, that this is far
below the number obtained from the nest of the
African ostrich (*Struthio camelus*) — in which as
many as sixty or seventy eggs are frequently found.
It would appear, therefore, that the greater the size
of the bird, belonging to this genus, the greater the
number of its brood. Both the American rheas
follow the peculiar habit of the true ostrich; that
is, several hens deposit their eggs in the same nest;
and the male bird assists in the process of incuba-
tion. Indeed, in almost every respect—except size
and general colour of plumage—the American and
African ostriches resemble each other very closely;
and there is no reason in the world why a pedantic
compiler should have bestowed upon them distinct
generic names. Both are true *camel birds :* both
alike the offspring, as they are the ornament, of the
desert land.

Another occupation in which the Patagonian en-
gages—and which sometimes rewards him with a
meal—is the snaring of the Pampas partridge (*No-
thuria major*). This is usually the employment of
the more youthful giants ; and is performed both on
foot and on horseback. A small species of partridge
is taken on foot ; but the larger kind can be snared
best from the back of a horse. The mode is not altogether peculiar to Patagonia : since it is also practised in other parts of America—both north and
south,—and the bustard is similarly captured upon
the *karoos* of Africa. During the noon hours of the
day, the performance takes place : that is, when the
sun no longer casts a shadow. The locality of the

bird being first ascertained, the fowler approaches it, as near as it will allow. He then commences riding round, and round, and round—being all the while watched by the foolish bird, that, in constantly turning its head, appears to grow giddy, and loses all dread of danger. The Indian each moment keeps lessening his circle; or, in other words, approaches by a spiral line, continually closing upon its centre. His only weapon is a long light reed—something like the common kind of cane fishing-rod seen in the hands of rustic youth in our own country. On the end of this reed he has adjusted a stiff snare; the noose of which is made from the epidermis of an ostrich plume, or a piece of the split quill; and which, being both stiff and elastic, serves admirably for the purpose for which it is designed.

Having at length arrived within a proper distance to reach the beguiled bird, the boy softly stops his horse, bends gently sideward, and, adroitly passing his noose over the neck of the partridge, jerks the silly creature into the air. In this way an Indian boy will capture a dozen of these birds in a few hours; and might obtain far more, if the sun would only stay all day in the zenith. But as the bright orb sinks westward, the elongated shadow of the horseman passes over the partridge before the latter is within reach of the snare; and this alarming the creature, causes it to take flight.

The Patagonian builds no house; nor does he remain long in one place at a time. The sterile soil upon which he dwells requires him to lead a nomade life; passing from place to place in search of game. A tent is therefore his home; and this is of the simplest kind: the tent-cloth consisting of a number of guanaco skins stitched together, and the poles being such as he can obtain from the nearest tract of thicket or *chapparal*. The poles are set bow-fashion in the ground, and over these the skin covering is spread—one of the bent poles being left uncovered, to serve as a doorway.

Most of the Patagonian's time is occupied in procuring game: which, as we have seen, is his sole sustenance; and when he has any leisure moments, they are given to the care of his horse, or to the making or repairing his weapons for the chace. Above all, the bolas are his especial pride, and ever present with him. When not in actual use, they are suspended from his girdle, or tied sash-like around his waist—the balls dangling down like a pair of tassels.

Only during his hours of sleep, is this national weapon ever out of the hands of the Patagonian giant. Had the wonderful giant of our nurseries been provided with such a sling, it is probable that little Jack would have found in him an adversary more difficult to subdue!

THE FUEGIAN DWARFS.

THE FUEGIAN DWARFS.

THE great continent of South America, tapering like a tongue to the southward, ends abruptly on the Straits of Magellan. These straits may be regarded as a sort of natural canal, connecting the Atlantic with the Pacific Ocean, winding between high rocky shores, and indented with numerous bays and inlets. Though the water is of great depth, the Straits themselves are so narrow, that a ship passing through need never lose sight of land on either side; and in many places a shell, projected from an ordinary howitzer, would pitch clear across them from shore to shore! The country extending northward from these straits is, as already seen, called *Patagonia;* that which lies on their southern side is the famed "land of fire," *Tierra del Fuego.*

The canal, or channel, of the Straits of Magellan does not run in a direct line from the Atlantic to the Pacific. On the contrary, a ship entering from the former, instead of passing due west, must first run in a south-west direction—rather more south than west. This course will continue, until the ship is about half-way between the two oceans. She will then head almost at a right angle to her former course; and keep this direction—which is nearly due north-west—until she emerges into the Pacific.

It will thus be seen, that the straits form an angle near their middle; and the point of land which projects into the vertex of this angle, and known to navigators as Cape Forward, is the most southern

land of the American *continent.* Of course, this is
not meant to apply to the most southern point of
American land—since Tierra del Fuego must be
considered as part of South America. The far-
famed "Cape Horn" is the part of America nearest
to the South Pole; and this is a promontory on one
of the small elevated islands lying off the southern
coast of Tierra del Fuego itself. Tierra del Fuego
was for a long time regarded as a single island;
though, even in the voyage of Magellan, several
large inlets, that resembled channels, were observed
running into the land; and it was suspected by that
navigator, that these inlets might be passages leading through to the ocean. Later surveys have
proved that the conjectures of the Spano-Portuguese
voyager were well founded; and it is now known
that instead of a single island, the country called
Tierra del Fuego is a congeries of many islands, of
different shapes and sizes—separated from one another by deep, narrow channels, or arms of the sea,
with an endless ramification of sounds and inlets.
In the western part — and occupying more than
three-fourths of their whole territory—these close-
lying islands are nothing else than mountains—several of them rising 5,000 feet above the level of the
water, and stepping directly down to it, without
any foot-hills intervening! Some of them have their
lower declivities covered with sombre forests; while,
farther up, nothing appears but the bare brown
rocks, varied with blue glaciers, or mottled with
masses of snow. The more elevated peaks are covered with snow that never melts: since their summits rise considerably above the snow-line of this
cold region.

These mountain-islands of Tierra del Fuego continue on to Cape Horn, and eastward to the Straits
of Le Maire, and the bleak islet of Staaten Land.

They may, in fact, be considered as the continuation of the great chain of the Andes, if we regard the intersecting channels—including that of Magellan itself—as mere clefts or ravines, the bottoms of which, lying below the level of the sea, have been filled with sea-water. Indeed, we may rationally take this view of the case: since these channels bear a very great resemblance to the stupendous ravines termed " barrancas" and " quebradas," which intersect the Cordilleras of the Andes in other parts of South America—as also in the northern division of the American continent.

Regarding the Straits of Magellan, then, and the other channels of Tierra del Fuego, as great *water barrancas*, we may consider the Andes as terminating at Cape Horn itself, or rather at Staaten Land : since that island is a still more distant extension of this, the longest chain of mountains on the globe.

Another point may be here adduced in proof of the rationality of this theory. The western, or mountainous part of Tierra del Fuego bears a strong resemblance to the western section of the continent —that is, the part occupied by the Andes. For a considerable distance to the north of the Magellan Straits, nearly one-half of the continental land is of a mountainous character. It is also indented by numerous sounds and inlets, resembling those of Tierra del Fuego; while the mountains that hang over these deep water ravines are either timbered, or bare of trees and snow-covered, exhibiting glacier valleys, like those farther south. The whole physical character is similar; and, what is a still more singular fact, we find that in the western, or mountainous part of Patagonia, there are no true Patagonians; but that there the water-Indians, or Fuegians, frequent the creeks and inlets.

Again, upon the east — or rather north-east of

Tierra del Fuego—that angular division of it which lies to the north of the Sebastian channel presents us with physical features that correspond more nearly with those of the plains of Patagonia; and upon this part we find tribes of Indians that beyond doubt are true Patagonians—and not Fuegians, as they have been described. This will account for the fact that some navigators have seen people on the Fuegian side that were large-bodied men, clothed in guanaco skins, and exhibiting none of those wretched traits which characterize the Fuegians; while, on the other hand, miserable stunted men are known to occupy the mountainous western part of Patagonia. It amounts to this—that the Patagonians *have* crossed the Straits of Magellan; and it is this people, and not Fuegians, who are usually seen upon the champaign lands north of the Sebastian channel. Even the guanaco has crossed at the same place—for this quadruped, as well as a species of deer, is found in the eastern division of Tierra del Fuego. Perhaps it was the camel sheep—which appears to be almost a necessity of the Patagonian's existence—that first induced these water-hating giants to make so extensive a voyage as that of crossing the Straits at Cape Orange!

At Cape Orange the channel is so narrow, one might fancy that the Patagonians, if they possessed one-half the pedestrian stretch attributed to the giants of old, might have stepped from shore to shore without wetting their great feet!

Perhaps there are no two people on earth, living so near each other as the Patagonians and Fuegians, who are more unlike. Except in the colour of the skin and hair, there is hardly a point of resemblance between them. The former seems to hate the sea: at all events he never goes out upon, nor even approaches its shore, except in pursuit of such game

as may wander that way. He neither dwells near,
nor does he draw any portion of his subsistence
from the waters of the great deep—fish constituting no part of his food.

All this is directly the reverse with the Fuegian.
The beach is the situation *he* chooses for his dwelling-place, and the sea or its shore is his proper element. He is more than half his time, either on it,
or *in* it—on it in his canoe, and in it, while wading
among the tidal shoals in search of fish, mussels,
and limpets, which constitute very nearly the whole
of his subsistence.

It is very curious, therefore, while noting the difference between these two tribes of Indians, to observe how each confines its range to that part of
the Magellanic land that appears best adapted to
their own peculiar habits—those of the Patagonian
being altogether *terrestrial*, while those of the Fuegian are essentially *aquatic*.

We have stated elsewhere the limits of the Patagonian territory; and shown that, ethnologically
speaking, they do not occupy the whole northern
shore of the Magellan Straits, but only the eastern
half of it. Westward towards the Pacific the aspect of the land, on both sides of this famous channel, may be regarded as of the same character,
though altogether different from that which is seen
at the entrance, or eastern end.

West of Cape Negro on one side, and the Sebastian passage on the other, bleak mountain summits,
with narrow wooded valleys intervening, become
the characteristic features. There we behold an in-
congruous labyrinth of peaks and ridges, of singular
and fantastic forms—many of them reaching above
the limits of perpetual snow—which, in this cold
climate, descends to the height of 4,000 feet. We
have seen that these mountains are separated from

each other—not by plains, nor even valleys, in the
ordinary understanding of the term, but by *ravines*
the steep sides of which are covered with sombre
forests up to a height of 1,500 feet above the level
of the sea: at which point vegetation terminates,
with a uniformity as exact as that of the snow-line
itself! These forests grow out of a wet, peaty soil
—in many places impassable on account of its bog-
gy nature; and of this character is almost the whole
surface of the different islands. The trees composing the forests are few in species—those of the
greatest size and numbers being the "winter's bark"
(*drymys*), of the order *magnoliaceæ*, a birch, and,
more abundantly, a species of beech-tree, the *Fagus
betuloides*. These last-named trees are many of
them of great size; and might almost be called
evergreens: since they retain part of their foliage
throughout the whole year; but it would be more
appropriate to style them *ever-yellows:* since at no
period do they exhibit a verdure, anything like the
forests of other countries. They are always clad in
the same sombre livery of dull yellow, rendering the
mountain landscape around them, if possible, more
dreary and desolate.

The forests of Tierra del Fuego are essentially
worthless forests; their timber offering but a limited contribution to the necessities of man, and producing scarce any food for his subsistence.

Many of the ravines are so deep as to end, as already stated, in becoming arms or inlets of the sea;
while others again are filled up with stupendous
glaciers, that appear like cataracts suddenly arrest-
ed in their fall, by being frozen into solid ice! Most
of these inlets are of great depth—so deep that the
largest ship may plough through them with safety.
They intersect the islands in every direction—cutting them up into numerous peninsulas of the most

fantastic forms; while some of the channels are narrow *sounds*, and stretch across the land of Tierra del Fuego from ocean to ocean.

The "Land of Fire" is therefore not an island—as it was long regarded—but rather a collection of islands, terminated by precipitous cliffs that frown within gunshot of each other. Ofttimes vast masses of rock, or still larger masses of glacier ice, fall from these cliffs into the profound abysses of the inlets below; the concussion, as they strike the water, reverberating to the distance of miles; while the water itself, stirred to its lowest depths, rises in grand surging waves, that often engulf the canoe of the unwary savage.

"Tierra del Fuego" is simply the Spanish phrase for "Land of Fire." It was so called by Magellan on account of the numerous fires seen at night upon its shores, while he and his people were passing through the Straits. These were signal fires, kindled by the natives—no doubt to telegraph to one another the arrival of those strange leviathans, the Spanish ships, then seen by them for the first time.

The name is inappropriate. A more fit appellation would be the "land of water;" for certainly in no part of the earth is water more abundant, both rain and snow supplying it almost continually. Water is the very plague of the island; it lies stagnant or runs everywhere—forming swamps wherever there is a spot of level ground, and rendering even the declivities of the mountains as spongy as a peat-bog.

The climate throughout the whole year is excessively cold; for, though the winter is perhaps not more rigorous than in the same latitude of a northern land, yet the summer is almost as severe as the winter, and it would be a misnomer to call it summer at all. Snow falls throughout the whole year;

and even in the midsummer of Tierra del Fuego
men have actually perished from cold, at no great
elevation above the level of the sea!

Under these circumstances, it would scarce be
expected that Tierra del Fuego should be inhabited
—either by men or animals of any kind; but no
country has yet been reached too cold for the existence of both. No part of the earth seems to have
been created in vain; and both men and beasts are
found dwelling under the chill skies of Tierra del
Fuego.

The land-animals, as well as the birds, are few in
species, as in numbers. The *guanaco* is found upon
the islands; but whether indigenous, or carried
across from the Patagonian shore, can never be determined; since it was an inhabitant of the islands
long anterior to the arrival of Magellan. It fre-
quents only the eastern side of the cluster, where
the ground is firmer, and a few level spots appear
that might be termed plains or meadows. A species of deer inhabits the same districts; and besides these, there are two kinds of fox-wolves
(*Canis Magellanicus* and *Canis Azaræ*), three or
four kinds of mice, and a species of bat.

Of water-*mammalia* there is a greater abundance: these comprising the whale, seals, sea-lions,
and the sea-otter.

But few birds have been observed; only the
white-tufted flycatcher, a large black woodpecker
with scarlet crest, a creeper, a wren, a thrush, a
starling, hawks, owls, and four or five kinds of
finches.

The water-birds, like the water-*mammalia*, muster in greater numbers. Of these there are ducks
of various kinds, sea-divers, and penguins; the al-
batross, and sheerwater, and, more beautiful than
all, the "painted" or "Magellan goose."

Reptiles do not exist, and insects are exceedingly
rare. A few flies and butterflies are seen; but the
musquito—the plague of other parts of South America—does not venture into the cold humid atmosphere of the Land of Fire.

We now arrive at the *human* inhabitants of this
desolate region.

As might be expected, these exhibit no very high
condition either of physical or mental development,
but the contrary. The character of their civilization is in complete correspondence with that of their
dreary dwelling-place—at the very bottom of the
scale. Yes, at the very bottom, according to most
ethnologists; even lower down than that of the Dig-
ger-Indian, the Andaman Islander, the Bushman of
Africa, or the Esquimaux of the Arctic Ocean: in
fact, any comparison of a Fuegian with the last-mentioned would be ridiculous, as regards either their
moral or physical condition. Below the Esquimaux,
the Fuegian certainly is, and by many a long degree.

In height, the tallest Fuegian stands about five
feet,—not in his boots, for he wears none; but on
his naked soles. His wife is just six inches shorter
than himself—a difference which is not a bad proportion between the sexes, but in other respects
they are much alike. Both have small, misshapen
limbs, with large knee-caps, and but little calf; both
have long masses of coarse tangled hair, hanging
like bunches of black snakes over their shoulders;
and both are as naked as the hour in which they
were born—unless we call *that* a dress—that bit of
stinking seal-skin which is slung at the back, and
covers about a fifth part of the whole body! Hairy
side turned inward, it extends only from the nape
of the neck to a few inches below the hollow of the
back; and is fastened in front by means of a thong

or skewer, passing over the breast. It is rarely so
ample as to admit of being "skewered;" and with
this scanty covering, in rain and snow, frost and
blow—some one of which is continuously going on
—the shivering wretch is contented. Nay, more;
if there should happen an interval of mild weather,
or the wearer be at work in paddling his canoe, he
flings this unique garment aside, as if its warmth
were an incumbrance! When the weather is particularly cold, he shifts the seal-skin to that side of
his body which may chance to be exposed to the
blast!

The Fuegian wears neither hat nor shirt, waist-
coat nor breeches—no shoes, no stockings,—nothing
intended for clothing but the bit of stinking skin.
His vanity, however, is exhibited, if not in his dress,
to some extent in his adornments. Like all savages
and many civilized people, he *paints* certain portions
of his person; and his "escutcheon" is peculiar. It
would be difficult to detail its complicated labyrinth
of "crossings" and "quarterings." We shall content ourselves by stating that black lines and blotch-
es upon a white ground constitute its chief characteristic. Red, too, is sometimes seen, of a dark or
"bricky" colour. The black is simply charcoal;
while the white-ground coat is obtained from a
species of infusorial clay, which he finds at the bottom of the peaty streams that pour down the ravines of the mountains. As additional ornaments,
he wears strings of fish-teeth, or pieces of bone,
about his wrists and ankles. His wife carries the
same upon her neck; and both, when they can procure it, tie a plain band around the head, of a reddish-brown colour—the material of which is the long
hair of the guanaco. The "cloak," already described,
is sometimes of sea-otter instead of seal-skin; and on
some of the islands, where the deer dwells, the hide

of that animal affords a more ample covering. In most cases, however, the size of the garment is that of a pocket handkerchief; and affords about as much protection against the weather as a kerchief would.

Though the Fuegian has abundance of hair upon his head, there is none, or almost none, on any part of his body. He is beardless and whiskerless as an Esquimaux; though his features—without the adornment of hair—are sufficiently fierce in their expression.

He not only looks ferocious, but in reality is so—deformed in mind, as he is hideous in person. He is not only ungrateful for kindness done, but unwilling to remember it; and he is cruel and vindictive in the extreme. Beyond a doubt he is a *cannibal;* not habitually perhaps, but in times of scarcity and famine—a true cannibal, for he does not confine himself to eating his *enemies*, but his *friends*, if need be—and especially the old women of his tribe, who fall the first victims, in those crises produced by the terrible requirements of an impending starvation. Unfortunately the fact is too well authenticated to admit of either doubt or denial; and, even while we write, the account of a massacre of a ship's crew by these hostile savages is going the rounds of the press—that ship, too, a missionary vessel, that had landed on their shores with the humane object of ameliorating their condition.

Of course such unnatural food is only partaken of at long and rare intervals—by many communities never,—and there is no proof that the wretched Fuegian has acquired an appetite for it: like the Feegee and some other savage tribes. It is to be hoped that he indulges in the horrid habit only when forced to it by the necessities of extreme hunger.

His ordinary subsistence is shell-fish; though he

eats also the flesh of the seal and sea-otter; of birds,
especially the penguin and Magellanic goose, when
he can capture them.   His stomach will not "turn"
at the blubber of a whale—when by good chance
one of these leviathans gets stranded on his coast
—even though the great carcass be far gone in the
stages of decomposition!   The only vegetable diet
in which he indulges is the berry of a shrub—a species of arbutus—which grows abundantly on the
peaty soil; and a fungus of a very curious kind,
that is produced upon the trunks of the beech-tree.
This fungus is of a globular form and pale-yellow
colour.   When young, it is elastic and turgid,
with a smooth surface; but as it matures it becomes
shrunken, grows tougher in its texture, and presents
the pitted appearance of a honeycomb.   When fully
ripe, the Fuegians collect it in large quantities, eating it without cooking or other preparation.   It is
tough between the teeth; but soon changes into
pulp, with a sweetish taste and flavour—somewhat
resembling that of our common mushroom.

These two vegetables—a berry and a crypto-
gamic plant—are almost the only ones eaten by the
natives of Tierra del Fuego.   There are others
upon the island that might enable them to eke out
their miserable existence: there are two especially
sought after by such Europeans as visit this dreary
land—the "wild celery" (*Apium antarcticum*), and
the "scurvy-grass" (*Cardamine antiscorbutica*);
but for these the Fuegian cares not.   He even
knows not their uses.

In speaking of other "odd people," I have usually described the mode of building their house; but
about the house of the Fuegian I have almost "no
story to tell."   It would be idle to call that a house
which far more resembles the lair of a wild beast,
and is, in reality, little better than the den made by

the ourang-outang in the forests of Borneo. Such as it is, however, I shall describe it.

Having procured a number of long saplings or branches—not always straight ones,—the Fuegian sharpens them at one end by means of his mussel-shell knife; and then sticking the sharpened ends into the ground in a kind of circle, he brings the tops all together, and ties them in a bunch—so as to form a rude hemispherical frame. Upon this he lays some smaller branches; and over these a few armfuls of long coarse grass, and the house is "built." One side—that to leeward of the prevailing wind—is left open, to allow for an entrance and the escape of smoke. As this opening is usually about an eighth part of the whole circumference, the house is, in reality, nothing more than a shed or lair. Its furniture does not contradict the idea; but, on the contrary, only strengthens the comparison. There is no table, no chair, no bedstead: a "shake-down" of damp grass answers for all. There are no implements or utensils—if we except a rude basket used for holding the arbutus berries, and a seal-skin bag, in which the shell-fish are collected. A bladder, filled with water, hangs upon some forking stuck against the side: in the top of this bladder is a hole, from which each member of the family takes a "suck," when thirst inclines them to drink!

The "tools" observable are a bow and arrow, the latter headed with flint; a fish-spear with a forked point, made from a bone of the sea-lion; a short stick—a woman's implement for knocking the limpets from the rocks; and some knives, the blades of which are sharpened shells of the mussel—a very large species of which is found along the coast. These knives are simply manufactured. The brittle edge of the shell—which is five or six inches in

length—is first chipped off, and a new edge formed by grinding the shell upon the rocks. When
thus prepared, it will cut not only the hardest wood,
but even the bones of fish; and serves the Fuegian
for all purposes.

Outside the hut, you may see the canoe—near at
hand too, — for the shieling of the Fuegian universally stands upon the beach. He never dwells
in the interior of his island; and but rarely roams
there—the women only making such excursions as
are necessary to procure the berry and the mushroom. The woods have no charms for him, except
to afford him a little fuel: they are difficult to be
traversed on account of the miry soil out of which
the trees grow ; and, otherwise, there is absolutely
nothing to be found amidst their gloomy depths,
that would in any way contribute to his comfort or
sustenance. He is therefore essentially a dweller
on the shore; and even there he is not free to come
and go as he might choose. From the bold character of his coast, there are here and there long
reaches, where the beach cannot be followed by land
—places where the water's edge can only be reached, and the shell-fish collected, by means of some
sort of navigable craft. For this purpose the Fuegian requires a canoe; and the necessity of his life
makes him a waterman. His skill, however, both
in the construction of his craft, and the management of it, is of a very inferior order—infinitely inferior to that exhibited either by the Esquimaux or
the Water Indians of the North.

His canoe is usually made of the bark of a tree—
the birch already mentioned. Sometimes it is so
rudely shaped as to be merely a large piece of bark
shelled from a single trunk, closed at each end, and
tied tightly with thongs of seal-skin. A few cross-
sticks prevent the sides from pressing inward;

while as many stays of thong keep them from "bulging" in the contrary direction. If there are cracks in the bark, these are calked with rushes and a species of resin, which the woods furnish.

With this rude vessel the Fuegian ventures forth, upon the numerous straits and inlets that intersect his land; but he rarely trusts himself to a tempestuous sea.

If rich or industrious, he sometimes becomes the possessor of a craft superior to this. It is also a bark canoe, but not made of a single "flitch." On the contrary, there are many choice pieces used in its construction; for it is fifteen feet in length and three in width amidships. Its "build" also is better—with a high prow and stern, and cross-pieces regularly set and secured at the ends. The pieces of bark are united by a stitching of thongs; and the seams carefully calked, so that no water can enter. In this vessel, the Fuegian may embark with his whole family—and his whole furniture to boot—and voyage to any part of his coast. And this in reality he does; for the "shanty" above described is to him only a temporary home. The necessities of his life require him to be continually changing it; and a "removal," with the building of a new domicile, is a circumstance of frequent recurrence.

Not unfrequently, in removing from one part of the coast to another, he finds it safer making a land journey, to avoid the dangers of the deep. In times of high wind, it is necessary for him to adopt this course—else his frail bark might be dashed against the rocks and riven to pieces. In the land journey he carries the canoe along with him; and in order to do this with convenience, he has so contrived it that the planks composing the little vessel can be taken apart, and put together again without much difficulty—the seams only requiring to be freshly calked. In the transport across land, each member of the family carries a part of the canoe: the stronger individuals taking the heavier pieces—as the side and bottom planks—while the ribs and light beams are borne by the younger and weaker.

The necessity of removal arises from a very natural cause. A few days spent at a particular place —on a creek or bay,—even though the community be a small one, soon exhausts the chief store of food—the mussel-bank upon the beach—and, of course, another must be sought for. This may lie at some distance; perhaps can only be reached by a tedious, and sometimes perilous water-journey; and under these circumstances the Fuegian deems it less trouble to carry the mountain to Mahomet, than to carry Mahomet so often to the mountain. The transporting his whole *ménage* is just as easy as bringing home a load of limpets; and as to the building of a new house, that is a mere bagatelle, which takes little labour, and no more time than the erection of a tent. Some Fuegians actually possess a tent, covered with the skins of animals; but this is a rare and exceptional advantage; and the tent itself of the rudest kind. The Fuegian has his own mode of procuring fire. He is provided with a piece of "mundic," or iron pyrites, which he finds high up upon the sides of his mountains. This struck by a pebble will produce sparks. These he catches upon a tinder of moss, or the "punk" of a dead tree, which he knows how to prepare. The tinder once ignited, is placed within a roundish ball of dry grass; and this, being waved about in circles, sets the grass in a blaze. It is then only necessary to communicate the flame to a bundle of sticks; and the work is complete. The process, though easy enough in a climate where "punk" is plenty, and dry grass and sticks can be readily procured, is nevertheless difficult enough in the humid atmosphere of Tierra del Fuego—where moss is like a wet sponge, and grass, sticks, and logs can hardly be found dry enough to burn. Well knowing this, the Fuegian is habitually careful of his fire: scarce ever permitting it to go out; and even while travelling in his canoe in search of a "new home," side by side with his other " penates" he carries the fire along with him.

Notwithstanding the abundance of fuel with which his country provides him, he seems never to be thoroughly warm. Having no close walls to surround him, and no clothing to cover his body, he suffers almost incessantly from cold. Wherever met, he presents himself with a shivering aspect, like one undergoing a severe fit of the ague!

The Fuegians live in small communities, which scarce deserve the name of "tribes," since they have no political leader, nor chief of any description. The conjurer—and they have him—is the only individual that differs in any degree from the other members of the community; but his power is very slight and limited; nor does it extend to the exercise of any physical force. Religion they have none—at least, none more sacred or sanctified than a vague belief in devils and other evil spirits.

Although without leaders, they are far from being a peaceful people. The various communities often quarrel and wage cruel and vindictive war against one another; and were it not that the boundaries of each association are well defined, by deep ravines and inlets of the sea as well as by the impassable barriers of snow-covered mountains, these warlike dwarfs would thin one another's numbers to a far greater extent than they now do—perhaps to a mutual extermination. Fortunately, the peculiar nature of their country hinders them from coming very often within fighting distance.

Their whole system of life is abject in the extreme. Although provided with fires, their food is eaten raw; and a fish taken from the water will be swallowed upon the instant, almost before the life is gone out of it. Seal and penguin flesh are devoured in the same manner; and the blubber of the whale is also a raw repast. When one of these is found dead upon the beach—for they have neither the skill nor courage to capture the whale—the lucky accident brings a season of rejoicing. A fleet of canoes—if it is to be reached only by water—at once paddle towards the place; or, if it be an overland journey, the whole community—man, woman, and child, start forth on foot. In an hour or two they may be seen returning to their hut-village, each with a large "flitch" of blubber flapping over the shoulders, and the head just appearing above, through a hole cut in the centre of the piece—just as a Mexican ranchero wears his "serape," or a denizen of the Pampas his woollen "poncho." A feast follows this singular procession.

Like the Esquimaux of the north, the Fuegian is very skilful in capturing the seal. His mode of capturing this creature, however, is very different from that employed by the "sealer" of the Arctic Seas; and consists simply in stealing as near as possible in his canoe, when he sees the animal asleep upon the surface, and striking it with a javelin, which he throws with an unerring aim.

We have already observed that the principal subsistence of the Fuegian is supplied by the sea; and shell-fish forms the most important item of his food. These are mussels, limpets, oysters, and other kinds of shell-fish, and so many are annually consumed by a single family, that an immense heap of the shells may be seen not only in front of every hut, but all along the coast of the islands, **above** high-water mark—wherever a tribe has made its temporary sojourn.

There is a singular fact connected with these conglomerations of shells, which appears to have **escaped** the observations of the Magellanic voyagers. It is not by mere accident they are thus collected in piles. There is a certain amount of superstition in the matter. The Fuegian believes that, were the shells scattered negligently about, ill-luck would follow; and, above all, if the emptied ones were thrown back into the sea: since this would be a warning of destruction that would frighten the living bivalves in their "beds," and drive them away from the coast! Hence it is that the shell-heaps are so carefully kept together.

In collecting these shell-fish, the women are **the** chief labourers. They do not always gather them from the rocks, after the tide has gone out; though that is the usual time. But there are some species **not** found in shallow water, and therefore only to be obtained by diving to the bottom after them. Of this kind is a species of *echinus*, or "sea-urchin," of the shape of an orange, and about twice the bulk of one—the whole outside surface being thickly set with spines, or protuberances. These curious **shell-fish** are called "sea-eggs" by the sailor navigators, and constitute an important article of the food of the Fuegian. It is often necessary to dive for them **to a** great depth; and this is done by the Fuegian women, who are as expert in plunging as the pearl-divers of California or the Indian **seas.**

Fish is another article of Fuegian diet; and many kinds are captured upon their coasts, some of excellent quality. They sometimes obtain the fish by shooting them with their arrows, or striking them with a dart; but they have a mode of catching the finny creatures which is altogether peculiar: that is to say, *hunting them with dogs!* The Fuegians possess a breed of small fox-like dogs, mean, wretched-looking curs, usually on the very verge of starvation —since their owners take not the slightest care of them, and hardly ever trouble themselves about feeding them. Notwithstanding this neglect, the Fuegian dogs are not without certain good qualities, and become important auxiliaries to the Fuegian fisherman. They are trained to pursue the fish through the water, and drive them into a net, or some inclosed creek or inlet, shallow enough for them to be shot with the arrow. In doing this the dogs dive to the bottom, and follow the fish to and fro, as if they were amphibious carnivora, like the seals and otters. For this useful service the poor brutes receive a very inadequate reward—getting only the bones as their portion. They would undoubtedly starve were it not that, being left to shift for themselves, they have learnt how to procure their own food, and understand how to catch a fish now and then *on their own account.* Their principal food, however, consists in shell-fish, which they find along the shores, with polypi, and such other animal substances as the sea leaves uncovered upon the beach after the tide has retired. A certain kind of seaweed also furnishes them with an occasional meal—as it does their masters,—often as hungry and starving as themselves.

In his personal habits no human being is more filthy than the Fuegian. He never uses water for washing purposes, nor cleans the dirt from his skin in any way. He has no more idea of putting water to such use, than he has of drowning himself in it; and in respect to cleanliness, he is not only below most other savages, but below the brutes themselves, since even these are taught cleanliness by instinct. But no such instinct exists in the mind of the Fuegian; and he lives in the midst of filth. The smell of his body can be perceived at a considerable distance; and Hotspur's fop might have had reasonable grounds of complaint, had it been a Fuegian who came between the " wind and his nobility." To use the pithy language of one of the old navigators, "The Fuegian stinks like a fox."

Fairly examined then in all his bearings,—fairly judged by his habits and actions—the Fuegian may claim the credit of being the most wretched of our race.

THE END.

www.ingramcontent.com/pod-product-compliance
Lightning Source LLC
Chambersburg PA
CBHW031828270326
41932CB00008B/592